UNUSUAL
UNDERTAKINGS

UNUSUAL UNDERTAKINGS

A MILITARY MEMOIR

by

LIEUTENANT GENERAL SIR JAMES WILSON

LEO COOPER

First Published in Great Britain 2002 by
LEO COOPER
an imprint of Pen & Sword Books
47 Church Street
Barnsley, S. Yorkshire, S70 2AS

ISBN 0 0 85052 905 0

A CIP record for this book is available from the British Library

Typeset in 10/12.5pt Plantin by
Phoenix Typesetting, Burley-in-Wharfedale, West Yorkshire.

Printed by
CPI UK

Dedication

To my wife, Jean, who has been involved with the project since its start, read and improved the text, and remained a wonderful support throughout. Without her help and encouragement this book would never have been published.

CONTENTS

PREFACE

This book does not amount to a comprehensive memoir in the accepted sense of that term. Its origins stem from a decision, taken soon after I left the Army, to record the main events of my life, so that my family would later have some idea how my life had been spent. The resulting account was discursive, much too long and unsuitable for publication, for which, of course, it had never been intended.

However, some of my friends reading the narrative felt that if I could reconstruct the manuscript in a more disciplined way, it might become possible for a sympathetic publisher to consider it for publication. Fortunately for me, Pen and Sword Books have turned out just such an organization; I owe them, and in particular Henry Wilson and Tom Hartman, a great debt of gratitude for their wisdom, patience and skill in helping me develop it all into a manageable concept. It tells the story of how an individual, who never considered a military career, found his steps directed that way; as the story indicated, I was exceptionally lucky in the opportunities with which I was provided and in those with whom I served. I remained an amateur at heart throughout my thirty-seven years' service, and owe much to the tolerance of my superiors and others whose approach to things military was more strictly professional.

In selecting the areas for detailed study, I have tried to choose those of general or historical interest – World War Two, for example, the early days of India and Pakistan, the Mau Mau emergency and my experience as a UN Chief of Staff and Acting Force Commander in Cyprus. The rest of my career, greatly though I enjoyed it, has been covered in a linking narrative, designed to show only how I arrived at the next significant opportunity. To have done otherwise would have been wearisome for the reader and disregarded the admirable advice of my publishers.

Apart from those at Pen and Sword Books, there are many people who have helped me at various times with support and assistance. In particular my friend, brother officer in The Rifle Brigade and superb Chief of Staff in Aldershot, David Pontifex, devised the list and collected many of the illustrative photographs. Others who helped in this way were General Wajahat Hussain, Pakistan Army and Ambassador for his country in Australia, Lieutenant General M.L. Chibber, Indian Army, Colonel Charles Baker-Cresswell and Patrick Maclure from Winchester College. Major Ron Cassidy from the Museum of the Royal Green Jackets at Winchester advised me on Regimental aspects, besides giving a home to the original manuscript before it was decided to make it suitable for publication.

My secretary, Mrs Julie Smith, has been with me since I left the Army in 1977. She has been involved in the book from the outset, and her patience, good humour and brilliant treatment of the manuscript have been beyond praise. Without her the project would never have reached fruition.

To summarise – I have as usual been fortunate in my friends, and hope they may feel that this book represents some sort of return for much encouragement and support. Where in the book I express judgement on events or individuals, these views reflect my personal opinions, with no other individual responsible. Finally I hope my readers will enjoy reading it, and perhaps reach the conclusion that Britain was well served by its armed forces, and the Army in particular, in the period described by the author.

September 2002
JAMES WILSON

Chapter One

ORIGINS

I did not intend a military career, but at least my birthplace, Camberley in Surrey, was military enough. I was born there in April 1921; my father, then a major in the Royal Engineers, aged 35, was a student at the Staff College.

My father's family were Lowland Scots by origin. My great grandfather came from Lockerbie in Dumfriesshire. He was not only Provost of Lockerbie but Factor to the Jardine family, and exercised considerable influence in both capacities. But the Wilsons never made much money; they were sensible, cautious, orderly folk with a typically Scottish regard for education.

My Wilson grandfather, a doctor, never lost his Lowland Scots accent; it survived a 10-year spell in Ontario – my father Bevil Thomson Wilson was born in Toronto in 1885 – and subsequent return to practice in Oxford Road, Manchester. I never met my Wilson grandmother; my father hardly remembered her either for she died in a fire while nursing his younger brother, Bunty. He said she was a beautiful, spirited woman and, from what he told me, she led my gentle Scots grandfather a considerable dance. She was doubtless the reason why the family failed to settle in Ontario and came back to Manchester. Nevertheless, the Wilsons owe her much for her spirit and character, which has greatly influenced the family.

My father, Bevil, was the eldest of three Wilson children. My grandfather was a considerable figure in Edwardian Manchester; he was a Fellow of the Royal College of Surgeons, a Deputy Lieutenant for Lancashire, and highly respected. Bringing up his three children, especially without a wife to support him, was an expensive business, and my grandfather took on extra work as an anaesthetist to meet its demands. The children were encouraged to fend for themselves, enjoying challenging and original holidays and were well educated. My father went to Clifton and followed his engineering bent through the RMA Woolwich into the Royal Engineers. His younger brother, Alex, always known in the family as Bunty, went through Osborne into the Royal Navy where he had a successful, if disappointing, career. He died in 1944, aged under 50, while Chief of Staff as a Commodore to Admiral Sir James Somerville, then C in C Far East and based in Ceylon. An attractive, handsome man and a fine sportsman, who boxed for the Royal Navy, he had a fatal weakness for women, especially those who flattered him. Despite his brilliant start and a spell of service on the Royal Yacht as a Commander, my father always doubted if his brother would have become an Admiral and attributed his early death to professional frustration. He was kind to me and I liked him, not least for introducing me early in life to the delights of gin and tonic, a drink which subsequently took me 20 years to abandon.

My mother's family origins were English, industrial and commercial. Her family, the Starkeys, came from Huddersfield in Yorkshire. They made money in wool in the early part of the 19th century and moved in 1870 to Nottinghamshire, where they bought a fine Georgian house, Norwood Park, Southwell. The Starkeys became country gentlemen and ran their estate admirably. My grandfather, John Starkey, inherited the Norwood estate from his father, Lewis, in 1910, having been elected Conservative MP for Newark in 1906. It was a distinct achievement to be returned as a Tory in that General Election which marked a Liberal landslide and the accession to power of the famous Liberal Government which lasted until the first Coalition of World War One in 1915. John Starkey was also later Chairman of the County Council, Chairman of Quarter Sessions, the first Starkey Baronet and a fervent supporter of everything that went on in his adopted county of Nottinghamshire.

John Starkey's son, the only boy amongst seven sisters, William Randle, was my godfather and a kind, if sometimes mischievous, person. He served in the Rifle Brigade and was the main reason for my becoming a Green Jacket.

The Starkeys were wool people, who became landowners. My grandmother Emily's family, the Seelys, were very different. The Seelys were coal owners, Liberals in politics, richer and more worldly than the Starkeys. The best known Seely was my great uncle, Jack Seely, later Lord Mottistone. He, like my Starkey grandfather, was an MP; as a Liberal he was in the Asquith Government before the First World War, a great friend of Winston Churchill and in 1914 the Secretary of State for War who so bungled the Curragh crisis that he had to resign. This left him free to join the Army at the start of the First War; he served first with the Yeomanry and ultimately ended as a much-loved Commander of the Canadian Cavalry Brigade. He was an engaging man, enjoying the good things of life, but not always the most modest of individuals. At the end of the First World War he was heard to say, reflectively, "It is sad my horse Warrior cannot be put in for a VC".

When one of his friends enquired the reason, my great uncle Jack blandly replied, "Well he has been everywhere I have."

I was fortunate therefore in my family origins. My ancestors were lively, energetic and patriotic. They worked hard, played hard and got the best from their active lives. Being a soldier's son, I was largely brought up by my relatives since for two out of three school holidays my parents were abroad and my sister, Priscilla, and I were "farmed out", happily usually together, with one or other member of the family. This meant Christmas either in Worcestershire with Aunt Isabel, or Gloucestershire with my mother's sister, Nell, more frequently the latter. We normally spent Easter at Norwood as guests of my grandparents, and another Starkey sister, Aunt Barbara, "in loco parentis". They were all kind and we owe them much. Separation from our parents was worse for my sister, Priscilla, than for me. I gained more than she did from what would now be described as 'male chauvinism' and our gypsy life made me unusually independent. I travelled around England a lot on my own and developed a great affection for the country, especially the Midlands and the North.

A word is due about my mother's sisters, of whom there were six. Without exception her sisters were brave, courageous, people, incredibly kind and generous to children, their own or anybody else's. They were very competitive; to play Racing Demon with the Starkey sisters was an experience which fitted one admirably for later life. Quickness of thought, absolute honesty and determination to fight one's corner were all essential, whatever the task. They were marvellous teachers, all the better because the lessons they taught were instinctive and not premeditated.

I have some early military memories, first of Wiesbaden, a spa town in the Rhineland of Germany, where my father was commanding 7 Field Company Royal Engineers, part of the Army of Occupation. My parents were not well off; nevertheless there were a nanny for Priscilla and myself, German servants and a soldier groom. My father bought the family's first car, an open tourer Citroen; it was the family's pride and joy but gave more pleasure to Priscilla and myself than to my father. He was brilliant with horses but never came fully to terms with the internal combustion engine. He drove the Citroen with distrust, my mother taking the wheel occasionally with abandon and limited regard for geography, or others on the road except dogs or horses.

My father was good in command of his field company – I remember seeing a bridge of boats his sappers built across the Rhine – and at his recreations, horses (and polo). The horses were provided by the Army and financed by occupation costs. There was a charger for him, and also a horse for my mother. There were polo ponies also at the polo club, to which we used to chug uncertainly in the car. My father had a good eye, was a fearless horseman and a competitive player. He enjoyed 'riding people off' and was ruthless in exploiting weaknesses of opponents with a distaste for physical contact. I was proud of my father and tried later to emulate his approach to games, though in my case it would be cricket and football rather than polo. He was also a very good fisherman, and this was probably what he was best at.

In the autumn of 1927 our halcyon life in Germany ended when my father returned to England – to a posting in York as a staff officer with the 49th West Riding Territorial Division. The plan for our move was simple. My father went straight to York, where he took over his new job, basing himself on the Mess at the Cavalry Barracks. To save money, my mother, Priscilla and I wintered in Belgium – at an unpretentious seaside resort, La Panne, half way between Ostend and Dunkirk. We found a small bungalow and settled in for the winter.

A lesser person than my mother would have accepted that there was 'nothing to do' at La Panne, rugged up in the bungalow and spent the winter complaining. She did nothing of the kind. We fed well on the wonderful fish with which the North Sea then abounded, but also with chicken, liver and bacon and memorable Irish stew as the basis of our diet. We learnt to bicycle, at first wobbling unsteadily down the Esplanade in the face of the fierce North East wind, and later, when we had mastered our machines, progressing rapidly downwind, weaving in and out of the lamp posts. We walked along the beach towards Dunkirk or in the firmer areas of the sand dunes; we learnt to read proper books, begun by my mother reading aloud till the story gripped us, and we read ourselves to satisfy our curiosity. *Kidnapped, Treasure Island, The Children of the New Forest,* Kipling's *Jungle Book,* these were our favourites. We had lessons, taught by my mother, a great achievement. Governesses at Norwood and two years at the Francis Holland School (near Sloane Square) had given her a solid grounding in the essentials. She taught us English (and proper spelling), history (plenty of dates to learn by heart), geography (capitals of countries and rivers) and arithmetic (sensible, practical, sums). Above all, we learnt French, which my mother spoke fluently and which we had to use when shopping every day. Sensibly, my mother used to give me a list and some money; I would then depart on my bicycle with a deadline by which the job had to be done. If I could carry out the mission more cheaply than the budget, I was allowed to keep the change or convert the proceeds into chocolate.

York, the next family base, provided more landmarks. Our house, 16 Fulford Road, was a tall Victorian villa on the south side of the city, not far from the Cavalry Barracks. The trams clanged cheerfully down Fulford Road towards their terminus at Heslington or northward through the city towards the road to Leeds. Sometimes our afternoon walks involved the tram. As a special treat, Marion, who looked after us for the first two months in York, would take us to the terminus at Heslington, a good base for further walking, especially to watch the trains on the main LNER line to London.

Marion was a marvellous person. She had been my mother's Lady's Maid at Norwood before 1914 and was an oracle on Starkey family matters. She was married to Frank Robinson, who ran a barber's shop in Southwell and served on the committee of the local football club. They lived in the Lodge at the bottom of Norwood drive. One called there to see Marion and hear the latest local gossip. Marion dominated her husband; she was, though without a formal education, highly intelligent, a wonderful mimic (especially of those above stairs who fancied themselves), and the life and soul of the Servants Hall. Periodically in times of family crisis she would leave Frank to look after himself and take charge of the family requiring help. It was in this capacity that she looked after Priscilla and me in York. Many years later she still did the same service for my own children in Germany and (her last excursion) at the RMA Sandhurst. She spoiled people, but there was no nonsense. If you broke the code, it was straight to bed and just bread and butter for tea; she might relent later, but it was unwise to count on it.

My own schooldays began in York. My parents arranged for me to go in the mornings to the York Girls College under the lee of the Minster. It was a sound basic education. I was the only boy and my mother's hard work at La Panne gave me a flying start in most subjects. In the afternoons the car driven by Driver Scholar, my father's groom, would pick me up and I would go to play games with the boys at St Olave's in Clifton, the preparatory school for St Peter's, York. I got some preliminary mickey-taking for being at a girls' school, but a few crunching tackles, and the odd "incident off the ball" soon established my credibility and there were no further problems.

Otherwise life centred round hunting, my parents' main interest. There were two horses, the Priest, my father's charger, a strong, brave animal who pulled like a train but jumped well. My mother's chestnut mare, Judy, was a classier performer. She was tubed – otherwise my parents could never have afforded her. She carried my mother, elegantly riding sidesaddle, successfully for two hunting seasons in York. Later my uncle, Bill Starkey, bought her and Judy won several races for him in Devonshire and Nottinghamshire. These two horses provided my parents with two days a week with the York and Ainsty (South); it was a good hunt, not so smart as the Bramham Moor, but very much in the First Division all the same. Priscilla and I often went to the meets and acquired a knowledge of hunt boundaries, classifications and customs. Twice my mother surrendered Judy to me for the day and I enjoyed the occasions, though they were to prove the summit and end of my equestrian career.

I was introduced to league football in York and it soon became my staple winter recreation. My father took me to watch York City, just elected to the Third Division (Northern Section) of the Football League. York's ground was then Fulford Road, ramshackle and primitive; they have since moved to better premises, but in those days Fulford Road was my Mecca and Valhalla combined. For years I followed York's fortunes in the league; I still look for their result today, though later I forsook them for Nottingham Forest and Notts County. It was a good start from which much enjoyment has since followed.

Altogether York, with its hunting, football and family life was a good period. All was to change, however, when my father was promoted Brevet Colonel and selected as Chief Staff Officer to the Sudan Defence Force in Khartoum. He was delighted at his promotion and at finding himself in what was 'the big time'. But for Priscilla and me it meant separation from our parents; after a short interlude in which we lived for six months in "rooms" at Seaford in Sussex, my mother followed my father to Khartoum and for the next 10 years we saw them only for the summer holidays. This was the accepted practice in those days and it never occurred to me then, thanks to the kindness of those who looked after us, that we were in any way to be pitied. But I am glad we had previously had such a happy and varied childhood, which helped me greatly in profiting from my schooldays.

Chapter Two

SCHOOLDAYS

I was lucky in my schooldays, both in the two schools I attended, and those who taught me there. I cannot deny, however, the desolation I felt in September 1930, when I arrived at Horris Hill for the first time. My parents were both in the Sudan and I did not know anyone at my new school. But, fortunately, I settled down quickly and the ethos of the school, competitive and challenging, suited my personality.

Horris Hill is near Newbury, on the border between Hampshire and Berkshire. The school, with a great Headmaster in 'Daddy' Stow – his two sons, Jimmy and Sandy, maintained the tradition and were in turn Headmasters to my two sons, William and Rupert – specialized in preparing its pupils for Winchester. Some went to other schools, Eton, Marlborough and Bradfield, though for about 60% Winchester was our destination. The school was based on competition. Each Sunday a Form Order showing one's place in class would be posted on the notice board after breakfast; we usually had a good idea where we would figure, but always confirmed our position. It was not done to be complacent; if one had achieved a high standing, you accepted the congratulations of the less fortunate with such modesty as you could muster. It would probably be different next week, and there were always subjects (Greek and Mathematics in my case) to bring you down to earth.

The same approach applied to games, which we took seriously and which provided our main interest and outlet. The team games, football and cricket, were well taught; we learnt the basic skills and were competitive both on the field and in our efforts to be selected for the teams representing the school. Horris Hill had a reputation to maintain in its outside matches against our main rivals, Cothill, Summerfields, Twyford and the Dragon School, Oxford. Horris Hill was the Arsenal of our preparatory school world and we were expected to win and also to play well. If one lost, as sometimes we did, if not often, reverses had to be accepted in the right spirit. "Win as if you were used to it, lose as if you liked it," 'Daddy' Stow taught. It was the right atmosphere in which to develop and the foundations on which the Horris Hill ethos depended still stand one in good stead.

The curriculum was limited and based essentially on the classics. Latin was taught even in the lowest form, and Greek embarked on at the age of 10. Mathematics were important; French, History, Geography and Divinity (detailed study of the Old and New Testaments) completed the range. We were not expected to think originally; our task was to master the basic facts. Such methods developed one's memory and taught one to work quickly and accurately.

The masters kept good order and gave our competitive instincts full scope. Generally they explained things well, often reducing matters to a rule of thumb, so avoiding subsequent error. The dirigiste nature of our early instruction may not, in theory, have encouraged creativity. Nevertheless Richard Adams, occupant of the next bed to mine for a year, and later author of *Watership Down*, had little difficulty, then or later, in developing his imagination. Even then he was a wonderful storyteller and delighted us each night with tales of mystery, unfolded in a whisper long after we were supposed to be asleep.

We were not an outstanding group, though we reached a good level of all-round competence. Among my Horris Hill contemporaries I can number two High Court Judges, two ambassadors, a Managing Director of the P & O Company and at least one Headmaster of distinction. Add Tony Pawson, who captained Oxford at cricket, represented the Gentlemen against the Players, won two FA Amateur Cup Medals for Pegasus, and played for Charlton in the First Division, and it can be argued we covered a good span of later activity.

In the summer of 1934, my last term at Horris Hill, I was entered with three other candidates, John Bates, son of a Northern Ireland High Court Judge, Derek Morphett and Tony Pawson for a Winchester scholarship. Tony and I were already booked firmly for Winchester. For us, therefore, the exam was less vital than for the other two, who needed to do well to be certain of entry to Winchester. 'Daddy' Stow led the expedition generously; we stayed in a 3 star hotel and were treated rather like valuable racehorses about to take part in a Gold Cup. After a splendid dinner with Hampshire strawberries, we slept like logs; next morning 'Daddy' Stow marched us down to the College, where we were to take the 2½-day Election Examination. The route took us past the Cathedral, then the Close, and through College, before we arrived at School, a fine 17th century building designed by Christopher Wren, where we were to sit the papers. Having nothing to lose, I was relaxed, while so good had been the Horris Hill preparation that most of the papers were as expected. My Greek, however, was dodgy, and my knowledge of geometry rudimentary. 'Daddy' Stow examined us briefly about the papers after we had finished the first day. He felt that John Bates had performed well, and that I, falling as usual on my feet, had done better than expected. But the Greek Unseen was still to come and there it was likely I would meet my Waterloo. "I do not imagine, Jim, that you will trouble the scorers much when it comes to the Greek Unseen," 'Daddy' Stow predicted.

Next morning I had a feeling that it would be my lucky day. Greek Unseen came first; I recognized it at once; it was about Porus and the elephants. I can remember little now about Porus except that he was a General who trained elephants for war, but in 1934 I had no such problems. For one of our practices at Horris Hill 'Daddy' Stow had set us this particular piece. Porus' problems had appealed to my imagination and now he seemed an old friend. There was a morning break after we had finished the paper; I handed it without a word to 'Daddy' Stow, who replied with a splendid wink. It was a stroke of luck for me and, when the results were announced a day or two later, Porus had won me an exhibition and thirteenth place on the roll. I walked proudly at Horris Hill for a day or two, my success the more agreeable for being unexpected. John Bates made it, of course, while Derek Morphett followed him deservedly the next year.

Joining Winchester that autumn was relatively easy. Election the previous June meant I knew the way around; there were also familiar faces from Horris Hill predecessors and contemporaries to help one settle down. I was lucky in getting an excellent bear leader for my first fortnight in Ronnie Buckland, later, after New College, to join the Coldstream Guards, and reach the rank of Major General. At the age of 14, Ronnie was well organized and made sure I became so too; with him as guide – learning my "notions" – the Winchester way of life was straightforward and my start in Phils (G House) easy.

At the beginning of my third year Jack Parr, my House Master, realized I needed to give up the classics and arranged for me to transfer to the Modern ladder, where I was to specialise in History and Modern Languages. The change transformed my education. French and German made more sense to me than Greek and Latin, while the study of History, especially of 19th Century Europe, immediately appealed to me. Even the mechanics of the feudal system were preferable to the classical texts, with which I had become disillusioned. I again enjoyed working, started to read widely, and for the last two years at Winchester made the best of the opportunities open.

I was fortunate in my House Master, Jack Parr, an unusual schoolmaster. He had been a classical scholar, good enough to achieve a First in Greats at New College, Oxford. But he kept his intellectual ability concealed; during the First War he had been a fighting soldier, first in Palestine, later in France, with the Highland Light Infantry. He had learnt much from this experience and was adept at getting the best from people. In Phils, therefore, everyone mattered; he took great pains to find activities which people could enjoy, even if they did not excel, while he realized how important it was to support the interest of others. So games players were not allowed to become "athlocrats", but found themselves supporting other people, and we became all-rounders as we learnt that everyone and their interests mattered. Phils had some good musicians; a little of their knowledge rubbed off on the Philistines as we listened to my friend Robert De Mowbray playing his French horn in Mozart's concerto, or were briefed by James Gammell, our senior prefect, about Brahms or Wagner before a gramophone concert in Jack's drawing room.

There was a Phils play-reading society and we performed a famous house play; Ronnie Hamilton, the producer, made T.S. Eliot's *Murder in the Cathedral* an outstanding memory. Many years later, when I was UN Force Commander in Cyprus negotiating with the wily Archbishop Makarios, my knowledge of the play and Eliot's analysis of Becket's character came in handy, as I shall recount. Then, however, I was too busy concentrating on my role as a Knight sent by Henry to murder the Archbishop to appreciate Eliot's subtleties; even so I can still recall much of the Archbishop's superb Christmas sermon, beautifully spoken by Jeffrey Earle, tragically to die in HMS *Glorious* three years later.

From 1936 onwards we lived in the shadow of the impending World War Two, which made us politically conscious with the current issues, the Spanish Civil War for example, often debated. In domestic politics there were also sharp divisions, especially for those like me, even then a Tory. In the spring of 1938 Jack Parr encouraged three of us to spend a week of our Easter holiday helping to dig allotments for the unemployed at Cleator Moor, near Workington in Cumberland. It was shocking to find there were people in our country so badly nourished they were unable to dig over a small garden and embarrassing to see how the small amounts we paid for our keep improved the family diet. Our approach to these problems might now be stigmatised as paternalistic; however, the week in Cumbria was memorable and helped me to understand the North of England and its ways.

Jack Parr also involved me in the Boys Club Movement with which I am still engaged. My involvement stemmed not from social conscience but from my love of Association Football and regret at being unable to play the game at Winchester in the autumn and early winter when Winchester's own football held sway. I escaped whenever I could, usually on the back of Phillips', the house butler's, motorcycle on Saturday afternoons to Southampton and Portsmouth to watch the Saints or Pompey. Jack was aware of these expeditions but turned a blind eye to them before suggesting

I might like to go to Hoxton periodically to play football legally on Hackney Marshes with the Crown Club, a recent addition to the Winchester College Mission. I jumped at the idea and went frequently, not only to play football, but also for cross-country running at which the Club excelled.

Football and cricket remained principal interests at Winchester; at cricket the quality of our coaching was exceptional. Harry Altham, the Cricket Historian, Rockley Wilson, formerly of Yorkshire and England, and Ted Bowley, Sussex and England, were inspired teachers with the knack of treating younger players as if we were more mature than we imagined. It was a happy time, and provided a foundation for games played subsequently, first at Oxford and later in the Army. We were taught that sport is basically a frivolous activity; it should be taken seriously, and one should perform as well as possible, but it must never cease to be fun. We were competitive, working hard to win, but laughter was never far away. Here Winchester was wise as, for all our enthusiasm, we retained a sense of perspective.

Inevitably, the prospect of World War Two loomed increasingly. The Munich agreement in October 1938 gave us an extra year of so-called peace, but we were aware we were living on borrowed time. I would like to maintain I opposed Munich; it would not be true, however, and I can still recall the relief I felt when our preparations for war that autumn – fitting together gas masks in Winchester Town Hall and digging slit trenches for the housing estate at Bar End – were suspended on Chamberlain's return from Germany.

Nevertheless, we continued to plan for the future as if war would somehow be avoided. It was decided I should go to Oxford; New College agreed to take me and I took their Scholarship examination as a Historian in December. To my and other's surprise, I was awarded an Exhibition, and gained the leisure to profit from my last two terms at Winchester.

By the end of August 1939 war was obviously inevitable and there was no Munich-style reprieve this time. My father, commanding 53rd Welsh Territorial Division, mobilized his formation; on 4 September I went by train to Birmingham and officially joined the Army. There was, however, no question of eighteen year olds being needed for some time to come. I was to go to Oxford as planned in October and obtain a law degree before joining the Army. It seemed certain to be a long war and I was relieved I would not be immediately involved.

Chapter Three

OXFORD AND THE PHONEY WAR

In October 1939 Oxford was still unchanged and retained a Brideshead ambience for the first year of the war.

I was lucky in New College, which was full of Wykehamists. Many were scholarly types with whom I had little in common, though I envied their intellects. But it was a large college, big enough to have other circles and I soon made new friends. Reading law, and deciding not to continue with history, turned out well, for David Boult, New College's law tutor, was an inspiring teacher. Not even David could make Roman Law interesting, but he was realistic enough to make one work at the subject in a disciplined way. But crime, constitutional law and later tort and contract were different, and I found mastering the law and arguing about its interpretation fascinating. It was good this proved so, since Law Moderations, the only examinations I took that year, proved enough, with the distinction I gained in each of the three sections to provide me with a degree. Thus, unlike many of my friends, I did not have to return to Oxford after the war to seek further academic qualification.

For the first two terms I lived in college, my room just above the main Hall. Hall Stairs was not one of the grander areas in New College; the smart Etonians inhabited the Garden Quad, which had bigger rooms and a lovely outlook. But Hall Stairs had a great advantage – I was completely on my own and for the first time in my life able to live more or less as I wished. It was certainly easier to work in my garret than when, in April, I moved into lodgings at 15 Ship Street, sharing with my friend, Marcus Dick, formerly Prefect of Hall at Winchester, a distinguished brain and a scholar of Balliol. Oxford provided other opportunities that year. Fear of bombing meant that London theatre struggled to survive while people adjusted to the blackout and wartime restrictions. So the Oxford theatre, nourished by stars from London, flourished as never before, or since. The New Theatre provided a series of brilliant London productions of which *The Importance of Being Earnest*, with John Gielgud, Edith Evans and Jack Hawkins, was typical. At the Playhouse, too, there was Oxford's own repertory company, with Alec Clunes, Rosalie Crutchley, and other fine actors; the standard of teamwork and good directors provided a string of Playhouse productions almost as good as the big name performances at the New Theatre. It was a great chance to learn about the theatre and we took advantage of our good fortune. Nor did we neglect the cinema, and I have never regretted seeing *The Wizard of Oz* so many times in a particular week that even today I know its script virtually by heart.

Games still figured largely in my life. I never achieved footballing heights, playing occasionally for the Centaurs (the University reserve side), regularly for New College and the Old Wykehamists. That winter, however, was unusually cold; throughout January and well into February there was continuous frost and skating on the frozen Christ Church Meadow became a staple pastime. Despite the cold, the sun often shone and the icy Meadow was a beautiful place.

In April I returned early to Oxford to practice in the Parks with the University cricket squad under the captaincy of Dick Luyt, a South African wicket keeper, and even better rugby footballer. The "Phoney War" meant a near normal cricket programme had been planned; we started with the usual Freshmen's Match and a subsequent full University trial. I managed a flying start and, stronger and fitter than I had been at Winchester, developed greater pace than ever before or since. To my delight, I found myself selected as the University's opening bowler, sharing the new ball with Tony Henley, my fellow Wykehamist. Sadly, the German invasion of the Low Countries on 10 May put paid to many of the fixtures arranged for us as cricket took a lower place in people's priorities.

Instead of cricket in the Parks, I now found myself, armed with a cavalry carbine from the South African War, patrolling the University Science Museum under the auspices of the OTC, wearing an armband marked Local Defence Volunteers, the predecessors of the Home Guard. Why we were patrolling the area was not obvious, and, since we had only five rounds each, I doubt if our resistance to German parachutists would have lasted long. Yet we took our activity seriously and at least felt we were doing something for the cause, as the news from Holland, Belgium and France grew daily worse.

Bad news from the battlefield coincided with a developing love life, which involved regular trips to London for dinner to take my attractive girlfriend to a nightclub, the Nuthouse off Regent Street. There, led by Al Burnett, we drank expensive quantities of gin till the small hours and sang a refrain, of which I can remember only the chorus, "The smoke goes up the chimney just the same"! Somehow we got back to Paddington in time to catch the milk train back to Oxford, where Marcus Dick would leave the window at 15 Ship Street open, while our landlady, the kind Miss Bannister, was too tactful to draw the College's attention to one's absence.

Meanwhile, my father was busy preparing 53rd Division for war. The first Christmas and Easter we spent at Saundersfoot, near Tenby in Pembrokeshire, where the Division had moved from Shrewsbury to train more realistically. At the end of April my father moved the Division to Northern Ireland, with its headquarters in Belfast. 53rd Division's task developed into the ambitious role of forestalling a possible German invasion of Eire. Though such military knowledge was not known to me, there was a happy consequence, since, after term ended on 20 June, I found myself bound for Ulster where my parents had taken a house on the outskirts of Belfast.

At first Northern Ireland seemed to interrupt my social life, but it was not long before I discovered that Ulster possessed compensations. For a start, I found a job as a "Learner" with a leading firm of Belfast solicitors, Lestrange and Brett, their offices about 300 yards distant from the Law Courts. Owing to the war, lawyers of any kind were in short supply and even a "war" degree in law made me useful. After about three weeks, while I learnt my way round Belfast, I was given regular assignments. I learnt to draft a will and found myself on the tram, rocking up the Antrim Road, to record the wishes of potential clients, often elderly widows, who wanted to make a testament. I recorded their requirements, consumed a cup of tea and returned to Chichester Street to report progress. If the will were simple, I would be allowed to attempt a first draft, basing it on a more professional version which I could copy. I found a good place to work in the Abercorn Public House where ham sandwiches, washed down by a pint of Guinness, proved a good brain stimulant. I retain fond memories of working there, stretching my drafts as necessary to make sure they covered two pages. This was vital since a single page testament was worth a mere 13/6d, while two pages rated 25/- and an accolade from the management back in Chichester Street. Sometimes, on a morning when one had done two or more wills, one would be allowed to put the Guinness, but not the sandwiches, on expenses – the firm had proper Ulster priorities!

Often I lunched in Donegall Square with Julian Brooke, an old friend from Winchester and also waiting to be called up into the Army. Julian was the eldest son of Sir Basil Brooke, later Lord Brookebrough, then Home Minister in the Stormont Government and for many years Prime Minister of Northern Ireland. It was a tragedy for Ulster that Julian, who possessed charm, a sense of humour and political understanding, should have been killed in 1943 while serving in North Africa with the Grenadier Guards. Had he survived, he would have played a key role in the history of Northern Ireland; it was obvious, even then, he had the character and imagination to take him to the highest places. Julian taught me much over the lunch table; not least he explained, what most English people do not appreciate, the almost total irrelevance of the facts in Ulster situations. Julian understood the political importance of events to Ulster people; later, on visits to Northern Ireland I found this knowledge invaluable and used it to advantage. From Julian, too, I learnt the Ulster Nod, a salutation which opens many doors and has provided many refreshing draughts of Guinness and subsequent friendships. Julian and I enlisted in the 'B' Specials, a branch of the Royal Ulster Constabulary, which executed the duties in England assigned to the Home Guard. I found myself with a stripe by virtue of the weapon training learnt under Jack Parr at Winchester, and became responsible for the defence of Shaws Bridge below the Malone Golf Club, and on a subsidiary route from Lisburn to Belfast. I doubt if our resistance would have been very effective; at least, however, my section had a bandolier of fifty rounds apiece for our old-fashioned Ross rifles, besides unlimited pugnacity. Militarily, however, I am glad we were not tested, and that Shaws Bridge remained just a marking on some staff officer's mapboard.

Ulster people were enthusiastic sportsmen and the local cricket league, run on lines similar to the Lancashire league, provided a competitive environment. I was lucky in getting an introduction to the North of Ireland Club and found myself promoted to the first team. The wickets were slow and often affected by rain; the bowling was better than the batsmanship. Thus the matches were usually low scoring and close; though North were one of the top clubs, none of the games were easy since our opponents were always keen to topple us. I was sad when the season came to an end, but at last my efforts to join the Army were starting to bear fruit.

I had enlisted in the Army in September 1939 and been a member of the University OTC at Oxford. The fall of France in June 1940, and the fact that by now I had acquired a war degree, made me anxious to join up as soon as possible. I went over to the mainland in late August, and, by badgering the recruiting authorities in Oxford, succeeded in persuading them to allow me to join as an ordinary soldier instead of waiting to be called up in my turn as a potential officer. Having made these arrangements, and persuaded the KSLI (King's Shropshire Light Infantry) to accept me, I returned briefly to Ulster to tidy up my affairs there and say goodbye to the family. I drafted a final will or two in the Abercorn and took some wickets for North against Waringstown before I had to catch the boat for England. Though I did not know it then, it was to be thirty-seven years before I returned to ordinary life.

Chapter Four

A LEARNING MILITARY CURVE

I joined the Army on 12 September 1940 at Copthorne Barracks, Shrewsbury, Depot of the KSLI. My recruit training was efficient and enjoyable. I played football for an excellent Depot side, fought, but narrowly lost, two novice boxing bouts and, by January 1941 was ready to move on.

The Royal Military College Sandhurst was my destination. It was lucky that I had chosen The Rifle Brigade as my regiment. Adrian Gore, later my Commanding Officer for much of the war, had been selected to run a pilot course at the RMC before assuming command of a special unit for the Green Jackets, on Salisbury Plain. He asked for any Green Jacket candidates in the pipeline to be sent to his B Company at Sandhurst; it was the first, but not the last, time the 'black mafia' favourably affected my destiny.

Sandhurst contained some interesting people. The Brigade of Guards C Company next door included on its staff Gerald Micklem, the Walker Cup golfer, serving as a Grenadier, and Mike Wardell, then in the Welsh Guards, later a key figure in the Beaverbrook newspaper organization. C Company had some star cadets too, notably David Fraser, later to reach Four Star rank and the Army Board, and Simon Phipps, future Bishop of Lincoln, better known then as a performer in C Company's excellent Concert Party. Their CSM, Jacky Lord, was an outstanding Grenadier. Later in the war he joined the Airborne Forces, dropped at Arnhem and survived the battle. He became a prisoner of war where he acquired fame and reputation with both Germans and Allies for the manner in which he maintained morale and discipline in his POW camp. Later Jacky Lord returned to Sandhurst as Academy Sergeant Major, where he became a legend in his lifetime, a wonderful example to everyone, from successive Commandants downwards. His bearing was perfect, his standards impeccable, and his turn of phrase and sense of humour a delight. It was obvious even in 1941 that Jacky Lord was a great gentleman – he never used bad language and in his off duty moments was as good a rugby football referee as anyone could wish.

Our own B Company was less distinguished, though Adrian Gore, our Company Commander, possessed a great sporting talent. As a soldier, he was an amateur, but a talented one, with natural tactical sense and, fortunately for those with whom he served, unusually lucky. Above all, he possessed a light touch, which helped him to get the best from others.

I was lucky, too, in my Platoon Commander, Reg Goodwin, of the Queen's Regiment. Reg was a wartime soldier; he had been a Labour politician on the London County Council in the Clem Attlee tradition. After the war he became Chairman of the LCC and its Labour leader for many years. He was also General Secretary of the National Association of Boys Clubs, and an inspiration there also. He did not find soldiering, or Sandhurst, congenial and, after our course had passed out in April 1941, found serving as a gunner on merchant ships in the Atlantic more to his taste. But his high sense of duty, modesty and unassuming leadership taught us much that spring.

My three months at Sandhurst passed quickly. There was one tragic moment, when a German aircraft, losing its direction to London, dropped its bombs on our New Building at Sandhurst. The bombs fell on C Company's block next door, killing three of their number outright. It was a shock, a foretaste of what was to come, as well as a salutary reminder that wars are real and that our happy, escapist life at Sandhurst would not continue forever.

Jacky Lord gripped the situation, parading his Company first thing next morning, expecting no loss of standards and reminding everyone that the best tribute there could be to their dead friends was to drill and soldier even better in their honour. It was an object lesson in leadership; "Never look back," said Lord. "Life must go on and being sorry for oneself is a form of selfishness soldiers cannot afford."

I admired Jacky Lord, but not the Academy RSM, RSM Brand (nicknamed the Bosom because of his remarkable shape). If Lord was a leader, Brand was a bully and someone to be avoided. He had missed the First War and reached the rank of RSM between the wars by scrupulous attention to the minor administrative and petty routine, which formed a large (too large, as Lord Carrington has since pointed out) part of life in the Brigade of Guards in the thirties. He was a terror on the drill square, getting results by fear rather than leadership. I only fell foul of him once. My light infantry training, where we marched at 140 paces to the minute, with its philosophy of the "thinking soldier", was to blame. In Green Jacket or Light Infantry drill, it does not matter on which foot words of command are given. Riflemen are intelligent enough to be able to carry out the required movement on the "next correct foot". In the Brigade of Guards, however, the command "Halt" needs to be given precisely as the "left foot passes the right". If so, the squad halts magnificently with an impressive crash of boots. But the slightest error in timing results in a broken down rattle of footwear, like old-fashioned coal trucks being shunted in a siding. My first appearance on the main square of Sandhurst was as Cadet Under Officer for B Company. Inevitably, I halted my outfit on the wrong foot and Brand appeared from his office inside the archway of the Old Building like the Demon King in a pantomime. I received the rocket of a century, including remarks about my ancestry, KSLI antecedents and Rifle Brigade future. I also got an instruction, with which I quickly complied, "to take my shower away and not bring it back again for a fortnight". B Company were due to pass out the next day, but, this time carefully coached by our helpful CSM Phillips of the Coldstream Guards, I managed to halt my colleagues correctly. Brand gave me a glare, but, as I had won the Belt of Honour and was due to be commissioned next day, that was as far as he dared go.

After Sandhurst and leave in Northern Ireland I reported on 15 April (two days after my twentieth birthday) to the 2nd Motor Training Battalion of The Rifle Brigade at Lucknow Barracks, Tidworth. Recruits for the regiment received basic training at the Rifle Depot in Winchester; after eight weeks they were posted to Tidworth where all subsequent training took place. 2 MTB was a happy, efficient place. Charles McGrigor, the Commanding Officer, was a reservist whose severe asthma disqualified him from an active command. But command of a training battalion was ideal for him and The Rifle Brigade owes him much.

The military training at 2 MTB was in the hands of the Chief Instructor, John Taylor, a terrifying figure, whose personality was a complete contrast to that of Charles McGrigor. John had fought in the First War and won the MC in France as a young officer. He never contemplated going to the Staff College and remained a regimental soldier all his service. When war broke out in 1939 he was commanding a motor company in the First Battalion (1 RB), and went with that fine battalion to Calais in 1940. At Calais he was seriously wounded and evacuated to England on one of the last vessels to get away. He knew the nuts and bolts of soldiering backwards and felt a compulsive duty to pass on what he knew to the next generation. He was a brilliant trainer at section and platoon level, but with a violent temper and famous rages. He suffered fools not at all, and few of us escaped criticism at his hands. I got to know him well, for Charles McGrigor selected me to command a demonstration platoon, whose role it would be to illustrate the tactical doctrines John Taylor wished taught. It was an exhausting job, for John Taylor was a perfectionist and we spent many hours practising again and again the drills he demanded. Much of John's training still remains with me; I never park my car, for example, without checking my route of withdrawal, and, on country walks, still think of ground and cover. But my main debt is that John taught me battle discipline, something quite different to the formal discipline of the barrack square. As Field Marshal Wavell put it, "Discipline is teaching which shows you the right, the proper, and the expedient thing to do". To learn this was worth enduring a summer of John Taylor's intolerance and, sometimes, sheer lack of reason; by the Autumn, indeed, we had become firm friends.

Not all the regular officers in The Rifle Brigade were as professional as John Taylor. George Troyte-Bullock, who commanded A Company, was a different character. Between the wars he had won a reputation in the regiment for dash in the hunting field and married turbulence. Once he and his wife, Nina, had a disagreement so violent that she locked poor George in the loo at the top of their flat in Half Moon Street and walked out of the front door in a huff, taking the key with her. George shouted in vain for attention; finally, in desperation, he managed to open the window and lower to the street a roll of loo paper on the bottom of which was inscribed the single word 'HELP'. In those days policemen on the beat were more frequent and George was duly rescued from his predicament by a patrolling Constable.

Christopher Congreve, commanding C Company, came from a family with at least one holder of the VC. Christopher, however, was a gentle creature, uninterested in soldiering; he had become a regular soldier by accident between the wars, but been too idle ever to resign his commission. I remember him on one of John Taylor's exercises – about the importance of 'all round defence' – happily oblivious to the tasks to be given the LMG on the flank, but busily engaged in making a daisy chain. Nor was unorthodoxy confined to the more senior regular officers. Amongst the wartime entry was Bunny Roger, later to become chief dress designer to Hardy Amies, and a keener follower of fashion than student of the military art. In June 1941 we were crowded round the radio in the anteroom of the Mess at Lucknow Barracks, listening to the nine o'clock news with its long catalogue of disaster – withdrawal from Crete, failure of the Battleaxe offensive in Libya, and the Nazi invasion of Russia. "There is one bit of good news," remarked Stuart Hibberd as the programme reached its end. "Lord Woolton has allotted us one extra egg in next week's rations". Bunny Roger's voice piped through the silence. "Oh Good! Now I shall be able to do my hair".

After six months at Tidworth I began to think it was time I moved on to an active battalion. By now The Rifle Brigade had four battalions, 1st, 2nd, 7th, and 9th involved in the Western Desert, and I thought I should find myself sent as a reinforcement to one of these. Instead Charles McGrigor told me that I was to go for nine months to the Oxford University OTC. Thereafter I was destined for 10 RB, part of 6 Armoured Division, which by next summer would be fully trained and ready for war. My job at Oxford, apart from being an infantry instructor, would be to supervise the Greenjacket potential officers studying at the University for wartime degrees, and, by discreet recruiting, add to their number. It was a tempting assignment, and there was, in any event, no opportunity for evading it – the Colonel made clear it was the wish of the Colonel Commandant, Jock Burnett-Stuart, that I should represent the regiment at Oxford and my posting was thus an order and not a basis for discussion.

Going to Oxford for nine months had the advantage of extending my busy social life. Tidworth had given me introductions to a wonderful selection of girl friends, all attractive and intelligent. Diana Gilmour and Jane Pleydell-Bouverie may have been the leaders, but Robby Lawrence and Patsy White were not far behind them. Jane, only 18, was at that time keeping house for her father, Lord Radnor, at Longford Castle, south of Salisbury. There was an open invitation to Jane's friends serving on Salisbury Plain to come to Longford any Sunday to have lunch, play tennis, or just relax. These were wonderful occasions, and our little group, John Russell, Nat Fiennes and myself from The Rifle Brigade, Roddy McLeod from the Scots Guards, Tony Bethell and Christopher Petherick from the Life Guards, took full advantage. It was happily not then accepted practice to 'go steady' with one particular girl friend; though one competed eagerly for their favours, there was safety in numbers and no harm in ringing the changes. There were frequent dances on Salisbury Plain, as well as racing every weekend at Salisbury, Newbury or Cheltenham. Sometimes there was a party in London – a theatre, followed by supper, generously financed by parents, who then tactfully withdrew so the young could continue at a famous nightclub, The Four Hundred, in Leicester Square.

There were numerous girls around, but the demands of wartime meant that 'men' were in short supply. It was a 'buyer's market', and I was lucky in it and my friends. It flattered one, for membership of our group meant you always had a pretty, and certainly one of the nicest, girls in the room with you at supper or on the dance floor. It set a standard for me through life; my wife, Jean, Diana Gilmour's first cousin, but then abroad with her parents in India, has maintained it for the forty or more years of our married life since we first met in 1958.

Life at Oxford was a change from Tidworth. At first I lived in New College and ate my meals in the Senior Common Room. I soon, however, recognized that this was too expensive; a subaltern, with a taste for New College port, clearly could not afford Lucullan living on such a scale for long. So, thanks to the kindness of Graham Greenwell, the doyen of the Officers Mess at Cowley Barracks, I found myself housed there with The Rifle Brigade's sister regiment, the Oxfordshire and Buckinghamshire Light Infantry.

Graham Greenwell, in peace a stockbroker, was an old friend of my parents, and his sister, Bridget, was my godmother. He had joined the 43rd in 1914 straight from school at Winchester at the age of 18; he not only survived the war, but, as his book *An Infant in Arms* makes clear, actually enjoyed much of it. He was a natural soldier, an enthusiastic Territorial Officer between the wars, and in 1942 elder statesman and HQ Company Commander at his regiment's Depot. With Graham as sponsor, I fell on my feet and my nine months at Cowley Barracks were a pleasure. The 43rd/52nd took the sensible view that any fool could be uncomfortable; life in their mess, though not luxurious, was well organized and the food plentiful and well cooked.

I soon established my regime, breakfast soon after 8.00, and a quick look at the papers. Onto my bicycle at 8.30 – petrol was too precious to drive into Oxford in my £16 baby Austin – and I would arrive at the University OTC in Manor Road about 8.50. I reported to the Adjutant, Bunny Romilly, a 40-year-old reservist in the Coldstream Guards, left my bicycle, and walked to the Town Hall, where the Infantry wing of the OTC was located. There, under the loose control of Stephen Green, a schoolmaster from Uppingham, commander of the Infantry wing, my fellow instructors and I would rough out the work for the day. I was lucky in my colleagues; David Mynors from the Scots Guards was a recent Boat Race 'blue', Desmond Eagar from the South Wales Borderers had represented the University at cricket and hockey. The drill fell into David Mynors' sphere; as a soldier, Desmond maintained an amateur status, but supervised weapon training, and, under his cheerful system, range classification, often dull, became an exciting amalgam of batting averages and 'Cuppers' (inter-College knock out competitions). This left me with tactics and organization, though the high sounding title of the subject amounted just to a study of an infantry battalion, and the outlines of infantry and armoured divisions. Map reading was a special subject taught by the poet, Edmund Blunden, who wore a World War I tunic, his cap bearing a General Service badge, which was new to me and caused me for a week or so, till I learnt better, to think of Edmund as something to do with the GPO. Edmund was a gentle person, but shy with us extrovert young officers. If, however, one was lucky, and you got him on your own, he would start to talk about his own experiences. He kindly lent me his book about the trenches, *Undertones of War*. I took it back to Cowley and discussed it with Graham Greenwell that evening, learning much in the process.

Tactically, I relied on what John Taylor had taught me at Tidworth, but I was aware of my limitations. Discussion at Cowley Barracks gave me a new idea; there was a new infantry technique, battle drill, sweeping through Home Forces. It simplified the tasks of junior leaders at section and platoon level, and, by providing simple drills for ordinary soldiers, made the job of infantrymen easier to understand and teach. The prime mover in the battle drill movement was General Utterson-Kelso, GOC 47 (London) Division, and its high priest Colonel Wigram, a Royal Fusilier who commanded the Divisional Battle School. Bunny Romilly's kindness, skill on the telephone – and the prestige of Oxford University – allowed me to spend three days at the Divisional Battle School in the New Forest early in February.

My visit was an eye-opener. I saw basic infantry tactics taught in a practical way, much as good coaches at football plan simple methods for their teams. In the stress and shock of battle an infantryman needs to react instinctively and to be confident that those round him will be reacting similarly. On first contact, for example, the Battle School reaction – DOWN, CRAWL, OBSERVE, FIRE – is so simple that I can remember exactly what to do sixty years later. There were similar drills for other situations; I was thrilled and returned to Oxford full of zeal, and proceeded to put the principles into action with my OTC Cadets. At first we practised our new skills in the limited setting of Christ Church Meadow. Later, as we became more professional, and fitter physically, we went further afield to Headington Hill, Cumnor, and a downland training area, at Churn near Didcot.

Desmond Eagar was won over, and I got support from Alan Brown, a don at Worcester College, but then serving in the Scots Guards, who had succeeded David Mynors. Stephen Green, like a wise schoolmaster, was content to let our enthusiasm have full rein; "It seems to keep the boys happy," I heard him say on the telephone to Bunny Romilly.

My enthusiasm for battle drill did not interfere with my social life, which had gained wider horizons from my move. Numerous intelligence organizations seemed to have found a place in or near Oxford, with Blenheim Palace the home of one such. I had no interest in their professional activities, which were secret and none of my business. My concern was with the many nice girls who seemed to run these outfits; we had some marvellous parties, either in Oxford or at Cowley Barracks.

Early in 1942 Diana Gilmour, Jane Bethell and Robby Lawrence joined the ATS and undertook their basic training at Aldermaston in Berkshire. It was not long before I received a 'cri de coeur' with clear instructions to be outside their camp gate next Saturday morning with transport, cigarettes and enough money to give them all lunch in the Chequers at Newbury. I went along obediently to find that, wisely, the girls had not put all their eggs in one basket and that some eight to ten officers from all the fashionable regiments were waiting outside the camp gate to conduct the recruits to civilization. It was the prelude to a superb party ending when we poured the girls back, Cinderella fashion, to their Aldermaston prison later that evening; unlike Cinderella, their time of return was fixed earlier than midnight and we had been to Newbury Races and not a palace ball, but the principles were not very different.

This good life came to an end in July 1942 when I reported to 10th Battalion The Rifle Brigade near Kilmarnock in Ayrshire. The move marked a decline in my lifestyle, but I had arrived at 10 RB at the right moment.

10 RB had developed from a second line Territorial battalion, the Tower Hamlets Rifles, formed in 1939 as part of the Hore-Belisha campaign to 'Double up and Double the TA'. Its first set of officers came from the City, the riflemen from Mile End, Hoxton and Stepney. All were volunteers, the great majority of whom joined the Territorial Army because they saw that war was inevitable and they preferred to face it in the company of their friends. If the officers varied in quality, the standard of the riflemen was outstanding. In 1939 there had been no dilution of the Cockney stock from East London. Apart from a talented Jewish element, the remaining riflemen were Cockneys to a man, younger 'mirror images' of Stanley Holloway in *My Fair Lady*. They were tough, loyal and sensible; importantly, they were young, with an average age of 20 or so in 1939, which meant that by 1942 they had matured enough to be the right age for service in an active battalion. They were also streetwise, pleasantly cynical, and with a wit and sense of humour which permeated the battalion and maintained its morale until 1945.

Adrian Gore had recently arrived to command the battalion; his second-in-command, Harry Nicholl, and one of the Company Commanders, Dick Fyffe, were both pre-war regular officers in The Rifle Brigade. Dick had joined 10 RB on returning to the regiment after a four-year secondment to the RAF, where he had served as an Army Co-operation Pilot. Like me, Dick had been in Phils at Winchester, though we had not overlapped, and he became my greatest friend and inspiration during my Army career. There were other old friends in 10 RB, Tony Henley, an exact contemporary at Winchester and Oxford, Tony Pawson, who had been with me at Horris Hill and Winchester, and Michael Welman, also a member of our Winchester cricket team in 1939. We had all been requested by Adrian Gore, and were initially viewed with suspicion by old-timers in the battalion from the THR.

10 RB formed part of 26 Armoured Brigade, the main element of 6 Armoured Division, whose divisional sign, the Mailed Fist, was sewn onto my battledress on arrival in Scotland. 10 RB, a motor battalion, comprised the only infantry element in 26 Armoured Brigade; three armoured regiments, the 16th/5th Lancers, 17th/21st Lancers, and a Yeomanry regiment, the Lothian and Border Horse, made up the remainder of the formation. 6 Armoured Division also possessed an infantry brigade, at that time 38th Irish Brigade, whose place was taken later, in Tunisia, by 1st Guards Brigade. The supporting arms, especially the divisional artillery (12 RHA and 152 (Ayrshire Yeomanry) Field Regiments) and engineers, were of

outstanding quality; so, too, became the Division's armoured car regiment, the Derbyshire Yeomanry. We had a new Brigadier, Charles Dunphie, an intelligent gunner, while our Divisional Commander, Charles Keightley, had just relieved John Crocker, who had formed the Division back in 1940 and now went, on promotion, to command a Corps. 6 Armoured Division was a special formation, and remained so throughout the war. 10 RB was fortunate in being in such an outstanding division.

In July 1942 10 RB inhabited a tented camp at Kennox Park, Stewarton, near Kilmarnock. Kennox was damp and the weather wet, even by Ayrshire standards. There was mud everywhere; one squelched about on duckboards, often as not in gum boots. Despite the weather, we worked hard and cheerfully, for it was obvious that 6 Armoured Division would soon be going abroad.

I joined B Company, commanded by David Elkington, a stockbroker, later senior partner of a famous firm, Sebags. His second-in-command, Teddy Goschen, in the same firm, also became senior partner in due course. Both had been in the battalion since its inception, but were different characters. David was a cold, shy man, difficult in the early mornings; he was certainly a good administrator, and ran B Company on well oiled wheels. Teddy, by contrast, was extrovert, bored stiff by administration, but, as he was to prove later, without fear in battle and with surprising tactical flair. Of my fellow subalterns, Ken Dale, who commanded the scout platoon, was the best. The others, Tony Naumann and Basil Evans, were pleasant enough, though neither was a kindred spirit, and both must have often thought my military enthusiasm too much of a good thing.

I was lucky in my 6 Platoon, and especially in my platoon sergeant, Bert Coad, one of the best fighting soldiers I have ever met. Bert had been a regular soldier in 2 RB, but had left that battalion in Palestine to return to civil life shortly before the war. Almost immediately, however, he was recalled as a reservist and sent to 10 RB to provide professional backing in that still amateur outfit. Bert was a professional to his fingertips; we got on excellently, sometimes arguing hotly, but nearly always agreeing about the best for our platoon. Bert complemented me perfectly, being good where I was weak. He was a splendid shot and could quickly master, and clearly explain, any new weapon. He was perfectly turned out, marching about the Kennox duckboards with a riflemanlike swagger which made him a man apart. He shared my views on physical fitness, and 6 Platoon became noted for our fleetness of foot, marching and footballing skill. Football was an area where Bert and I agreed to differ; he had little time for games, which, in his view, interfered with the pursuit of 6 Platoon's excellence. His only weakness was map reading, where his navigation was uncertain. But, as a practical tactician, once an objective had been pointed out on the ground, his expertise was great and his determination absolute. He was a fine man; I admired him then, and still do now.

Perhaps our mutual regard can best be understood when I recount the pleasure, over twenty-five years later, on becoming a Major General, of receiving a rare letter from Bert Coad. He congratulated me on my promotion and asked if I would send him a signed photograph of myself in uniform for his 'front room' in St Pancras. "I always thought 6 Platoon was good," he wrote. "I should like to be reminded of it." I was proud that Bert Coad felt I had arrived. When he was my platoon sergeant, though he was too polite to say so, I feel he sometimes wondered if I would.

Bert and I did all we could to make 6 Platoon excel. We made a feature of marching – both fast over short distances and the ability to cover 30 miles in a day. There was method in this apparent madness, not just military masochism; I had heard about Vic Turner, then with 1 RB in the Desert – how he had been captured by the Germans, somehow escaped, and walked back to freedom through sheer determination. 6 Platoon's ability to march not only made us immensely fit, but developed the platoon's morale. Later, in Tunisia, our ability to march was to give just the confidence we needed at an unpleasant moment, but in Scotland that still lay in the future.

We had no idea then where 6 Armoured Division was to fight. We were told we would be going overseas that autumn, but where was anyone's guess. Nor did DRYSHOD, the final large exercise for Force 110, as our expeditionary force was called, provide the answer. We heard that General Alexander, who was to have been our Force Commander, had been removed to the Middle East. General Montgomery followed him there a day or two later, which confirmed many in their view that the Desert would be where we should fire our first shots in anger. Had we but known, Ex DRYSHOD, an imaginative piece of training, contained the key, though no one could have guessed it. The exercise was based on an assault landing from the sea, with troops being allowed into the operation only in accordance with previously planned shiploads or assault craft. The sea was imaginary, a line drawn across the Lowlands from Ayr eastwards, but the Lowland hills south of that line resembled the contours of Tunisia, as we discovered when we arrived there later. The tactics we developed with Dumfries our objective were therefore identical to those we should need to employ later in our assault on Tunis. But no one guessed and when we embarked at Greenock on 26 October we still did not know our destination.

After Ex DRYSHOD preparations for going abroad developed apace. Our vehicles became unavailable for training as the drivers worked on waterproofing them against the possibility of an amphibious landing. It was a frustrating time of order, counter-order and regular disorder, and Bert

Coad and I decided our strategy would be to get 6 Platoon daily out of Kennox Camp, so avoiding the worst of the hassle.

For a week I was taken away from 6 Platoon, and, with Ian Blacker, an old friend who had come to 10 RB after being Adjutant at Tidworth, sent to learn about anti-tank gunnery. 10 RB was to have its own anti-tank platoon; Ian Blacker was to be its first commander and I was to be his substitute; or succeed him if he should be promoted. We spent a strenuous week with the 72nd Anti-Tank Regiment Royal Artillery learning about the 2 pounder, a marvellous gun technically, but by then too small in calibre to penetrate the front armour of the main German tanks.

At the end of September news emerged about our overseas role. A regimental battle group, based on the 17th/21st Lancers and commanded by their former Commanding Officer, Dick Hull, was to precede the division. Dick Hull was promoted full Colonel to command the group, known as Bladeforce. Apart from the 17th/21st Lancers, Bladeforce included a motor company (our own B Company), a battery from 12 RHNA, an armoured car squadron of the Derbyshire Yeomanry, as well as supporting anti-tank and anti-aircraft batteries, and, of course, a sapper squadron. Though we did not know our task it was obvious that we would form an advance guard; we studied this role on model exercises, planning which proved invaluable later.

The 17th/21st Lancers, wearing their famous skull and crossbones cap badge, had been one of the first cavalry regiments to be mechanized. They adopted their new role enthusiastically, and under Dick Hull, later to become a Field Marshal and CIGS, became an outstanding armoured regiment. Dick Hamilton-Russell, who took Dick Hull's place in command, was an admirable commanding officer; their squadron leaders, with Val ffrench-Blake a charismatic star, were excellent too. We riflemen admired them greatly and B Company felt honoured to work with them, a view we continued to hold and never altered.

Early in October Kennox Camp became uninhabitable. The battalion moved to temporary winter quarters in billets at Darvel, a small, hospitable Ayrshire town 20 miles away. B Company, who were to go abroad earlier with Bladeforce, moved to a snug hutted camp at Prestwick, on the edge of the championship golf course. We left from Prestwick railway station for Greenock and embarkation on 26 October. By then the news of Eighth Army's assault at Alamein had broken; we assumed, wrongly, that our task would be to exploit their success.

At Greenock B Company with most of the 17th/21st embarked on SS *Cameronia*, a former Anchor Line Ship of 17,000 tons, which in peacetime had also doubled as a trooper. Bert Coad knew *Cameronia* well, having travelled to and from India on board her some years previously. He was typically resourceful in getting 6 Platoon established on their troop deck in the 24 hours or so before we sailed from the Clyde.

Ken Dale and I shared a three-berth cabin with David Elkington – it was a dry ship, but David, never a man to be parted from his gin for long, had foreseen this contingency and was kind enough to provide a libation each evening for those like myself who had been less provident.

When our convoy (KM2) left the Clyde, we headed far west, beyond Ireland, out into the Atlantic. Though it was rough at first, *Cameronia* was a steady ship and there was enough space on deck to take exercise and maintain our fitness. After six days at sea Bladeforce opened our orders. We were to land at Algiers, exploiting an earlier assault landing by the Americans and the British 78th Division. Subsequently, overcoming any resistance offered by the Vichy French military forces, we were to advance as fast and far to the east as possible – final objective Tunis and ultimate aim to link up with the Eighth Army's advance from Egypt. It was an imaginative project and excited us all as we examined its possibilities.

Chapter Five

TUNISIAN TURNTABLE

"In the first advance on Tunis, we made virtually every mistake in the book. Staff Colleges in future should study our operation as an example of how not to do it."

GENERAL DWIGHT D. EISENHOWER
Supreme Allied Commander in the Mediterranean 1942–43

Cameronia sailed past Gibraltar and Oran, where half the convoy carrying American troops left to join their compatriots in Western Algeria. We heard over the ship's loudspeaker that the French had decided not to offer further resistance to the Allied landings and intended, under Admiral Darlan's leadership, to resume fighting the Axis. It was confusing as we attempted to explain the politics to the riflemen, who were relieved at merely having the Germans to consider.

Cameronia anchored off Algiers on 12 November, we disembarked without incident and with amazingly no German air attacks. While the drivers waited under Teddy Goschen to collect their vehicles, I marched the rest of B Company to the Jardin des Essais – the Algiers Zoo – where local maps and transport were waiting to take us to L'Arba, our assembly area. There the vehicles and our luggage joined us, and we reloaded the vehicles in preparation for our long move eastwards towards Tunis. Bert Coad was critical about the amount of luggage we (and especially the officers) brought with us. "Trouble with these officers is that the Mediterranean means the South of France to them. They don't realise we are here to fight a war." Since Darlan's decision to join the Allies, Eisenhower had no need further to bother about overcoming French military resistance in North Africa. Political affairs would remain a problem, but they were no concern of ours. For us it was a question of a race for Tunis against the Germans; though Bladeforce did not immediately see the campaign in such terms, the stakes had become clear enough by 25 November when Anderson and First Army launched their attack on Tunis and Bizerta.

First Army resembled its high-sounding title only in name. The forces available on the ground were small – 36 Infantry Brigade on the northern

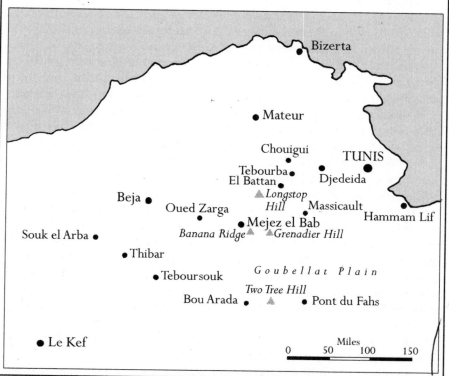

Mediterranean Sea

Sicily

ALGIERS
Bône
Bizerta
Cape Bon
TUNIS
Constantine
Hammamet
Sousse
Kairouan
Fondouk
Pass
Kasserine
ALGERIA
Sfax
TUNISIA
Gabes

0   50   100 Miles

Bizerta

Mateur

Chouigui

Tebourba
El Battan
Longstop
Hill
Djedeida
TUNIS
Beja
Oued Zarga
Massicault
Hammam Lif
Souk el Arba
Mejez el Bab
Banana Ridge
Grenadier Hill
Thibar
Teboursouk
Goubellat Plain
Two Tree Hill
Bou Arada
Pont du Fahs
Le Kef

Miles
0   50   100   150

axis to Bizerta, 11 Brigade directed on Mejez and the main road to Tunis. Bladeforce, reinforced by elements of a Parachute Brigade dropped haphazardly into the area south of Tunis, and some American armour sent forward from Oran, operated between the two infantry brigades. Bladeforce's mission was vague – to establish a 'tank-infested area' near Chouigui, ready to operate against Mateur or Djedeida as opportunity dictated. Command of this untidy plan was delegated to Vyvyan Evelegh and 78th Division. Since the Germans had command of the air and held the best airfields in Tunisia, especially the one at El Aouina, near Tunis itself, it is now obvious that 78th Division's task was quite unrealistic; in the circumstances, though mistakes were made and opportunities missed, perhaps it is surprising First Army performed as well as it did.

B Company's move forward to the battlefield was generally smooth, though, for me, it had its moments of drama. We started from L'Arba on the afternoon of 15 November and for two days our advance to Constantine in brilliant sunshine resembled a military picnic. We gorged ourselves on beautiful oranges bought in the bazaar at L'Arba, admired the scenery and dozed away between times.

At Constantine the weather broke. With the rain's arrival, our holiday mood disappeared. David Elkington returned from Dick Hull with news that the French in Tunis had given in to German pressure and that we would not get to Tunis unopposed, as some optimists had hoped; we were to move eastward as fast as possible, which meant a night drive to Souk Ahras, starting at midnight. We snatched a short sleep, and, with our drivers still tired, and everyone grumpily half asleep, were again on the road.

We had driven 10 miles from Constantine when disaster struck 6 Platoon. Our convoy was going through a military motoring phase when one oscillates between a slow crawl and frenetic speeding to catch up the vehicle in front. We were driving on sidelights only and those in front were setting a rapid pace. One cannot therefore blame my driver, Rifleman Gough, for skidding on the wet cobbles, being unable to correct his error, and ending up in the ditch between the road and the main railway line running east towards Tunis. The next vehicle, carrying Corporal Dingwall's section, was too close to our tail and ran into our back; thus 6 Platoon found itself reduced to a mere two sections. I transhipped gloomily to Corporal Johnson's section truck; there was just time to pick up my small pack containing washing and shaving materials. I left Bert Coad, whose map-reading skills were limited and who knew no French, to sort matters out without expecting we would meet again before Tunis. When morning broke, I walked up the company column and broke my news to David Elkington, who received it without enthusiasm.

Before lunch Ken Dale's carriers materialized as they were unloaded by apathetic Arabs from the flats on which they had travelled by rail from

Algiers. By the time we left for Bladeforce's final assembly area at Souk el Arba, with the exception of the truncated 6 Platoon, B Company was complete. We drove to Le Kef and leaguered for the night well into Tunisia to carry out our first operational task, protecting Bladeforce's southern flank from surprise attack. For 6 Platoon this involved blocking a crossroads, through which moved a continuous stream of French soldiers of the XIX Corps, their orders to extend the Allied line to the south of Medjez el Bab, forty miles further to the east. I consulted the map and thought this plan sound enough, though the antique equipment of the Tirailleurs Tunisiens, their pack transport, and horsedrawn 75 Millimetre (the famous soixante-quinzes of World War I) artillery seemed unlikely to halt a serious German thrust. Memories of the French débâcle in 1940 often caused us to underrate the French in Tunisia; they fought with valour despite their lack of modern equipment. It was from the Tirailleurs Tunisiens that I got some tangible enemy intelligence; the Germans had occupied El Aouina airport between Carthage and Tunis as early as 9 November. The French estimate was that the Germans had been landing some 1,000 soldiers a day since then; by now (19 November), therefore, we were likely to be opposed by at least 10,000 Axis soldiers, and, being aware of our long Lines of Communication back to Algiers, one realized the German build-up would be as quick as, and probably faster than, our own. "How do you get your information?" I asked the French, naively in my best Wiccamical French. They looked at me in the way intelligent French often regard thick Anglo-Saxons. "*Mais, naturellement, on telephone tous les jours directement à Tunis.*" It was clearly an odd war, and David Elkington was unconvinced by my information when I reported it next morning.

My knowledge of French, however, and the fact that 6 Platoon was still incomplete, gained me an interesting job. While B Company concentrated with Bladeforce, I was to motor forward along the main road to Teboursouk, carrying out a road reconnaissance, before returning to Souk el Arba by Thibar and Souk et Khemis. It was a fascinating and beautiful drive of 80 miles. We moved semi-tactically by bounds, one vehicle covering the other; fortunately we met no opposition and my military confidence recovered as the day wore on. I discovered, too, that Thibar produced Tunisia's best wine and returned to Souk el Arba with about three day's supply for Teddy Goschen and myself, the only addicts in the company. David Elkington stuck resolutely to gin, and the riflemen dismissed all wine as 'gut rot' and pined only for beer, which was non-existent.

I was more cheerful, therefore, when I had finished my report and seen it off by dispatch rider to Bladeforce HQ. As I regained 6 Platoon's area, where everyone was 'brewing up' and discussing our patrol, there came a memorable moment. Up drove Bert Coad with our Platoon HQ truck, standing up grinning broadly as he saluted triumphantly. Rifleman Gough had recovered his balance and my other section commander, Corporal Dingwall, was equally delighted to be back. "How did you do it, Bert?" I asked as soon as a welcoming mug of tea had been thrust into his hands. He described how he had persuaded the local garage in Le Krib, scene of the accident, to mend Gough's broken axle by trading a box of compo, and some of the cigarettes I had brought for the platoon, in exchange for the repair. "Splendid botchers, them Frogs," remarked Bert, as he marched off regimentally to clock in with the CSM. It was wonderful to have him back; Dingwall had helped with the map reading – but it was Bert's drive, determination and fear that somehow he might miss the battle which had saved the day. I slept happily that night; next morning the 'compo' sausages tasted good, while Bert walked proud for a day or two and deservedly too.

The real battle began for B Company on 25 November, when we moved forward, as part of Bladeforce, to establish our tank-infested area between 36 and 11 Brigades. We went through Beja as it was getting light; one could see rubble and damage caused by a fierce Stuka raid the previous afternoon. We took the road to Sidi Nsir; B Company was good at march discipline, each vehicle spaced out at the regulation 20 vehicles to the mile (88 yards between vehicles). As we reached Sidi Nsir two German ME 109s, reconnaissance aircraft, flew fast down the column. Sensibly, no one engaged them; even so, if the Germans did not know the location of Bladeforce or the direction of First Army's armoured thrust they now would. About a mile short of the T roads, our first objective, the column halted. Leaving Bert Coad to get 6 Platoon's vehicles off the road, I jumped on the back of Rifleman Hedgecock's motorcycle and got a lift to Company HQ where the Company 'O' Group was assembling. Teddy Goschen, busy on the radio to RHQ 17th/21st Lancers, told us David Elkington had gone forward to where the Derbyshire Yeomanry had identified the enemy opposition. We could hear the rattle of Besa fire from their armoured cars as they engaged our opponents; there was no reply yet from the enemy, apart from the odd mortar round which burst about 150 yards away. Bert Coad, meanwhile, had disembarked 6 Platoon and I could see him leading them steadily forward along an English style ditch and stream which ran parallel with the road 100 yards or so to the right. 7 and 8 Platoons followed Bert's example, so our battle procedure was working perfectly, just like an exercise. Soon Teddy told the platoon commanders to go forward 300 yards down the road to meet David. Ken Dale had already deployed his carriers and would join us there.

David's orders were clear; the enemy were holding a farm on the right of the road and also a ridge to the left about 1,200 yards beyond the T roads. The scout platoon had already found a way round on the right for the 17th/21st tanks, who would get above the farm and so be able to dominate it. 6 Platoon were to advance on the right of the road, 7 Platoon on the left.

8 Platoon would stay in reserve. "Ready to move in 15 minutes as soon as the supporting artillery stop firing and you see the tanks going forward across the road." It was well timed; I was just able to brief the section commanders and point out our objective (the farm) on the ground before the RHA battery opened up. They were spot on target, and some smoke fired by the tanks helped too. We moved steadily uphill towards our objective, spaced out in arrowhead formation. About 200 yards forward of our objective, the tanks roared in from above, setting a haystack on fire in the process, while a few token shots were fired at us. There followed a mass fluttering of white handkerchiefs and down the hill trooped sixty unhappy Italians, most of them already disarmed and all clearly intent on surrender. It was embarrassingly easy; Bert Coad detailed two sensible riflemen to escort our prisoners down to the T roads. Remembering what I taught in the OTC at Oxford, I kept 6 Platoon going through the objective and we exploited forward about 1,200 yards till we reached the Mateur road at the top of the ridge. There Ken Dale caught me up in a carrier, and relayed orders to go firm for the moment. "I think there is some trouble on the left," he said.

Ken's information was correct. 7 Platoon, advancing on the left of the road, had nearly reached their objective when an isolated German section, armed with a Spandau machine gun, opened up from point blank range. Corporal Mister, the leading section commander, was killed instantly; Tony Naumann, the platoon commander, was desperately wounded and, though we did not know this till later, never recovered his sight. Sergeant Rutherford, the composed Scots platoon sergeant, took control and 7 Platoon completed their mopping up, killing several German parachutists. 8 Platoon, under their platoon sergeant, came up through 7 Platoon on my left; I then expected the trucks to come up and for Bladeforce to resume its advance. Through my field glasses I could see two Italian medium tanks which had survived the engagement at the T roads making tracks back towards Mateur; so easy had our triumph been that, despite 7 Platoon's misfortune, Bert Coad and I felt we could have captured Mateur single-handed with just 6 Platoon (and a tank or two in support, of course).

My enthusiasm for pushing on, Prince Rupert fashion, towards Mateur was misplaced. The T roads had been our objective, and now the task of the infantry in Bladeforce was to hold it firmly. Dick Hull had also heard that not only had 36 Brigade's attack in the north failed to capture its objective, but 11 Brigade's attack on Mejez had been equally unsuccessful. Bladeforce therefore needed to pause for consolidation.

Two days later, while B Company were still sitting at the T roads protecting the armour overnight, the American tanks in Bladeforce achieved a masterstroke. Debouching from the Tebourba end of the

Chouigui Pass, they surprised a German flank guard and advanced un-opposed to Djedeida. The Germans on the airfield were taken unawares; thirty-seven fighters and bombers, grounded by bad weather, were destroyed in situ. Not only did this action briefly reduce the scale of air attack on Bladeforce, its impact caused the Germans to decide they were over-exposed and should withdraw from Mejez – a decision for which Kesselring, his Commander in Chief, criticized his subordinate Nehring fiercely and later, on 10 December, relieved him of his command.

The German withdrawal from Mejez, back to the high ground between Djedeida and Tebourba to protect their airfields, allowed 11 Brigade to advance quickly to beyond Tebourba. It was the high water mark of 78 Division's attempt to reach Tunis, and on 30 November Bladeforce and B Company drove over the Chouigui Pass to a concentration area near Chouigui village whence next day it was planned to launch an armoured drive to Tunis, a concept which was over-optimistic. As 6 Platoon cowered that evening in its slit trenches round Chouigui church, the Luftwaffe hovered continuously overhead and I was not surprised to get a change of orders. The armoured raid on Tunis was postponed 'sine die'; instead Bladeforce was to take up position on the left flank of 11 Brigade, covering the approaches to Tebourba from the north. B Company's task in this new role was to block the road leading from Chouigui to Tebourba; we occu-pied our new position at first light on 1 December, dug ourselves in energetically and tucked our trucks away on the reverse slope behind our position. 6 Platoon were forward on the left with a good field of fire covering the road itself; 8 Platoon were higher up the ridge about 500 yards to our right. 7 Platoon with Company HQ were on a ridge behind about 1,000 yards back. Behind B Company 17th/21st Lancers embarked on vital main-tenance; the sun came out and, after I had walked round my platoon position, congratulating people on their digging and checking the camou-flage, I felt pleasantly content. I opened my shooting stick, relaxed in the sun and surveyed the high ground about Chouigui through my binoculars. It was, briefly, like an interval between races at a Nottinghamshire point to point.

I had been sunning myself for half an hour when I saw a long column of tanks and trucks moving in our direction about three miles away. The Derbyshire Yeomanry had seen them too, and alerted the duty squadron of the 17th/21st, who moved forward of my position to the left to deal with the threat. I watched intently through my glasses, confident in the ability of our armour to deal with the threat.

What I saw was, in fact, the right wing of a German pincer movement to re-establish their position to the west of Tunis. On 30 November, while Bladeforce was being bombed in its concentration area at Chouigui, Field Marshal Kesselring had visited Nehring. "He who holds Mejez holds

Carthage," the Field Marshal had said, quoting the old Carthaginian adage; Nehring was to counter-attack at once, first recapturing Tebourba. Nehring delegated this task to Major General Fischer, commander of the 10th Panzer Division; he rightly appreciated the weakness of 11 Brigade, with its three battalions strung out loosely in 'line astern' from Djedeida. Fischer's plan was simple – to attack 11 Brigade frontally from Djedeida with the bulk of his infantry and some forty tanks. The rest of his armour, about sixty tanks, would simultaneously move round to the north, brush Bladeforce aside and seize the Tebourba Gap. 11 Brigade would thus be encircled and could be destroyed at leisure. It was a bold plan and came near success. B Company, a pawn on a larger chessboard, was to undergo a frightening experience as the German plan developed.

I watched fascinated as 10 Panzer Division deployed. They had little artillery, since only a few shells screamed over our heads to land among the tanks hurriedly completing their maintenance behind us. Their move from the single file in which I had first observed them moving over the pass into battle formation was stately and menacing because of its sheer lack of haste. About 1,500 yards short of us they halted and took up 'hull down' positions. It was obvious the panzers were waiting for something; our own tanks, outnumbered by over two to one, sensibly did not open fire since at that range a Crusader six pounder could not penetrate their opponents' armour. The reason for the German delay then became clear; overhead appeared a dozen Stukas like sinister black crows. They circled the area, carefully identifying their target, then dived one after another to release their bombs. From the direction of their dives, my guess was that Bladeforce HQ was their target, but by now it did not matter since the German armour was starting to move forward. Our own tanks opened up, but got the worst of the engagement. Soon two Valentines and a Crusader were in flames, as the mass of Mark IIIs and IVs moved purposefully forward. I feared for the two Rifle Brigade two pounders, deployed on the reverse slope of our ridge. Earlier that morning I had helped them choose their positions, but had not since been to check them. I hoped they had practiced our camouflage teaching, but one could only hope for the best.

Just then, imperturbable, cheerful as usual, Teddy Goschen arrived behind me on a motorcycle. "Pack up, Jim," he said. "Straight down the road into Tebourba. Look out for Company HQ, who will have found a harbour area on the El Battan Road. I rushed round my three sections to pass on these orders, leaving Bert Coad to get Platoon HQ on the move and alert the drivers. The riflemen as usual reacted superbly when it came to quick movement; soon we were all in the dead ground behind our ridge, jumping on our trucks like a load of football supporters leaving a lost match. Thank God, too, I had remembered my training; the trucks were parked facing the exit, so we could go straight out of our area and onto the

Tebourba road. We bumped agonizingly over the rough field between us and the tarmac, followed by our anti-tank guns; once on the firm surface, Rifleman Gough and the others put their feet down. It had been a near thing, and only as we drove into Tebourba past a 5.5 medium gun, sighted to fire down the road in an anti-tank role, did I realize that I had left my shooting stick behind. Doubtless 10 Panzer Division kept it for the rest of the campaign, and perhaps it got back into Allied hands when the Germans surrendered next May. More likely, however, a Chouigui Arab collected it; if so, I hope he is still using it, as he walks round his cornfields inspecting his crop.

Tebourba was a small township, with a railway station and two important road junctions. We found there what Field Marshal Montgomery would have described as a 'scene of considerable military confusion'. Neither the pell-mell withdrawal of Bladeforce, nor the arrival in the town of B Company, helped greatly. Though we were exhilarated by our narrow escape, we had taken part in a retreat so headlong as to constitute a near rout. An officer in the East Surreys said later, "It was like Dunkirk all over again". We found an olive grove on the south edge of the town and concealed our vehicles before starting to dig ourselves a new set of slit trenches. The arrival overhead of a fresh lot of Stukas made digging a priority.

As soon as 6 Platoon were organized, I walked over to Company HQ to try and establish 'the form'. It was not encouraging; Ken Dale, who had been sent in a carrier to tell 8 Platoon to withdraw from the Chouigui position had reached the top of the ridge only to see them overrun by a troop of Mark IIIs accompanied by a platoon of Panzer Grenadiers. 8 Platoon were 'in the bag' as the saying went; B Company now had only two motor platoons and Ken Dale's scout platoon, itself reduced by casualties and mechanical failures to about two-thirds of its proper strength. Though Teddy Goschen put a good face on our situation, David Elkington, who had commanded B Company since the start of the war, was shattered at the losses it had suffered. Though, for the next couple of months, he maintained a stout front, David was never the same man again. We depended increasingly on Teddy Goschen from now on.

I gradually established the main outlines of the military picture in the Tebourba area. To the south, where affairs seemed least confused, the East Surreys held the El Battan bridge securely; towards Djedeida and Tunis the Northamptons and the Hampshires (a magnificent battalion, superbly led, detached and sent ahead from 1st Guards Brigade) were under attack from tanks and infantry. Behind us on the Mejez road the Germans occupied the Tebourba gap; an American counter-attack was being mounted to clear the road. Inside Tebourba, there was a jumble of supporting arms, supply echelons of the 11 Brigade infantry battalions, and, of course, B Company.

The rest of Bladeforce had withdrawn to reform on the Mejez side of the Tebourba gap. B Company were to move back to rejoin the rest of Bladeforce as soon as the road could be cleared. "What happens if the American attack is not successful?" I asked, not altogether helpfully. "Well," said Teddy, surprisingly cheerful for someone who never marched a yard if he could help it, "it looks like a long walk in the dark to Mejez." I returned to 6 Platoon to brief Bert Coad and the section commanders. Though it would be humiliating to abandon our transport, the prospect of a long night march did not daunt them. "How far to Mejez?" asked Bert Coad. "About twenty miles? Nothing to what we did in Scotland." Their confidence did me good and was a great support for the next 36 hours of order, counter-order and Stuka attack as the battle for Tebourba ebbed and flowed round us.

As usual, the gunners, field, medium, anti-aircraft and anti-tank, stood out above the others in Tebourba. They had a vital job to do, with the 25 pounders in particular responding to regular calls for defensive fire from the infantry protecting our perimeter. But, above all, their communications worked and they seemed to know what was happening. It was from one of the field regiments, for example, that we first heard the American counter-attack had been postponed and later proved successful, though no one knew how long the Mejez road could be kept clear. The Hampshires, we heard, had beaten off a fierce German infantry attack, information confirmed through Bladeforce when we got orders for our night move back behind Mejez after dark on 2 December.

No one was sorry to leave Tebourba. At the back of our minds there was regret at leaving a sinking ship. But at the time my reaction was of relief at the prospect of being able to fight again another day, coupled with gratitude and admiration for those – the Americans, the Hampshires, the East Surreys, the Northamptons and, not least, the gunners – who had made our withdrawal possible. The drive back in the dark to Mejez was tense, but uneventful. We went into reserve behind Mejez at a farm above Oued Zarga, to lick our wounds, re-fit, and await the future.

The next three weeks were a jumble, as B Company moved about behind Mejez for a series of tasks, none of which, happily, materialized. First Army was suffering from a typical British military disease, a superfluity of chiefs and a shortage of Indians. By mid-December, for example, First Army had its own staff, as well as the newly arrived 5 Corps, and two divisional Headquarters to direct the activities of two incomplete British divisions. Add the French XIX Corps and the US II Corps, both of them directly responsible to AFHQ in Algiers, and one can understand the regrouping and constantly changing plans. The Axis forces gained most from the confusion, with some important features being abandoned by the Allies, sometimes without a fight, in efforts to obtain a breathing space. Some of the positions – the Tebourba Gap and the famous Longstop Hill, for example – were not recaptured till the following April, and then only at the cost of many lives. It was not a distinguished period, and steady rain and resulting mud did not help our morale.

On 20 December the weather relented and B Company became involved in First Army's next attempt to resume the attack on Tunis. This required our sitting isolated on a long low hill, later famous as Banana Ridge, covering the Mejez–Tunis road about a mile to our north. Behind us on Grenadier Hill were the 3rd Battalion Grenadier Guards, who made no concessions to mud and rain, behaving as on an exercise from Pirbright. There were old friends around from Oxford days as we laughed and gossiped outside their HQ, The Cave, on Grenadier Hill, while David Elkington got his orders from their Colonel, Algy Heber-Percy. Our task was simple, militarily dodgy and, in the winter weather, unpleasant. B Company were to man an outpost line a mile and a half in front of the Grenadiers on Banana Ridge; we were also to patrol vigorously to discover what defences the Germans held along the main road from Mejez towards Tunis. Any information would help to make the plan for First Army's renewed assault on Tunis. In principle, we gathered that the attack, mounted by our own newly arrived 6 Armoured Division, would be launched on Boxing Day. It was to be preceded by an attack by the Coldstream Guards on Longstop Hill the other side of the Medjerda. Like the Grenadiers, this fine battalion formed part of 1st Guards Brigade. It sounded all right on paper, but the weather and a wary cynicism, born of our Bladeforce experience, made B Company jaundiced about its prospects.

6 Platoon's position on Banana Ridge proved as disagreeable as expected. There was no cover against the driving rain, while the ground was too rocky for our picks and shovels to dig proper slit trenches. The only protection was to build North-West Frontier style sangars on the reverse slope, rigging gas capes and groundsheets over the top to keep out some of the rain and sleet. Fortunately the enemy seemed unaware of our existence; there was no shelling and, apart from reconnaissance flights down the valley each morning, no hostile air activity either. We devised a routine by which half our number went down by day to the more sheltered area where the trucks were; here the drivers provided tea and a hot meal. By night our position was fully manned – with double sentries in each section, and the remainder snatching what rest they could in their sangars. It was a dismal Christmas.

Though life on Banana Ridge was disagreeable, we were luckier than the Coldstream Guards involved in bitter fighting for Longstop Hill five miles away across the valley. We could see the gun flashes from the artillery on each side and measure how things were going by the flares put up by the

Germans as they indicated their positions and called for defensive fire. On the morning of 23 December we heard that the Coldstream attack had been successful; they had handed over to some Americans and withdrawn into reserve round Mejez station ready for the next phase. It looked as if, despite the weather, First Army's Boxing Day attack might start as planned.

That evening I was told to lead a patrol with two tasks – first to discover the going on the low ground below Banana Ridge and beyond it off the road along which 26 Armoured Brigade would have to advance, second to estimate where the enemy's FDLs (forward defended localities) were sited. Though our position on Banana Ridge had given us good observation over the area in daylight, we had seen no enemy movement apart from the odd armoured car or motorcycle moving cautiously along the muddy tracks. Though I guessed there was an infantry and anti-tank screen, we had no idea where it lay. Our patrol was therefore important; it was in any case no hardship to leave Banana Ridge in the safe hands of Bert Coad and set off in the dark with just Corporal Dingwall and another rifleman as companions.

My patrol technique was always to make maximum use of the half-light just before it gets dark. By moving quick at this time one gets a flying start and a chance to check one's reverse compass bearing in half-light against the feature one is leaving. So our party were near the main road as darkness came down and I determined to lie up for half an hour to listen for sounds of enemy activity. Twenty minutes after dark we heard the clanking sound of tracked vehicles about a mile beyond us. The Germans seemed unaware there was anyone near them, for there was plenty of shouting, as they went into leaguer for the night. We listened intently until, half an hour later, comparative silence ensued, broken only by the unmistakable noise of a battery charging engine. We moved forward cautiously towards the sound; the going was appalling, thick glutinous mud, impassable for wheels and in which I judged our Crusaders and Valentines would probably also get stuck. Our progress on foot was slow – 1,000 yards in the hour at best. After about ninety minutes homing on the charging engine, we saw the outline of a cactus grove; stopping again, we saw what seemed the glow of a cigarette at the corner of the clump. German sentries, like their counterparts in the British Army, clearly 'had a drag' at night when their Feldwebel was not watching. The sentry finished his cigarette and we heard him plodding slushily round the clump, presumably to make contact with his half section the other side. Inside the cactus we heard the odd vehicle start up and briefly run its engine. A heavy half-tracked vehicle drove up from the direction of Massicault, its arrival followed by a burst of shouting as the drivers were roused and re-fuelled.

The pattern was clear now and I felt I knew enough to answer the questions set me. Slowly we headed back towards Banana Ridge. Once across the main road, we moved more confidently, though I checked frequently to ensure I was returning to 6 Platoon's position exactly where I had agreed beforehand with Bert Coad. A quiet challenge; the first word of the password – thank God I remembered the response – and we were safely back. A shot of rum for the three of us then I made my way down to Company HQ to report my conclusions. These were simple – the going was far too bad for movement even of tracked vehicles across country. Wheels would be restricted to roads only. There was little German infantry about, but an advance could expect to meet a German defensive screen of tanks and anti-tank guns about 2 miles west of Banana Ridge. It was not my place to say so, but clearly the proposed advance by 26 Armoured Brigade was not on; Teddy Goschen thanked me nicely and back I went to 6 Platoon and Banana Ridge.

On Christmas Eve we heard the attack was off. It is tempting to think the decision was taken on the evidence of our 6 Platoon patrol; this was not the case, for greater men had been involved. First the Americans, taking over from the Coldstream Guards on Longstop Hill found the feature had not been cleared of enemy. This made them victims of a typical German counter-attack and the Coldstream, the only reserve available, were called back to attack Longstop again for the second time in 24 hours. With great gallantry, the Coldstream attacked again on Christmas Eve and regained the feature, only to find themselves overlooked by the even more dominating Djebel el Rhar. It was a stalemate, and certainly not the start for which the generals were hoping. Fortunately Eisenhower had come forward from Algiers to confer with Anderson, arriving early on Christmas Eve. He had seen the conditions from his car on the way up, stopping to watch six soldiers struggling to free a motorcycle stuck in the mud. Disappointed, he decided rightly to postpone the attack, so saving 6 Armoured Division for a later occasion. It would have been folly to have done otherwise.

B Company's presence on Banana Ridge had now lost its tactical meaning. We struggled back to Mejez after dark on Boxing Day, and joined our parent 10 RB (newly arrived and anxious to hear our news) at Sidi Ayed. There was a great reunion with our friends; we dried our clothes and shot a line or two about Bladeforce. There were letters from home, beer and cigarettes for the riflemen, and even a bottle of gin for Bert Coad and I to share that evening. It was good to be back with our battalion.

I soon learnt my days as an ordinary platoon commander were numbered, for Adrian Gore confirmed I was to take over the anti-tank platoon from Ian Blacker, who was needed elsewhere. I was warned to learn about the six pounder with which we were to be re-equipped, while John Chadwyck-Healey soon arrived and briefly shadowed me in 6 Platoon. He was a delightful person and I was happy to hand over to him, though it was sad to leave the platoon with whom I had shared so much.

There was, however, a major battle before I left. For the first weeks of January 10 RB occupied Bou Arada, at that time the southern end of the First Army front. We patrolled at night towards Pont du Fahs and occupied OPs on either side of the Bou Arada valley by day. It seems, and was, amateurish, but we were short of infantry and did not realize the Germans would seize our key OPs as soon as they had enough troops to do so.

On 10 January the inevitable trouble developed. That day the Germans forestalled us by occupying the dominant feature, Two Tree Hill, on the north side of the Bou Arada valley. This position gave observation not only over Bou Arada itself, but also the Goubellat plain to the north. Various attempts were made to recapture Two Tree Hill. They followed an unwise pattern; insufficient force was used in the first instance, and when a stronger attack was launched the enemy's defences were well organized. The decision to mount a full-scale assault was delayed until 16 January; the Irish Brigade reached their objective, only to be ejected by the inevitable German counter-attack.

6 Armoured Division now decided to guard against being similarly forestalled on the south side of the Bou Arada valley. Two companies of 10 RB – C under Dick Fyffe and B still under David Elkington – were ordered forward to occupy Argoub el Hanech, a scrub-covered feature about 4 miles east of Bou Arada, giving observation as far as and sometimes beyond Pont du Fahs. We moved there in the dark, a nightmare of a move, skidding in the mud, and arrived just before first light. We tucked the trucks away; 6 Platoon had drawn the best job, establishing an observation post on the forward edge of the Argoub, shared later with a gunner OP from 12 RHA. In an attempt to arouse enthusiasm for observation I had offered a financial reward to the first rifleman who could produce a piece of worthwhile information. I was not surprised therefore when a panting Rifleman Murray, an Irishman from Kilburn, approached me over my early morning brew-up claiming to have seen a large number of German tanks advancing down the road from Pont du Fahs. Reluctantly relinquishing my tea, I went up the hill to check and found that Murray's story was all too true. A column of tanks, mixed Mark IIIs and IVs, followed by infantry in lorries, stretched back down the road towards Pont du Fahs. There was a delay at the bridge over the wadi below the Argoub; perhaps there was some disinclination on the part of the leading tanks to deploy off the road onto the open ground to the right for fear of getting bogged. Behind the tanks we could see the following column of vehicles concertina; 10 Panzer Division had forgotten their march discipline. Just then our gunner OP set up shop near Rifleman Murray's original position. He was through to his guns behind Bou Arada immediately. The ranging was good and delicate enough not to disturb the target. The regimental shoot was devastatingly effective; the German infantry from the Panzer Grenadier regiment of 10 Panzer Division

de-bussed in confusion and made for the dead ground behind Hir Mogra, a feature across the wadi about 2,500 yards from our position on the Argoub. The tanks deployed quickly to the right of the road, resuming their advance on Bou Arada, but separated now from their supporting infantry.

Those on the Argoub had a dress circle view of the battle raging below. It was dominated by our artillery. Had the Germans not attacked that morning, it was 6 Armoured Division's intention to mount their own overdue assault on Two Tree Hill. Thus, in the gun area behind Bou Arada, there was an extra field regiment, 17th, borrowed from 78 Division, besides the best part of a Medium Regiment to provide extra weight to the fire which followed the German armour wherever they went. If those on the Argoub had dress circle seats, A Company on a low ridge just in front of Bou Arada were in the front row of the stalls. Luckily the infantry who should have been around to clear them away had been scattered behind Hir Mogra by that first devastating shoot directed from the Argoub. Finally, the German armour, having had several tanks destroyed by 17 Field Regiment firing over open sights, sullenly withdrew in late afternoon leaving eight of their number knocked out. A further six were bogged in the mud; our gunners happily harassed the German teams who bravely tried to recover them. The only jarring note for 6 Armoured Division came at the end of the day. The Lothians were ordered to send a squadron of their Valentines to follow up the retreating Germans; four of them were picked off in quick succession by a Mark III, armed with a long-barrelled 75 mm, left behind by the Germans with precisely that aim in mind.

Fighting patrols after dark kept up the pressure. Tony Pawson's was the most successful; he laid mines on the main road and stayed around long enough to hear a Volkswagen blow up with a satisfying explosion. My own sortie against the Germans holding the bridge over the wadi between the Argoub and Hir Mogra went well at first; we shot two Bren magazines into a group standing on the bridge at a range of about 100 yards. While we were getting away down the wadi, however, an armoured car opened up – first with bursts of Spandau fire, which went harmlessly overhead, then a lucky shot with a 75 mm, which killed Rifleman Highbloom. I felt terrible about his loss; he was a gentle person, in no way military, but he had battled successfully in 6 Platoon. He was shortsighted and should not have been on a night patrol, but he had begged me to let him come. Weakly, against Bert Coad's advice, I had given in. I thought of his parents, who owned a small tailoring business behind Aldgate – I had been to introduce myself during our final embarkation leave in September – and now had to write to tell them what had happened. It was a sad note on which to end my time with 6 Platoon, but probably it was time to go. I had become over-identified with my outfit, it was starting to affect my judgement and Adrian Gore was right to see a change was needed.

I left Bou Arada for my six pounder course on 12 February, and so missed 10 RB's epic involvement in containing Rommel's advance after the American débâcle to the south of First Army. Adrian Gore, given the task of commanding the withdrawal from Kasserine to Thala, and Dick Fyffe, with his C Company, played key roles in stabilizing the situation. I returned only after the position at Thala had become firm, so the battle, a key one at the time, gets only a passing mention here. I recall just the fierce shelling as the Germans, after deciding on withdrawal, fired off their stock of shells, and our relief next morning when 10 RB's carriers, probing forward, discovered that Rommel had gone.

For the next three weeks 6 Armoured Division, split into penny packets, moved up and down the First Army front like plumbers reacting to a freeze up. I acted as second in command of B Company, but had little to do except read Tolstoy's *War and Peace* until we finally left the Argoub and went to retrain at Sakiet on the Algerian frontier.

Here I took over the anti-tank platoon, but this command proved a military disappointment, despite the quality of the riflemen and some superb sergeants, especially Northfield and Bargery. The reason was simple; 26 Armoured Brigade, now equipped with Shermans and brilliantly commanded by Pip Roberts, completely dominated their German and Italian opponents. There was, in consequence, never a job for towed 6 pounders, though we did not know that at the time, and still thought in terms of a Tunisian 'Snipe' action like that of Vic Turner at Alamein. At least, however, I had a marvellous battle position – in my scout car driven by 'Chalky' White – behind Adrian Gore and able to watch Pip Roberts direct his armour and control the battle. I saw, too, some superb feats of arms – the steady advance of the Welsh Guards as they moved up Djebel Rhorab to clear the way for the armour at Fondouk, followed by the Balaclava-style charge of the 17th/21st Lancers as they cleared the floor of the valley. This last operation was, as Pip Roberts recognized, a complete misuse of armour; it was ordered by the Corps Commander, John Crocker, to redeem the failure of 34 US Division on our right to capture the southern flank of the pass. The stakes were high, for failure might have meant an unhindered withdrawal for the enemy armour opposing Eighth Army. As it was, next day, 9 April, saw us, for the only time in the war, adopt the box formation we had discussed long ago in Scotland. It was an exhilarating experience as we raced across the Kairouan plain, the spring flowers contrasting with the grimness of the mountains behind. Since this is a personal account and in no sense a war history, there is no need to recount the detail of 6 Armoured Division's fighting round Kairouan, or later in the fierce unsatisfactory attempt to break through in the Goubellat Plain north of Bou Arada. The anti-tank platoon had its bad moments – a series of Stuka attacks beyond Kairouan, and two days unpleasant shelling below

Djebel Kournine in the Goubellat battle. By then, however, it was obvious we would win; it was merely a question of how and when.

Though there was never a real job for the anti-tank platoon, I saw enough of our commanders, as they visited 26 Armoured Brigade, to form a judgement of their worth and contribution to the final victory. Tolstoy maintained that generals have little impact on the battles they think they are directing. I do not agree now, nor did I then. Some reflections on our commanders in Tunisia are therefore relevant; they indicate what I thought at the time, and are only slightly modified by later study.

We saw much of Charles Keightley, who commanded 6 Armoured Division throughout the Tunisian campaign. There was no time for Keightley to alter the style of the Division during the short period he had with us in Scotland; even had he wished to do so, he would have been unwise to attempt it, for his predecessor John Crocker's foundations were sound and stood the test of both Tunisia and Italy.

Keightley had a reputation for being ambitious and ruthless; at the time he came to 6 Armoured Division he was the youngest Major General in the Army. He commanded our respect, if not particularly our affection. His leadership lacked warmth and he did not bother much about communicating with junior officers, let alone developing relationships with the soldiery.

He made an unfortunate remark early in his command of the Division; its consequences were long to dog him. Callum Renton, a distinguished rifleman, had just returned from the Desert where he had been commanding the famous 7 Armoured Division. About three weeks after Monty's arrival, Callum fell out with the Army Commander and was sent home. He came to talk to 6 Armoured Division in Scotland, where we listened intently. It was just what we needed to hear, and valuable as he described how to cope with the Afrika Corps. Callum remarked, without intention of giving his hearers an inferiority complex, that we would find the German tanks superior to our own in many respects. Keightley was distressed, and intervened at the end of the talk to restore our morale, "I can assure you, gentlemen," he emphasized, speaking in the ponderous slow manner used by the military establishment when forced on the defensive, "that the Crusader and Valentine tanks in 6 Armoured Division will be more than a match for anything we may meet in Africa." It was unwise to stick his neck out and gave the cynics a field day whenever, as happened later, the quality of our tanks came into question. Keightley affected a quasi-episcopal touch as he drove round his formation, inclining from the waist in his armoured car, and giving people the odd de Gaulle-style wave as he passed. There was no doubt, though, about Keightley's ability, even if he sometimes lacked a sense of timing and judgement of ground in handling armour.

Keightley may have lacked tactical instinct, but was without doubt an admirable organizer who not only ensured the administrative side of his formation worked like clockwork, but was sensible enough to defer to the tactical judgements of those like Pip Roberts who possessed genuine flair. Later Charles Keightley was to command the 78th Infantry Division with success in Italy, and ended the war in command of 5 Corps in Austria. Harold Macmillan in his diaries makes clear that he had a high opinion of Keightley's competence. Possibly he was one of those commanders who appealed more to his superiors than to his juniors, and, in this respect, like Hubert Gough in the previous war, he may have followed a certain cavalry tradition.

Despite the reservations some of us felt about our Divisional Commander, we had great affection for our first Brigade Commander, Charles Dunphie, and his successor for the last two months of the campaign, Pip Roberts. They were very different characters – Charles Dunphie a former horse gunner of charm and courtesy, Pip Roberts a professional from the Royal Tanks of real quality, who was flown across from Tripoli to provide an experienced commander for our armoured brigade after it had been re-equipped with Sherman tanks. Charles Dunphie was unlucky to be taken away from his Brigade to help re-train the Americans after conducting a brave and determined defence against Rommel at Thala. He soon became a Major General; after the war, retiring from the Army, he proved an excellent chairman of Vickers.

Pip Roberts was a natural commander of armour and a master tactician. All day he operated from the turret of his command Sherman, the Brigade Major, Tony Kershaw, below, operating the radios and feeding his commander tea and bully beef sandwiches. Pip watched the battle through field glasses, coming on the air occasionally to adjust the position of his regiments. Behind him, part of his small Tactical HQ, were his gunner, John Barstow, CO 12 RHA, and our own Adrian Gore, his motor battalion commander, in case the battle developed an infantry bias. Pip Roberts was indefatigable and unruffled; he was always in the right place and a jump ahead of the opposition. As the anti-tank platoon commander of the motor battalion, I was told by Adrian to position myself a tactical bound behind; from my dingo scout car I watched the battle develop and tried to anticipate possible tasks for 6 pounder anti-tank guns. I need not have worried; Pip Roberts, like some armoured team manager, organized things so well that infantry were seldom needed till last light when they would be called forward to protect the armoured leaguers. As soon as this moment came, Pip Roberts felt able to switch off. Up would come the main part of his Brigade HQ, with a 3 ton lorry carrying a piano. Sometimes the piano would be unloaded and Pip would relax over its keys – he was a jazz pianist with a delicate touch – till he was needed for a decision or, as often happened, Charles Keightley called for advice on what he should do next day. It was true professionalism; Pip Roberts was a leader who realized that being good at one's job and enjoying life were not mutually exclusive.

Other commanders in Tunisia were more remote. Though he did not arrive in Tunisia till February, we admired Alexander; he had the distinction of bearing and ease of manner typical of the Brigade of Guards. He was a great regimental soldier, who knew exactly what one should be doing as a battalion or company commander. History now suggests that he was no strategist and that he had problems in controlling strong-willed subordinates. But Alex's style, and the fact that he was plainly a commander to whom problems did not adhere, gave us confidence when he arrived from Cairo to direct the final battles in Tunisia. Generals like Alexander need a good Chief of Staff, and he was certainly not effective without one. Fortunately in North Africa there was Dick McCreery for him to lean on; later in Italy, John Harding filled the same role.

The First Army Commander, Anderson, was an unlucky general. 6 Armoured Division saw little of him, though his decisions often affected us. He took risks in launching the initial drive on Tunis, which failed, not because of deficiencies in Anderson's generalship, but due to the quicker Axis build-up. Subsequently circumstances forced Anderson to throw in reinforcements piecemeal; soon British, French and Americans were inextricably mixed up, and the battlefield was never tidied up until Alex and McCreery arrived and sorted things out. Anderson was a reserved character, whose Orders of the Day reflected a certain pessimism. But his conduct of the final battle in Tunisia was impressive and to dismiss him, as Monty did, as just a 'good plain cook' was less than fair.

I have always felt Corps to be a specially difficult level of command. It is the first level at which generals become remote from actual fighting soldiers. Divisions, fixed teams of all arms, move round between Corps as required; though the Corps Commander will know his Divisional Commanders well, he will not have the same direct contact with their units. Those, like Horrocks, who possessed a real flair for command at Corps level seemed able to overcome this problem. Others, like Allfrey, an excellent gunner, who commanded 5 Corps throughout the Tunisian campaign, found it difficult to achieve the same identification with the battalions and regiments serving under them. I recall Allfrey, for example, turning up at our OP on the Argoub in a shiny military mackintosh, which would have been instantly visible to the German OPs on Hir Mogra opposite, had we not politely drawn attention to the Corps Commander's sartorial failings, and caused him to leave his Burberry and red hat behind. Yet Allfrey became a thoughtful commander, who handled the hard infantry battles in the later stages of the Tunisian campaign with skilful competence.

While we were waiting near Bou Arada for the next stages of the Tunisian battle to develop 1 Armoured Division joined us from Eighth Army, including 7th Motor Brigade, all Greenjackets, and we enjoyed the reunions with old friends who had come all the way from Alamein. Within the regiment, good manners prevented too much patronising of First Army by those accustomed to Eighth Army's continuous record of victory. Yet there were fundamental differences of approach, of which dress was not the only one. First Army had been trained in England and remained essentially European in outlook; our experiences in the hills, valleys and enclosed country of Tunisia had made us cautious and pawky compared with the expansive outlook of those from the desert where there was usually space and room to manoeuvre. First Army's vehicles, camouflaged and painted a sober green and brown, contrasted sharply with the sand-coloured appearance of those from Eighth Army. We concealed ourselves under trees and what shrubbery we could find; if there was a valley or a re-entrant we tucked ourselves away in the dead ground provided. The early days of air inferiority made us aware of the threat of air attack. By contrast, Eighth Army relied on wide dispersal and had become used to superb support from the Desert Air Force; they took air superiority for granted and regarded our insistence on track discipline as pedantic and unnecessary.

If 1 Armoured Division had ever thought fighting in Tunisia would be easy they were soon disillusioned by Operation Vulcan. Vulcan visualized two armoured divisions, 1 on the left, 6 on the right, passing through 46 Infantry Division and driving north-east towards Tunis across the Goubellat Plain. This mass of armour, over 300 tanks, operated under command of IX Corps (John Crocker); further north the infantry under Allfrey's V Corps were to continue their slogging advance towards Tunis up the Medjerda Valley and in the hills dominating it from the left.

For the armour it was tough going from the start. 46 Division proved unable to provide the clear break which the Corps Commander needed to launch his armour; the tasks given to the infantry were far too ambitious. By midday on 22 April Two Tree Hill still defied capture and Crocker, as he had done at Fondouk, felt he could wait no longer. He ordered both armoured divisions to advance regardless of the unfinished business on their flanks; it was a messy start and the prelude to a disappointing and untidy battle. The German anti-tank defences were skilfully placed; they were supplemented as required by tanks of 10 and 21 Panzer Divisions supported by artillery fire, which Pip Roberts described as the heaviest he had ever experienced. The armoured advance thus came to a halt beneath the twin peaks of Djebel Bou Kournine; there was insufficient infantry available to capture the feature and by 26 April the stalemate was complete and obvious. Re-grouping and a change of plan was clearly required.

I was largely a spectator in this unpleasant battle. My anti-tank platoon followed a tactical bound behind the armoured regiments until being deployed to protect the southern flank of the advance just north of the salt lake (Sebkret el Kourzia). We dug ourselves in too near the Djebel Kournine for comfort; no enemy tanks materialized, but we survived some disagreeable bouts of shelling, when the enemy periodically grew tired of concentrating on our tanks and switched elsewhere. It was a relief when 6 Armoured Division were withdrawn to re-group; we moved north behind Mejez to await our role in the new plan.

During the re-planning stage John Crocker, our Corps Commander, who never quite found his touch in Tunisia, was wounded while watching a demonstration of a new infantry anti-tank weapon. A piece of armour dislodged during the firing flew back and hit the Corps Commander. "Well," remarked Douglas Darling, then in charge of 7 RB, cynically, as John Crocker was carted away in an ambulance, "these projectors may or may not be able to deal with a Mark VI, but at least they seem to be good for promotion." Crocker was replaced by Horrocks, who came round from his Corps in Eighth Army, where Montgomery admitted that even he was stalled by the mountain barrier facing him at Enfidaville.

At this time Horrocks was at the top of his form as a Corps Commander. He was rightly confident after his spectacular success in outflanking the Mareth Line a month earlier and possessed a touch and timing our previous generals in First Army had lacked. His impact on the final drive on Tunis was immediate and salutary.

Horrocks' personality got down to the lowest levels; he possessed the personal touch and seemed never too busy to stop by the roadside and chat up the humblest passing officer or soldier. A Corps was probably the ideal level for his particular skills, and we were certainly lucky that he arrived when he did.

Before describing the IX Corps plan for the final offensive, one should not give the impression that our armoured operations had been the only pressure on the Germans during April. There had been significant happenings elsewhere. Of these, the redeployment and reorganization of II (US) Corps had the greatest long-term consequences. I have alluded earlier to the rawness and lack of experience of the Americans when they first arrived in North Africa. The soldiers were splendid material, but, regrettably, at first lacked the leadership they deserved. Fredendall, their first Corps Commander, has been described as thinking one could command a Corps on active service by adopting the "mores and manners of a movie Mogul". He certainly had no idea what to do when faced by an attack from a professional like Rommel, while his insistence on his own personal safety – he seldom left his dug-in HQ near Tebessa – did little for his soldiers' morale. Nor did his unconcealed dislike for the British help inter-Allied solidarity. In short, Fredendall was a disaster and greatly responsible for the malaise, unwise dispositions and lack of training which caused the Kasserine débâcle.

Eisenhower finally recognized Fredendall's failings and replaced him by the famous George Patton, at the time still relatively unknown. Within a month Patton, by strict insistence on basic military discipline, had revolutionized II Corps; not all of the battles under his command had been successful, but enough had been won to restore the soldiers' self respect and to make them feel a match for the Germans. When Patton left the Corps at the beginning of April – on promotion to plan the invasion of Sicily as an Army Commander – Alexander was happy for the II (US) Corps to be squeezed out and, under its new commander, Omar Bradley, allotted an unimportant task in the final stages in Tunisia. He had, however, reckoned without American pride and Eisenhower's determination that the United States should play a proper role in finishing the campaign. During the third week in April, therefore, Bradley's Corps moved north to take over the task of advancing via the coastal route on Bizerta. It was a formidable task, but Bradley overcame the obstacles. By meticulous planning, first Hill 609, then Green and Bald Hills, and finally Mateur fell to the Americans before Operation Strike was launched in the Medjerda Valley. Bradley's success represented a great feat of arms and needs to be remembered in order to get the American performance in Tunisia in proper perspective.

Equally, V Corps' fighting for the high ground either side of the Medjerda Valley involved some of the toughest battles of the campaign. The recapture of Longstop Hill by 78 Division, the 1st Division's achievement in seizing Djebel Bou Aoukaz, and 4th Division's desperate struggles round Ksar Tyr – all these engagements set the stage for the final triumph, but at great cost, and in much slower time than had originally been hoped.

These April battles had in fact brought the Germans to the brink of exhaustion. In such circumstances, Horrocks' IX Corps plan was perfectly designed as a knock out blow. The concept was simple: 4th Indian Division on the left, 4th British Division on the right were to make the initial breakthrough by means of a night attack. As soon as the way was clear, 7 Armoured Division (another arrival from Eighth Army) and 6 Armoured Division were to pass through and aim for Tunis. There was a formidable artillery plan and a massive daylight air assault. Intelligently, 1 Armoured Division, supplemented by a mass of dummy tanks, had been left behind in the Goubellat Plain in order to deceive the Germans into thinking that the Allies would repeat their armoured attack in that area.

In the event all worked superbly and there was little real opposition. Both armoured divisions passed through the infantry about mid-morning and achieved a subsequent advance of some 15 miles before nightfall. Though the advance was not a cavalry charge – more a steady progress from one feature to another – such headway was unprecedented in Tunisia. 'Chalky' White and I bumped along cheerfully in our dingo in the wake of the armour with, for once, nothing to worry about except to make sure that the anti-tank platoon was following us. We had some tea in a thermos, from which we refreshed ourselves periodically. It was like going to Epsom on Derby Day, but with no racing to concern one at the destination.

That evening, 6 May, we leaguered near Massicault, still pinching ourselves to make sure our progress was real. At first light next morning Adrian Gore told me to reconnoitre some positions to the south of the main road in case an anti-tank screen were needed against any enemy armour flushed back our way from the Goubellat Plain. We investigated two or three farms and came back with a couple of prisoners draped across our dingo; they told us they had stayed behind when their flak battery moved out. They had had enough and complained hotly about how long it had been before we British arrived to accept their surrender. Both clutched leaflets dropped from the air, the theme seemed sensible to me – "Why fight on in the Bridgehead without a Bridge?"

About seven miles short of Tunis we heard that armoured cars (Derbyshire Yeomanry and 11th Hussars) had entered the city. The armour was to wheel south, cut across the routes leading to the Cape Bon Peninsula and subsequently advance towards Eighth Army. It came on to rain, a fine steady drizzle, and for the moment we seemed to have missed the party. We harboured for the night somewhere in the rich farming country to the south of Tunis; after nearly six months of anticipation the actual capture of the city seemed an anti-climax.

Next day the extent of German disintegration became more obvious. We passed ration dumps and transport parks, evidently hastily abandoned. There were signs everywhere telling the Germans to make for the Cape Bon Peninsula. With memories of Dunkirk in mind, 6 Armoured Division pushed on, anxious to cut off as many enemy as possible. Overhead flew a steady stream of Allied aircraft flying to attack the Cape Bon beaches; plainly, any large-scale evacuation would be difficult.

Nevertheless, the enemy still showed no sign of general surrender and, about midday on 8 May, 6 Armoured Division encountered determined opposition at Hammam Lif. Here the main road from Tunis to Hammamet ran through the town, which forms a narrow defile a mile wide, between high ground on the right (the menacing Djebel Bou Kournine) and the sea on the left. It was obviously an ideal place for a stand and we soon heard that the armour was to halt while the Guards Brigade came forward to capture the high ground above the town. I found space for the anti-tank platoon to harbour, guessed (rightly) that we should be there for the day and settled down in the sun to write letters and read a book. There is never much to be gained by creating activity, and, in my experience, the best active service soldiers are those who have learnt how and when to re-charge their batteries.

Next morning, however, we heard that the Welsh Guards' attack on the high ground had been only partially successful, and that the armour would have to force a way through the town. Though I did not know this till later, Bert Coad and 6 Platoon were to play a key role here. B Company first had to establish whether Hammam Lif was still held and, if so, where the main centres of resistance lay. 6 Platoon was given this task, during which John Chadwyck-Healey was wounded with two other riflemen. In face of sniping and mortar fire, Bert somehow got the three casualties back to a place of comparative safety. He then assumed command of the platoon and stayed in position, observing the enemy, until ordered to withdraw. Later the same morning, B Company undertook a full-scale company attack on the positions which Bert had identified. 6 Platoon suffered more casualties, and the neighbouring platoon commander was killed and his platoon sergeant wounded. Bert Coad then took charge of both platoons, rallied and encouraged them so effectively that they were able to withdraw, stage by stage, when ordered to do so. His DCM was well earned.

While B Company was engaged along the line of the main road into Hammam Lif, the Lothians had launched what can only be described as a cavalry charge into the town, unsupported by infantry and in face of fierce anti-tank fire. By all the rules, this operation should have ended in disaster. Instead two troops of tanks found a way through along the beach and somehow, half an hour after the start of their assault, the Lothians found themselves beyond the town and in a position to take the enemy defences from behind. It was an astonishing feat by the Lothians, made possible by their sheer determination to get forward at all costs.

This success loosened the situation. Soon the rest of 26 Armoured Brigade were pouring through Hammam Lif, my anti-tank platoon bumping along with the rest. Adrian Gore stopped us in the middle of the town and directed me, with the scout platoon of D Company under command, to establish a defensive flank in the hills to the right of the road. Our task was to prevent any enemy coming back into Hammam Lif and cutting the road behind the advancing armour. It was a simple role, but provided me and my two platoons with a fascinating day as we watched the Guardsmen slowly clearing the hills ahead of us, and below along the coast road the jam-packed progress of 6 Armoured Division southward towards Hammamet.

All day, as we sat sweltering above Hammam Lif, a steady trickle of prisoners came to surrender. They were not, unusually, the weaker brethren who had somehow become detached from their units. By contrast, these prisoners came from the best-known German units in Tunisia – the Hermann Goering Division, Colonel Koch's paratroopers, and some even from the famous 90th Light Division. We felt no animosity, rather admiration, towards these splendid soldiers, who, whatever the abysmal quality of the Nazi regime, had fought bravely and correctly. One particular officer came in about the proper time for afternoon tea. He was a kindred spirit, replying in perfect English to my welcome in Wiccamical German, "Well done, lads, you took your time, but better late than never." He gave me his field glasses – I have them still, and find them perfectly suited to watching cricket at Lords and Trent Bridge. "These will be more use to you than me from now on. But do not imagine war in Europe will be sport like it has been in Africa." Reflecting on Tebourba and Thala, I doubted if our views on sport were identical, but nevertheless he made a good point well. 'Chalky' White brewed the three of us some tea and gave him a cushion out of the dingo to sit on while we all drank our brew together. I wish I had kept his name; he was from 90th Light Division, not our usual opponents, 10 Panzer Division, but knew all about 6 Armoured Division. Pointing to my mailed fist divisional sign he remarked, *"Elite und königlicher Division,"* a chivalrous reference to the armoured regiments of 26 Armoured Brigade and our supporting 1st Guards Brigade. Apparently the Germans had tracked our progress all over Tunisia by the style of our radio conversation – there was no disguising the professional efficiency of our soldier opera-tors, and the confident amateurism of the Eton/Winchester/Oxbridge element of the officers called to the set. We had more laughs together in similar vein before I sent him down the hill in a carrier. I hope he survived to make his fortune as a businessman later; I still recall our conversation, which confirmed my views about the folly of wars within Europe.

Adrian Gore called in our flank guard about an hour before nightfall and we motored down to Hammam Lif to join the flow of transport surging slowly down the road south towards Hammamet. In the opposite direction, some on foot, many in their own transport, moved a steady stream of Germans and Italians intent on finding a prison cage to which they could surrender. It was all over, though the end did not come formally till 13 May after fifty-four Bostons of the US Air Force had dealt the Axis positions a final devastating pounding, and given General Messe, the Italian C in C, an opportunity to surrender without losing face. Opposite 6 Armoured Division the end had come about 6 p.m. the evening before when General Graf von Sponeck, the Commander of 90th Light Division, immaculately dressed in green uniform and greatcoat with red facings, surrendered to Charles Keightley and General Freyberg, commanding the New Zealand Division in Eighth Army, who had come round especially to take the surrender of his old opponent. Von Sponeck was clearly a fine commander; as his soldiers went by him on their way to captivity they cheered or saluted him as evidence of their respect. Dick Fyffe and I, watching from nearby, admired von Sponeck's dignity and composure; a rifleman came up to ask the German general's name, and, when told, merely remarked, "Never heard of him, Sir," before turning away to his evening 'brew up'.

The final German surrender in Tunisia came just over six months after we had left Scotland. It had been a remarkable period. We had passed through many different stages, starting with the early days in Bladeforce, when both sides were weak but the Germans prevailed because of their shorter communications and quicker build up. Next a phase of inferiority, when the Germans were superior because of better organization, better tanks and great professionalism. In the end Allied material superiority began to tell, until finally our dominance, especially our total control of the air, won us an overwhelming victory.

We saw Alexander at his best during the later stages of the Tunisian campaign. With McCreery at his elbow as Chief of Staff, he had someone around to keep the battlefield tidy; equally, his subordinates did what he asked, and there was no Mark Clark about to damage the pattern of operations by his pursuit of personal glory. Even Montgomery was helpful, making available the cream of his formations from Eighth Army to assist First Army in their final battle.

The impact of Horrocks' arrival to command IX Corps was remarkable. I have never forgotten his flair, style and sense of timing. He was wounded later by a piece of shrapnel while watching an air raid on Bizerta; though he returned to duty with distinction in North West Europe, I doubt if he was ever again physically capable of reaching the heights he did in Tunisia. It was a privilege, too, to watch a masterly commander of armour like Pip Roberts, and to have had a job which gave me such a good opportunity of seeing him at work. Altogether I had been lucky and hope that, even then, I realized it.

Chapter Six

ITALIAN STRUGGLE

After the German surrender in Tunisia 6 Armoured Division expected to go home to take part in the Normandy invasion the following year. It made sense, therefore, for the division to stage westward into Algeria and retrain round Philippeville and Constantine. It did not work out that way, however, for once Montgomery was appointed to command the invasion force, he preferred to have with him his trusted formations from Eighth Army, 50th and 51st Infantry Divisions, and the original Desert Rats, 7 Armoured Division. So 6 Armoured Division, denied the nod, realized early in 1944 that Italy would be our destiny.

Though, at first, we were disappointed at this change in destination, we quickly became reconciled to the new reality. 10 RB did not waste its time training in Algeria. It was a better battalion, better equipped (armoured half tracks and White scout cars in place of 15 cwt trucks), and strengthened by some high-grade reinforcements which landed at Naples in mid-March 1944. Though we had lost Adrian Gore (on promotion to command a brigade at Anzio), we felt relaxed and professional.

By now I had been Adjutant for five months and, still aged 22, had gained confidence in the job. Both Adrian Gore and Dick Fyffe, during his period acting in command, had trusted me and left me alone to operate in my own way. 10 RB had hoped Dick Fyffe would succeed Adrian in command; it was a disappointment that Dick Southby, a stranger without previous war experience, should have been appointed instead. But there it was, and we hoped our new Colonel would realize what a good outfit he was inheriting.

Our 1st Guards Brigade had preceded us to Italy at the end of January and became involved in some unpleasant fighting in the mountains above the Garigliano south-west of Cassino. We read their reports with disquiet; plainly there would be no taking up where the Tunisian campaign had ended. The German defence in Italy was well organized, while grim stories about Cassino and the Gustav Line, where the Allied advance had stopped for the winter, did little to raise morale. In January it seemed the Anzio landing might restore a degree of mobility to the campaign; all too soon, however, the Allies were bogged down there also, and were struggling desperately to avoid being driven into the sea. It was a thoughtful 10 RB as we contemplated our return to the battlefield.

Dick Fyffe, acting in command, went ahead with the advance party; I followed later with the main body. The journey from Philippeville to Naples, on the *Ville D'Oran*, a peacetime ferry from France to Oran, was eventful; the ship was fast, but known to be unstable. On our voyage the *Ville D'Oran* excelled itself; about three house out from Philippeville, while travelling at top speed, it developed an alarming list to starboard. OC Troops, who had experienced this phenomenon before, reacted with quick common sense. We were told to report to the boat deck immediately; there we received a life jacket and instructions to muster on the port side of the vessel. The riflemen reacted enthusiastically, and after a long ten minutes the *Ville D'Oran* recaptured an upright position. We walked ashore relieved, across the wrecks of two sunken ships, on arrival in Naples.

Naples was in the throes of a typhus epidemic, the population were short of food and there was no housing to cope with the swollen population. We went straight from the dockside to a concentration area 30 miles in the foothills of the Abruzzi Mountains. The nearest town, Piedimonte D'Alife, two miles from our camp, was a glorified village, normally a small holiday centre where rich Neapolitans avoided the summer heat. In spring, our unheated tents were cold and indicated the hardships which winter fighting in the mountains had entailed. We settled down to train hard in the new conditions; there were few distractions, though our campsite provided a grandstand view of the Luftwaffe's raids on Naples, and, for two days, Vesuvius, as it erupted fiercely to add to the worries of those living beneath it.

Dick Southby arrived to take over and Dick Fyffe left us to command the Royal West Kents in 78 Division. Bobby Selway, a diplomat, became second in command and Jim Lonsdale, a rugged former Guardsman who worked in peacetime for the Bank of England, succeeded him in command of A Company. Jim Lonsdale was a natural fighting soldier who always led from the front. Jim's A Company, with support from Teddy Goschen in a different style with B Company, were to play leading roles in carrying the battalion through the next difficult months.

Our preparations in Algeria had been thorough enough for little reorganization to be needed. Dick Southby, as a new Commanding Officer, found it frustrating to take over a going concern, which was used to being left alone to get on with things. Dick had missed the fighting in the desert, but had latterly been second in command to Douglas Darling in 7 RB, and learnt

Chain of Command – Italian Campaign – May 1944 (Operation DIADEM)

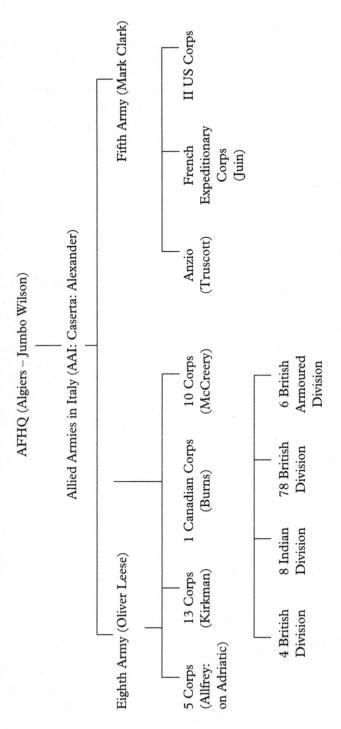

AFHQ (Algiers – Jumbo Wilson)

Allied Armies in Italy (AAI: Caserta: Alexander)

Fifth Army (Mark Clark)

Anzio (Truscott)

French Expeditionary Corps (Juin)

II US Corps

Eighth Army (Oliver Leese)

13 Corps (Kirkman)

1 Canadian Corps (Burns)

10 Corps (McCreery)

5 Corps (Allfrey: on Adriatic)

4 British Division

8 Indian Division

78 British Division

6 British Armoured Division

SWITZERLAND
AUSTRIA
Villach
Klagenfurt
Belluno
Predil Pass
Caporetto
Milan
Lake Garda
Lombardy Plain
Treviso
Padua
River Po
R. Adige
Venice
Trieste
YUGOSLAVIA
Genoa
Ferrara
Cavanazza
Bologna
Ravenna
GOTHIC LINE
Forli
Rimini
Pisa
Prato
Pesaro
Florence
Siena
Arezzo
ADRIATIC SEA
Monte Rentella
Lake Trasimene
Monte Malbe
Perugia
Pescara
GUSTAV (HITLER) LINE
ROME
R. Rapido
Aquino
R. Sangro
Anzio
R. Liri
Cassino
Monte Trocchio
R. Garigliano
Mignano
Naples
Bari
Salerno
TYRRHENIAN SEA
Palermo
Reggio
Sicily
Catania
Venice
Monselice
R. Adige
R. Po
Cavanazza
Poggio
Renatico
Ferrara
San Nicolo
Ferrarese
Lake Comacchio
Argenta
R. Santerno
Bologna
Imola
Ravenna
Tossignano
R. Senio
Fontanelice
Castel del Rio
Forli
Rimini
Prato
Muraglione Pass
Florence
Dicomano
R. Arno
Vallombrosa
Arezzo
Siena
Lake Trasimene
Corciano
Perugia
0 km 30
ITALY
0 50 100 150 Miles
0 100 200 km

a different approach. Our motor companies were used to a double loyalty – as much to the armoured regiment with whom they worked as to 10 RB. As Adjutant I had grown up this way and employed a velvet glove with the Company Commanders. It was hard to adopt a different style; I hoped it would all work out when we started operations.

Alexander, delegating the tactical conduct of the Cassino battle to Freyberg and the New Zealand Corps, had just launched a final assault against the Gustav Line and its lynchpin Monte Cassino. On 15 March a thousand tons of bombs and 1,200 artillery shells landed on Cassino. Little of the town survived, but the debris prevented the New Zealanders advancing quickly enough to prevent the German paratroops re-entering the rubble as soon as the bombing stopped. By 22 March it was obvious that the attack was yet another failure and that to continue battering away would put a spring offensive in jeopardy. Alexander called Freyberg's battle off and allowed his staff, under his recently appointed Chief of Staff, John Harding, to concentrate on preparations for the May offensive.

10 RB were not concerned in Freyberg's battle. Bobby Selway and I, however, playing truant from Piedimonte, jeeped forward at different times to have a look at the battlefield, to satisfy our curiosity and get an idea of what scope there might be for 6 Armoured Division. We returned abashed and unhappy about the future. We were not surprised when we heard the New Zealand attack had been halted; it was obvious from looking at the battlefield for a couple of hours through field glasses that a new look was needed.

Early in April 10 RB was warned to take over a sector at Cassino, to allow the present occupants to be withdrawn and re-trained. Dick Southby and I went up to the Cassino area and reported to the HQ of 2nd Parachute Brigade under whom we would come for the ten days we expected to be in position. We had an admirable briefing and a good look at our sector from the vantage point of Monte Trocchio, which gave excellent observation over Cassino, the River Gari and the Liri Valley beyond. To hold the line for ten days as ordinary infantry meant some reorganization before we took over position south of Cassino on 7 April, but 10 RB was accustomed to improvization and adjusted easily.

Cassino was an alarming battlefield; with the Monastery looming over one, it was impossible to forget how completely one was dominated. As a motor battalion we were spared the worst areas, Cassino town and the railway station. Here the New Zealanders, the month before, had fought an epic battle, but left a third of the town still in German hands. Positions were incredibly close, often just thirty yards apart; life, like the trenches in World War One, involved regular exchanges of sniper fire and grenades. These positions were now occupied by our Guards Brigade, while 10 RB held the line of the Gari about a mile south of the town itself.

At least 10 RB had a river and some 200 yards of water meadow between ourselves and the Germans; even so the riflemen in the front line were totally overlooked. Any movement by day brought down observed mortar or artillery fire; though the Germans were supposed to have logistic problems caused by the Allied command of the air, they never seemed short of shells here, doubtless because Cassino was on Route 6, their main supply line.

At Battalion Headquarters, half a mile behind the front companies, we lived in a farm building, which had so far survived the fighting. We had a few vehicles with us; as Adjutant, I covered the paperwork from the command half track with the back door open, so I could jump easily into an adjacent slit trench whenever the shelling came close. Apart from shelling and mortar fire, our main concern was the German multi-barrelled mortars or 'nebelwerfers', new to us, and therefore alarming. One heard down the valley six or ten eructations – not unlike the emissions of a 'lager lout' – followed by a hissing sound as if several flocks of lethal geese were heading in your direction. Then followed a series of simultaneous explosions as the bombs landed. Though terrifying, nebelwerfers were inaccurate, so one suffered less from them than from more conventional artillery or mortars. But for those who were short on the 'dono di coraggio', they were a disagreeable feature of Cassino life.

Here, for the first time, 10 RB encountered the symptoms of 'bomb happiness' from which we had been largely immune in Tunisia. Though we had been bombed and shelled periodically in North Africa, and briefly experienced withdrawals rapid enough to be almost routs, our high morale and freshness to war helped us recover quickly from our experiences. One felt, when the shelling stopped, like exhilarated school children who had been out scrumping apples and miraculously escaped retribution.

In Italy it was different. It was somehow all more serious. In Tunisia you could often move round and talk to your friends, but at Cassino there was strictly no daylight movement. Officers and riflemen became isolated; sitting with just one companion in a slit trench meant there was less opportunity for laughter and badinage, and greater inclination to take counsel of one's fears.

There was a further factor, though not one which I then understood. Courage, as Lord Moran had discovered in World War I, is an expendable quality. No one had yet briefed regimental soldiers about this, perhaps as well since our hypochondriacs could well have talked themselves into 'battle fatigue' long before this state genuinely developed.

Nevertheless, progressively, some of those who had carried the main burden in Tunisia and earlier in Italy itself became exhausted. Often battle fatigue took the form of extreme caution; those affected were normally content to stay in a particular position, but when it came to a question of moving on there was a tendency to lose the way or become separated from the main body. After a particular action was over the battle-exhausted often turned up again at a rear company or Battalion headquarters with a specious account of how they had become lost. As we moved up Italy during the long summer of 1944 the actual fighting was executed by fewer and fewer of those on the paper strength of a battalion – by early August perhaps forty in each motor company, or a total of under 200 in any one battalion.

The pressure of battle fatigue was less evident in people who had a specialist task. The signallers, for example, who had a tricky job keeping communications going, were rarely touched by 'bomb happiness'. Perhaps they were more intelligent than the average, certainly they knew better than most what was happening; whatever the reason, they maintained their morale superbly and were always a tonic. There were differences between companies and, within them, between platoons, depending on the quality of leadership provided. The 'come on, boys, follow me' style of leadership cut no ice with the riflemen; they worked better and endured longer with quieter leaders whose professionalism they respected, and on whom they felt they could rely for coolness and common sense in a crisis.

It was difficult for Dick Southby, our newly arrived Commanding Officer. He had come late into battle fighting, having missed an apprentice-ship at a lower level of platoon and company command because he was kept behind in England to run the Green Jacket OCTU (Officer Cadet Training Unit) on Salisbury Plain. He was intelligent, ambitious, and charming – he had been an ADC to the Viceroy in peacetime, and had the reputation of a 'coming man'. Cassino suggested, however, that Dick Southby was not the right leader in battle – at least for a battalion like 10 RB, with a successful campaign in Tunisia behind us, and our own method of working. He inherited me as his Adjutant; though we got on well at first, having friends and interests in common, we fell out once active operations de-veloped. His predecessor used to tell one what he wanted you to do and then leave you to get on with the mechanics, intervening only if he saw something going awry. Dick Southby, by contrast, liked to sit on the end of a wireless set, demanding 'sitreps' from busy and overworked company commanders. It was a system which might have worked two years before when we were still training in Scotland, or several years later on peacetime post-war exercises in Germany. Now it was the wrong method; in four short months Dick Southby drove himself into a state of exhaustion, from which he was only rescued by Adrian Gore, by then back as our Brigadier, who wisely arranged for him to return to the staff, where he was in his element and again effective.

So Cassino proved a difficult time during which we learned the realities of the Italian campaign. Even the approach to Cassino was an exercise in re-education. There was no space, harbour areas were cramped and allotted by the staff; because the Cassino battle had been in progress since January, there was rubbish everywhere and the flies were starting to proliferate. One moved up to Cassino along what had once been the main railway line from Naples to Rome. The rail tracks had been removed and the sappers had ingeniously converted it into a throughway called the 'Speedy Highway'. You got a strict timing to join the route, on which vehicle movement was in the dark and without lights; the Germans intervened periodically with bursts of shelling, which were disagreeable, frightening and often accurate. Being shelled in a 'soft' vehicle – though our half tracks and White scout cars were lightly armoured and protected one from splinters – is far more unpleasant than on foot; in the latter case you go to ground in a ditch or any available cover and resume activity when the opposition stop. On the Speedy Highway you had to keep going; the noise of the engine prevented you hearing the shells arriving and, importantly, how close they were.

Our sector lay in front of Monte Trocchio and opposite the strong point of Sant Angelo on the far side of the Rapido. Our job was to patrol the territory on our side of the river and ensure the Germans got no inkling of the attack by Eighth Army the following month. It was not an easy task; by day there was no movement outside the ruined houses in which we lived. We were overlooked by the Germans, so any visible activity meant retribution by shelling, mortaring and nebelwerfers directed with precision, speed and, apparently, plenty of ammunition. The Germans had been holding the Gustav Line for three months and so been able to build up their stocks.

All activity therefore was by night; the space available for patrolling was limited and there were mines everywhere, left by the Germans before they withdrew across the Rapido. Most unpleasant were 'Schu' mines, small wooden affairs, almost impossible to detect, but powerful enough to blow off the foot of anyone unlucky enough to step on one. One of our best officers, Angus Macnaughton, was wounded in this way and we were lucky not to have more casualties. We captured a prisoner one night who provided a useful identification of our opponents, 15 Panzer Grenadier Division. By comparison with our cheerful riflemen, he was a melancholy, pasty individual, clearly relieved to be captured. We had little doubt, however, that he and his colleagues would have fought hard had we attacked them, as 8 Indian Division, who relieved us, discovered later when they captured Sant Angelo.

Our spell holding the line at Cassino did not greatly erode our reserves of courage. Nevertheless we were now properly realistic about fighting in Italy. There was little glad confidence about the 1944 campaign, despite the imaginative concept for Operation DIADEM, as the May offensive was known.

Operation Diadem entailed Eighth Army leaving the Adriatic and becoming the main striking force at Cassino with four Corps under command. There was only one option for the main effort – up the Liri Valley. The way to win a decisive victory was to encircle the German armies south of Rome; to do so required a correctly linked sortie from the Anzio beachhead. Thus the main Fifth Army effort would be from Anzio, though the remainder of Mark Clark's troops (II US Corps) would attack along the coast astride Route 7. Key tasks were given to Juin's French Expeditionary Corps, charged with attacking in the mountains on the southern side of the Liri Valley. In fact this action by the French proved the decisive factor in achieving victory; this outcome was not visualized during the planning and the French have never received full acclaim for their brilliant performance. The task of capturing Monte Cassino fell to II Polish Corps under their General Anders; it was a hard assignment, with the outcome of the battle dependent on it. While Cassino remained in enemy hands, the main drive down the Liri Valley, entrusted to Kirkman's XIII Corps, with 1 Canadian Corps available to exploit success, could not succeed.

The Allies had overwhelming superiority in the air and massive artillery resources. Appropriately Kirkman was himself a gunner. He was an experienced professional, under whose command we were to operate for most of 1944. We were fortunate to serve under a Corps Commander with much practical common sense; a more ambitious general, with less regard for realities, would certainly have incurred more casualties and not achieved so much. We then knew little about Kirkman – to us he was just another Eighth Army gunner – and not much more about Oliver Leese, Monty's successor as Eighth Army Commander. What little we knew about Leese did not impress us; he had been a successful Commander of XXX Corps under Monty, and before that founding father of the Guards Armoured Division. Our assessment turned out not far wrong. Leese was over-promoted, a view now confirmed by the Alanbrooke diaries; admirable when employed as a Corps Commander under Monty, but unconvincing when deprived of the master's direction. He was a forceful leader, but devoid of subtlety. 10 RB never admired Leese and shed no tears when he left Italy (further over-promoted) that autumn to command the Army group in Burma. For Alexander, our C in C, we retained admiration and affection; he had rescued us from a sticky patch in Tunisia. We were always pleased to see him and felt that, outstanding regimental soldier as he was, he understood our difficulties.

The close country of the Liri Valley meant that there was at first no role for 6 Armoured Division. Instead its component parts were divided; the Guards Brigade had the task of holding Cassino town while, to the south near where 10 RB had held the river line in April, 4 Division and 8 Indian Division were to undertake the main assault crossings. 26 Armoured Brigade went under command of the reserve formation, 78 Division, thus renewing their Tunisian association with its present commander, Charles Keightley. The only mobile troops able to exploit early success consisted of the Derbyshire Yeomanry, the armoured reconnaissance regiment equipped with Shermans, and 10 RB. The Derbyshire Yeomanry were easy to work with; under a professional Commanding Officer in Peter Payne-Gallwey, a former 11th Hussar who had learnt his trade in the desert, the regiment worked like clockwork with communications as slick as those of our armoured regiments. If there was a success to exploit, we hoped to do so well.

The preliminaries to Diadem were well organized by the staffs at both Eighth Army and XIII Corps. Our move to an assembly area near Mignano went smoothly, helped by the Allied complete control of the air. By now the staffs in Eighth Army were young, experienced and, largely, former civilians; most had moved to the staff after serving in a regiment at the 'sharp end'. They were thus helpful, understanding and sought practical solutions. There was never any animosity towards the staff such as existed during the 1914–18 War. We were admirably served and grateful for the support we received.

Less welcome were the personal messages from senior commanders which arrived before major attacks. Monty had started this fashion and doubtless his famous missive before El Alamein about 'hitting Rommel for six' had its effect. By May 1944, however, the novelty had worn off and the impact of such messages on the riflemen was negligible. People were, however, interested in a detailed briefing about the operational plan. In 10 RB we took care over this aspect; before Operation Diadem I explained the plan for the battle to all in Battalion Headquarters and answered some pertinent questions. Here again, Eighth Army staff were good in making information available; one could quote, for example, the exact number of guns to be involved in the fire plan, besides an outline of the air support. We were bothered about being overlooked from the Monastery. It helped our morale to know there were plans for a continuous smoke screen until Monastery Hill fell into our hands. Though the smoke would not affect the amount of enemy shelling, it would reduce its quality and improve the chances of the sappers bridging the Gari. It was upon the success of the bridging operation that the battle hinged; until the river was bridged, and some real estate obtained on the far side, our superiority in armour meant little.

The fire plan was far from being a thoughtless bombardment by the 1060 guns involved; particular attention was paid to enemy gun positions, while the central control of the British artillery, far superior to that on the German side, ensured that opportunity targets were engaged as necessary. Again the gunners served us superbly, while credit, too, is due to the air forces, who so dominated the battlefield by day that one hardly saw an enemy aircraft. The Luftwaffe's intervention amounted to just sporadic night bombing which, though alarming to those in the vicinity, had little impact.

Nevertheless, we soon guessed that the battle was not going to plan. By midday on 12 May we learnt that the attack by the Poles on Monastery Hill had failed and the news from the divisions south of Cassino was not encouraging. There was no move for us that first day and we heard that 4 Division and the Indians had secured small bridgeheads only, and that 4 Division had been ordered by the Corps Commander to build a bridge that night 'at all costs'.

Though 10 RB played only a small part in this huge battle, we were near enough to appreciate the courage of the Poles attacking the Monastery. Less obvious was the achievement of the two assault divisions in the valley below. If 8 Indian Division were the more successful at first, tribute is due to 4 Division who, overcoming a bad start to their operation, finally got a bridge across in their sector on the second night. By first light on 13 May all three squadrons of 17th/21st Lancers were across; the way was now clear for the reserve brigade of 4 Division and later for 78 Division. Some idea of the cost of the bridging operation can be seen from the casualties to the sappers concerned, eighty killed or wounded out of 200 engaged in the project. It makes one feel ashamed that one took those bridges almost for granted.

On the afternoon of 14 May we were called forward to a harbour area short of the bridge across the Gari in the 8 Indian Division sector. The bridgehead was still only a mile deep and there was no room for soft transport on the far side of the river. Some of the Derbyshire Yeomanry tanks and two of our scout platoons got over the river. The rest of 10 RB spent a disagreeable 24 hours sheltering in slit trenches from shelling. It was an unpromising start to our battle, but we were lucky only to have a few casualties, though these included the RSM, Taffy Crocker, who blew himself up on a mine while harbouring Bobby Selway's vehicle. Happily his injuries were not too serious and he soon rejoined us.

On 16 May there was finally space across the river for the Derbyshire Yeomanry Group to embark on our task. This was my first experience of an Adjutant's eye view of battle; it was frightening and frustrating. The narrow Liri Valley lanes were choked with transport; visibility was limited and the situation confused. My task was to man the command set and deal with the rear link and instructions from the Derbyshire Yeomanry. At least I had a job to do and good company in the shape of Corporal Eric Young, the operator on the command set. Young was a brilliant operator of the 19 set and combined this skill with a cynical sense of humour. He kept the command half track happy, even if his repartee was sometimes too much for those without the wit to compete. Bobby Selway was also good company and a calming force. Though Bobby considered his job in battle a sinecure, I admired his loyalty and the help he gave Dick Southby, who was usually away from Battalion HQ in a scout car with his own driver and operator. The close country made map reading a nightmare; one seldom knew for certain one's own position and for the companies up front, fighting a tenacious and determined opposition, it was harder still. Poor Dick Southby found the loneliness of command and untidiness of battle difficult. He had a logical mind; given the facts of a situation marked clearly in chinagraph on a map, he could plan sensibly, but it was not that sort of battle.

The leading Company Commanders, Jim Lonsdale's A Company on the right, Teddy Goschen with B Company on the left, attacked brilliantly on the morning of 17 May. After being repulsed the previous evening, they used a shoot by the 78 Division artillery to occupy their objective. A devastating concentration of artillery struck the Germans as they were leaving their trenches for a counter-attack and 10 RB exploited the confusion. On 17 May, too, the Poles finally captured Monastery Hill, and the Germans decided they now had no option but to withdraw from the Gustav Line. 10 RB pressed on slowly up the valley, but snipers and bazookas prevented quick exploitation.

For a brief moment, late on 18 May, it appeared a coup might be within our grasp. On the Derbyshire Yeomanry net the leading squadron reported that part of the squadron were in Aquino, which, incredibly, seemed unoccupied. Hastily we checked and re-checked the codenames and map references; Aquino was undoubtedly where they claimed to be. Yet Aquino, so our trace of the defences indicated, was within the framework of the Hitler Line. If the information were true, therefore, the Germans were in such disorder that they had failed to get people back from Cassino in time to man their switch line. It was possible, but, we felt, unlikely.

It is obvious now that the Derbyshire Yeomanry's information should have been checked out at once by an infantry patrol from their supporting motor battalion. Regrettably, however, the Tactical HQ of the Derbyshire Yeomanry and our own were not co-located – an elementary mistake, but understandable. The Derbyshire Yeomanry were not used to working closely with a motor battalion, while Dick Southby, in his first major battle, seldom positioned himself correctly and relied too much on his radio to follow events. The armoured reconnaissance squadron had moved so fast that Main HQ 10 RB was three miles behind Aquino, caught in the traffic, which that day was even worse than usual. The Divisional Commander, Charles Keightley, took the Yeomanry report at its face value and decided to attack next morning with an infantry brigade supported by 100 tanks from the independent Canadian Armoured Brigade.

It was an expensive error. Early next morning, 19 May, Ralph Stewart-Wilson, probing forward on the left of the main attack with B Company's scout platoon, discovered the truth. There was a thick mist that morning, which first helped but later hindered the attackers. Ralph's leading section were quickly faced by a roadblock covered by small arms and anti-tank fire. Ralph took his reserve section to find a way round to the left. As the leading carrier went round a bend in the lane it came face to face with a heavy German anti-tank gun, which its crew had just manhandled into position. The leading carrier commander, Lance Corporal Hennell, killed or wounded the entire anti-tank gun crew and set their gun tower on fire but retribution arrived in the shape of supporting German infantry. Ralph put down smoke with his 2 inch mortar, while Hennell skilfully withdrew his carrier; almost immediately afterwards, however, Ralph's own carrier was hit and set on fire. Ralph, now without a wireless, baled out, supervised the withdrawal of the rest of his platoon, remaining on his own within 100 yards of the enemy for several hours before making his way back to the battalion. We were thrilled to see him, having given him up for lost, and his information explained the previous evening's misunderstanding.

The Derbyshire Yeomanry were a great regiment, but on this occasion the commander concerned had either read the map wrong or not appreciated that a ravine lay behind the forward edge of the village. Behind the ravine, steep enough and deep enough to stop a tank, were sited the Hitler Line defences. The Yeomanry were correct in claiming to be in Aquino (or at least its outskirts) the previous evening; it was likely that their part of Aquino had not yet been occupied by the enemy. The latter, thin on the ground and arriving in haste, would naturally have taken up an initial position in the Hitler Line defences themselves – behind the ravine. The party encountered next morning by Ralph Stewart-Wilson were edging forward to give their position extra depth.

It would be wrong, therefore, to blame the Derbyshire Yeomanry for the failure of 78 Division's attack the next morning. Ralph's information arrived too late to affect the plan; as soon as the fog lifted, the Ontario Regiment tanks were caught in the open, suffering heavy losses. When the supporting infantry arrived, they faced uncut wire, covered by heavy machine-gun fire from the Hitler Line. The Germans knocked out nine Ontario tanks, two 78 Division COs were killed and a major disaster was only averted by a smoke screen fired by the divisional artillery. Keightley intended to resume the attack after dark that evening, but the Army Commander, Oliver Leese, intervened. In his view the chance of 'bouncing' the enemy out of the Hitler Line had gone; instead a deliberate assault, featuring 1 Canadian Corps in the lead role, was planned for 23 May. The

Derbyshire Yeomanry and 10 RB withdrew for a couple of days; we got some sleep, caught up with the mail and I made a flying jeep trip to the Reinforcement Centre near Naples to collect some riflemen to fill our depleted ranks.

With Aquino glory denied us, the Yeomanry Group returned to the treadmill. Under 6 Armoured Division we had an unspectacular role filling the gap between the Canadian Corps on our left and the rest of our division on the right. From 23 to 26 May, as great things were happening elsewhere – on 23 May the Canadians broke the Hitler Line to our south by opportunism and sheer courage, while the French, under Juin were almost unnoticed winning the Diadem battle for Alexander in the mountains – we worked our way forward against solid opposition. The Germans still thought, wrongly now, that Eighth Army's advance up the Liri Valley was the main threat to their withdrawal; we, in turn, though that 6 Armoured Division must have been committed with a pursuit battle in view. Our slow progress up to and across the River Melfa was, therefore, disappointing and an affront to our armoured 'machismo'. We had yet to understand the facts of Italian military life.

Rifle Brigade thoughts were distracted by an impending reorganization which was to affect the regiment for the rest of the campaign. As we have seen, there was no role in Italy for an armoured division with equal balance between armour and infantry. The proportion of infantry needed to be increased. Accordingly, 6 Armoured Division would, in future, include two infantry Brigades – the original 1st Guards Brigade and a new formation 61st Infantry Brigade, three battalions of The Rifle Brigade, commanded by Adrian Gore, who returned from Anzio to take over the new job. Two of 61st Brigade's battalions were already available; 2 and 7 RB had come from Egypt, and, modifying their character as motor battalions, were reorganizing as 'ordinary' infantry, while 10 RB were to leave 26 Armoured Brigade, but remain as a motor battalion, able to operate in our specialized role with the armour whenever required.

This reorganization seemed in theory to give 10 RB the best of both worlds. We were to retain our vehicles, and the extra comfort and independence this implied. Equally we were to come under command of Adrian Gore who, as our former Commanding Officer, knew how to use a motor battalion properly. It was sad to leave 26 Armoured Brigade, but, on balance, it seemed a good deal, though, in the early stages, jealousy and patronage of the other two battalions, veterans of the desert with exceptional records, did not always make for easy relationships. In practice, 10 RB fell that summer between two stools. We lost some of our previous expertise at working with armour and were often too vehicle-bound when acting as infantry.

Meanwhile, between 30 May and 1 June, 10 RB reorganized and I found myself out of a job. Dick Southby had found me hard to work with – he was probably tolerant to have put up with me for so long – and understandably wanted to have his own man as Adjutant. The formation of 61st Brigade altered plans for me to go to the staff and I was to remain with 10 RB as second-in-command of a company; the decision made sense and turned out well for me in the end. At the time, however, it was disappointing, and the next three weeks' advance up Italy, past Rome, to Perugia were for me a low point.

In early June the Allies missed their best chance of destroying the German armies. History has cast Mark Clark, Fifth Army Commander, as the villain of the piece; his contempt for the British led him to disobey Alexander's instructions and divert his Army's breakout from Anzio towards Rome instead of following his orders to cut off the German withdrawal down Route 6 at Valmontone. Clark's disobedience allowed the Germans under their Corps Commander, von Senger und Etterlin, to regain control; by the time we reached Perugia the German withdrawal to the Gothic Line had become orderly. They held a series of lines across Italy, invariably based on excellent defensive features, and withdrew from them at their own choosing only when the pressure became dangerous. One of these defensive lines, running east and west either side of Lake Trasimene and slightly north of Perugia, faced 61st Brigade, as we squared up to Perugia on 17 June, after a long advance of some 200 miles.

Throughout the flog up Italy we always expected the Germans to withdraw to the Pisa-Rimini position, known as the Gothic Line. It is hard to see why we were so confident that this would be the German plan. Perhaps it was due to information from ULTRA; more probably because it was what the British would have done in similar circumstances. Our expectations proved wrong, since they ignored Kesselring and his concept of defensive fighting. Kesselring was perhaps the best defensive general on either side in the Second World War; he fought always as far forward as possible, occupying ground which provided good observation, and withdrawing only when a position was likely to be turned. In mid-June round Perugia and Lake Trasimene we encountered a typical Kesselring intermediate position. It should have been obvious that only hard fighting would turn the enemy out; instead a facile optimism prevailed and we had heavy casualties. It was not a good period for 6 Armoured Division; it is always easy to think you are good, vastly more difficult consistently to remain so. Perhaps the Normandy landings, two days after the capture of Rome, subconsciously affected our attitude to the Italian campaign. Italy had become a secondary theatre; the impending removal of an American Corps and the French Expeditionary Force added to the feeling that the 'D Day dodgers' were becoming a forgotten Army. There was no alternative but to 'keep on keeping on', our role for the rest of a disagreeable summer.

In mid-June we experienced a week of unseasonable but heavy rain. The Divisional Commander, Vyvyan Evelegh, considering the high ground round Perugia unsuited to armour, determined to employ both his infantry brigades simultaneously. 1st Guards Brigade on the right were to clear Perugia itself and the high ground to the north. 61st Brigade had the job of capturing the hills to the west between Perugia and Lake Trasimene; subsequently we were to open up the main road from Perugia to Arezzo, Route 75.

At this time The Rifle Brigade technique was to advance at night and aim to be installed at first light on our objective. Usually these attacks were 'silent'; artillery support would only be called for when the attack encountered opposition. In all these battles there was little chance of reconnaissance and no time for patrolling. Our tactics required a high standard of map reading and cross-country navigation; on a dark night the attackers had no exact idea of their whereabouts. Often it was a night compass march, hoping somehow one would end up in the right place.

10 RB's first attack of this kind on the night of 18/19 June proved successful. It was a pouring wet night, and Jim Lonsdale and Teddy Goschen did brilliantly to get A and B Companies onto their objectives. When dawn broke, Teddy Goschen gave up the compass in favour of following a railway line and found his B Company had slipped through the forward elements of the enemy in the darkness. Teddy,whose modesty and sense of humour rarely deserted him, remarked afterwards, "We made so much noise going along that railway line, I think the Germans must have taken us for Panzer Grenadiers". In fact, B Company had cut Route 75; they soon knocked out a Mark IV as well as two enemy trucks and a motor-cyclist motoring along the main road unaware of the situation. With Jim Lonsdale's A Company safely installed on Monte Lacugnano, south of the road, a considerable success was achieved. A further twenty prisoners were picked up later in the day; that night the Germans, after resisting the Guards Brigade stoutly for two days, decided with withdraw from Perugia.

The next night 7 RB, using similar tactics, captured the dominant Monte Malbe. It seemed too easy and a reverse was inevitable. 2 RB were the first victims of over-confidence; the problems also resulted from indecision about whether to push on and exploit success or pause to consolidate. This uncertainty meant that 2 RB's plan for the next phase was not made till after dark, and next morning they were nowhere near their objectives. An unpleasant day followed with 2 RB pinned down astride Route 75, and completely dominated by enemy still holding the villages of Corciano and Castelvieto (on the right and left of the road respectively) as well as the key feature Monte Rentella. 10 RB were now ordered to capture Corciano and Monte Rentella on the night of 21/22 June.

The notice was short, unnecessarily so, since the plight of 2 RB had been obvious since early morning, and there was therefore plenty of time for reconnaissance and preparation. The task required three companies up, and, understandably, Dick Southby decided to keep B Company in reserve as they had borne the brunt of the earlier successful advance three nights before. This meant Ian Blacker, inexperienced as a motor company commander, being launched into his first battle as the head of new hotch-potch of former support platoons. There was little alternative, but it was unfortunate that D Company's baptism of fire should occur in a situation so testing. 10 RB's plan was simple. A Company on the right of Route 71 were to go for Corciano, too large a village to be the objective for a motor company with a rifle strength of only some fifty or sixty. But if anyone could take the place, Jim Lonsdale's determination would do so. On the left of the main road D Company in the centre were to capture the main feature, Monte Rentella, some 1,200 feet high. It was a sharp, wooded hill, rising steeply from the valley; since it obviously provided excellent observation in both directions, the Germans from 15 Panzer Grenadier division, one of their best formations, were unlikely to give it up without a struggle. C Company, under David Bassett, had another tricky task on the battalion's left. Their objective was an unnamed extension of Monte Rentella 400 to 500 yards to the west; a gully ran between the two hills, providing a natural forming-up area for enemy counter-attack. Because of the haste with which the operation was mounted, the company com-manders had no chance to study the ground beforehand. Otherwise this factor would surely have been appreciated and a plan made to cope with the likely consequences. To make matters harder for C Company, they were ordered to 'mask' the village of Castelvieto, which 2 RB's failure the previous day had indicated was held by the enemy. It constituted a dangerous enemy position in 10 RB's left rear, as well as yet another forming-up area for counter-attack. B Company, in reserve, were to occupy a position round the buildings at La Torre at the foot of Monte Rentella. This was a sound aspect of the plan and provided balance throughout the battle.

Ian had gone forward with his signaller, Corporal Carlton, to make what reconnaissance he could; we arranged on the air that I would bring D Company up in their vehicles to a harbour area Ian had selected near a road junction just beyond kilometre 9 along Route 71 out of Perugia. The move involved dodgy map reading in the dusk as our convoy threaded its way through the western suburbs of Perugia. Our drivers were, however, skilled at this sort of movement and made the trip without becoming en-tangled with other parts of the battalion also moving at the time. In the harbour area Ian gave clear orders off the map to his platoon commanders, who had had no chance to look at the ground; anyway it was by now too dark for them to have seen anything. They, in turn, briefed their section commanders off the map as best they could. I wished Ian and the others luck as they moved off into the darkness and penetrating rain. I was left, inglorious, in charge of the vehicles, which I was to bring forward onto the objective the next morning. I hoped for the best, but my tactical instinct warned me of impending trouble.

The night passed quietly apart from a few bursts of Spandau fire and the odd flare from the direction of Castelvieto; by first light both D and C Companies were reported on their objectives and to be digging in. Back at the vehicles, I felt relieved that my forebodings had apparently proved groundless. About half past six, however, we heard heavy mortar fire from the direction of Monte Rentella; soon afterwards the sound of small arms confirmed that a German counter-attack was in progress. Battalion HQ warned me over the radio to come forward with more ammunition; Jock Hamilton, D Company CSM, whom Ian, to Jock's disappointment, had left out of the night advance, started to load a White with an appropriate selection.

About 7.30 a.m. we got the expected summons. Jock Hamilton accompanied me and we nosed our way carefully onto the main road. As we went over the crest we could see the battlefield and Monte Rentella clear before us. Enemy mortar and artillery fire aimed at the top of the feature had ceased, though we could still hear small arms fire and the noise of exploding hand grenades. Just then German mortar and artillery fire re-started, their targets A Company held up short of Corciano and some tanks of the 16th/5th Lancers who were milling about in the valley below. I decided to make for Teddy Goschen and B Company in their position near La Torre to discover what was happening.

It was a dodgy drive on treacherous tracks; Rifleman Gudge needed all his skill to avoid joining several 2 RB carriers ditched and abandoned in the fighting of the previous day. By the time we reached La Torre and found Teddy Goschen, it was 8 o'clock. It was soon obvious that things had gone badly wrong with C and D Companies. I found Corporal Carlton, Ian's signal corporal, who had volunteered to take a message back from the top of Rentella, and told me what had happened.

The mortar fire aimed at Rentella earlier that morning had been the support programme for a well-executed counter-attack by 15 Panzer Grenadier Division. Under cover of this fire, some 100 infantry had moved into the valley between C and D Companies, and then gone on to envelop the Rentella feature. It was a professional performance and the speed with which it was executed prevented our artillery and mortars from intervening – partly because they had no obvious targets, but more for fear of hitting our own troops, still digging in. To make matters worse, communications with both C and D Companies had collapsed, leaving them out of touch with Battalion HQ at the critical moment. Though

Teddy Goschen had a gunner OP from 2 RHA and there was another with Jim Lonsdale near Corciano, no gunner was available for the other forward companies; it was planned for the OP from La Torre to go forward onto Rentella once the feature was secure, but the German counter-attack had been too quick. There had been sharp hand-to-hand fighting near the summit of Rentella with casualties to both sides. Ian Blacker and eight riflemen had been killed, while Pat Wilding, commanding the platoon of C Company nearest to Rentella, was also dead. The stretcher bearers, who excelled themselves that morning, evacuated about thirty casualties, but there were nearly seventy missing, mostly from D Company. C Company had been less directly attacked, but with both his flanks now exposed, David Basset rightly withdrew. He took up a position on Teddy Goschen's left and prevented any threat developing from Castelvieto. Altogether the battle had been a chapter of accidents, many avoidable, and we were fortunate to avoid a worse débâcle.

10 RB were saved by the common sense of Teddy Goschen and James Booth, the support company commander, at La Torre, and the magnificent fighting of A Company under Jim Lonsdale. A Company's position near Corciano Church gave observation onto the Germans behind the Rentella feature and 2 RHA took advantage of this situation to bring down devastating 'stonks' on any Germans wishing to exploit the success their counter-attack had won them. Jock Hamilton, Corporal Carlton and I – with a B Company section to protect us – edged forward to the bottom of Rentella to see if we could pick up any D Company missing, lying up in the scrub and hoping to rejoin the battalion after dark. It was a sad mission; the Rifle Brigade in general, and 10 RB in particular, had suffered a humiliation. Though between them Teddy Goschen, James Booth and Jim Lonsdale had saved the day, it remained a disaster for D Company, and also for C Company, whose retreat had been almost as precipitate as my own earlier withdrawal from Chouigui eighteen months earlier in Tunisia.

In war no situation is ever as bad as first appears. Though 22 June ended with a feeling that 61st Brigade had suffered a reverse, the Germans had not had a good day either. The magnificent shooting of 2 RHA had damaged the enemy considerably. The steady pressure exerted by A Company round Corciano and the threat posed by 7 RB's hold on Monte Malbe must have made 15 Panzer Grenadier Division worried about being outflanked. There was also a threat from the other side of Lake Trasimene where 78 Division had come up from reserve and clearly intended an early attack. The Germans decided enough was enough; when, during the night, A and B Company patrolled cautiously forward they found Corciano Village and Monte Rentella both unoccupied.

The next morning Jock Hamilton, Corporal Carlton and I reached the top of Rentella; it was easy to see what had happened. Ian Blacker, shot at close range, lay in his half-dug slit trench. His Thompson sub-machine gun, which he was firing at his attackers, lay in his hands. He looked peaceful and at rest; gently we helped the stretcher bearers lift him up, covering his face before he was carried away. There were half-finished slit trenches all over the feature; most were little more than scrapes and few would have provided much protection against the shelling and mortaring to which D Company had been subjected. Without communications to the rear, D Company had no chance of maintaining their position. They were easy meat for a well-timed German counter-attack. It was the sort of operation at which our opponents excelled and to which 10 RB had yet to find the answer.

I had first to persuade Dick Southby that it was worth re-forming D Company. The alternative would have been to disband it and split the assets between the existing motor companies. Fortunately, Dick agreed to give me a try, a decision for which I was grateful. The other company commanders also wanted D Company back in the frame and their attitude and encouragement were a support. I started with a complete Company HQ, an outstanding CSM in Jock Hamilton, a full set of vehicles and drivers, but only one composite platoon of riflemen. Jim Lonsdale gave me one of his best platoon commanders, Maurice Day, to come on promotion as second-in-command. This was a promising start and for the next nine months Maurice and I formed a good partnership. We were very different but complemented each other well. Maurice was sound on administration; he and the Colour Sergeant, Tibby Watson, formed a strong team and quickly swung into action to re-equip the Company. This left me free to rustle up some soldiers; I left early next morning in a jeep, driven again by Chalky White, two three-ton lorries trailing behind, on operation Pied Piper to see how many riflemen I could collect from the reinforcement units near Naples.

10 RB was such a happy battalion that no one sick or wounded spared any effort till they got back. By good fortune, too, a number of officers and riflemen had returned to the market when the Anzio operation came to an end. During the winter infantry reinforcements were so short that officers and riflemen sent out as Rifle Brigade reinforcements had been compulsorily re-badged and sent elsewhere. Now that 10 RB and the other battalions in 61st Brigade were suffering casualties, such expatriate riflemen became available to return to the fold. There were fine people among them and, having served as 'ordinary' infantry, they possessed skills and techniques which the Rentella disaster had shown 10 RB lacked.

My journey, therefore, went well. I returned with enough former members of the battalion to bring A, B and C Companies up to their required strength and also a small increment which Dick Southby gave me to get D Company back on the road. He decided that when the battalion returned to active operations D Company should find a campsite about 10–15 miles behind the front line to retrain and absorb the extra reinforcements which I knew were on the way. Vitally, I obtained some high-grade platoon commanders returning to the regiment; Henry Hall, who had been at Anzio with the Green Howards, took over 13 Platoon, formed mainly from Rentella survivors, while Jimmy Stevens, back from a spell in hospital, started 14 Platoon. Soon Peter Beazley, also returning to the regiment after service elsewhere, arrived and an embryo 15 Platoon emerged under his energetic command. I thought it would be too difficult to form a complete scout platoon, so kept just a section of the original D Company platoon under the admirable Sergeant Watson. Thus by the middle of July we had a proper Company HQ, three viable motor platoons and an effective reconnaissance element.

Modern regular soldiers will be surprised at the degree of free enterprise practiced in reorganizing D Company. There will be muttering about 'private armies', and concern about the informality of my methods. Nothing so amateurish would have been allowed in 21st Army Group, where tighter control existed over all aspects of military activity. Fortunately, however, in Eighth Army some privateering spirit, developed in Africa, still existed. In The Rifle Brigade, too, initiative was encouraged and I am grateful for the freedom I was given and hope the cause benefited from our enthusiasm.

I based our training on Rentella. We discussed what had gone wrong and how to avoid similar mistakes. Rentella showed clearly the need for better and more thorough reconnaissance; a mere company commander could not always be the master of his destiny, but we should aim for platoon commanders to have a sight of ground beforehand, and for section commanders to be shown objectives properly. We would try and avoid tumbling into battle; nevertheless, we must retain our ability to think and plan on the move.

We spent time, too, in curing the communication weaknesses which had bedevilled Rentella. There was no alternative but to rely on our unreliable manpack radios within the company, but we needed to carry forward a high-powered 19 set to operate when the objective was captured. If Ian Blacker had possessed this facility on 22 June our artillery might have broken up the German counter-attack before it started and his Company would not have been left isolated. We needed to pay attention to selecting artillery and mortar defensive fire tasks beforehand and checking them on the ground when we arrived on the objective. All of this was elementary, but to us in D Company then it seemed like Columbus discovering America. We were learning, in fact, that, while to be ponderous is unriflemanlike, projects should still be carefully planned and thought through.

Every three days or so, leaving my platoon commanders to get on with their training, I jeeped forward with Chalky White to see how the battalion were faring. For 10 RB it was a hard, hot summer; just occasionally there would be a burst of 10 miles when the armour could take the lead, but the Germans never lost control; 6 Armoured Division would soon find itself again brought up short by the next intermediate defensive position. There was unpleasant fighting round Arezzo, where the New Zealand Division was called in to help the Guards Brigade crack the Dora Line, then disappointment soon afterwards when the 16th/5th Lancers saw a bridge over the Arno blown up in their faces with the leading tank only 100 yards short of its capture. 10 RB soon after fought a fierce encounter with elements of the crack German 1st Parachute Division. This last battle, round Renacci, was Robby Selway's finest hour; with Dick Southby ill in hospital, suffering from the ulcers which caused him to hand over command later, Bobby handled a tricky situation with calm determination. Each advance was difficult, and all increased the human toll, especially the loss of leaders who could no longer be replaced with people of similar quality. The loss of John Bodley, blown up with his carrier on a mine, was a special tragedy. He had only just found his way back to A Company after being wounded in the Liri Valley; he had been involved in so many near things that everyone had begun to feel he bore a charmed life. By the end of July, in fact, 10 RB's three motor companies were exhausted and it was time for D Company to share the load.

About now 6 Armoured Division experienced some changes in command. Vyvyan Evelegh left us on 27 July. By now, after nearly two years commanding a Division in active operations, he was a tired man. Though we were sad to see him go, it was the right decision. 6 Armoured Division was in a rut and required a new mind to remove its developing pessimism and loss of dash. Gerald Templer, a new broom if ever there was one, took over; we were just starting to feel the impact of his very different style when he was wounded by a mine on the side of the road, set off by a Guards Brigade lorry. In the back of the vehicle there was a grand piano, liberated by the Grenadier Guards. Out flew the instrument, pinning Gerald Templer beneath it; when, ten minutes later, he was extricated, there was no question of his continuing in command and he was evacuated back to England. The accident, however, may have proved a blessing in disguise. I doubt if Gerald Templer's technique, well suited to the Anzio beachhead, would have been equally fitted to nursing 6 Armoured Division through a period of convalescence.

I had only one encounter with Gerald Templer during his short time as our Divisional Commander. It was just after my new D Company had taken the field; we were sitting on a ridge in the Arno Valley acting as flank guard to the Division against incursions from the Prato Magno, a mountain mass on our right. It was late afternoon and there was more enemy shelling than usual; the methodical Germans, disliking waste, often used to fire off any spare ammunition before withdrawing to a new position. My task was to occupy a ridge closer to the Prato Magno, and so widen the front for the divisional advance up the Arno Valley. Using our new techniques, we were studying the ground over which D Company aimed later to make a night advance of 2,000 yards. Gerald Templer arrived, having left his jeep and ADC below the crest. I saluted smartly and introduced myself as D Company Commander; I explained the local situation and pointed out on the ground where I thought the enemy positions were. My exposé was not popular; "Well," remarked Gerald Templer, "and what are you going to do about it, Sonny?" I blanched visibly – Company Commanders, especially those aged 23, do not find being addressed as 'Sonny' improves their credibility. "Wait till it gets dark, when I expect the Germans will go away. Then we will patrol forward 2,000 yards and occupy their ridge." It seemed sense to me then, and still does now. However, this concept of operations failed to convince our new general. Slipping below the crest, he arranged for powerful artillery support to be made available half an hour later, and told me 'to take my finger out' and mount an attack. He then left in a cloud of dust, attracting some German shelling; I assembled my O Group and reluctantly issued orders for a daylight advance. It might have cost casualties, if probably not too many, but it was the negation of our D Company philosophy which irked me. Henry Hall and the others were too courteous to point this out, but I noticed the general silence as my team went off to brief their subordinates. Five minutes before we were due to start, over came the familiar hisses of 2 RHA's 25 pounders providing Gerald Templer's promised support. The shells landed perfectly and I walked across to Jimmy Stevens, whose 14 Platoon had drawn the short straw of leading our advance. Just then Corporal Carlton raced up from my jeep below with a message form, beaming all over his face, "Message from Own Sunray, Sir. Pay no attention to what very Big Sunray told you. Circumstances have changed. Revert to earlier order." We breathed a sigh of relief, though it was only later that I learned we had a Grenadier piano to thank for our reprieve.

That August D Company, fresh and fortunate in having had the chance to consider our methods, settled down operationally. Rightly, the main burden of 10 RB's work briefly fell on us. The other companies needed a rest and we were content to give them a break. Luckily the battalion's role – flank protection – was well suited to D Company's tactics and some early successes in patrolling increased our confidence.

That month there were, however, forces at work on a high level. Operation Anvil, the invasion of Southern France, led to the equivalent of seven divisions being withdrawn from the Italian campaign. Once the debate over Anvil went against him, Alexander had to halt and re-deploy to fill the gap left in his Fifth Army by this loss of resources. Alexander's job, to contain Kesselring, remained the same, and his Chief of Staff, John Harding, concluded that a further offensive was required with the weight concentrated on the western side of the Apennines. The Adriatic side was initially discarded, the alternation of ridges and river valleys which had plagued Eighth Army the previous autumn being the main reason. The main road over the Apennines from Florence to Bologna seemed to offer better prospects, and this plan would probably have been adopted but for the intervention of Kirkman, our commander in 13 Corps and an original thinker.

Kirkman had commanded 13 Corps throughout the long advance from Cassino, but, by early August, his command had been halted south of the Arno either side of Florence. The natural defences of the mountains ahead offered little scope for a mechanized army; the eastern end of the Gothic Lane, on the Adriatic, seemed to him the better option, where Eighth Army's main assets, a mass of tanks and large amounts of artillery, could be deployed. Kirkman put his plan to Leese, the Army Commander, and found him receptive – not only for reasons of strategy. Leese had found it hard to deal with his opposite number, Mark Clark, and disliked him personally, besides finding him an uncongenial neighbour as an Army Commander. He had resolved never to fight shoulder to shoulder with him again, if he could avoid it, and Kirkman's persuasive tactical arguments gave Leese a solution to his dilemma. Leese put the idea of making Eighth Army's main effort on the Adriatic to Harding and Alexander on 4 August; typically the latter accepted the change in plan without demur.

Alexander now had to sell the revised concept for his autumn offensive to Clark, who agreed in principle with the revised plan, but insisted a main role be given to his Fifth Army. Clark realized that if he accepted a secondary role in Italy, he risked his Army being transferred to France – not a prospect he welcomed. He therefore struck a bargain with Alexander by which Kirkman's 13 Corps remained on the west side of the Apennines and came under command of Fifth Army. 13 Corps' task would be to protect the right flank of Fifth Army's main effort; in accordance with the original plan, this offensive centred on the main road from Florence to Bologna over the Futa Pass.

It was ironical that Kirkman, who had conceived moving Eighth Army to the Adriatic, should remain behind under Mark Clark. The latter made no secret of his lack of confidence in his British allies, whom he considered slow and cautious. Mark Clark also had no time for British generals, despising their reluctance to incur heavy losses or drive their subordinates as he forced his American commanders to do. The new plan was thus a bad personal deal for Kirkman, who had much to endure from his Army Commander that autumn. Nor, militarily, was the decision to leave

13 Corps behind above criticism. It deprived Eighth Army of an effective reserve, while two armoured divisions, 6th South African as well as 6 Armoured, were deployed where there was little scope for tanks.

This high-level bargaining was unknown to us. While the measures to move Eighth Army across to the Adriatic were being implemented, 10 RB and D Company continued leaning on the opposition south of Pontassieve. For D Company it was a splendid time; we occupied the Villa Bensi, as stately a home as Tuscany could provide. We ate our meals in the drawing room, facing across the Arno valley, and opening onto a delightful veranda. There was a grand piano for the riflemen to strum, and even an organ for skilled musicians to practice on. The gardens produced marvellous fruit; I still recall the peaches we consumed as we planned our patrols up the hill towards Vallombrosa. We worked hard on our tactics, edging steadily forward, identifying enemy positions and then giving them devastating 'stonks' from 2 RHA, directed by their OP on the Villa Bensi roof. Retaliation came our way sometimes from enemy artillery or mortar fire, but the walls of the Villa Bensi were thick and the sandbag defences organized by Jock Hamilton efficient, so that little harm resulted. Our co-operation with 2 RHA at this time was so good, and that regiment's shooting so accurate, that we dominated the Germans opposed to us. We captured a prisoner from Vallombrosa, our immediate objective; we gave him a cup of tea in the Villa Bensi and discussed the British 'trommel feuer', which he said was worse than anything he had experienced in Russia. A feature of 2 RHA gunnery was how close their support was; once, when Peter Beazley and his platoon were in difficulties, he reminds me now that I brought the fire of 2 RHA down on his slit trenches to solve the problem. I remember also selecting SOS tasks only 100 yards out, confident that 2 RHA's precision would see us through. It was a sad day when 2 RHA had to leave us to return to their own 1st Armoured Division, who were now in Italy and about to take part in the attack on the Adriatic coast. Good though their successors, first 57 Field Regiment, and later 104 RHA (Essex Yeomanry), proved, 2 RHA set a standard of infantry support in a class of their own.

At this time our new Divisional Commander, 'Nap' Murray, visited 10 RB. We liked him at once; he came from command of a brigade of 51st Highland Division in Normandy and understood exactly 6 Armoured Division's feelings after so much continuous action. His term "Leaning on the enemy" made sense by saving infantry casualties, but also exploited the areas where we were superior. Murray's other nickname – the 'Nap', short for Napoleon, referred to his tactical ability – was Mr Punch, whom, with a red face and prominent nose, he somewhat resembled. He had joined the Cameronians as an ordinary soldier, and kept goal for his regiment and then the Army, before being commissioned. He had limited talk for officers, but great ability to take people into his confidence; I cannot remember anyone better at talking to soldiers individually or in a group. His sense of humour, never far from the surface, was a delight and, like all good regimental soldiers, he remembered people's names. "Quite a card, Sir," observed Chalky White as we drove away from Battalion HQ, past the signs reminding one "Drive Slowly – Dust is Death", on our return to the Villa Bensi. I hope I do not trivialise Nap Murray by portraying him as a politico-military Doctor Cameron; certainly 6 Armoured Division were fortunate to have someone like the sage of Tannochbrae to conduct our convalescence and, like Dr Cameron's patients, the beauty of the cure was that we did most of the work ourselves.

Suddenly, one night, our opponents withdrew. I wish I could pretend that we had leaned on them so successfully that we had forced this action upon them; in fact Eighth Army's attack on the Adriatic made Kesselring withdraw across the Arno and occupy his main Gothic Line positions north of Florence. Our job now was to take up the slack, never a pleasant task, with the enemy able to choose the point of first contact. In D Company's case our first attack went well and we occupied a village on the high ground above Pontassieve, but the objective and surrounding tracks were thick with mines. We lost, in quick succession, first Jimmy Stevens, who died of his wounds soon after, Peter Beazley, another, happily less serious, victim of an 'S' mine, and Sergeant Northfield, Henry Hall's platoon sergeant and as good a man as one could wish for. Northfield had been with D Company since the earliest days; he had been Ian Blacker's right-hand man in the anti-tank platoon, and his loss and the news his leg had been amputated were hard to bear.

The Sieve valley up which we moved towards Dicomano was dominated by high ground on the left. 8 Indian Division wisely took their time clearing this area, not to our disadvantage, since this meant that 61 Brigade's battalions took turns at following up in the Sieve valley. Most people managed a break in Florence in the next ten days; the Germans had left the Ponte Vecchio intact but demolished the other bridges before they withdrew. We soon knew Florence well, since Adrian Gore had friends owning a house just south of the city. The Villa Capponi not only provided people with a bed, bath and 48 hours complete rest, it was also a reminder of ordinary life. To have a civilised drink before dinner in a drawing room, followed by a meal served on china plates, washed down by admirable 'vino', provided just the break one needed from the sharp end. The Italian girls, many speaking fluent English, were good for our morale; just to roll back the carpet, dance with a pretty girl and talk about something other than the war, reminded one that sometime it would end and that proper life remained at the end of the tunnel.

Dick Fyffe's return to command 10 RB was another good feature. He had struggled with 7 RB, who were used to Douglas Darling and his 'hands on' approach. Dick's calm ability to decentralize suited 10 RB better and our military convalescence advanced steadily. We reached Dicomano, where our conversion to proper infantry continued as we first used the mules who were to figure largely in our lives all winter. The enemy opposing us were 715 Infantry Division, a moderate outfit by any standards, but even poor troops can damage those on the wrong end of a Spandau. I was pleased therefore with D Company's debut in the mountains, as we passed through B Company in a Scotch mist early on 21 September. Climbing steadily, passing one platoon through another, as I had seen the Indian Division doing earlier, we established ourselves by evening at the top of the Muraglione Pass with the way downhill to Forli apparently open.

But, though we had penetrated the fixed defences of the Gothic Line, our problems were just beginning. The Germans were under pressure, from Eighth Army on the Adriatic, and from the Americans attacking on the Florence-Bologna axis; Kesselring, however, appreciated it was easier to defend the back end of a mountain range with short communications behind one, rather than sitting forward and being supplied over inadequate mountain roads. Well planned demolitions prevented 13 Corps bringing their superiority in tanks and artillery to bear and Kirkman could deploy only the troops he could supply. The advance slowed as September ended, the rain poured down, and 6 Armoured Division found itself frustrated.

Just as Route 67 over the Muraglione Pass became a possible axis, the weather broke. I have never seen such rain, as we sat in vehicles nose to tail hopefully about to start a drive on Forli. It was a miserable time, and the downpour washed away any hope of a 26 Armoured Brigade breakthrough. It was so cold, also, that a rifleman in 7 RB, working in the mountains to our left, died of exposure before he could be evacuated. October saw us back to the old routine of leaning on the opposition and waiting for the Germans to withdraw when it suited them.

Though 6 Armoured Division were making slow progress, the Italian front as a whole was not becalmed. All September Eighth Army battered away on the Adriatic. There was an opportunity early in the offensive when Leese (shades of the Liri Valley) omitted to provide the Canadian Corps with a proper reserve; thus, when the Canadians and Keightley's 5 Corps broke through, success went unexploited. A week later, on the Coriano Ridge, 1st Armoured Division suffered a Balaclava-like reverse, for which indifferent generalship was largely responsible. But Eighth Army maintained their pressure and when McCreery relieved Leese at the start of October progress continued, despite obstacles provided by the rivers running into the Po Valley. When McCreery took over, he identified Eighth Army as a tired old steeplechaser good for just one more race, and did a good job that autumn; while keeping his Army in being for a spring offensive, he cleared some tricky fences which would later make the way down to the start easier. In Fifth Army, Mark Clark, rudely criticising 13 Corps' slow progress, forced his American formations forward until halted by Monte Grande 12 miles north of Bologna. He had driven his troops into the ground; they were exhausted and Clark now had to wait for the spring and their recovery. As usual, he made the British the scapegoats for his failure to reach Bologna. "We were caught in the British Empire machine," he wrote to an American colleague to justify his failure.

Mark Clark's attacks in the mountains north of Bologna forced the British to shift their boundaries westward and take over more of Fifth Army's front. In mid-October this process involved 6 Armoured Division; first the Guards Brigade, and then 61 Brigade, switched to the Santerno valley with Imola as a distant objective.

Before we left Route 67, D Company enjoyed a modest tactical Indian summer. It was only a minor success, but we were proud of it then and I have returned since to savour our achievement. It began with the successful use by the 17th/21st Lancers of a scissors bridge (an ingenious device carried on the front of a Valentine tank); we had never seen one used before and I cannot remember any repeat performances. On this occasion the Germans were surprised; the tanks managed a quick three-mile advance until being held up on the outskirts of Portico, a small town on the main road. D Company, following up, took over the high ground on the left, and, as night fell, attacked Cannetole, a group of farm buildings over a mile to the left, which gave good observation down the valley towards the German gun area in Rocca San Casciano. For the only time that autumn I commanded D Company from a carrier, driven by Rifleman Christmas; it was an exhilarating interlude and a rare break in our pedestrian progress.

Our subsequent night attack on Cannetole was, however, too methodical. Though it was finally successful, I should have done better to have let Henry Hall and John Goddard, who had taken over 14 Platoon and rapidly become an excellent performer, have their heads. Instead I wanted 15 Platoon, who had not yet recovered from the loss of Peter Beazley, to lead as a fighting patrol at their own pace. Though my motives were correct and I needed to develop the platoon's self confidence, the burden was too much for them. I should have understood this sooner and passed the others through; 15 Platoon finally made it, but by the time we arrived at Cannetole the Germans had withdrawn and we captured only one prisoner, a deserter in disguise, instead of a larger haul which faster exploitation of the 17th Lances' success would have provided. Had we been less deliberate, we could too have patrolled forward from Cannetole and gained more valuable ground. Though Dick Fyffe was very civil on the radio, I was aware of missing a trick and, when daylight came, the vista ahead confirmed my judgement.

The Cannetole complex dominated Portico, which was now ours for the taking. Further down the valley we could see into the German gun areas round Rocca San Casciano, about five to six miles beyond Portico. Dick Fyffe came up that morning on foot since the Germans still held Portico and controlled the road junction off Route 67 to Cannetole. D Company's vehicles had made it the previous evening in the wake of the tanks, and while the Germans were still off balance. They soon recovered their form, however, and Dick's arrival coincided with a damaging bout of shelling on Cannetole itself. Though this confirmed the threat our penetration presented, it made Dick pause to think how Cannetole could be maintained and whether it would not be sensible to mark time on our flank until 2 RB on the right cleared Monte Orlando and came up level with us across Route 67. I thought his decision right then, and can defend its wisdom now. Equally, however, we missed another trick by not exploiting the success we had gained on the left, and we should certainly have pushed on more boldly. It is a British failing that we like to keep in line, disliking salients and exposed flanks. In the event the 2 RB attack failed partly because it was hurried, but also because the Germans had recovered their balance, and, anticipating 2 RB's attack, defended Monte Orlando more strongly than expected.

There was now deadlock; the next six days saw D Company holding firm at Cannetole, with a tricky maintenance problem each night, and restricted to patrolling into Portico and to the north. Each night we secured the road junction leading to Cannetole, so that Maurice Day, proceeding at a snail's pace and without lights, could bring up supplies. It was an unattractive assignment and I admired the calmness with which Maurice executed his blockade running. Otherwise the main feature of life was an artillery duel, the Germans betraying their anxiety about another attack down Route 67 by steadily shelling Bocconi, where Battalion Headquarters and the 17th/21st Lancers were located. We retaliated on the German gun areas further down the road; for once, Cannetole provided the better observation and, by taking compass bearings on the German gun flashes, we gave more than we received.

In mid-October we left Cannetole for good. Maurice Day thinned out our vehicles over two nights' dodgy motoring, while mules arrived to evacuate our other stores. A Polish division took over the sector and we moved to our new area for which Castel del Rio represented the main base. The route to Castel, through Firenzuola, was spectacular and one could only admire the fine American achievement the capture of its heights represented. US II Corps, who had been responsible for this fine feat of arms, had come a long way since their troubles at Kasserine and Fondouk eighteen months earlier; perhaps Mark Clark's unpopularity in his own country prevented the exploits of his Fifth Army that autumn getting the acclaim they deserved.

The approach to Castel del Rio was down the Santerno valley through a deep gorge, in places a mere 100 yards wide. The sappers had done marvels clearing the demolitions left behind by the retreating Germans, but the valley remained hopelessly congested. One needed a block timing to use it; even then, the route was controlled by military police. Castel del Rio resembled a boom town in the gold rush; vacant accommodation of any sort was seized on immediately, with a tumbledown shed considered great luxury. The German artillery treated Castel as a favourite target; only shortage of ammunition prevented them doing more damage. It would be hard to imagine a worse place to site the administrative areas for two divisions (6 Armoured and our old friends 78 Division), but there was little alternative.

D Company's contact with Castel was fleeting. Leaving our vehicles and Maurice Day to find a home for them, we set off right-handed up the hill to relieve the London Irish Rifles on Monte Capello. It was a warm afternoon and we sweated profusely as we climbed. About one and a half hours walking from Castel we reached our destination, a cosy group of farm buildings, which provided cover for everyone and were easily adapted into a tactical framework. We settled in and analysed the situation. The Irish had left us out of touch with the Germans, so our first task was to patrol forward and re-establish contact. It proved easier than expected, and steadily over the next weeks, taking it in turns by companies and battalions, we edged our way forward above the main road to Imola. 78 Division on the left attacked more formally, and had some heavy fighting; we were able to profit from the pressure they exerted. Our opponents, again 715 Division, included a fair proportion of Poles and Alsatians, neither of whom had their heart in the conflict. Patrol clashes consistently went our way and during the next month 61 Brigade inflicted seventy casualties on the enemy, including the capture of thirty-seven prisoners of war, without losing a single prisoner ourselves. Life, despite heavy rain, might well have been worse; nearly everyone had a 'casa' as a base. We became used to the tempo of mule supply, while the routine of 14 days at the 'sharp end' followed by a week at the battalion's base, Grassina, south of Florence provided variety. By the first week in December the line seemed to have stabilized for the winter opposite a feature, the Veno del Gesso (Vein of Chalk), a topographical feature, which dominated our lives for the next three months.

So convenient was the Vena del Gesso for the Germans that it might have been constructed by their own engineers. Opposite us – in the Santerno valley – it was a cliff face, sheer in places, and impossible to scale without specialized equipment and training. On the German side, however, the feature sloped away gradually, providing admirable terrain for reverse slope defensive positions at which the enemy excelled. There was only one gap in the Gesso in our sector – the Santerno valley itself, which opens out to a width of a mile round the small town of Borgo Tossignano. The Borgo gap, however, was dominated by the town of Tossignano, nestling on the Gesso ridge; from a distance Tossignano resembled a mini-Cassino and dominated the Santerno valley and the surrounding area like its famous counterpart had done in the Liri valley. It was a difficult objective, and at the beginning of December, by when 61 Brigade had closed up to the Gesso, it seemed we would stop there for the winter. The main Fifth Army attack south of Bologna had stalled through the heavy casualties suffered by the American infantry in breaching the Gothic Line further back. An impending reorganization of the Allied Command in Italy, involving promotion for both Alexander and Mark Clark, and the departure of Field Marshal Jumbo Wilson to Washington to replace the dead Sir John Dill, suggested a pause in Italy before anything further occurred. As part of the reorganization 13 Corps reverted to command of Eighth Army, and its patient commander, Kirkman, worn out by arthritis and squabbles with Mark Clark, returned to England.

So unlikely did an attack on Tossignano seem that 10 RB went back complete to Florence for a rest on 2 December. The winter plan visualized the 61 Brigade front in the Santerno valley being held by two battalions at a time, the third being left to recuperate round Florence, alternating fort-nightly with one of those in the line. Such a policy made sense and Field Marshal Jumbo Wilson, who as our Colonel Commandant inspected 10 RB in our Florence base at Grassina on 7 December, never suggested that any variation from it was under consideration. It was good to meet Jumbo Wilson, my much more distinguished namesake and brother rifleman; he had a reputation in the regiment for military sagacity, while his appearance and bulk were certainly elephantine enough to justify his nickname. I sat near him at lunch and enjoyed his comments on life in general and relations with Winston Churchill in particular. When he came round my Company later, he displayed his practical experience as a frontline soldier in World War I by telling us how to avoid trench foot, a malady just starting to become fashionable in Italy. Bert Coad, by now CSM of A Company, was impressed – the Field Marshal was the sort of visiting fireman he could cope with; Jock Hamilton, by contrast, a wartime soldier, was as distantly polite as only an intelligent Scotsman can be to a Sassenach with whom he is not in complete sympathy. I sat on the fence at the time; the Alanbrooke diaries indicate Bert Coad's view was right, and Jumbo's reputation for wisdom justified.

Suddenly rumours began to circulate about an impending attack by 2 RB on Tossignano. At first I paid no attention; the idea did not appear sensible or likely. Henry Hall and I took Rifleman Christmas and my jeep shopping in Florence – Chalky White had left me after Cannetole to 'improve himself' by driving for Adrian Gore. I missed his perky presence for a week or so, but he had been at the sharp end so long that it would not have been right to stand in his way; Jock Hamilton reminded me, too, that D Company would now have its own friend at court at Brigade HQ. It was also true that Rifleman Christmas deserved a good job on the strength of his efforts since D Company had been back in the line. Christmas proved an equally delightful, if calmer, jeep driver than Chalky White, who never completely lost the effervescent style perfected on the 'dingo' in Tunisia. I was lucky to be so admirably looked after by both of them, and with Ken Ives, my radio operator minding the 19 set at the back, jeep journeys were never dull. That afternoon Henry Hall, Christmas and I returned to Grassina by way of the Villa Capponi, where we called for afternoon tea and the latest gossip. The Tossignano story was true, so we heard, and D Company would be needed; we gulped our tea, swallowed a sandwich or two, nicked a slice of cake for Rifleman Christmas and sped back to D Company at Grassina.

I found that Maurice Day had already given preliminary orders for a move over the Giogo Pass the next morning, 13 December. Though the timing we had received from 13 Corps was an early one, I reckoned the Company could not be complete in our assembly area behind Fontanelice till early afternoon; I decided therefore to go ahead myself with my jeep party to try and discover the form before the main body arrived. Dick Fyffe dropped in and told me that the whole battalion would be following D Company as soon as suitable block timings over the pass could be arranged. Meanwhile I was to go ahead, prepared to go under command of 2 RB for 24 hours till the main body of 10 RB arrived back in the operational area. Dick approved my decision to go on ahead of my main body; he had already rung Hugo Baring, the Brigade Major, and arranged for me to be briefed on arrival. All that could be done seemed to have been done; there were no details available about the 2 RB plan for the attack, except that H Hour would be that night, 12/13 December. 2 RB, commanded by Owain Foster, the second-in-command – Chris Sinclair had gone home at the end of October – consisted of only three rifle companies. It seemed that a boy was being sent on a man's job, but there was nothing D Company could do about that; I went to bed early, slept well and was still asleep when Alfie Moore, my orderly, woke me next morning with a cup of tea.

Since Tossignano was to prove the worst military experience of my career, and for The Rifle Brigade one of its worst setbacks of the war – only Calais exceeded it in casualties and numbers of people captured as prisoners of war – one should consider why it was selected as an objective. Once again 61 Brigade, as it had done at Rentella, was tumbling untidily into battle; some background to the whole operation is therefore required to set it in perspective.

As we have seen, the main offensive in Italy was over by the end of

November when Mark Clark's Fifth Army ran out of infantry reinforcements. Eighth Army, to whose control 13 Corps, including 6 Armoured Division, had reverted at the end of the month, still contrived a series of limited attacks. McCreery, the Army Commander, wisely concentrated on picking up any tricks that might be going at the end of the season; he had two aims in mind – to give Eighth Army the best possible line on which to winter, and, equally, a position which offered a springboard for a spring offensive. At the end of November Kirkman handed over command of 13 Corps to John Harding. The latter naturally favoured a contribution towards Eighth Army's fighting in the Lombardy Plain; an attack, even just a holding affair towards Imola, seemed a reasonable way to achieve this aim.

It is hard to be too critical of Eighth Army and 13 Corps for making offensive demands at this late stage of the campaigning season. The Italian campaign was designed primarily to tie down opposing Germans; clearly, to continue limited attacks was a more certain way of doing so than merely 'rugging up' for the winter, however welcome such a policy would be to the formations at McCreery's and Harding's disposal. Doubtless, too, 6 Armoured Division and 61 Brigade were less exhausted, and had experienced an easier passage through the Apennines, than most others.

It is less easy, however, to defend the way in which the Tossignano operation was mounted within 6 Armoured Division, and 61 Brigade made several errors, in both planning and execution. On the strength of his time in Italy, I had heard our Divisional Commander, Vyvyan Evelegh, remark, "Successful operations in Italy are either section attacks or full-scale Brigade assaults. There is nothing worthwhile in between." This was good sense, and, at Tossignano, it should have been obvious that 61 Brigade's skirmishing techniques were inappropriate. We were the prisoners of our own previous experience; though we knew all about dominating features and reverse slopes, we had given little thought to the street fighting tactics which would be required to clear a town like Tossignano. Nor, too, were proper reserves available to exploit success; Adrian Gore's policy of limited liability, so often successful on previous occasions, now proved ill-conceived. I doubt, too, if 2 RB were the right battalion to choose for this mission; they were a Company short, many of their riflemen had been abroad for over three years, and Owain Foster, acting in command, was the least experienced of the commanders available. Nearly everyone involved made mistakes at some stage or another; the only real satisfaction to emerge from an unhappy battle was the cheerfulness and courage of the riflemen involved. I feel, though, that on this occasion they deserved better leadership and planning than their leaders, and the staff, provided.

None of this wisdom after the event was available to me as Rifleman Christmas, Ken Ives and I jeeped down the gorge through Castel del Rio towards Fontanelice. It all seemed normal, apart from a swirling mist, which reduced visibility to about 50 yards, and then cleared briefly to allow a normal view. At last we came to Brigade HQ, a house about ¾ mile short of Fontanelice; it was an ill-chosen location, for the German gunners knew all about it and harassed it consistently whenever they had nothing better to do. Hugo Baring, the Brigade Major, briefed me about the battle and D Company's likely role in it that night. It was not an encouraging tale.

2 RB's plan the previous night had been simple. Tossignano could only be approached from the two entrances on the west side of the town – the upper entrance via point 282, and the lower via point 222, where there was a small group of farm buildings. The main entrance from the Imola direction lay on the reverse slope; it offered better access than the two western approaches, but there had been no patrolling round the back so too little was known about this route to consider an assault from that direction. In any event Owain Foster had too few troops to contemplate an alternative to a frontal attack by the two western approaches. There were feint diversionary attacks on his flanks – by 8 Indian Division on the right from Casola Valsenio and 1st Guards Brigade on the left, who had only recently captured the dominating Monte Penzola. These feint attacks, and a similar effort by 7 RB from Borgo, managed to disperse the enemy's defensive fire to some extent, but otherwise provided little help to the unfortunate 2 RB. Owain Foster's plan provided for his B Company, under John Reader-Harris, to attack the top right-hand entrance via point 282; C Company, under John Brown, were assigned the left-hand entrance via point 222. There was a tiny reserve of two platoons, but apart from the scout platoon working on their feet under John Wood, Owain Foster was never able to use them. A Company, under Dick Flower, held Casas Monteleto and Poggiolo as firm bases, and stayed there throughout the operation.

2 RB's attack began at 0200 hours with strong artillery support, but got off badly. A barrage had been chosen as the most effective form of supporting fire, perhaps because there had been no time for patrols to identify the exact location of the enemy defences. When B and C Companies were heavily shelled on their way to the Start Line, it was impossible to discover whether or which of our guns were responsible; it could equally well have been enemy defensive fire, but all our guns were told to lift their fire by 400 yards. Most of the barrage thus went over the top of the defending Germans and fell harmlessly on the empty slopes behind the town. B Company were stopped by heavy Spandau and mortar fire covering a block across the track leading to point 282; however, a platoon of C Company forced their way in via point 222 and John Brown followed up at once with the rest of his Company. By first light at 0630 hours John Reader-Harris with his two reserve platoons had followed C Company into the town and there was a brief moment of optimism about the battle.

Soon, however, reverses occurred. The enemy, whose knowledge of the town was much better than our own, brought down accurate mortar fire on the exact area occupied by 2 RB. The defending Germans came from 334 Infantry Division, who, apart from the parachute Divisions, had the reputation of being the best German infantry formation in Italy. Certainly the Tossignano battle showed that they had professional leaders and they made few mistakes throughout the operation. John Brown and two of his platoon commanders were wounded in the first mortaring, and C Company, now without an officer, were driven to cover in the nearest buildings. John Reader-Harris and his two platoons from B Company had fewer casualties from the mortaring, but John himself, who had gone forward to contact John Brown, was pinned down in another building and, thanks to the inefficient man-packed 38 sets, out of touch with everyone, including his gunner OP. By 0830 that morning, in fact, while Rifleman Christmas, Ken Ives and I were still driving up the Giogo Pass, the 2 RB presence in Tossignano was no more than isolated groups of riflemen putting up a fight in different houses. It was brave enough certainly – and one should remember the dash of John Brown and his Company who had forced their way into the town in the first place – but, militarily, the position was already beyond repair.

The picture Hugo Baring gave me was not so clear. John Reader-Harris was still coming through periodically on the air, though reception was appalling, doubtless because he was transmitting from inside a house. Owain Foster, at his battalion HQ in the valley 1,000 yards behind point 222, was desperate to do all he could to rescue his two Companies cut off in the town. D Company were to go under 2 RB and do what we could to improve the position – an unpleasant assignment, but there it was, and we would do our best.

I reckoned I would have two hours at my disposal before Maurice Day and the Company arrived after their journey from Grassina. I had never even seen the town of Tossignano, let alone had a look at the place through field glasses; I decided therefore to go to a viewpoint near Longhina, a mile beyond Fontanelice, hoping the mist might clear sufficiently for me to get a sight of the place. Christmas drove brilliantly and we got a good way up the track towards Longhina before I decided to do the rest of the trip on my feet. I waited about at the viewpoint, hoping against hope for the weather to clear, and managed a brief ten minutes which enabled me to identify the main positions, and, in particular point 222 where Owain Foster would meet me that night to arrange our relief operation. Tossignano itself seemed ominously quiet as I examined the town through field glasses; the visibility was clearly too bad for our own artillery to do much except harass known German gun positions behind Tossignano. Moreover, as Hugo Baring's briefing had told me, communications with 2 RB in the town were too bad to get an indication of their whereabouts.

By contrast, the Germans had plenty of targets and were making the approach routes to Tossignano as unpleasant as possible. I doubled back down the hill to rejoin Christmas and the jeep; Ken Ives, as usual, was through on the air and I sent a message to Maurice Day letting him know I would soon be with him.

I called in at Brigade HQ, and collected some air photographs of Tossignano, which Hugo Baring had arranged for me while I was away on my reconnaissance. It was now about 4 p.m., there would be no chance for my platoon commanders to see the ground, so the air photographs would have to serve for the orders I would shortly give out. Hugo had also arranged for some transport to ferry us forward after dark; we were to rendezvous short of Borgo where a guide from 7 RB would take us via Casa Cogalina across the steep and muddy valley directly to point 222. Hugo and his staff could hardly have done more; I was grateful for their help and also for the cup of tea I gulped while the air photographs were explained to me. They were not, by the high standards of the RAF, particularly good prints; there had been too little clear weather that month for photo-reconnaissance. But they were better than nothing and gave a general idea of the ground to supplement what we could get from our maps.

Back with the riflemen, Maurice Day had excelled himself. There was a hot meal – a piping stew – before we moved off, and the cooks had sensibly knocked up sandwiches for people to take with them. As this was to prove our last meal for 36 hours, it was as well Maurice had thought ahead so well; he also made everyone fill their water bottles from the cart, so that with the tea and powdered milk we all carried we could manage a brew on our tommy cookers – a D Company gimmick, which had served us well before. I did my best to give optimistic orders, but doubt if I was convincing. We knew too little about everything and I never liked playing operations in the mountains by ear. But, equally, we had to do our best for 2 RB, and it was a resolute party who clambered aboard the trucks when they arrived soon after dark.

The road forward through Fontanelice to Borgo was a favourite target for German harassing fire, but that evening the opposition had fired their 'hate' at the bridge in Fontanelice immediately after dark. A guide from 7 RB met us at the rendezvous to take us up to Casa Cogalina, where another guide, also from 7 RB, would take us across country by a short cut across the intervening gorge and thence up to point 222. Amazingly, there was little enemy shelling as we made our way, heavily laden and slipping about in the mud, up to Cogalina.

The effect of mud on one's morale, and its inhibiting effect on soldiering, is well known. Perhaps Italian mud did not quite measure up to its Passchendaele or Somme counterparts; in December, nevertheless, especially after six weeks' consistent rain, it ran Flanders a good second.

The tracks, running like Devonshire lanes between steep banks, suffered from the nightly passage of the mules we used for replenishment; even someone as athletic and sure-footed as I then was reckoned to fall periodically. The walking stick I carried helped to keep my balance, but the riflemen, less used to the conditions, had a difficult time. On normal ground one reckons to cover three miles in an hour; when climbing on an Apennine track, a mile in a similar period represented good going. Add delays for interference by enemy shelling and mortaring, which were always unpleasant and frequently lethal, and one can see that even a simple move to Cogalina was no easy stroll.

The atmosphere at Cogalina resembled Robert Louis Stevenson's description in *Kidnapped* of David Balfour and Alan Breck's arrival with James of the Glens after the Appin Murder. The 7 RB Company concerned may have been pleased to see us come, but they were certainly anxious to see us go again quickly. One cannot blame them; they were in the middle of their nightly replenishment and feared an accurate German 'stonk' which the passage of D Company was likely to provoke. A guide to point 222 was forthcoming; he seemed to know little about the route, so Henry Hall, Jock Hamilton and I determined to check our route by compass bearings, which, providentially, we had worked out roughly from the map before leaving Gaggio.

All my life I have disliked asking the way and in the war I never relied on a guide if I could help it. This particular guide lacked confidence to start with and quickly went from bad to worse. A check on the compass soon confirmed what I had suspected – that he was heading too far to the left down the hill towards Borgo. The route he was taking led nowhere near point 222 and I knew that between Borgo and the lower edge of Tossignano the ground was mined and that the German gunners had enjoyed a field day the previous evening breaking up 7 RB's feint attack. It was best to cut our losses, return to Cogalina and make our way up to point 222 by the longer but secure route round the rim of the valley. A burst of shelling 50 yards to our left confirmed me in my decision, and slowly, in the darkness and pouring rain, we turned the D Company column and regained Cogalina.

Here the James of the Glens atmosphere had improved somewhat. Their replenishment was complete; I returned the guide, without being too scathing about his performance. 7 RB undertook to report what had happened so that Owain Foster would know the reason for our delay, and, after giving the Company a badly needed breather, we set off on the steady climb up the rim of the valley towards Dick Flower's position, Casa Monteleto. We made what speed we could, but it was slow going and the affair of the guide had not increased our confidence.

Eventually we reached Dick Flower's position at Casa Monteleto a little after midnight. Dick was marvellous, a tower of strength, as he had remained throughout 2 RB's long campaign in the desert and up Italy. I gave D Company a rest and picked Dick Flower's brains about the situation inside Tossignano. It was a profitable ten minutes; Dick doubted if there was still any organized 2 RB resistance inside the town. Neither John Reader-Harris nor any other officer had been heard on the air for several hours. The doctor, 'Nell' Gwynn, who throughout the battle was tireless in his care of the wounded and in getting stretcher bearers forward to evacuate casualties, had been into the town earlier in the day, but had returned without being able to contact John Reader-Harris.

We plodded on, down the hill past 'Nell' Gwynn's Aid Post and 2 RB's Tactical HQ, where I called in and got a clear briefing from Alan Cowan, their Intelligence Officer. Alan, cool, composed and tireless, was a hero of this battle; merely to hear his voice on the 2 RB command net was a tonic and he was a great source of support to D Company for the next 36 hours. Finally, up a steep slope and through some of the worst mud, we arrived at point 222, where Owain Foster was waiting. While I was talking to Alan Cowan there had been a sharp and nasty piece of German shelling. One of Corporal Carlton's best signallers had been killed and two other riflemen in 15 Platoon wounded. Jock Hamilton's leadership, magnificent throughout our demanding march, played a vital part in keeping everyone together, but it was a weary Company who reached point 222. It was three in the morning and I told Owain at once we would need a break to give out orders and provide the riflemen with a rest before we tackled the final climb to Tossignano.

I have seldom admired anyone more than Owain Foster that morning. It was his first battle in command; he had seen his battalion thrown into an attack which he must have realized was beyond their scope. He had modified his initial plan and achieved amazing success before the loss of John Brown had led to 2 RB's disintegration inside the town. The move of D Company to reinforce 2 RB had been a chapter of accidents; he could have been excused for feeling bitter and critical about the way he had been let down by others and the lack of reserves available to fight an impossible battle. Instead Owain was cool, courteous and realistic; we put our heads together and made the best plan we could.

Owain, though he had been at point 222 most of the night, had little idea what was happening inside the town. He was naturally reluctant to admit he was fighting a lost battle, and our plan was thus a compromise. 14 Platoon, under John Goddard, were my freshest outfit; 15 Platoon, who had never quite recovered from the loss of Peter Beazley three months before, the least confident. Furthermore their platoon commander had sprained his ankle on our marching marathon and was in no state to lead what I felt might be a forlorn hope. I aimed to keep Henry Hall, with his consistent 13 Platoon, and Sergeant Watson's dismounted scout section under my own hand as long as possible. They were the most experienced part of D Company and I planned to use them to influence the battle when its crisis appeared.

Owain and I agreed that the first step must be to try and discover what 2 RB elements were still holding out and where such pockets of resistance were. We could not use the artillery at our disposal until we knew where we could fire without endangering our own troops. I decided, therefore, to send John Goddard and 14 Platoon forward into the town acting as a fighting patrol to try and clear up the uncertainty. I gave John two tasks – first to make contact with John Reader-Harris and get a message back so that a proper plan for his relief could be developed; second to secure the southern entrance to the town so that the rest of D Company and other relieving troops, in due course, could follow up in support. We arranged a simple fire support programme for the 14 Platoon operation – all available 25 pounders were to concentrate on point 282 at the top of the town, where we knew for certain the Germans were strongly posted and there were no riflemen. Other artillery was to be used for counter-bombardment, the aim being to silence the German mortars which had broken up the 2 RB move into the town 24 hours previously. By now Corporal Carlton and his signallers had established a field telephone link from point 222 to 2 RB Battalion Headquarters; amazingly, this line remained intact all day and thanks to Alan Cowan's linking skill my rearward communications were surprisingly good.

I gave John time to organize and brief his platoon; stacking the heavier elements of the loads they had carried forward below point 222, they were to advance in normal fighting order with just small packs and a bandolier of reserve ammunition only for each man. It was still dark, but near enough to daylight for John to treat it as a dawn attack; he decided to advance in arrowhead formation across the open ground until the leading section reached the entrance to the town. A quick rush then to clear the entrance; John and the rest of his platoon would follow through to try and establish contact with 2 RB.

It worked well at first. 14 Platoon suffered only two or three casualties crossing the open; perhaps the Germans were taken by surprise, or the visibility was not yet good enough for their small arms fire to be accurate. We heard two searing bursts of Spandau fire as John's own group forced their way into the town; next some isolated thumps and bangs, probably grenades, followed by silence. I reported our initial success to 2 RB over the radio, and then, just as I was about to tell Henry Hall to follow up into the town, all hell broke loose with point 222 as the epicentre for some unpleasant mortaring. Jock Hamilton, typically moving about outside getting things organized, was hit almost at once; Henry Hall managed to get his platoon under cover in the buildings at the back of point 222. With only two or three casualties in 13 Platoon, things might have been worse, but the Germans had taken advantage of their mortar 'stonk' to come to life with a vengeance. There were a couple of Spandaus aligned on point 222; any movement brought down a hail of fire and our own gunners could not operate for fear of hitting 14 Platoon, who had gone into the town not far from where the Spandaus were firing. Henry Hall crawled up to my position; we agreed that there was nothing to be done for the moment. "Pinned to the ground" is a military expression often used in training to describe this sort of situation; it was the only time in the war when I found myself so placed and I was too frightened to be frustrated by my impotence. Gradually my mind cleared. Miraculously, the field telephone was still working. I spoke to Alan Cowan and told him what had happened; he acknowledged my instructions to keep 15 Platoon out of trouble in the dead ground behind point 222. There was no room for them in the cover our buildings provided, and no role for them anyway. By now it was fully light, with that perfect visibility which often follows a night of rain. I arranged with Alan for the gunners to fire some smoke shells in front of point 222; this gave us cover for the stretcher bearers to evacuate Jock Hamilton, fortunately not too badly wounded, and the 13 Platoon casualties. We still, however, were unable to reach the 14 Platoon wounded earlier who lay out in the open between point 222 and the southern entrance to the town. For the moment it was stalemate; I concluded that the only course of action was to hold firmly onto point 222 at all costs. If that position was lost 2 RB's Battalion HQ would be completely exposed. I spoke to Owain Foster on that incredible telephone line and was glad he agreed.

Suddenly the deadlock broke. First there was an outbreak of firing from the houses in Tossignano nearest to us at point 222. Next came the crash of what must have been bazookas fired at the buildings, two of which were soon afterwards observed to be in flames. Down the hill towards us burst about ten riflemen, all from 2 RB, while two others, one armed with a Bren, the other with a sub-machine gun, did their best from improvised fire positions in the rocks to cover their withdrawal. When the main party of the riflemen escaping from the town reached the open ground, the Spandaus opened up; three or four riflemen fell, while the rest found what shelter they could amongst the rocks at the bottom of the slope. Sergeant Watson put down some smoke with the scout section 2 inch mortar, under cover of which Lance Corporal Dyer, leader of the dash to freedom, made his way over the open ground and reached the relative safety of point 222.

By now it was about nine o'clock and Dyer's story, told me with surprising clarity, explained what had been happening in Tossignano that morning. Apparently the enemy had attacked the house in which he and his 2 RB platoon were holding out shortly after first light that morning. Perhaps this attack accounted for the comparative ease with which 14 Platoon had gained entry to the town at about that time. Though the first attack had been beaten off, thanks largely to Dyer's work on the defending Bren gun, after the original gunner had been killed, a later attack with bazookas, and involving the use of petrol to set fire to the house, had forced Dyer and the remains of his platoon to withdraw down the hill. Dyer, his platoon commander (later captured), and Rifleman Aldridge (then lying wounded just below the rocks) had covered the withdrawal; of the three, only Dyer had managed, despite being wounded in the leg, to reach us at point 222.

Despite his wound, Dyer's concern continued to be for the 2 RB wounded under the rocks and in the open ground in front of point 222. We put down smoke to provide cover for their withdrawal, but more fugitives from Tossignano were hit as they attempted to cross the open. Dyer found a Red Cross emblem from somewhere – perhaps one of the stretcher bearers had one with him – and went forward several times in face of fierce machine-gun fire to help wounded riflemen to safety. Finally, and to their credit, the enemy recognized Dyer's efforts and his Red Cross emblem; their firing died away and the stretcher bearers were able to go forward and bring in the wounded. Altogether twelve casualties were brought in; the informal truce lasted for over two hours while this operation was in progress and the Germans, punctiliously, made no attempt to interfere with the arrangements for further evacuation down the hill behind point 222. Dyer's initiative, bravery and disregard for himself constituted courage of the highest order; an immediate award of the DCM reflected the nature of his achievement.

Many years later, I remain staggered by Dyer's courage. I have often reflected on what drove him on. He was a typical old 'sweat' – of a kind which 2 RB, as a former regular battalion, still possessed. They had been regular soldiers before the war started and been through it all from the early days in the desert. If those like me in 10 RB felt sometimes that we had 'done our stint', and that it was time someone else had a go, old 'sweats' like Dyer had ten times more excuse for taking things steady. He clearly had enough experience to have realized that Tossignano was unlikely to be a success and that his battalion were playing a losing hand. What then prompted Dyer's surge of adrenalin, and led him, against all the odds, to act with such heroism? One can only guess; perhaps it was a reaction against the sheer bloodiness of the situation, a feeling that nothing worse could possibly befall him and his platoon. Whatever it was, Dyer was inspired for nearly half a day; I shall never forget him and am proud to have seen him in action. Such courage leaves one humble, but also ennobled; we all felt sustained by Dyer's example and found ourselves fortified for the rest of the action.

Dyer's truce enabled the wounded to be evacuated and also gave me a breathing space and chance to reorient my own ideas. From what Dyer had told me, the situation inside Tossignano was lost and quite incapable of being redeemed by any action of which my D Company, now down to two weak platoons, was capable.

While we welcomed the truce as a chance to evacuate our wounded, sort ourselves out at point 222 and make some sort of a plan for the rest of the day, the pause was probably also welcome to the Germans. I expect they used the ceasefire to round up the 2 RB survivors inside Tossignano, aware that, while the truce lasted, there would be no shelling. They also doubtless started moving their considerable haul of prisoners towards the rear. At all events the Germans seemed in no hurry to restart the battle, and, finally, it was we who signalled the end of the break by vigorous waving from point 222. We gave them ten minutes' notice and then confirmed the resumption of play by a hearty stonk fired by 104 RHA on both entrances to the town.

During the ceasefire Dick Fyffe came through to me on the telephone. He told me that he had arranged with Brigade HQ to take over the Tossignano front from Owain Foster; "Your friends are being relieved," he explained in coded speech, which would have deceived nobody but nevertheless satisfied the conventions. Between us we made a new plan, D Company would hold point 222 as a firm base till the evening; now that there were no longer any problems about using our artillery for defensive fire in front of point 222 I had no worries on that score. Visibility and communications were both now good and I could not see the Germans being stupid enough to leave their entrenched positions in Tossignano and mount an attack in daylight on point 222. After dark it might be different, but there would be time enough to think about that later. Dick told me that he felt in honour bound to Owain Foster and 2 RB to have a final probe round Tossignano to confirm my impression, based on what Corporal Dyer had told me, that there was no longer any organized resistance inside the town. Accordingly C Company, under Bob Fairweather, would move up behind point 222 after dark and send forward strong fighting patrols to both entrances to Tossignano. If, as we both expected, there was no answering response from within, the operation would be discontinued.

The rest of that day dragged by somehow; neither the Germans nor I wanted to stir matters up. There were other matters on my mind. I could not help feeling that I had let John Goddard and 14 Platoon down. Though my head told me I had been right not to throw in the rest of D Company earlier that morning, my heart pricked me for not having been bolder. Perhaps a less calculating company commander might somehow have got into Tossignano while the Germans were still pre-occupied with rounding up the 2 RB remnants. But I doubt if it would have made much difference;

more of D Company would have become casualties or joined 14 Platoon as prisoners of war, for the outcome of the battle had been settled long before. The original attack had been carried out with insufficient forces, with no proper reserve available to Owain Foster, and the arrangements for feeding D Company into the battle had been bungled and incompetent.

61 Brigade had been the victims of their own previous experience. Neither Adrian Gore nor his staff had ever executed a deliberate attack on a position the Germans really intended to defend. Even at Rentella, the scene of our earlier failure, the Germans had been prepared to go when put under sufficient pressure. At Tossignano they had no such option; if they lost the town their whole position in the Santerno valley would have crumbled, and in the Lombardy plain beyond this would have meant withdrawal from Imola. There had, in fact, been a misappreciation of the situation by everyone from the Corps Commander downwards, for which the unfortunate 2 RB were left to pay the bill. It was an expensive lesson, costing over 200 casualties, of whom, happily, about 140 turned out later to have been made prisoners of war, though some of these were also wounded.

Though Tossignano continued to bulk large in our thinking for the next three months, there is no need to discuss its sequels here. Bob Fairweather's fighting patrols confirmed that there was no organized resistance left in the town; before first light next morning Dick Fyffe told me to pull back from point 222, and, picking up 15 Platoon en route, a truncated D Company reassembled behind Monte Taverna, safely out of view from Tossignano.

Reorganization, first within 10 RB, and the whole of 61 Brigade, now dominated our affairs. At the end of November we realized that shortage of reinforcements would mean that one of the battalions of 61 Brigade would have to be disbanded. To prevent speculation, Adrian Gore had announced that, when the time came, 10 RB would be the unlucky victim of this process; we were the junior battalion, and this decision, however sad, was accepted as inevitable. But 2 RB, dying on its feet as its longer serving members became due for Python (a scheme by which those who had served abroad for four years were posted home to the UK), had now been mortally wounded by the losses at Tossignano. It was decided, therefore, that though in theory 10 RB remained the battalion selected to disappear, in practice it would remain as the basic entity, merely changing its title to that of 2 RB. This sensible military pragmatism now dictated my immediate future.

Dick Fyffe, in the light of the impending reorganization and the need to absorb those elements of 2 RB not eligible for Python, decided against re-forming D Company. I arranged for the excellent 13 Platoon to go complete with Henry Hall to join Bob Fairweather's C Company. 15 Platoon, which had never really come alight since Peter Beazley left wounded in September, was to be dispersed, most of its riflemen going to B Company.

Fortunately, there was a command slot for me in B Company, where Teddy Goschen was leaving to be Military Assistant to the new commander of Eighth Army, Dick McCreery. At the same time Ken Dale, who had been with B Company since the days of Bladeforce, was to join David Elkington on the staff directing the affairs of the partisans in Northern Italy. It was one of Italy's many tragic ironies that Ken Dale, who had survived so many hair's breadth escapes as a scout platoon commander in Tunisia, should have been killed in a jeep accident in Florence a mere ten days after taking up his new assignment. It made a sad start to 1945 for those of us who attended Ken Dale's funeral at the Military Cemetery outside Florence; in a curious way, one felt his death in such circumstances to be more wasteful than those of his fellow musketeers and great friends, Jack Toms, Jack Dust and Ron Sturgess, all killed in Tunisia. The old 10 RB seemed to be falling apart and of those officers who had left Scotland in 1942 only Dick Fyffe, Bobby Selway, Jim Lonsdale, James Booth, Bob Fairweather and myself remained at the 'sharp end'. Perhaps it was as well that we were to change our title in March.

B Company, though outwardly cheerful, were in a state of convalescence when I took over just before Christmas. The Company had achieved great success during the late autumn period of patrolling in the Santerno valley. The prime mover had been Charles Morpeth, at first glance the most unmilitary of officers, but who possessed genuine flair as a patrol commander. He had a string of coups to his credit, until sadly, in December, he was badly wounded by the infamous clutch of 'S' mines which made the environs of Borgo Tossignano such an unpleasant neighbourhood. The remaining star, Roger Parker, was, however, a great character whose influence played a key role in B Company's steady recovery.

It is no surprise to me, or anyone who served with him in Italy, that Roger Parker has proved such a successful barrister, becoming first a very young Queen's Counsel, next a High Court Judge, and, finally, a Lord Justice of Appeal. Roger had a great personality supported by a robust sense of humour, and with a brilliant talent for mimicry; his forensic potential, even then, was clear. He had an idiosyncratic style on the air, the despair of more serious individuals who worried unduly about security, but which gave infinite delight to me and other users of the B Company net. "Hello Three," Roger would say when instructed by me to follow some course of action whose practicality he doubted; a telling pause would follow; then "Dear Old Sir and Honoured Chief, the situation does not appear to me in quite the colours in which you have ably but inaccurately described it." In other words, Sunray was being over-optimistic and needed to think again. I do not know what the Germans intercept service made of it – probably much less than the judges and jurors whom Roger was to persuade later as his legal career developed. We had endless laughs, too, as Roger imitated either the Führer or an imaginary 'U' boat captain and often a dialogue between them. He was a tonic, in fact, and just what we needed as we regarded Tossignano and were reminded of our failure to capture it.

It was not until the New Year that the idea of a renewed attack on Tossignano was dropped. 7 RB were to have done the initial assault, with B Company under Douglas Darling for the operation, in view of the specialized knowledge I had acquired of the entrances to the town as a result of my unhappy day and night at point 222. This time there was to be no tumbling into battle; we spent days looking at Tossignano through binoculars from a variety of different viewpoints. After a heavy snowfall on Christmas Eve, the weather turned bright, clear and frosty. The RAF were thus able to provide superb air photographs; we patrolled, professionally and methodically, round the back of the town with Roger Parker at his most incisive and intelligent in discovering where the German defences were sited and how they maintained their garrison. But it was obvious that another attack on Tossignano would be expensive and, finally, after Field Marshal Alexander had paid us a personal visit, it was decided to abandon the idea. B Company were delighted, for none of us wished to renew acquaintance with point 222 or the southern entrance, which was to have been B Company's objective. Though it was galling that the Germans had beaten us at Tossignano, it was a reverse I preferred to live with rather than lose more good riflemen in what, at best, would have been a Pyrrhic victory.

Tossignano remained in German hands till April; it was then liberated, as the Germans withdrew voluntarily, by the Italian Friuli Group trained and organized by Dick Southby, and local partisans from Imola. I have been back to Tossignano twice since. Nowadays there is a restaurant in Tossignano with a Michelin guide star; it serves superb pasta and the excellent wines from the surrounding Romagna, which wash it down, maintain the standard.

The rest of the winter, January and February, were spent in that excellent military pursuit, 'holding the line'. There was snow, but the sun shone more often than not; we wore white snowsuits and found protected slops in the dead ground where we could safely toboggan. Life was a Jorrocks style conflict – the image of war with no feelings of guilt. The gunners were rationed to just five rounds of 25 pounder ammunition a day; once, while holding the sector forward of Casola Valsenio, we saved our allotment up for a week and used them in a spectacular Chinese attack – all fire and no movement – on German positions in the Vena del Gesso. The Germans realized it was a hoax and hardly bothered to react, though next morning my orderly, Alfie Moore, improving the runners on his toboggan, was hit in the backside by one of the few German mortar bombs of the week. Luckily the wound was not serious and he was back again, cheerful as ever, by the end of February. Just once the Germans showed signs of nerves; one evening towards the end of February they unleashed 500 missiles of all sorts and uncounted quantities of small arms ammunition, at a B Company position just to the left of Borgo. No one was hurt by this display, but it was a reminder all the same that Tossignano still held, and that the Germans had defeated us in the Santerno valley.

Chapter Seven

ITALIAN TRIUMPH

Our winter of discontent in the Apennines ended at last. Tossignano, looming above us, mocked us, while our German opponents demonstrated their high morale and sometimes a good sense of humour. At Christmas we were treated to a leaflet bombardment; the leaflets were in Christmas card form and contained, besides a list of those recently captured in the battle of Tossignano, a poem sympathizing with those still fighting in the mountains. The final words of the poem have remained in my memory:

> "The Q has got no puddings plum,
> So I am afraid you have had it, chum."

At the end of February the snow and ice which had been with us since Christmas vanished. An Italian Gruppo Folgore arrived to take over our positions; they were cheerful, well trained and delighted at being treated as Allies. We had a splendid supper of pasta, vino and British compo to mark the take-over, before returning to Florence. 6 Armoured Division was to move round to the Adriatic coast, re-train near Cattolica (a seaside town south of Rimini), before taking part, under command of Eighth Army, in a final offensive in April. Meanwhile Ralph Stewart-Wilson and I were given ten days' leave in Rome and were soon on the road there.

The weather was lovely, cold and crisp at night, bright warm sun by day, and plenty to see on our journey. Ralph and I heard the riflemen singing in the back of the truck – Bob Hope's "We are off on the road to Morocco" – with Alfie Moore leading the choruses.

The beauty of Siena and the setting of Orvieto, its cathedral sited superbly on top of a hill, have remained with me always and I can still re-capture the sheer exuberance of that drive to Rome and civilization. In 1945 the Rome traffic, though heavy, was not so anarchic as it now is. It was possible to drive almost anywhere, park, leaving someone to guard the

Chain of Command – Italian Campaign 1945 – Final Battle

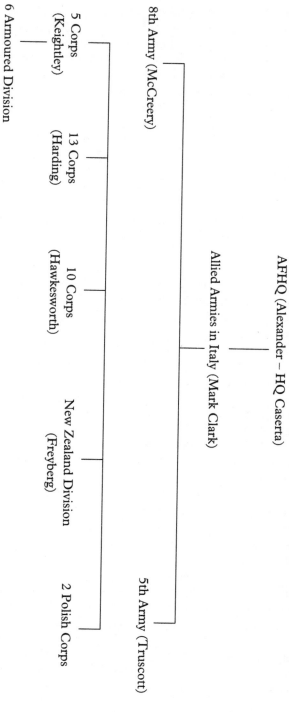

AFHQ (Alexander – HQ Caserta)

Allied Armies in Italy (Mark Clark)

8th Army (McCreery)

5th Army (Truscott)

5 Corps (Keightley)

13 Corps (Harding)

10 Corps (Hawkesworth)

New Zealand Division (Freyberg)

2 Polish Corps

6 Armoured Division

vehicle, and then visit your particular tourist objective. St Peter's Square was an exception, and we walked there and to the Sistine Chapel. Otherwise we drove, often overcome by the splendours we saw, but always, like the riflemen, ready for restorative cups of tea. We did not plan our itinerary, taking the Eternal City as it came, so that Imperial Rome, the Renaissance, and Mussolini's grandiose concepts soon became an agreeable jumble. One objective was to see the Palazzo Venezia, where Mussolini addressed the Fascist mob, before we realized how feeble in fact was the Duce's regime. It was surprising how low the balcony turned out to be; perhaps the Duce got Dutch courage from the mob below. We visited Anzio, the beachhead which had promised so much in January 1944, but in the end delivered so little. It was too far to re-visit Cassino, and to go so far out of Rome would have disrupted the social life which, thanks to the introductions we had brought with us from the Villa Capponi in Florence, quickly developed.

We stayed in the Hotel Eden, then an Officers' Leave Centre, for which one paid an absurdly small sum in occupation currency – 3 shillings a day. We shared a lovely room with a balcony, but the food in the restaurant consisted just of Army rations supplemented by pasta. Ralph quickly made touch with the 'circuit'. It seemed to operate like the 'list' in London, with Ralph and I accepted into the Roman equivalent of the 'season'. To our enjoyment, Ralph's telephoning produced numerous invitations, and our evenings were spent in charming company, usually in old-fashioned night-clubs, just like the Four Hundred in London. The girls were fun, beautifully turned out, and pulled our legs unmercifully; we enjoyed it all greatly. Did the Germans, our predecessors, have a 'list' too, I wondered idly? I doubt it somehow, and, anyway, Ralph's and my Greenjacket good manners prevented us from asking our girlfriends awkward questions and I am glad we did not. War is a stupid business and I am grateful to those attractive, lively and well brought up girls for their timely reminder that there was life beyond 10 RB and that the fighting would not last forever.

One engagement was altogether different, and the most memorable of our stay in Rome. A friend in Florence – probably a grown-up visitor to the Villa Capponi – had given me the name of Prince Doria. He was a relation of the King, Victor Emmanuel, who had just been persuaded by Harold Macmillan, then head of the Allied Control Commission, to abdicate in favour of his son, Umberto. She told me little else – just that "the Palazzo Doria was full of lovely things." When we got to Rome I debated whether I dared use such a vague introduction to someone who was so distin-guished, certainly busy, and by now had probably had more than his fill of brash young Allies. Without telling Ralph, I wrote a letter, which Rifleman Christmas and I delivered personally one afternoon while Ralph was still out to lunch with one of the prettier girls. I must have struck the right note – or perhaps Prince Doria's kindness to the young was responsible – for that evening in our pigeonhole at the Hotel Eden was a letter asking us to come to tea next afternoon.

Round we went therefore, dressed in our best uniforms, and found ourselves in a different world. I did not know then what a great man Prince Doria was. Harold Macmillan describes him in his diaries as "A remarkable man – a real mediaeval saint, of spotless reputation". Nor was I aware that the Prince had written in 1940 to his cousin, the King, begging him not to go to war with England and forecasting accurately what would happen and stressing Mussolini's cynicism and immorality. The King did not even have the courtesy to reply to his cousin's letter. Instead he handed it to Mussolini, who threw Doria into prison. I was unprepared for the level of Prince Doria's conversation; it was like arriving, without having done one's homework, for a tutorial with a tolerant Oxford don, who, despite one's mental failings, was anxious to spare you embarrassment. Luckily both Ralph and I were sensible enough to realize that if we could persuade our host to talk himself we would avoid exposing our own ignorance and learn something into the bargain. It was a great experience; I learnt how loyalty can be a complex business, that Italy was still not completely united, and how much of Cavour's concept for the nation remained incomplete. Prince Doria stressed the individualism of Italians, which made them great artists, but also made the mechanics of democracy difficult. It was political wisdom of a quality then well above my head, but an unforgettable example of how much courtesy and kindness to the young on the part of the obviously great are appreciated. The time sped by; we listened intently, munched tomato sandwiches and drank tea poured from a silver teapot.

When the time came to go, we walked out past a whole gallery of pictures to which there was no time to give more than a passing glance. There was one exception – a portrait by Velasquez of the 'Red Cardinal', a marvellous work, which taught me the special insight into characters and personality possessed by great artists. I remembered we asked, and were allowed, to call again the next morning to see the Red Cardinal in better light. If the world 'entertain' means to occupy agreeably, Prince Doria and his family were masters of hospitality, and I still remember their kindness and warmth.

Back at Cattolica, Dick Fyffe's plan for the reorganization of the battalion involved careful linking of former 2 and 10 RB elements. Bobby Selway had gone home; there was a new regular second-in-command in Tony Palmer, who had begun the war in 2 RB, commanded a battalion of the Wiltshire Regiment, and been wounded in Sicily doing so. Dick Worsley, later to reach the Army Board as Quartermaster General, came from 2 RB as Adjutant and his competence soon won our respect. Alan Cowan, hero of Tossignano, accompanied Dick as Intelligence Officer, and altogether the new team were properly professional. In B Company I lost Maurice Day to go and help an incomer from 2 RB, but gained Michael Brown, a graduate from Sandhurst in the autumn of 1939; he came from the Ulster Rifles, but his battalion had been converted into anti-aircraft artillery and his way back to the infantry had been through a staff appointment at 61 Brigade Headquarters. He was efficient, friendly and easy to work with; B Company was in luck, and my two new platoon commanders, Hugh Carey and Ian Mitchell, confirmed this judgement. Hugh Carey took over my old 6 Platoon; he was a historian, and intended, after the war, to become a schoolmaster. He did so successfully, becoming second master at Stowe, before leaving to serve as Chief Executive of Voluntary Services Overseas and to die tragically young in his late fifties. Hugh's donnish qualities contrasted with Roger Parker's forensic talents; Roger teased him unmercifully, but not unkindly, and we soon grew to respect Hugh for his integrity and the pastoral way he looked after his riflemen. Ian Mitchell was more of a fighter pilot – fearless in battle, but wild as a hawk outside it. I used to hide his light under several bushels whenever Dick Fyffe or others in the military establishment favoured B Company with a visit. But as a fighting platoon commander, Ian had few equals.

A great asset was the Sergeant Major, Willie John Lawson, also from the Ulster Rifles. Willie John possessed the qualities I had come to admire when I lived in Northern Ireland in 1940; his Ulster accent, sense of humour, love of a party, and courage marked him out as a leader. His sergeants' mess was a happy place and many were the parties we shared with them; Willie John taught us traditional Ulster songs, but also Irish country dancing with The Walls of Limerick a speciality. I can still see the Homeric terpsichorean conflicts, often between Willie John and Roger Parker, which developed on these occasions. Altogether B Company was fun, often riotously so, as we became optimistic about the future.

We embarked on a training period, which proved the best I can remember anywhere. We practised our techniques, regained lost skills and confidence with our weapons, and developed sensible methods for operating in the Po valley where Eighth Army's offensive would be launched. Apart from the few vehicles in Company HQ, I did not have to bother any more about those in individual platoons; as part of the reorganization our White scout cars from the RASC now came to us on call like taxis. It was a welcome change and, once the RASC drivers had grasped their responsibility for providing tea for the riflemen on all conceivable occasions, the system worked smoothly and well.

The weather was lovely and by early April 2 RB was a different and more confident battalion than any of us had served in for over a year. There were other factors involved too; for the forthcoming battle individual rifle battalions were to work with specific armoured regiments in 26 Armoured Brigade. In 2 RB's case this meant association with the Lothians, a superb armoured regiment particularly well commanded by a young former territorial from Edinburgh, Gordon Simpson. He and Dick Fyffe struck up a special relationship, which quickly spread down to the level of squadron and company commanders. B Company, for example, worked with B Squadron of the Lothians, under Gordon Goodrich. The armoured commander took command when the situation was one where tanks were in the lead; the infantry commander took over at night, or in circumstances where infantry became the predominant arm. The tactical headquarters of armoured and infantry elements moved together; in my case this meant that Corporal Clay, my signal corporal (a Bladeforce veteran who had been with B Company throughout), and I travelled in a Honey tank loaned us by the Lothians. We took post behind Gordon Goodrich's command tank, so one was able to react quickly when called upon. The main body of B Company moved a tactical bound behind under the control of Michael Brown; in this way I hoped to keep them away from the shelling which the tanks attracted, so the platoons would be fresh when needed. All this was discussed and rehearsed beforehand; we got to know each other well and mutual confidence grew daily. For the forthcoming battle B Company were given our own gunner from 104 RHA; he was Philip Pawson, elder brother of Tony, and my respected senior at both Horris Hill and Winchester. Philip proved a tower of strength and fitted perfectly into our professional team.

We left Cattolica for a concentration area behind the Senio on 8 April; here the plan for the final defeat of the German armies in Italy was explained to us in detail, with plenty of time to brief the riflemen. After the botched battles of 1944, this April campaign opened with a proper aim – the destruction of the German armies in the field by means of double encirclement. It was a classic recipe for victory, besides being in accord with the best principles of war.

Mark Clark, now the Army Group Commander, found himself forced, as Alexander had been, to defer in planning to the views of his Army Commanders, Truscott and McCreery. In typical fashion, Clark wanted a territorial objective for the offensive – in this case Bologna, presumably because its capture had eluded him the previous autumn. Instead, however, Truscott and McCreery between them persuaded him to aim for a more ambitious idea; their design involved each Army Commander fighting his battle in his own way, with successive assaults timed so the massive air support available could be deployed to help each Army in turn. Eighth Army were to attack first on 9 April across the Senio, aiming to develop two thrusts, one along Route 9 towards Bologna, the second, highly imaginative, an attack further north, using the low lying ground round Lake Comacchio to outflank the German positions based on the River Reno. The Comacchio attack was combined with a more conventional operation by 5 Corps, directed, after crossing the Santerno, at the bridge over the Reno at Bastia, and designed to open the Argenta Gap. Through this gap, but only when the opening was really clear, 6 Armoured Division would drive northwest to link up with Fifth Army's advance from the Apennines west of Bologna. Eighth Army's attack began on 9 April; Fifth Army, which Clark, still distrustful of his British allies, regarded as the main effort, jumped off on 14 April, two days late because bad flying weather in the mountains on 12 and 13 April prevented the full use of air power. In the event, the delay was providential; by 14 April Eighth Army had broken the German winter line and attracted many of the limited German reserves. Fifth Army, driving northwards, thus had an easier task, an advantage they exploited well.

Eighth Army's attack on the Senio was a set piece affair (over 1,000 guns and air support on a huge scale). There was, however, a subtle difference between McCreery's handling of the battle and that of his predecessors. He declined to commit 6 Armoured Division until the gap in front of Keightley's 5 Corps at Argenta was finally yawning and ripe for exploitation. Only then did he release the Armoured Division to Keightley's control with orders to make for the Po crossings flat out and at whatever cost. It was perfect timing and revealed McCreery as a great Army Commander.

For a full week, while McCreery waited patiently for the opportunity to develop, 6 Armoured Division moved with growing impatience from one concentration area to another. Alan Cowan, Intelligence Officer, reported daily that one German formation after another had been sucked into the battle and been either severely mauled or eliminated. At last, on 19 April, we received our long-awaited orders. B Company, under our affiliated B Squadron of the Lothians, were given the task of securing a crossing of the Po de Primaro south of the village of San Nicolo Ferrarese. We drove forward, in Tunisian style, for once relatively unfettered by the going. It was an exhilarating advance of some six miles, with A Squadron and A Company on our left reporting similar progress, and only ended, towards nightfall, when resistance stiffened; the Lothians were opposed by a strong anti-tank screen from 26 Panzer Division, who clearly intended to hold the bridge over the Po di Primaro at San Nicolo as long as possible. Aggressive infantry fighting patrols went forward as soon as it was dark; Roger Parker reached the river, but found the obstacle firmly held. Just after midnight there was a mighty explosion in San Nicolo and it was obvious that the bridge there had been blown. The next morning, therefore, faced us with a difficult battle, which gave our battle group the opportunity to put the principles of our training into practice.

Gordon Simpson's plan for capturing San Nicolo next morning was simple. A Company, supported by A Squadron, would first clear the village and protect an armoured bulldozer which the sappers reckoned could make a causeway across the Po di Primaro. Once the causeway could take tanks, B Squadron, with B Company under command, would pass through and make headway on the far side. The previous night's patrols had prepared us for a hard struggle and the fierce shelling which greeted A Company and A Squadron as they advanced to clear the village confirmed these expectations.

A Company were outstanding that morning. It was a typical Jim Lonsdale operation, well planned, clearly directed and methodical. Clearing a village is never easy, though, and it took time to complete the process. It seemed as if we had managed to surprise the enemy, since a German colour sergeant drove into the middle of the battle, the street fighting at its height, with his horse and cart, carrying supplies for the garrison. He was slow to recognize his predicament; when eventually the penny dropped, he turned his equipage on a sixpence and drove off, Keystone Cops fashion, through a hail of Bren-gun fire until an anti-tank projector blew off the wheel of his cart. The horse, happily, survived; A Company turned him loose into the meadows behind the village, where he grazed calmly for the rest of the battle.

Gordon Goodrich and B Squadron did not find it easy to get through the village and over the causeway across the Po di Primaro. Following in my Honey tank, I realized that, though the causeway would just about take the tanks, it would be impassable for wheeled vehicles until the sappers were able to improve it. I decided, therefore, after a word on the air with Gordon, to bring just one platoon on foot through San Nicolo to provide anti-infantry protection for B Squadron on the far side of the obstacle. The country was close, ideal territory for enemy armed with bazookas to sneak up and attack the Shermans. I chose 8 Platoon for this tricky task; it seemed well suited to Ian Mitchell's flexible style and proved a good selection. At the same time I moved the rest of the company forward into an assembly area not far behind San Nicolo, where they would be available to operate on foot on the far side of the village. This last operation sounds simple and straightforward; in fact, it required much skill and training. We used a system worked out and practised during our recent training period. Many years later the technique became fashionable in BAOR, where it became known as 'trickle' movement; at that time, however, B Company had not invented this high-sounding term. It involved an intelligent advance man – Willie John Lawson – going forward to choose an assembly area with cover, plenty of room, and firm enough underfoot to prevent vehicles getting bogged or delayed by soft going. The assembly area once selected, Michael Brown would feed the vehicles forward individually as opportunity offered and taking advantage of any distractions which might cause the enemy to be looking elsewhere. To bring off a move like this successfully needed judgement, good map reading and, above all, communications which worked smoothly, otherwise the opportunities for confusion and unnecessary casualties were considerable.

There was no problem about the radio link between Michael Brown and myself, since we both had high-powered sets on the B Squadron frequency. We needed, however, to use this frequency sparingly, for this was the net on which Gordon Goodrich controlled his tanks. For talking to our own platoons, however, whether dismounted or still in their vehicles, we were less well placed. The portable 48 sets on which we had to rely were temperamental. They were also easily 'screened' so that good communication depended on the aerials being intervisible. Houses or operating the set inside a vehicle caused 'screening'; to make matters harder, a high-powered set operating in the same vehicle as a manpack one cut out the transmissions of the weaker set, often in the middle of a key message. These communications problems threw a weight on Corporal Clay, B Company's signal corporal, as good in his own way, if different in method, as either Eric Young or Corporal Carlton. Eric Young obtained his results by his ability and power of repartee; Corporal Carlton depended on courage and willpower. Clay, by contrast, relied on sheer niceness; if he approached one with a request, personal or professional, it was hard to turn him down. His supporting team, with my jeep operator, Ken Ives, as his No. 2, backed him loyally because they liked him. He was good company, with perfect manners; San Nicolo was now to prove that, on top of all these qualities, Clay was a man of great courage, determined enough to maintain his bravery over a period.

When our Honey tank settled behind Gordon Goodrich's command tank at the back edge of San Nicolo, I could see from Clay's expression that he was worried about keeping me in touch. A formidable German 'stonk', partly artillery, but mostly mortars, did not help my own concentration; Clay, however, seemed oblivious to these distractions as, calmly, he established touch on the 48 set net with the various platoon commanders. Just then, as B Squadron's leading troop of tanks began to cross the causeway, Gordon Goodrich's net burst into a frenzy of disciplined activity; it was an impressive education to hear the calm Edinburgh/Borders dialogue on the air, as the tank battle developed. My own job was to keep off the air, but acknowledge enough to let Gordon know that I was following events and that 8 Platoon were moving forward to provide the support he needed. Clay, reading the battle perfectly, realized I would soon need to talk to Ian Mitchell on the 48 set to pass on the information flowing back on the armoured nets. There was no hope of my doing so while the high-powered sets around us jammed our manpack system. Without a word, Clay put his 48 set in an exposed position on the flattish platform outside our Honey tank, where, luckily, it was not jammed by the more powerful tank network. He then settled himself in an exposed position where he could keep the set tuned and dropped a jumper lead down to me in the bowels of the tank. Clay stayed in this vulnerable position for the next four hours, never displaying any sign of fear, despite regular hostile shelling and mortaring. It was an example of coolness, skill, and disregard of his own safety which I have never forgotten; it made yet another reality of Sir John Moore's ideal of the 'thinking fighting man', and Clay's modesty, then and later when he received an immediate award of the Military Medal, made one proud, and humble too, at serving with such fine people.

Meanwhile, Ian Mitchell had been edging forward during the breaks in the shelling and mortaring. By now B Squadron's leading tanks had established a small bridgehead 800 yards deep on the far side of the obstacle; here they ran into a typical anti-tank screen of German tanks, self-propelled guns and infantry. It was a classic damage limitation exercise, at which 26 Panzer Division were known to excel. Despite casualties, Ian established 8 Platoon on their objective on the far side of the river, to the flank but parallel with the leading tanks of B Squadron. Here he spotted a party of enemy infantry forming up to attack and used tracer ammunition to attract the tanks' attention. It was school solution stuff; B Squadron got the message immediately and soon killed, wounded or put to flight the enemy party.

Nevertheless, as Gordon Goodrich and I set up a Squadron/Company HQ on the far side of the Po di Primaro, the situation remained dodgy. There seemed plenty of German armour about and 26 Panzer's tanks were well sited and used their guns as well as ever. Soon three Lothian tanks were in flames and it required a tremendous shoot from Gordon Goodrich's supporting 12 RHA OP, well supplemented by Philip Pawson, who had found himself a good position in San Nicolo itself, before relative security was assured. I brought Roger Parker and Hugh Carey forward with their platoons to strengthen our position, but, as darkness fell, it seemed a German counter-attack would be inevitable. Philip Pawson came up; we fixed the closest defensive fire and SOS tasks we dared, and, as the tanks withdrew to refuel, hoped for the best.

B Company spent an anxious night, while A and C Companies behind us in San Nicolo also expected to be attacked, but in the event nothing happened. Next morning's news brought an explanation, while we had been engaged with 26 Panzer Division across the Po di Primaro, further south the 17th/21st Lancers and 7 RB had managed to cross an anti-tank obstacle at Segni. With their left flank protected by the Reno, they had broken into the open country beyond and created a chance for 6 Armoured Division to reach the Po before the retreating Germans. If we could bring this off, the main part of the opposing Army Group would be encircled, caught in a grip between Fifth and Eighth Armies. The Lothians and 2 RB were to hand over our bridgehead at San Nicolo to 8 Indian Division and move round to exploit the opening created on our left. Our feelings were mixed; we were reluctant to hand over what we had worked so hard to win the previous day. But the decision was wise, for by drawing most of 26 Panzer Division to San Nicolo our efforts had weakened the German defences elsewhere.

Soon we were following the other armoured regiments through the Segni gap towards Poggio Renatico. As we did so, signs of German disorganization became evident; first abandoned guns and other materials, and soon large numbers of prisoners escorted by grinning riflemen from the other battalions. At planning sessions for our deployment on 22 April, the intention paragraph of Gordon Simpson's orders became ever more optimistic. The atmosphere was infectious; it was like the best of Tunisia all over again.

Final orders were for the Lothians Group to secure the bridge over the Panaro at Bondeno, thus sealing one of the few remaining exits from the rapidly closing trap between the Apennines and the Po. C Squadron and C Company bore the brunt at first, meeting desperate opposition from German infantry armed with bazookas determined to keep the Bondeno bridge open as an escape route. C Squadron lost eleven tanks in this unpleasant fighting but opened the way for Gordon Goodrich and ourselves on the right. I took an early decision to dismount B Company; Corporal Clay's performance at San Nicolo had given me confidence in our ability to control the platoons on foot while keeping touch with the armour. Once on the ground, the tactics developed at Cattolica for movement in close country worked well; soon we and the Lothians, after a dismounted advance of over two miles by the motor platoons, were within 400 yards of the bridge. German traffic was still using the road across it and we aimed to secure the bridge intact. We had made such plans earlier in the campaign, but the Germans had always proved too quick for us. This time it really seemed as if we had succeeded, but just as B Squadron's leading tank edged onto the approach road with Roger Parker's 7 Platoon moving up the ditch beside them, the enemy blew their charge. By German demolition standards, this was an indifferent job, but it was enough temporarily to halt the armour. Roger Parker and his platoon scrambled across the debris to secure the far side, while Gordon Goodrich and I got orders for the night from Gordon Simpson and Dick Fyffe. The latter decided to hold the Bondeno complex by means of three company groups, each supported by tanks; B Company's task was to hold the area round the bridge itself, with A Company to the south protecting our rear and C Company providing depth to the position on an embankment further along the Panaro. This plan involved some difficult motoring in the dark for nearly everyone; by midnight, however, the regrouping was complete.

Dick Fyffe decided to allot most of the Lothians to his left flank, fearing that enemy armour might attack us from that direction at first light. B Company were left with just a troop of tanks to hold the Bondeno bridge, and the line of the Panaro in its vicinity. To make up for my lack of tanks, Ralph Stewart-Wilson and his mortar platoon and Michael Bury, with a platoon of Vickers medium machine guns, both arrived. We held some houses which dominated the bridge and also the low ground on the far side of the Panaro. After B Company had settled for the night in their new positions, Willie John Lawson and I enjoyed a tactical 'nip' of Scotch together before going to sleep; it had been a good day for B Company and we both felt that tomorrow might prove even better. Corporal Clay came over to wake me up while it was still dark. Some infantry, a Mark IV tank and, surprisingly, a towed 88 mm gun had appeared opposite A Company behind us. B Company stood to and awaited developments. Soon we heard over the air that the Mark IV tank, allowed to proceed down the road till it was almost on the muzzle of Gordon Goodrich's tank, had been destroyed, the 88 mm gun abandoned, and the infantry had dispersed into the mist. Alan Cowan came on the air with identifications of enemy involved in this affray; they were a hotch potch, and Alan concluded that the opposition had no idea of what had happened to them and were hopelessly disorientated. C Company reported capturing two enemy lorries, who had apparently been routed to Bondeno by their traffic control organization. As daylight broke, I heard Bob Fairweather report that he was using most of C Company Brens to engage more lorries trying to make for Bondeno along another embankment. It was obvious B Company's turn would soon come.

It was daylight when it did. A rifle company of Germans advanced across the open ground the other side of the Panaro. We watched them, fascinated; they clearly had no idea that we already held the Bondeno bridge, far less that we were sitting in houses on the far side of the river and completely dominated their position. I gave my orders over the air, Clay having as usual arranged perfect communications for the critical moment. No one was to open fire till ordered; H hour for doing so would be in approximately 15 minutes. This gave time for Philip Pawson to get the services of 104 RHA complete, and an extra battery of 12 RHA for good measure. Ralph Stewart-Wilson's mortars had time to prepare a full quota of bombs with a mere quarter charge; the range was only 250 yards. Our first burst of fire was devastating, as it was clearly the last thing our opponents were expecting. They had started to dig in behind the river, exhibiting the lack of enthusiasm for the shovel common to all infantrymen; there was a good deal of shouting and more gesticulation as their platoon commanders came round and allotted areas of fire. I almost felt I was cheating when I gave the order to open fire. Philip and Ralph had co-ordinated the respective times of flight of guns and mortars to perfection; thus at least 100 projectiles of various calibres arrived on target simultaneously. All activity stopped; the enemy went to ground, and, whenever they moved for the next two hours, Ralph or Philip opened up pitilessly. Our Brens and the machine gunners joined in as opportunity offered, with Willie John Lawson in his element on the command vehicle LMG; I doubt if this weapon had seen action since Bladeforce in Tunisia. It made a complete revenge for the humiliations endured at Rentella and Tossignano. There was nothing the Germans could do in their unenviable situation; they tried to get a Spandau or two firing back at our houses, but to no effect. Either Philip or Ralph were on to them at once.

The Germans endured for nearly two hours, before, suddenly, there came a massed blast of whistles as they broke and ran in disorder. I had never seen Germans disintegrate like this before; one felt no sense of triumph about the situation, which had developed into a massacre. I was relieved when their stretcher bearers appeared, bravely waving a Red Cross flag; with memories of how well the Germans had behaved when the boot was on the other foot at Tossignano, we got the fire stopped and allowed the enemy to carry away their dead and wounded.

Later that morning the Lothians reached the Po itself, where they re-fuelled at leisure. It was obvious there would be no effective defence of the river; soon news reached us that the 16th/5th Lancers and 1 KRRC had joined hands with the Fifth Army at Finale d'Emilia, an appropriate name for such an event, and that the battle for the Lombardy Plain was over. There remained only pursuit and exploitation; and that evening, after the New Zealanders had relieved us at Bondeno, we retired into harbour to catch up on badly needed sleep. That night a lone enemy self-propelled gun crossed the Po and fired about fifty shells at random into the battalion area. It was ironical that Tony Palmer, who had been wounded on so many previous occasions, should have been the only casualty, and the news placed a damper on any celebrations Willie John Lawson and I might other-wise have contemplated.

While we were sitting in our rest area near Bondeno orders came through that 2 RB were to move early on the morning of 26 April across the folding boat bridge built by the New Zealanders over the Po; our task would be to protect the right flank of the New Zealand Division, as they moved up to cross the Adige. This last river, little inferior in size to the Po, was con-sidered a major obstacle; so, too, it would have proved if the Germans, adopting the strategy the Allied intelligence services had long devised for them, had withdrawn six months or so earlier, while they still possessed enough troops to man the position properly.

Our excitement at being included in the New Zealand Division team for the next phase of the pursuit to the Alps was tempered by sadness at having to leave the Lothians behind. The folding boat bridges over the Po were of Class 9 classification only; the largest armoured vehicles able to cross were armoured cars, so the Shermans would have to wait until a proper Bailey bridge could be constructed. For the remainder of the pursuit battle, the only tanks available would be the amphibious Shermans of the 7th Hussars. It shows how absolute had been the German defeat south of the Po that the pursuit northward could continue with such limited tank support. 2 RB would miss the Lothians; it was good, though, to have fought in an armoured/infantry battle group, where co-operation had been on such an exceptional basis, and the experience proved valuable to me later.

We crossed the Po early on 27 April, with orders to move on the right flank of the New Zealand Division, our objective a ferry site on the Adige at Lusia which the Germans were thought to be using in their withdrawal northward. At this time there was talk of the Germans having plans for a National Redoubt, based on southern Germany and Austria, where the last Nazi extremists and picked formations, like the SS and parachute divisions, would hold out after the main resistance had collapsed. In the event, these stories had no substance; nevertheless the concept made us anxious to cut off as many Germans as possible before they could cross the Adige. 2 RB made good progress all day, meeting only scattered opposition; there were many small bodies of enemy about, but we hardly bothered to take prisoners, just instructing those we met to march or drive southwards till they could find a prisoner of war cage to accept their surrender. That evening, however, as we approached the Adige and our objective, Lusia, we encountered organized opposition. A Company became involved in a fierce battle to clear the village of Saguedo. While their fight was still in progress, Dick Fyffe told me to loop round the village to the north and get as far forward on foot as I could towards Lusia during the dark. B Company dismounted and we set off on a memorable night march. At first flames from burning houses in Saguedo gave us some visibility, besides being a helpful landmark. Soon, however, we were making our way by compass along any floodbank which led in the right direction. The country was close, boggy away from the floodbanks, like Sedgemoor in Somerset. It was a hilarious scramble, and, for once, it did not matter how much noise we made. The Germans were totally disorganized and speed was the point. It was impossible to keep Dick Fyffe informed of our progress – most of the time I had little idea of our position and halts to talk on the radio would only have slowed us down. About three o'clock that morning I reckoned we had covered five miles. We emerged from a maze of floodbanks onto a narrow metalled lane; there was a house nearby into which we broke to set up our maps, find out our position and establish rearward communications. Someone found a signpost; CAVANAZZA 1 km, LUSIA 4 km, it told us. I looked at the map; Lusia seemed too ambitious an objective; Cavanazza, however, looked a good alternative. It was a road centre and traffic for Lusia would have to go through Cavanazza to reach the ferry.

I made a plan and issued orders. 8 Platoon under Ian Mitchell were to go ahead as a fighting patrol to secure the crossroads in Cavanazza. The rest of B Company would stay where we were as a firm base, report back to Dick Fyffe, get Michael Brown to bring the transport forward now that Saguedo was clear, and generally tidy up our operation. As soon as the vehicles arrived, we could consider moving on Lusia.

I listened to Ian delivering his orders, watched Clay check that 8 Platoon's radio was working and properly netted to ours, and wished 8 Platoon luck. It was still dark; I had a feeling Cavanazza would be occupied and that we would have a battle on our hands. While we waited, and, incredibly, got through to Dick Fyffe, passing our messages through Eric Young and the A Company set in Saguedo, Willie John Lawson organized a brew of tea. We had sweated copiously on our cross-country scramble – "just like the County Down Farmers' Race at Downpatrick", Willie John described it – so the tea went down well.

Suddenly there came firing from Cavanazza, a Verey light or two, and the thump of hand grenades, then more firing, mostly Spandau, but often enough the slower reassuring stutter of 8 Platoon's Brens. Ken Ives gave me the headset as Ian Mitchell came on the air. "Hello Three," he said. "Have run into trouble. We are holding a house which covers the cross-roads. Enemy strength approx one company holding remainder of village." Apart from being a bit breathless, Ian was wonderfully calm. I could hear a Bren firing in the background as he reported. It was obvious that 8 Platoon were pinned down in their house; Ian reported that their first contact had cost them two or three casualties, but he sounded confident of being able to maintain his position. I decided to wait till daylight and then lay on a proper attack to support 8 Platoon. A surge forward in the half-light without proper fire support might add to the confusion and prove un-necessarily expensive. It was not a difficult decision and Ian accepted it confidently and at once. I talked to Dick Fyffe, who had come forward to Saguedo. He had arranged for a troop of 7th Hussar tanks to support us and they were on their way through Saguedo. Ralph Stewart-Wilson's mortars were in action beyond Saguedo and could give us full support. There would be a battery of 104 RHA available and a gunner OP was on his way forward with the 7th Hussars. This was Dick Fyffe at his best, thinking ahead and entirely supportive. I was glad he did not suggest coming forward himself to Cavanazza; I was happier to fight the battle myself, and, now that I had the means, it was not hard to make a sensible plan. We needed to identify 8 Platoon's house as clearly as possible, a task achieved by their Bren firing tracer out of the window as vertically as possible, supplemented by the odd Verey light. I wanted the infantry platoons, 6 and 7, to arrive on the objective together with the tanks, and this we planned to manage by moving the 7th Hussars on a different axis on the flank of the advancing infantry. They could thus continue firing in support of the motor platoons till the last possible moment. A section of David Pontifex's scout platoon arrived to provide extra covering fire, and we arranged for them to move up onto the objective as soon as it was captured, where the Brownings on their carriers would help in dealing with any counter-attack. Dick had also sent forward a Wasp flamethrower mounted on a carrier, thinking this would come in handy if the opposition holed themselves up in houses and proved difficult to remove. Finally, 104 RHA and Ralph's mortars were to produce a smoke screen by firing directly at the enemy positions; 8 Platoon had identified some of these and intelligent guesswork did the rest. Altogether the plan looked good; we allowed ourselves time for orders to be given out and, with H Hour an hour after first light, we were on our way.

The plan worked perfectly. There were no hitches; everyone did his stuff exactly right. Even the Wasp was useful; it needed only a token blast of flame into the first house in the village and the opposition came tumbling out, happy to surrender. Our covering fire, the excellent shooting of the tanks and 8 Platoon's own efforts accounted for about twenty enemy; we took thirty prisoners and the rest of the garrison were put to flight. B Company were on top of the world, as we consolidated in Cavanazza and prepared to be counter-attacked.

We had certainly struck the retreating Germans a damaging blow; the capture of Cavanazza denied them the use of the Lusia ferry on which they had been building their hopes for getting troops and vehicles over the Adige. They tried several counter-attacks that morning, but none were well co-ordinated and there was little fire support. B Company inflicted more casualties and took another thirty prisoners. Altogether Cavanazza was a minor triumph for B Company, and, personally, I felt satisfied that Rentella and Tossignano had now been amply avenged.

Our only casualties occurred in 8 Platoon at the very start of the battle. I felt specially sad at the death of Rifleman Duncan, Ian Mitchell's radio operator, who was an obvious target for the Germans as they ambushed 8 Platoon entering the village. 8 Platoon's fight had been a distinguished affair; without it, Cavanazza would not have been captured so early, and their battle, about which Ian Mitchell and Sergeant Thompson told me at intervals that day, merits more description.

Ian reached the crossroads in Cavanazza without difficulty, but soon afterwards 8 Platoon were counter-attacked by about fifty enemy. The platoon had about eight casualties, of whom Rifleman Duncan was the only one to be killed. Sensibly Ian established the platoon in a house covering the crossroads, and, fortunately, despite the operator being killed, the set was not damaged and they remained in touch with us throughout the operation. Sergeant Thompson, bravely and coolly, went forward under fire and pulled two of the casualties to safety. He next recovered a Bren abandoned by one of the casualties; for the rest of the battle he manned the gun personally and did deadly execution, killing seven enemy himself, and wounding others. 8 Platoon were able to help the other two platoons forward by producing covering fire at a key moment of our attack. It was a model platoon battle; Sergeant Thompson won a richly deserved MM, and Ian Mitchell, who had already been awarded an MC for his efforts at San Nicolo, was mentioned in dispatches.

Cavanazza was a personal highlight. I felt proud of how B Company had performed, and that our tactics, carefully rehearsed beforehand, had worked when put to the test. It was the last real battle of the war for 2 RB, and it was good to end on such a note.

After Cavanazza the rest of the campaign was less spectacular, though B Company continued to have some excitement and incident. On 29 April, for example, after crossing the Adige to continue our role as right flank protection for the New Zealanders, B Company reached Monselice after a rapid advance with little opposition from Germans increasingly intent on surrender. We entered the town in triumph; our arrival was a dead heat with the New Zealanders, Bernard Freyberg, their famous Divisional Commander, following in his jeep immediately behind the leading section of David Pontifex's scout platoon. Bernard Freyberg told me his Division's job was now to make for Triest with all speed in order to forestall the city's occupation by Tito and the partisans. It was our first intimation of the problems which peace would bring, but we thought little of it at the time, being busy with more immediate matters.

After a night's rest near Monselice, we were directed north in the middle of the following night through Padua and Treviso towards Belluno. Here A Company, a squadron of the 27th Lancers and Dick Fyffe between them negotiated the surrender of a German Corps HQ and two more or less complete divisions, 65th and our old opponents from Fontanelice, 715th. It was a remarkable situation and on 3 May, while we were still at Belluno coping with a mass of prisoners and equipment, we got official confirmation that Vietinghoff, the German Army Group Commander in Italy, had surrendered to Field Marshal Alexander, and that, officially at least, our particular war was over. In practice, however, for the next few days, it was not greatly to affect 2 RB's role as we struggled to comply with our orders to make for Austria by means of the Isonzo valley and over the Predil Pass to Tarvisio and Villach.

B Company moved first, and spent a night of pouring rain under command of the Welsh Regiment (who had taken the place of the Coldstream Guards in 1st Guards Brigade) at Plezzo. Next morning the rain eased off and finally stopped altogether in time to provide a glorious spring morning, as B Company, Roger Parker's 7 Platoon in the lead, advance up the Isonzo valley towards the Predil Pass and our objective, Tarvisio. It was not long, about 5 kilometres, before we came to the first blow; Michael Brown harboured the company off the road and gave orders for a brew. We had a sapper with us, and a bulldozer was soon at work getting the road back into use. Roger and I, aware of Vietinghoff's surrender and having been briefed that force was not to be used except in self-defence, negotiated the blow on foot and 7 Platoon followed with instructions to look as peaceful as possible as they advanced. We plodded steadily up the pass in bright sunshine; it was a beautiful scene and a memorable walk. Just short of the summit there was another demolition. On the far side waited a German parachutist, whose troops, well concealed as if the war was still in progress, covered the obstacle with Spandaus and patent professionalism. Roger and I indulged in a shouted dialogue across the demolition; Roger's German, honed to a high level by his imitations of the Fuhrer in the Sergeants' Mess, was impressive in its grammar, as well as 'name dropping' the names of our main opponents, Kesselring, Vietinghoff, and the opposing Army Commander, Herr. His eloquence, however, cut little ice with the parachutist who, coming across to our side of the blow, revealed himself as a fluent English speaker with a pseudo-Wodehousian style and vocabulary. His Drones club accent explained the dilemma; the troops defending the Predil Pass and behind them in Tarvisio did not belong to Vietinghoff's Army Group and had received no orders to surrender. 97th Corps, to which they belonged and whose HQ we discovered later were in Tarvisio, formed part of Army Group South East. This formation's job was Jugoslavia, and their task was to secure the withdrawal of the Germans remaining there who had been involved in fighting Tito's partisans. It soon became obvious that on our level we were deadlocked. General Loehr's Army Group SE felt themselves in no way concerned with the Allied Armies in Italy, except where we impinged on their mission of withdrawing in face of the 'Tito Leute' or 'Tito Banditen' to whom our parachutist scathingly referred. I got through to Dick Fyffe on the radio; 2 RB Headquarters, fresh from the triumph at Belluno, had moved forward of Plezzo and were busy getting comfortable in the White Horse Inn equivalent at Bretto di Sopra. Dick told me to try and get the facts of military life into the head of my parachutist. It was obvious that any delay to the advance of Eighth Army would give the 'Tito Leute' their best chance of settling themselves down in Carinthia; once installed, they might prove hard to dislodge. I was also to explain tactfully that 7 Platoon, Roger Parker and I represented the mere tip of a formidable military iceberg. It would be unwise for anyone, whether Commander 97 Corps or General Loehr himself, to obstruct our passage. We returned to the demolition and resumed our dialogue armed with new facts about progress on the main axis from Udine to Tarvisio via Pontebba. The demolitions on this road were even worse than our route through Plazzo, where they were formidable enough. If Eighth Army did not get through to Carinthia, the province could easily fall to the advancing Russians; 97 Corps' private conflict with the local partisans would seem irrelevant in such circumstances.

These arguments were new to my parachutist and so much beyond his previous ken that he agreed to report them back to his superior in Tarvisio. Consideration would take time, he warned; we arranged to meet again, on our level, early next morning. I reported back to Dick Fyffe on the radio; he accepted the delay, reluctantly, but could see the logic of the argument that we were not in fact losing time since the sappers still had so much to do lower down the pass. A sapper had already been forward to the demolition near the top of the pass, so no time would be wasted if our parleys proved successful. Dick was good at trusting one's judgement; Roger and I were allowed to continue parleying next morning, though Dick, wisely, backed himself both ways by instructing David Pontifex and the scout platoon to look for an alternative route into Austria over the tracks further to the east, and across what was then the Jugoslav border. Their search was finally non-productive, with their way forward blocked by snowdrifts, but it represented an extra parleying card.

When Roger and I regained the blow on another lovely morning, our parachutist met us and greeted us with a proper military style salute, supported by appropriate heel clicking. There was a Volkswagen, nose pointed towards Tarvisio, waiting on the German side of the demolition; I was to go forward, unescorted, to Tarvisio to meet the 97th Corps Commander and tell him myself about the wider picture I had discussed with his liaison officer the previous day. Roger was given the task of telling Dick Fyffe this new and exciting piece of form; I was blindfolded, then climbed into the back of the Volkswagen and we were off down the road to Tarvisio. I was not surprised by the blindfolding protocol; six years before, at Winchester, Robin Ridgway, who taught us German imaginatively, had used a book *"Wir fordern Rheims zur übergabe auf"* to give us some military vocabulary he felt would soon come in handy. Knowing the drill for surrender, I therefore chatted away correctly to my escort, and refrained from cheating by glancing under my blindfold until we drew up outside Corps HQ in Tarvisio. My blindfold was removed and an ADC conducted me to a large billiard room with wide plate glass windows. Tarvisio is a pretty place and the view of the surrounding mountains in the May sunshine was sensational. Soon the Corps Commander, Lieutenant General Felmy, arrived; I accepted a cup of coffee and, despite the early hour, a glass of Kümmel of impressive proportions.

Suitably mellow, I embarked, in my best German, on my parleying script; the Drones club parachutist helped out when my vocabulary failed and, between us, we got the message across. The General explained that, though he had received no orders from Army Group Loehr to let Eighth Army through, he saw the logic of the position. However, as a General Leutnant, there could be no question of his surrendering to me, a mere Major of 24. More formal arrangements would be required. If he undertook to use his

1. My parents at
   Norwood Park in 1956.

2. Horris Hill football team, 1934. *Back row:* H.S. Morshead, A.J. Wilson, R.B. Adams,
J. de C. Mitchell; *Seated:* R.W.H. du Boulay, R.S. Clarke, H.A. Pawson (captain),
M.A. Bankier, I.P. Bankier; *Front:* R.H.A. Mackenzie, M.J. Goddard.

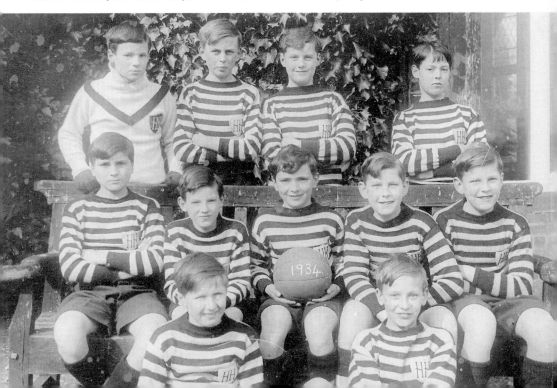

3. "I was fortunate in my housemaster, Jack Parr, an unusual schoolmaster" (p9).

4. Winchester College Chapel.

5. The author when first commissioned in 1941.

6. Brigadier A.C. Gore, DSO, my commanding officer for much of the war.

7. CSM Bert Coad, DCM, "one of the best fighting soldiers I have ever met" (p24).

8. Brigadier Pip Roberts, DSO, then commanding 26 Armoured Brigade, with Field Marshal Alexander; Major General Charles Keightley, GOC 6 Armoured Division, stands behind them.

9. Adrian Gore *(left)* and Dick Fyffe conferring in Tunisia. Between them is Lieutenant H.B. Shepherd, Signals Officer 10 RB.

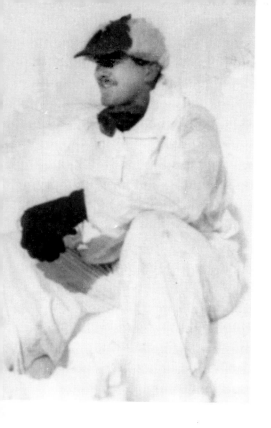

10. Major J.F. Lonsdale, DSO, in a snowsuit; "a natural fighting soldier who always led from the front" (p55).

11. Monte Cassino seen from the War Cemetery.

12. The upper approach to Tossignano.

13. The author, with walking stick, at Battle School, March 1942.

14. Chetwode Building, IMA Dehra Dun.

15. Brigadier A.B. Barltrop, OBE, MC. Commandant IMA. Dehra Dun 1945-47; "an unusual man" (p128).

16. Brigadier Barltrop with Field Marshal Auchinleck, 1946.

17. RSM J. McGarrity, Irish Guards, (see p. 127 et seq).

18. The author when Adjutant IMA, 1946.

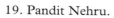
19. Pandit Nehru.

20 Indira Gandhi.

21. Qaid-e-Azam
    Mohammed Ali Jinnah.

22. Liaquat Ali Khan.

23. Wajahat Husain, "delightful, courteous and well educated" (p166). ADC to C-in-C Pakistan, 1948.

24. Pakistan Test Trial – Rest of Pakistan v. C-in-C's X1, Rawalpindi, 1948.

25. "My own team included two stars in Charles Baker-Cresswell *(right)* and Ned Ram *(left)*" (p191).

26. Jean, 1958.

27. Army FA team who defeated Heart of Midlothian, Scottish League Champions 1958, 5 – 3 in December 1957. Bobby Charlton at front on right.

28. A change of regiment: the author as CO 1st Lancashire Fusiliers with his Adjutant Ian Cartwright in 1962.

29. The author as Chief of Staff and Acting Force Commander, UN Forces in Cyprus, 1964–66.

30. Lieutenant General Sir Richard Fyffe (1912-72). "He became my greatest friend and inspiration during my Army career" (p.23)

31. Carlos Bernandez, UN Secretary General's Representative in Cyprus 1964–66.

32. The author with Irish troops when Chief of Staff UNFICYP.

33. With Jean and Archbishop Makarios, Easter, 1966.

34. GOC NW District 1970–72.

best offices with General Loehr, perhaps I could arrange for him to have a dialogue on a higher level, more fitting his rank and command. On this note, our meeting ended and General Felmy withdrew; the ADC offered me another beaker of Kümmel, which I declined, before, again blind-folded, entering the Volkswagen and being driven back up the pass to rejoin 7 Platoon. While I had been away in Tarvisio, the road behind had been improved so that my command vehicle with its high-powered set was only just down the road. I was soon on the air to Dick Fyffe, who proved as usual resourceful. I was to arrange for General Felmy to come to the blow himself that afternoon; he suggested four o'clock, in time for tea. I was then to drive him down to Battalion HQ at Bretto di Sopra, where Dick would arrange for him to be suitably received. I rightly took this to mean that the Divisional Commander would be there, and, plainly, this would be a bull point in persuading General Felmy to give us passage.

I returned to the demolition and explained our proposal to the para-chutist. We arranged for General Felmy to cross into our lines at the time appointed; I walked back down the hill to confirm the plan with Dick Fyffe. At a quarter to four Rifleman Christmas, perfectly turned out in green beret and camouflage smock, with Ken Ives in the back, radio on net to Battalion Headquarters, was waiting with me and our jeep by the demolition. The jeep looked a picture, its two formation signs, the 61 Brigade bugle and the mailed fist of 6 Armoured Division, polished up for the occasion. Punctually at four o'clock General Felmy arrived in a Mercedes more magnificent than any staff car I had ever seen. I conducted the General across the rubble, which energetic shovelling by the Germans and 7 Platoon had made easier to cross than earlier that day. I installed General Felmy in the front seat of my jeep, with the windscreen down; Christmas joined Ken Ives in the back, which meant there was no room for the parachutist. He looked a bit miffed, but General Felmy did not seem to mind, and there was no way I intended to do either Christmas or Ives out of their moment of glory. No blindfolding; Dick intended the General to see our medium artillery which had already moved into position ready to support our attack if we had to make one. I drove slowly and carefully; having landed our Corps Commander, it would be a disaster if anything happened to him at this stage. It was difficult to make good conversation, though the General remarked that the way British officers drove their own vehicles appealed to him as an indication of the 'sporting' approach we adopted towards warfare. Mr Crocker, the RSM, had organized an admirable reception; the riflemen had been briefed to stand to their front, as the General passed, but there was to be no saluting. It was good to see Tim Marten, who had joined us as second-in-command in place of the wounded Tony Palmer; his German, I knew, was perfect and there would be no problems of interpre-tation. General Nap Murray's jeep was there too, and I just had time to explain to Felmy that he would be meeting the Commander of 6 Armoured Division.

I need not have worried about the outcome of the high-level parley Dick Fyffe had arranged so perfectly. As soon as General Felmy met our Divisional Commander he handed over a note signed by General Loehr in person authorizing him to discuss the unopposed entry of Eighth Army into Austria. Since our first encounter on the Predil Pass, Admiral Doenitz, Hitler's successor, had ordered a general ceasefire. The Germans were therefore anxious for Eighth Army to occupy as much of Austria as possible before the Soviets or the Jugoslavs could arrive. There would be no problem about our move over the Predil Pass the next day, and the way would be clear for us to Klagenfurt, and for the Guards Brigade who were to follow us over the pass as far as Villach.

Next morning, therefore, found us, after harbouring for the night at Tarvisio, waiting on the road just short of the Austrian frontier. It was 8 May and VE Day was being celebrated in London. 2 RB's scout platoon were the first troops of Eighth Army to cross the frontier into the Greater German Reich. Hard though it was to believe it, the war in Europe was over.

Austria looked beautiful as we drove to Klagenfurt; apart from 2 RB, there was no traffic and hardly a sign of war. In Klagenfurt B Company found a hutted camp which nicely fitted our numbers. We named our new home Tredegar Road Barracks (after the drill hall at Mile End whence 10 RB had sprung in 1939).

Klagenfurt was far from dull. On the night of VE day I drank white wine from the bonnet of the command half truck while talking on the radio to Battalion HQ, as Roger Parker and 7 Platoon rushed to control a group of partisans looting a train. Corporal Clay had tuned into the Prime Minister on another set, so Churchill's voice competed with Roger's progress from his rail yard and 2 RB briefing us about German troops withdrawing through our position next morning. It was all confusion, with the 'Tito Leute' making the running and 2 RB unable to identify their enemy.

The partisans dominated our lives, but, though we had come to regard Tito and his supporters as heroes, we were soon disillusioned. The 'Jugs' were dirty, undisciplined and unreliable; they had no right to be in Carinthia and their presence in Klagenfurt was evidently unwelcome to the locals, with whom we quickly sympathized. The Jugoslav argument that Carinthia was a Slovene province was nonsense, and their practice of daubing 'Zivel Tito' in blue paint on walls and roads did not convince us. Willie John Lawson identified what we all felt; the sooner they went back over the Loibl Pass to Jugoslavia the better.

To add to the instability, 2 RB began to disintegrate. Dick Fyffe was warned he would be required at home to instruct at the new Joint Services

Staff College, while the Ulster Rifles were asking for Michael Brown and Willie John Lawson. I won a draw for LIAP (Leave in Addition to Python) and began looking over my shoulder. I was to leave Klagenfurt on 23 May; Dick Fyffe allowed me to drive to Naples to catch a boat home at the end of the month. Riflemen Christmas and Gough, the drivers taking me to Naples, and my orderly, Alfie Moore, began preparations for the journey. Assuming that I would be rejoining B Company, I negotiated the transfer of David Pontifex to join it as second-in-command, first to Michael Brown until he returned to the Ulster Rifles, and then, as I expected, to myself. Nevertheless, one felt 2 RB could never be quite the same again.

While in Klagenfurt, I 'owned' a superb green Mercedes, acquired on arrival in Carinthia. It had been the property of the Nazi Gauleiter of Carinthia and was even more magnificent than General Felmy's staff car. I reported its acquisition to Dick Fyffe, Rifleman Christmas decorated it with a mailed fist and we obtained a captured vehicle number. The car was so splendid, however, that a mere Company Commander could not hope to retain it long. Dick wisely imposed restrictions on its use; it was not to appear at Battalion HQ, nor to be used on military business. Picnics by the Wörther See were therefore almost the only journeys allowed, but it was a great car and gave me much pleasure.

B Company had a final excitement. On 19 May I was in the jeep with Hugh Carey and Ken Ives, prospecting for a battalion cricket ground. I kept my set tuned to Battalion HQ, and it was as well I did so for orders came for me to meet Dick Fyffe 'soonest' at Brigade HQ. B Company were placed at 30 minutes notice for an operational task from eleven o'clock. I dropped Hugh Carey back at Tredegar Road Barracks to mobilize 6 Platoon and went to meet Dick.

The assignment for B Company was delicate. Dick said B Company had been chosen for the mission because of our previous success in diplomatic parleying in the Predil Pass and at Tarvisio. We were to persuade the Jugoslav partisans presently occupying the municipality in one of Klagenfurt's main squares to evacuate the building and move in RASC transport back over the Loibl Pass into Jugoslavia. The Jugoslavs had accepted withdrawal from Carinthia in return for their claim to part of the hinterland round Trieste and other compensation elsewhere. I never discovered the details of the deal; it probably included the Predil Pass, the two Brettos and Plezzo, for these all now form part of Slovenia. The partisans, despite the agreement, however, showed no signs of leaving the Klagenfurt municipality, though elsewhere in Carinthia they were moving back within their borders. B Company, therefore, were to use diplomacy in our task of persuasion; force was only to be employed as a last resort. In the latter event, two troops (Shermans) of the Derbyshire Yeomanry were placed under B Company's command, but Dick's last words stressed that force should be avoided, unless it was the only way to achieve our aim.

I gave out orders at Tredegar Road Barracks. In view of the need to avoid force, I decided to keep the main body of B Company and the two troops of tanks out of view under Michael Brown to be called forward only as a last resort. 7 Platoon, under Roger Parker, and the RASC transport, four troop carrying vehicles, would parade openly in the square in front of the municipality building. 7 Platoon were briefed to present arms to the Jugoslavs as they emerged from the building – a tribute to our Allies for their achievements in our common victory. To make certain that the partisans understood the ceremonial nature of 7 Platoon's role, Roger, helped by Willie John Lawson, was to carry out some practice 'presents' while they were waiting outside. I would go into the building accompanied just by Willie John; the latter had injunctions to avoid fighting talk and only to give encouraging salutations in the shape of the Ulster nod, though whether this greeting, peculiar to Belfast, had reached Slovenia was uncertain.

By 2 p.m. the stage was set. 7 Platoon fronted the municipality, pretending they honoured the partisans. The RASC drivers stood by their vehicles, smoking discreetly, whenever they thought Willie John was not looking. The remainder of the force were concealed round the corner. Michael gave the order to brew up; it seemed a situation which would develop slowly.

At 2 p.m. Rifleman Christmas dropped me outside the partisans' temporary headquarters. Willie John and I walked slowly, looking more confident than we felt, into the building, where we asked to see their commander. We were taken to a room at the back of the building, where we encountered an unprepossessing group, describing themselves as the 'leadership'. I embarked on a carefully prepared speech in my best German; I hoped that the Brigade staff's assurance, "Don't worry, Jim, the Slovenes were part of Austria-Hungary; they all understand German," was not over-optimistic. My address conveyed the compliments of Eighth Army to Marshal Tito and his partisans and our pride in having fought the Nazis with them, shoulder to shoulder. Now it was time for peace and for us to return to our own countries and garner the fruits of victory. This last sentiment fully taxed my limited German, besides being of doubtful validity where the Jugs were concerned; four years of Nazi occupation had probably left little for them to garner inside Jugoslavia, but I felt the sentiment was sound. Where fruits of victory were concerned, the ground was stronger, ten days of partisan looting in Carinthia had liberated plenty for them to go home with. Willie John and I had both noticed signs of hasty partisan packing and numerous bulging suitcases.

As a mark of 6 Armoured Division's respect for their Jugoslav comrades, I explained that my general had sent me to provide them with transport and a guard of honour to escort them to the Loibl Pass. The guard of honour,

7 Platoon, were already in position to pay them the respect they deserved. The transport was outside and would take them to the Loibl Pass. The road had been cleared for their move and I asked them to board the trucks at 1500 hours. It is now, I concluded, without quite daring to invite the leadership to synchronise watches, 1415 hours; are there any questions?

There were none, but, as Willie John and I withdrew, we had no idea how my speech had gone down. Perhaps I should have been blunter and not left quite so much to the partisans' imaginations. Impressive though 7 Platoon and Roger Parker appeared, perhaps I should have organized a bigger and more obvious show of force. It was too late to play things differently now, I returned to the jeep, reported my speech to Dick Fyffe over the air and spent a long forty minutes waiting to see what happened.

By five minutes to three there had been no sign of reaction from the municipality building. Plenty of noise and movement from within, but there was no indication whether this meant preparations for joining the transport, or for fighting it out with B Company. At four minutes to three my nerve failed me; I summoned a Derbyshire Yeomanry Sherman forward into the square and asked the tank commander to load the 75 mm gun obviously and then traverse the turret menacingly. At the same time the remaining tanks were to start their engines and 'rev' them up threateningly in the background.

Brinkmanship achieved what oratory had failed to deliver. At one minute before three the first 'Jug' appeared, so loaded with loot he could hardly carry his rifle. 7 Platoon presented arms, the first RASC vehicle drove up to the front door, and, happily, we were in business. It all took longer than we had expected, but, by 4.30 p.m., the partisans were clear of Klagenfurt, no longer a responsibility of 61 Brigade and safely en route to the Loibl Pass.

Three days later I handed over B Company to Michael Brown and left for Italy in the Mercedes, Rifleman Christmas at the wheel. Dick Fyffe had arranged for me to hand the car over to Gordon Simpson, still with his regiment south of the Po. I had a safe conduct in a letter signed by Dick, explaining my mission, and another to Gordon himself giving him and the Lothians 2 RB's renewed greetings and gratitude. It was enough to satisfy the authorities in 6 Armoured Division's area; once beyond Tarvisio, I doubted if we should have any problems. This departure was the last I was to see of the regiment for over four years. I am glad I had no idea of what was in store; I hate farewells and saying 'goodbye' to B Company and 2 RB even for a couple of months was something of a wrench. If I had known that the parting was to prove so final it would have dampened an otherwise light-hearted departure.

Chapter Eight

INDIA

1945 London proved a disappointment when I returned there from the Italian campaign. It was marvellous, of course, to be back with my mother; she had been wonderful throughout the war, for the first two years as a general's wife in Shropshire, South Wales, and Belfast, and since 1941 running a family flat in London. She had been involved in six moves over the period, maintained a base for us all, and worked a full-time stint in the Registry of MI6. Blitzes, flying bombs, rockets – she took them all in her stride – supported by a fierce Corgi of high intelligence, Taffy, who, next to the family, was the light of her life. It was lovely to see her, and for the next ten weeks her flat in Sloane Gate Mansions was my base.

But it was unrealistic to expect to find the capital as one had left it in 1942. It was not long, therefore, before I contacted the Training Battalion at Ranby in Nottinghamshire – 9RB it was now called and, luckily for me, Vic Turner was in command. Vic had been greatly responsible for my joining The Rifle Brigade in the first place; he was an old friend of the family, had been my Uncle Bill Starkey's best man and often stayed at Norwood before the war. Vic went abroad in the desert with 1 RB in 1941, was captured in the Benghazi débâcle of early 1942 and regained our lines only after a memorable march back across the desert. At the Battle of Alamein Vic had commanded 2 RB in a famous exploit by that great battalion. His heroism at the Snipe action, and the performance of his battalion, had won Vic the Victoria Cross; he was worshipped in The Rifle Brigade and respected throughout the Army. I could not have had a better counsellor and friend than Vic, and, after my visit to Ranby, I knew my future would be in good hands.

At the end of July Vic asked me to lunch with him in London. He came quickly to the point, giving me the bad news first. "The Colonels Commandant have decided that it would be a good idea if you were to have a break from regimental soldiering for a year or two. This means you will not be going back to 2 RB, as I know you wanted to do." I looked downcast and wondered what I had done to deserve relegation. So Vic went on quickly, "They want you instead to go to India to take over as Adjutant of IMA Dehra Dun. This establishment was the Sandhurst of India before 1939, and the Government of India want to get it re-established as a fully-fledged Military Academy as soon as possible. The Rifle Brigade have been chosen to provide the Adjutant; a new RSM is going at the same time from the Irish Guards. The Colonels Commandant are honoured that the Regiment should be asked to find this appointment, and I know you will understand how lucky you are to have been selected."

I was overcome. Vic told me a bit about Dehra Dun. It was a beautiful place in the foothills of the Himalayas about 160 miles north of Delhi, and a centre for training the Gurkhas, which meant that there would be kindred spirits in black buttons nearby. I owed my selection to Dick Fyffe's reports on me as a Company Commander in 10 and 2 RB; it was an advantage that I had been an instructor in the Oxford University OTC and had obtained a good degree at Oxford. The academic side of the IMA would be important and I should be involved in that side of the training, probably teaching military history. It was obviously a great challenge for a 24-year-old, and I was sufficiently humble to realize that it would not be an easy job.

I had naturally to do as I was told, and was grateful to the Colonels Commandant and Vic for giving me the opening. The next days were a blur, spent in chasing round tailors, organizing my luggage and arranging to get myself to India by the end of August when India wanted me to be in post. All available shipping space was booked for the Japanese war; though the atom bomb meant a Japanese surrender, the problems involved in rounding them up in Burma, South-East Asia, Malaya and the Netherlands East Indies remained immense. There was no obvious priority for someone going out to re-establish a peacetime establishment like Dehra Dun, about which 'movements' had never heard. Finally a solution was found. A million pounds in gold bars needed to be taken to India to pay agents and others in resistance movements in Burma and elsewhere; the gold bars, at present in the Bank of England vaults, required an escort to deliver them in Bombay. I got the job and the air passage which went with it.

I took a taxi to the Bank of England to collect my bullion and the meter ticked quietly while the gold was loaded. There were no security companies in those days, so I dropped my million pounds at the Knightsbridge Barracks guardroom for the night. The Guard Commander was surprised when I said I would call in a taxi next morning to collect the gold; the Household Cavalry have perfect manners, however, and laughed politely when I said I hoped no one would put the lot on the 2.30! Too busy to be homesick, I took Penelope Forbes out to dinner and to the Four Hundred, before finishing my packing.

Next morning I had so much luggage of my own that there was little room in the taxi for the gold. I joined my flight to India in a seaside hotel at Poole, the Transit Camp for RAF Hurn. We were to travel by Dakota, three days flying and night stops at Malta and Cairo. I had never really flown before; I tried to seem sophisticated, but could not conceal my excitement next morning when I sat down in a window seat at the rear of the aircraft, the gold safely stowed behind me. The Dakota was slow and deliberate, and I enjoyed every minute of our flight. Malta – no time sadly to leave the airfield at Luqa – Cairo, after a brief stop at Benghazi, and the Heliopolis Palace Hotel. A night refuelling break at Sharjah on the Gulf and we arrived in Karachi early next morning. I negotiated an onward journey to Bombay and arranged for the pay authorities to meet me in Bombay to take the money off my hands. I was not sorry to part with the gold; I found a Transit Hotel, drank a celebratory glass of beer and consumed my first Indian curry lunch.

Wartime movement in India was as difficult as at home. I was lucky to find a berth on the Frontier Mail to Delhi next morning. I arrived ahead of time at the station and settled myself in a two-berth cabin. By now I owned a bedroll, but still lacked a bearer since the IMA had signalled there would be an incumbent waiting at Dehra Dun. I laid my bed down untidily, there-fore, in the compartment, and anxiously awaited the arrival of my travelling companion. To my delight, it was Ronnie Hamilton, dressed as a full Colonel; he had been a master at Winchester and producer of Phil's famous 1938 production of T.S. Eliot's *Murder in the Cathedral*. He was now 14th Army's Chief of Intelligence, under the newly arrived General Dempsey. The Japanese surrender had altered every plan; Ronnie was on his way to Delhi to negotiate an early release and quick return to Winchester, who badly needed him back. It was a great encounter; Ronnie, well equipped as always, had some gin with him. His bearer, as efficient as his master, produced glasses and tonic water, and our journey taught me much about sub-continent life.

Ronnie, of course, knew all about the IMA; he had been to Dehra Dun twice already. It was the apple of the C in C's eye; Claude Auchinleck re-alized the vital importance of training good young Indians to take over from their British predecessors. Ronnie told me that he would be staying with the 'Auk' in Delhi; Robin Ridgway, another don from Winchester, was with Auchinleck as his Private Secretary. I would clearly have some friends at court in India, but that meant I had better be good and get it right. Ronnie, wisely, declined to mark my card about the IMA itself; "It's a wonderful place", he said. "It will be up to you to make it work the way the Chief expects."

All too soon we found ourselves running into Delhi and about to be enveloped by the confusion of arriving at a main station. Ronnie's bearer rolled up my bed, organized my luggage and pushed me into a taxi. I chose the Cecil Hotel, knowing it to be in Old Delhi, and remembering my parents had stayed there in 1939. Ronnie Hamilton waved me goodbye; "I expect the Chief will give you a month or so," he said, "but with Robin around it won't be long before he pays you a visit. Best of luck, and enjoy yourself. You will find it a marvellous job."

The Cecil Hotel was what I had expected. Old fashioned, relaxed and still comfortable. I unpacked, changed and ate a leisurely dinner; being owned by the Swiss, there was still wine to be had, and I retired to bed, pleasantly tired and able to savour my good fortune. I spent next day sight-seeing in Delhi and embarked on the train journey to Dehra Dun that evening with a blend of anticipation and anxiety.

I drank my early morning tea as the train chugged slowly at about 15–20 mph up the long incline towards Dehra Dun. It was my first view of the jungle and already the air was cooler and fresher than in Delhi, where the end of the monsoon had made it sticky and oppressive. My predecessor as Adjutant of the IMA met me at the station and introduced me to my bearer, Attar Singh. The latter was an Indian Gurkha from Dehra Dun itself; Pat Stubbs, of the 2nd Goorkhas, with whom I was to share a bungalow, had engaged him on my behalf and it proved a great success. Attar Singh, shy, honest as the day, and wonderfully reliable, soon won my heart; we exchanged Christmas cards till his death fifty years later.

The IMA station wagon bumped us five miles through tea plantations towards Chakrata. We passed the impressive Forest Research Institute and, a mile beyond, entered the IMA ground. I had arrived and there could now be no turning back.

I had reached India at an interesting time, even if it did not appear so to my new colleagues at Dehra Dun. In their view, training young officers, now that the war was over, was an anti-climax. Their interest now became returning home if they were wartime officers, or getting back to peacetime routine for regulars. A sense of duty helped them struggle on, but IMA training, based on preparing cadets for the Burma war, seemed irrelevant.

If the officers lacked motivation, the morale of the British warrant officer and NCO instructors was worse. Many had been abroad since before the war, others had been sent back wounded or unfit from Burma; they were mostly too old for their existing role, let alone for learning new tricks. My first visit to the Sergeants' Mess was depressing when I compared the dismal absence of talent and enthusiasm to the marvellous teams I had served with in 10 and 2 RB. My RSM, Joe McGarrity, from the Irish Guards, had arrived two days before me and was also disappointed by his first impressions. Next day we decided that something must be done, though quite what we could not determine; more thinking was needed if the training and atmosphere at the IMA was to match the environment and facilities Dehra Dun provided.

The Academy had been built originally as a Staff College for the Indian Railways. The main building itself was imposing, if not beautiful; it was like St Pancras Station nestling beneath the Himalayas. But it was comfortable to work in; I have seldom had a better office, while the library, classrooms and the main Chetwode Hall were all well designed. Accommodation for the cadets was excellent; everyone had his own room, while the grounds were beautifully maintained. The officers lived mainly in spacious bungalows, each with their own garden; at this stage there were still few wives, but for them an IMA bungalow represented far better accommodation than anything the normal Indian Army cantonment could provide. McGarrity, the RSM, and his wife had their own detached house and soon made it delightful; the general standard of rooms for the warrant officers and sergeants was also good, and their Mess far and away the best its members had encountered in India.

The IMA's facilities, too, were excellent – superb pitches for any team game, good tennis and squash courts, a riding school – it was a splendid establishment, but that September the atmosphere required to profit from the advantages was absent. This, so the Commandant, Brigadier Barltrop, told me at our first interview, was why Joe McGarrity and I had been brought from England; it was up to us to change things and set the scene for the Academy to re-open in February 1946 and train the first intake of future regular Indian officers. Meanwhile the existing 600, mainly British cadets – just 10% were Indians – would complete their training for emergency commissions as planned; the last such company to pass out would do so on 20 January 1946. This would mean only a three-week interval before the first intake of Indian cadets arrived on 10 February. It sounds an impossible task, but the arrogance of youth is such that I do not remember then considering it very difficult.

The Commandant, known as 'Groppi', was an unusual man. He owed his nickname to a famous cake shop in Cairo, 'Groppis', where, as a young officer in the First World War, he had evidently been a keen customer. A former 3rd Gurkha, he had fought in Iraq in the First War; between the wars he had combined regimental duty with a spell as a staff officer in charge of the independent States Forces. He had never bothered to attend the Staff College, but had developed a broad knowledge of India and its problems. He had been Commandant of the 3rd Gurkha Training Centre in Dehra Dun and had made this centre into the best training establishment in India. On this basis he was selected to command the IMA. He had a flair for training, while his interest in methods of instruction made him ahead of his time. He knew how to delegate and wished to work as much as possible through me as his personal staff officer. He had plenty of ideas and these concepts flooded into my tray in the form of scribbled notes at intervals each day. It was my job to examine them further, to discuss their implementation with others, and report progress to Groppi. He operated the Chief of Staff system; it was a similar method to that of Adrian Gore in 10 RB and I naturally welcomed it. He liked a short exchange of views, a quarter of an hour only, each morning at 9.30 when he came in; the aim would be to plan activities for the day and assess progress in getting the Academy onto the right line.

It was fortunate that two people, different in personality, age and interests, should have complemented each other so well. We shared the same aim and that bound us together. In the two years we worked together I cannot recall any conflicts and I remain grateful for the way I was trusted and given so much scope.

I have since wondered how Groppi, unmilitary in appearance, apparently gentle, always courteous, could have become such an effective Commandant. Perhaps he was a Headmaster who had missed his vocation; he reminded me of Walter Oakeshott, who had taught me at Winchester, became a successful Headmaster, and afterwards an equally good Master of an Oxford College. Certainly one of Groppi's strengths lay in his ability to understand schoolmasters and the relationship he established with Arthur Foot, Headmaster of the Doon School (the Eton of India) down the road, served the IMA well.

One must now consider the political situation in India. The Viceroy, Lord Wavell, remarked that if India had not been ready for war in 1939, the country was certainly quite unprepared for peace in 1945. Throughout the war India had been vital to the Allies, both as a base and an important source of military manpower. The country's progress towards independence had slowed after the outbreak of war. Defence and security became the prime consideration; the Congress party's equivocal attitude towards the war soon led to the dismissal or resignation of elected Congress administrations in those provinces held by them in 1939. Thus Hindu India, and notably the main provinces of Bombay, Madras and the United Provinces, were ruled by provincial Governors under Section 93 of the India Act. By contrast, the Muslim League, representing the Moslem community, generally supported the war effort; Muslim League governments therefore stayed in power in Bengal, Punjab, Sind and the North-West Frontier Province, with those Governors acting in a constitutional role. The Viceroy until 1943 was Lord Linlithgow, who was content for this situation to continue. He saw his main priority as the Indian war effort and considered the Congress politicians likely to promote instability. At home, Churchill, a bitter opponent of independence for India, had no wish to change the position; only once, therefore, in 1942 did HMG attempt a political initiative. This move, the mission by Sir Stafford Cripps, was undertaken primarily to satisfy American susceptibilities; once the Cripps' mission failed, as it was bound to do, given the attitude of the Congress politicians, and Gandhi in particular, there was no need to do more until after the war was over. The Congress leaders were interned, and after the suppression of the 'Quit India' campaign in 1943, general stability existed for the next two years.

Wavell owed his appointment in 1943 as Viceroy to follow Linlithgow partly to his personal qualities, but also to a hope on Churchill's part that, as a soldier, he would not rock the boat by thinking of political progress. Churchill underestimated Wavell's abilities and neglected his progressive nature, but, in June 1945, before the results of the UK General Election were known, Wavell finally persuaded the UK Government to let him convene a political conference to discuss the way forward for India. Though the conference, held at Simla in the early part of July, failed to reach agreement, largely because of the Muslim League leader Jinnah's intransigence, the stage was set for future initiatives. The election of a Labour government provided, too, a further stimulus towards independence. Our plans for reconstituting the IMA on a peacetime basis would need to accommodate such factors; it would not be possible just to revert to the original small concept of the IMA. A more ambitious, and much larger, IMA would be needed.

A visit by the Commander in Chief to Dehra Dun at the end of September helped to make us understand these new facts of Indian life. We got about ten days' notice of the Auk's visit; Robin Ridgway, his Private Secretary, rang me up from Delhi. I had known Robin well at Winchester; he had been with Auchinleck, who enjoyed Robin's effervescent approach to life, much of the war. Robin, now a Lieutenant Colonel, was an outstanding Private Secretary to his Chief, and knew well how to manage Delhi's often tricky corridors of power.

I asked Robin what sort of programme his boss would like. "A good drill parade, a gossipy breakfast, and then a walk round whatever training is going," I was told. "Nothing special, whatever you do. He will certainly ask the cadets if they have had an extra practice for the drill parade, and be annoyed if they had." I passed this invaluable briefing on to Groppi and told Joe McGarrity what was required. It was the RSM's first chance to show what he could do and he excelled himself. Good but simple; a general salute, the usual inspection, a march past in quick time and a final advance in review order. I decided that this first parade, and all subsequent ones, would be commanded by the cadets themselves. Only the RSM and the CSMs would be on parade, apart from the cadets; I explained this polity to the cadets and decided to stick to it, when the IMA reformed next year in its new role.

The Auk's visit went well; he was relaxed, interested and said all the right things to everyone, and especially to Joe McGarrity, who was pleased by how well his design for the parade had worked out. Over breakfast I listened carefully as the C in C told Groppi how he saw the IMA's future developing. One angle especially made me prick my ears. "You will need to get more Indian officers here pretty quick, and they will need to be good." Under the Indian constitution, the C in C doubled as Defence Member; in the climate of a move towards earlier independence for India, a large concentration of British officer instructors, however good, at the IMA would be difficult to defend both in Cabinet, and against Congress questioning. "You had better send young Jim Wilson down to Delhi to fix things with my staff. Tell him to arrange it with Robin Ridgway." So it was arranged; I would motor down to Delhi on 15 October, stay the night in the Commander-in-Chief's house, and the next day visit GHQ and arrange staffing the Academy with the best Indian officers available. There would be no problem, the Auk said, about retaining Joe McGarrity and a supporting staff of British WOs and NCOs; we needed, however, to improve their quality and reduce their average age, and this would not be easy.

In retrospect, I am surprised Groppi should have delegated all this to me so early in our relationship. Perhaps he recognized that my interests lay in the field of organization and people; certainly, it was a help that such a young Adjutant had contacts in high places. It allowed Groppi to concentrate on his main interest, the organization of military training. He had little idea of what sort of academic training we should develop at Dehra Dun; here again, trusting in my education at Winchester and New College, he told me to obtain the best educator I could, and we could determine this aspect when he arrived.

Meanwhile, we needed to watch the final short service courses, improve the atmosphere of the Academy and provide a good background for the British cadets finishing their training at Dehra Dun. We decided to relax the tempo, to spend more time on games and to begin the development of the clubs and other activities which would be needed in the reorganized IMA.

Luckily the IMA had inherited some admirable talent and we set them to work in their own spheres of interest. Pat Stubbs, the delightful 2nd Goorkha with whom I shared a bungalow, had been badly wounded winning his MC in North Africa, but this had not interfered with his love of horses and equitation became his responsibility. Soon he was to be joined by Ronnie Holman, recruited for the job of GSO 1 (Training Plans); it would be his task to plan the successive regular courses, the first of 9 months only, the second of 15 months duration, and finally the third course which would be the first two-year affair and a model for all subsequent courses. Ronnie, a thoughtful gunner, proved a good planner; as importantly, he was a fine horseman, had ridden in the Grand National, and possessed great talent at teaching people to ride and look after horses. Cricket and football fell into my sphere, CSM Woodcock of the KOYLI emerged as a superb swimming coach, while Dick Graveston, from the Rajputana Rifles, took on athletics.

Music, debating, a history group and a dramatic society soon followed when we recruited an educational staff. Arthur Foot from the Doon School was full of ideas and every morning I found my tray full of slips from Groppi with requests to initiate or examine new propositions. It was an exciting time and our ingenuity often surprised us.

But, as the Auk had said at breakfast, all depended on the quality of the Indians we could attract as instructors. Here the C in C's support ensured that the IMA got the best, and we were lucky in the talent made available. As Senior Instructor there came Lieutenant Colonel Mahadeo Singh, a successful CO in 10th Indian Division, veteran of the Italian campaign, and the holder of a DSO. Mahadeo was a delight; a landowner in the United Provinces, he had perfect manners, high standards and great integrity. Later, after independence in 1947, he became the first Indian Commandant of the IMA, and ultimately a successful Quartermaster General. As a company commander we received Attiqur Rahman, educated at St Paul's in England, awarded the MC in Burma and a man of originality, intellect and quality. He reached three-star rank in the Pakistan Army, served as Governor of the West Punjab, and in retirement developed into a successful writer on strategy and military history. Of equal distinction was A.C. Iyappa, recently released from Japanese captivity, where his courage in refusing to join the Indian National Army, despite being tortured and placed in solitary confinement, had won universal admiration.

Two other stars, again very different, were Zorawar Singh, an extrovert Rajput from Jaipur, another Italian veteran, and Tikka Khan, a determined gunner, later to be Commander in Chief Pakistan Army, to be imprisoned as a political opponent of President Zia, and finally Governor of the West Punjab. We needed an outstanding Indian staff officer and obtained Mohan Thapan of the Rajput Regiment, who quickly became a great friend, pulling my leg by correcting my English, often with justification, whenever he saw the least opportunity.

Another outstanding person was Inder Gill, who had won renown while serving in the British Army by blowing up the Gorgos Potamos railway bridge in Greece, the most spectacular exploit of the Greek resistance. Inder was the son of a Sikh, but with a Scottish mother. Educated in England, he was a clean-shaven or 'mechanized' Sikh, who had joined up in Britain, been commissioned into the Royal Engineers and qualified as a parachutist. He loved a party, was as tough as they came and a great example and inspiration to the cadets. Inder was a natural commander; it was no surprise that he held successive high command appointments, retiring in the end as Commander of India's Northern Army and largest troop command.

It was difficult even for Groppi to realize just how much Indian talent we had acquired as a result of the Auk's instructions to his staff. It was my job to see these able Indians were given their heads and full scope to influence events. Some of the British officers did not immediately appreciate the speed at which events were moving. Where such problems occurred I admired the loyalty to both sides which Mahadeo displayed; nearly always we managed to remove the log jam and it was seldom necessary to bother the Commandant for a solution. Mahadeo and I found our hands strengthened early in the New Year with the arrival of 'Pom' Power as Deputy Commandant. He had been captured in Burma early in 1942 while commanding a battalion of his regiment, the Dogras. Though his health was badly damaged by his time as a prisoner, and he never recaptured it completely, he proved a tower of strength. He had been an instructor at Dehra Dun before the war and possessed a wonderful touch with everyone.

With all this talent on the military side, we needed to develop an academic team strong enough to provide a balance. Again the Academy was fortunate. Ernest Gould, the Assistant Commandant RAEC, was an imaginative educationalist; aged only 31, he had an instinct for what was required, and could be achieved by his supporting staff. His right-hand man, a historian, Donald Washtell, helped to create a good nucleus. It was clear that, with so much military talent, the soldiers would need to help get the academic side off the ground. Soon Ernest Gould devised an excellent medium for this purpose, adapting the Oxbridge tutorial system so that individual cadets came in pairs to read their essays to selected officer tutors. Ernest's concept proved a success; of my own group of students, two, Bhopinder Singh and Harish Dutta, were both to reach three-star rank in the Indian Army and have remained my friends. Our discussions covered a wide field, usually over a cup of tea in the garden of my bungalow and with sandwiches and a chocolate cake as a brain stimulant. Perhaps our chief success lay in persuading our cadets, who in my case were only four years younger than I was, of the opportunities and responsibilities which independence would provide. We discussed the role of armed forces in a democracy. It was not always easy to persuade the young to avoid getting involved in politics. Happily this lesson became appreciated by the Indian Army, who have wisely avoided such involvement; in Pakistan, sadly, democracy never developed firm roots and the Army's involvement in politics has proved the rule rather than the exception.

I have rushed ahead in my description of our aims for the IMA, and may have given the impression that it was all part of a preconceived plan, unrolled with measured regularity. It was nothing like so organized, though there was a general directive from GHQ in Delhi, providing sound general principles. But it was up to us at Dehra Dun to fill in the detail; our methods were essentially pragmatic, depending greatly on Groppi's bright ideas, stemming from his vivid imagination, often supplemented by Arthur Foot from the Doon School, and increasingly by views advanced by our strong team of Indian officers. We studied, too, the working of similar institutions, West Point especially, and also RMA Sandhurst; we were six months ahead of RMA Sandhurst in developing our post-war existence, and, by the time the Sandhurst concept emerged, were already well down our own track. Soon we prided ourselves on having pioneered a definitively Indian establishment and determined to keep our Academy that way.

A main problem was to obtain enough British warrant officers and sergeants good enough and sufficiently flexible to implement our ideas, which were not always orthodox. McGarrity and I thought hard about how to overcome this difficulty. It was easy to identify and remove our dead wood; replacing it was a different matter. AG Department in Delhi delivered the answer. We were to be given access to all British reinforcements of any rank below Sergeant in the Depot at Deolali near Bombay with eighteen months or more to serve overseas; from this field we could select any forty we wished, train them ourselves at the IMA, and retain the twenty odd we needed to fill our establishment. The idea appealed to me; I recalled that 10 RB, which had possessed an outstanding group of senior NCOs, had chosen its NCOs early in the war in just this way. Joe McGarrity relished the challenge – he had great confidence in basic military virtues and in his ability to instil them in others. He went by train to Bombay to select his candidates, having devised a simple but imaginative cadre course for them on arrival at the IMA. We based our course on teaching the new arrivals what they required to know and exactly how to teach it – drill, weapon training, and minor tactics. We also decided to employ the education wing of the IMA and our distinguished group of Indian officers to brief them on the main elements of Indian history, present politics and the likely attitudes of Indian cadets. We stressed the importance of good manners, the need to avoid bad language, how to lead and not to drive. Between us, we managed to develop an effective amalgam between the best Brigade of Guards training and a riflemanlike reliance on Sir John Moore's concept of the 'thinking fighting man'.

Thanks to McGarrity's personality and example, our plan worked admirably. The material given us was splendid; they were excited at being brought to Dehra Dun, given proper accommodation and treated intelligently. Altogether they responded superbly and I learnt another lasting lesson. The British soldier has great capacity for understanding complex issues if these are explained to him clearly and without any attempt at talking down. Given this sort of briefing, the British soldier's enthusiasm and ability knows no bounds. I was to see these qualities again in Kenya later, and also as a Commander of the British element in the UN Force in Cyprus. McGarrity and I were thrilled at the response our training pattern elicited; we now had a young Sergeants' Mess at the IMA, trained the way we wanted, and on which we could rely to handle Indian cadets in the right way. For the next two years there was never a complaint from any of the Indian officers, far less any of the cadets, about the conduct and behaviour of the British staff. Given the political stresses in India and the constant denigration of the Raj in the newspapers, this situation reflects much credit on the British individuals concerned. It also indicates the cohesion which soon developed between British and Indian elements at the IMA; we wanted the best possible training for the future officers of the Indian Army and understood that only teamwork and co-operation could produce it.

While we were planning the start of the new IMA, there had been movement on the political scene. The new Labour Government soon announced their intention of pressing on towards Indian independence. The Viceroy went to London for consultation, and, on his return, repeated HMG's 'determination, in conjunction with the leaders of Indian opinion, to promote the early realization of full self-government in India'. There were to be provincial elections and a further attempt to reconstruct the Viceroy's Executive Council on a representative basis. A strong Parliamentary Delegation came out from home at the beginning of January, followed in March by a full Cabinet Mission, made up of three front-rank Ministers, Pethwick-Lawrence, the Secretary of State for India, Stafford Cripps, and A.V. Alexander.

This meant that the IMA would have less time to get off the ground than expected. It was important for the Academy to deliver its first crop of newly commissioned Indian officers as soon as possible; hence the first nine months course with a small intake of just 126 cadets, starting in February 1946 and passing out on 20 December. In purely military terms, this decision made little sense, but, against the urgent political background, we needed to do the best we could. Fortunately the quality of the first intake was high and we decided to relegate to the second course any for whom a commissioning date in December was premature. There was pressure on us to turn out the maximum numbers as soon as possible; wisely the Commandant determined not to lower standards, but to do all we could to explain our methods to the press and public. Our attitude proved more easily sustained than might have been expected. It helped that the key decisions about the destiny of our cadets were taken considerably by the high-grade Indian officers we had been able to recruit; the Auk's foresight in this respect quickly paid off.

There is no need to give a detailed account of the IMA's progress. Routine is important in a training establishment and we worked hard to develop continuity. A typical day for me began early; an early morning jog, a cup of tea from Attar Singh, a shower, and I was in the office at 7 a.m. with half an hour to plan my day before the flood of callers arrived. About 7.15 came Groppi's overnight flow of new concepts; unlike me, he worked late, and we had a system by which an orderly collected his 'out tray' early in the morning so, by the time the Commandant came in about 9.30, progress had already begun. Breakfast in the mess – usually about 8.30; Attar Singh, perfectly dressed in a rifle green pugri and with a shining Rifle Brigade badge, stood behind one's chair and negotiated with the cook for one's choice of eggs. Back to the office before 9 and a stream of callers requiring information and often a decision. We made it a rule that one did not use the telephone within the Academy for the discharge of normal business. It was the practice, instead, to get up from one's chair and walk along the passage for a word with whoever one needed to speak. The Commandant liked to see me for a quarter of an hour at 9.30 – to get a quick progress report on how his ideas were being developed, to check respective plans for the day, before going off in his car to watch the training. By 10.30 Mr Sood, a brilliant stenographer, would appear with the first of the letters and notes I had dictated before breakfast. I would sign or amend my drafts, dictate Academy Orders, and then walk round the Academy, calling on the various departments, sitting at the back of classes and getting the feel of things.

I would return to the office for half an hour before lunch for another session with Mr Sood and a talk to anyone who wanted to see me. By three o'clock I was clear of the office and involved in games thereafter. My activities were varied – coaching Academy sides at cricket and football, followed by tennis or squash, was my norm, but there were many other activities which required a visit. Though Indians love games, and are fanatical about sport, we did not neglect the cultural side. There was a music circle, a flourishing dramatic society and a well-attended debating club, besides other more specialized pursuits.

Cricket was, however, my main love. The facilities were marvellous and the matting wicket on which we played provided an excellent surface, giving equal opportunity to both batsmen and bowlers. We soon developed a good side, class players emerging steadily. Perhaps the best two were Ramesh Chandra, an elegant batsman from Government College, Lahore, our first captain and later to represent the Combined Services, and Khanna, from the Doon School, who was to make 149 against RMA Sandhurst, when the IMA team toured England just before independence in 1947. But there were others not far behind – Manohar, opening batsman and an off spinner who came into his own during the tour of England, Mohoni, the wicket-keeper and captain in succession to Ramesh, and Belwalkar, a leg spinner and no slouch with the bat.

There was some criticism of the importance attached to representative sport at Dehra Dun. I was unrepentant then, and am even more so now when I reflect that of the IMA cricket team, three, Bhopinder Singh, a talented Sikh from the Doon School, Manohar, and Mohoni all reached three star rank, while several others became Major Generals. One is only nineteen or twenty once in one's life and opportunities to pursue a chosen sport or pastime in depth seldom recur. Interestingly, Mohoni, later a distinguished head of his service, the Ordnance Corps, when I met him again in 1979, told me that cricket had "saved his career after being relegated from the first course at the IMA". I consoled him at the time by appointing him captain of cricket for the next term, a job which led to his leading the IMA team in England the following summer. Here he learnt leadership, diplomacy and the ability to conduct himself well in public in a way which might not otherwise have come to him. As a result it was a different, more confident, Mohoni who was commissioned from the IMA in December 1947. We were right to have relegated the immature, slightly uncouth young man from Nagpur the previous year; a year later he was a different prospect and it is nice to think that sport played such a key role in his redevelopment.

Thus, throughout 1946, the IMA grew in numbers, confidence and reputation. The Auk came to take our first passing out parade just before Christmas, having spent the previous day looking at all aspects of our training.

Jawaharlal Nehru, Prime Minister of an interim government at the centre, came with his daughter Indira and Sardar Patel to visit the IMA in February 1947. It proved a memorable 24 hours. Nehru and Patel in succession addressed the Academy in the Chetwode Hall; afterwards we gave them lunch and a chance to see the full range of our training. In the evening we reassembled in the Commandant's garden for an informal drink and a chance to discuss the day's impressions. I found Nehru an attractive person; he was beautifully turned out, had fine features and natural charm and dignity. His speech was tactful and liberal in tone. Sardar Patel was also impressive but in a different way; in his Congress style dhoti, he resembled a Roman senator and there was no hint of 'non-violence' about his approach to life. He was obviously as tough as they came, and it was no surprise when, after independence, he carved up the various Princes and rulers with speed and ruthlessness. I sat next to Indira at lunch and we got on well; she was, I think, surprised to find how well we knew individual cadets, and impressed by our tutorial system and the genuine freedom with which people were encouraged to express their views. Many years later, in 1982, I attended the ceremony to mark the fiftieth anniversary of the IMA's foundation, Indira Gandhi, then Prime Minister, was the Guest of Honour and took the salute; afterwards one of my Indian general friends, a former cadet, reminded her of her earlier visit to the Academy and mentioned that I was among those present. I was flattered to be invited to join her party for the rest of her programme and to find she recalled our conversation and my assurance that future Indian officers would be worthy of the responsibilities certain to come their way. I remember Nehru remarking to me that he was surprised at the 'effortless ease' with which young British officers got on with the Indian cadets for whose training they were responsible. He inquired how we managed to motivate our cadets so successfully and contrasted the atmosphere of learning he had found at Dehra Dun with the anarchic conditions at many Indian universities. I explained that discipline was the answer but not, of course, the repressive variety. At the IMA we realized that only self-discipline would serve, and this was the basis on which we aimed to build.

Our Indian officers were less impressed by Nehru's visit than we British. Muslims were starting to think in terms of Pakistan. I think they regarded Nehru's views on the evils of communalism as either insincere or ineffective; Attiqur Rahman, for one, preferred Sardar Patel. "At least one knows where one stands with him." The attitude of the Hindu and Sikh officers was also critical, reflecting suspicion of all politicians in principle. Inder Gill and Zorawar both expressed a fighting soldier's approach, "They are all the same, Jim. Yours or ours – it makes no difference." These reservations, however, failed to dim my own respect for our visitors and I was pleased to have met them.

Soon after Nehru's visit to Dehra Dun, news came of Wavell's replacement as Viceroy by Mountbatten. It was sad to see Wavell go, but I realize now that it was the right decision. Wavell was tired and had shot his bolt in dealing with Indian politicians. He was worried, too, at the deterioration of the administrative machine, and by his inability to rectify it. But it was impossible for any of us to understand the lack of understanding Wavell was getting from the Government at home. In circumstances of such mutual incomprehension a change was the only answer.

My principal interest that spring was more frivolous, involving a plan for the IMA cricket team to tour England that summer, the highlight being a challenge match in late June against the RMA Sandhurst. We had developed a good side at Dehra Dun and were playing a two-day match early in February against the Roshanara Club in Delhi. We outplayed them, batted and fielded beautifully, and made a good impression. I sat for some time with the Nawab of Pataudi, who had just returned from captaining the 1946 Indian side on its tour of England. He was thrilled with the aptitude and attitude of our players. "You ought to get them to England," he advised. "It would do much for India, and for the IMA." Greatly daring, I repeated this remark to the Auk, with whom I was staying, and found him receptive and enthusiastic. I was told to go back to Dehra Dun and come back in a fortnight's time with a possible fixture list and an outline of what such a tour might cost.

Fixtures were not hard to plan. The Indian Gymkhana at Osterley was an obvious starting point; the Auk, a Governor of Wellington College, fixed us a game there. RMA Sandhurst embraced the project enthusiastically. Watford Grammar School had a former IMA Instructor on their staff, while Edwin Calvert, from 6 Armoured Division, was now back in charge of the cricket at Cheltenham. I arranged a game in Nottingham with the City Police; the Chief Constable, Captain Popkess, was a cricket fanatic and his team included four or five former Nottinghamshire professionals. The Royal Navy agreed to play us at Portsmouth and we arranged with Bournemouth for us to play the local club on the county ground at Dean Park. MCC were supportive; I had earlier qualified as a playing member and Harry Altham, Treasurer of MCC and highly influential, helped us greatly. We would be allowed to practice in the nets at Lords and the club would give us an official lunch in the Tavern. My mother, fortuitously, was running a YMCA hostel in the Cromwell Road; we could be accommodated there and the hostel would be our Headquarters for the tour. The Auk had promised us free travel to and fro by troopship, with an air passage for me to make arrangements the other end. I estimated the cost of the expedition, 16 players, two officers besides myself, John Dalvi and Dick Graveston, at about £20,800 (1946 prices) or ¼ million rupees, provided the players themselves paid a contribution towards the trip. It was not an insuperable financial target, given the generosity of people in India, and we achieved it with surprising speed. By mid-March we were in business, with just the training and ability of our players to worry about. Would they adapt to English conditions? Would the food be a problem? How could we keep them fit on the troopship? Gradually answers emerged and we became confident of our ability to do ourselves justice in England.

Such concentration on cricket, while the key negotiations for Indian independence were in train, may now appear misplaced. At the time, however, we had no idea of the speed of events in Delhi, and, in any case, there was nothing those at our level could do about the situation. There was much to be said for having an outside interest, and the generosity of those who supported and financed our tour indicated that the Indian public agreed with our priorities.

Mountbatten's success in reaching agreement owed much to the secrecy with which his negotiations were conducted. In Dehra Dun we knew that the Viceroy was in daily contact with the Indian political leaders, but there was no reason to suppose that he would make more progress than his predecessor, while the news of communal trouble in the Punjab, and especially round Rawalpindi, was not encouraging. In April Mountbatten paid a visit to the North-West Frontier Province, where only his personal courage, standing on an embankment in face of a huge and hostile demonstration, redeemed a dangerous situation. Though there was now more political talk about partition, no one seemed to consider its military consequences; certainly none of our officers at the IMA – Muslim, Hindu, or Sikh – yet thought in terms of a divided Army. Thus the announcement of Mountbatten's partition plan, and its acceptance by all the political leaders, on 2 June came as a complete surprise.

By then I was in London, putting finishing touches to plans for the cricket tour and preparing to meet the players when they arrived after their journey from Bombay to Liverpool by troopship. I got in touch with the Military department of the India Office; they knew no details at first of the plans being developed in Delhi to divide the armed forces, but soon told me that the intention was for the IMA to remain intact and continue its role of training officers for both India and Pakistan. Such a decision seemed sensible; no one foresaw the scale of communal disorder, which was to disfigure independence two months later. It briefly appeared as if the Mountbatten plan might provide a peaceful transfer of power in circumstances which would allow the two new Dominions to start their existence in relative stability.

Our IMA tourists showed great maturity. They were constantly in public view, leaving by bus from their Cromwell Road hostel, practising at Lords, attending an official luncheon given by MCC and travelling round the country to fulfil the fixtures arranged for them. There was no bad behaviour, while their courtesy, immaculate appearance in uniform or plain clothes, and perfect manners on the field won them respect and friendship. They were admirable ambassadors for India and Pakistan, and one felt proud for them and for the IMA. They made friends easily, and Belwalkar, our leg spinner, seemed invariably to attract a pretty girl wherever we went. We travelled by bus; I hired a car and usually took three or four passengers with me, often for a detour to show them an interesting site en route. John Dalvi, an Indian Christian from Bombay, later, as a Brigadier, sadly to see his formation overrun and be captured himself during the confrontation with China in 1962, was a great support; so, too, was Dick Graveston, whose sense of humour was an asset, especially when it came to packing up in a hurry to reach the next engagement.

In our most important fixture against RMA Sandhurst we excelled ourselves, outplaying the home side, and only time stood between us and victory. Khanna with a superb innings of 149 was the star, but our bowlers, Mazumdar, an excellent seam bowler, and the spinners, Manohar and Belwalkar, supported him well. The fielding was brilliant and Mohoni led his team well from behind the stumps. In none of the other matches, where we sometimes faced strong opposition, were we disgraced, and where we lost, as against the Royal Navy by nine runs, Bournemouth by a similar margin, and the Nottingham Police, the margins were close and exciting.

The reactions of the cadets were of great interest. They were, naturally, patriotic and looked forward to freedom for their countries; equally, there was gratitude for what Britain had done in India; a sentiment often expressed charmingly to those they met. I took them to Norwood for tea while we were in Nottinghamshire; Myrtle Starkey laid on a lovely spread with strawberries and cream, as well as delicious sandwiches and cakes. She had also invited some of the younger Nottinghamshire generation, who got on well with the IMA party; they went round the farm, visited a pedigree Jersey herd and learnt from Bill Starkey about growing apples, before piling into the bus to attend a civic reception given by the Lord Mayor of Nottingham. Next day, the City Police gave us a tour of their HQ, and two of the party, in uniform, spent a morning on crime prevention in a police car. It was undoubtedly an experience for both sides wherever we went, and many of the IMA party, most recently Bhopinder Singh, now retired as a three star general from India's Central command, and Kemal Rabbani, a Pakistani two star general, have told me since they have never forgotten it.

Return to India and a visit to GHQ in Delhi proved an unpleasant return to reality. The decision to divide the Army simultaneously with the political division was a mistake, though it is hard to see a better alternative, which would not have involved grave risks. Mountbatten had only managed to secure agreement to his plan with great difficulty. It was remarkable to have persuaded Nehru and Jinnah to accept his solution and the Viceroy must have been terrified that either or both might regret their decision. Hence his insistence on the need for speed; it was rather like learning to ride a bicycle and being forced, through fear of falling off, to pedal faster and faster. One should remember, too, that Gandhi, who still retained great capacity for wrecking agreements, never accepted the principle of partition. Thus the practical military solution of dividing the armed forces before formal granting of independence probably appeared too risky a political option; a squabble in this area might have led to the collapse of the whole rickety structure of partition.

The military consequence were, however, disastrous. On Independence Day neither of the two new Dominions possessed effective armed forces under their own control; they were thus incapable of maintaining order within their own boundaries, while the main area of communal trouble, the Punjab, remained the responsibility of a special Boundary Force responsible to neither of the two Governments but instead to Field Marshal Auchinleck, whose title of Supreme Commander had no political backing. It was a recipe for tragedy; one felt deeply for the Auk, who had presided over the dissolution of the magnificent Indian Army and now attempted to control the troubles in the Punjab without either the necessary military means or a proper governmental base. No wonder he became withdrawn and bitter, as the carnage in the Punjab grew and the Boundary Force, despite the efforts of its commander, Pete Rees, became increasingly impotent.

I discovered in Delhi that the IMA was to remain intact until December; for four months, therefore, after independence we would be required to train cadets for both India and Pakistan. Meanwhile we were to divide the assets of the IMA on the basis of 70% to India and 30% to Pakistan. Such a task would have baffled Solomon, but there was no point in arguing. The British staff officers in GHQ were working conscientiously to achieve a fair division of assets, but it was already obvious that growing acrimony between India and Pakistan would make this impossible. In practice the location of equipment and installations usually proved the decisive factor, with physical possession nine-tenths of the law. In this 'gold rush' India was better placed than Pakistan; at least, Delhi provided a capital city and political base, while Pakistan had to start from scratch with an embryo government in Karachi and its Army HQ 700 miles away to the north in Rawalpindi. The scope for sabotaging a fair division was considerable, and India had all the advantages since most installations lay on their side of the inter-Dominion boundary.

After the unpleasantness of Delhi, it was a relief to get back to Dehra Dun. The Doon valley still seemed beautiful and the Academy itself peaceful and unaltered. Joe McGarity and I discussed the form our Independence Day Parade on 15 August should take; it was an occupation sufficiently normal to make one forget one's apprehension of the rocks lying ahead. The cadets were away on leave till 1 August; I was confident they would not be affected by communal feelings and that the traditional harmony of the IMA would continue.

Nevertheless we needed urgently to examine the local situation. The IMA is four to five miles from Dehra Dun itself, surrounded by tea gardens and small villages where the proportion of Muslims to non-Muslims was about 35 to 65 per cent. Inside the Academy itself the military Indian other ranks and the civilian employees were also mixed in composition. If communal trouble arose in the city we should undoubtedly face problems. The Commandant had wisely given instructions in May for the matter to be examined. It was simple, therefore, to put our preliminary precautions into operation. We increased the guards and organized a mobile column from the cadets when they returned from leave on 1 August. As I had hoped, their relations with each other were as good as ever, a situation which, happily, remained unaltered, much to their credit.

Independence Day provided a problem which, however petty, could have had repercussions if we handled it wrong. By now patriotic sentiment was running high; newspapers, local politicians and the politically conscious public vied with each other in expressions of extreme nationalism. In Hindustan such feelings centred round the national flag, the green, white and saffron tricolour with the Asoka wheel superimposed. Ceremonial flag-hoisting became a national sport and was conducted by local dignitaries whenever possible. Naturally the Indian Military Academy as a national institution would be expected to mark independence on 15 August. But which flag or flags should we hoist? After all the Academy still represented the cadets of both India and Pakistan. The obvious solution seemed to be to replace the Union Jack by both Dominion flags simultaneously, and to remove the Pakistan flag when their cadets finally departed for Pakistan. However, the local political leaders indicated that this compromise would be regarded as a final attempt to 'divide and rule'; to fly a Pakistan flag in Hindustan territory would be a mortal affront. It would, however, be equally inappropriate to fly the Indian tricolour by itself, since this would have disregarded the Pakistani element in the Academy. Finally we decided quietly to remove the Union Jack a few days before 15 August and, un-obtrusively, to replace it with an Academy regimental flag. There would be no flag-hoisting on 15 August; instead Joe McGarity organized a special advance in review order and General Salute in honour of independence. Since everyone could put their own construction on this tribute, we hoped no one would take offence; in the event the decision either satisfied or was equally unsatisfactory to all parties, for no more was heard of the problem.

It was too much to hope, however, that the Doon valley would remain for long remote from events in Delhi and the Punjab. Though Independence Day in Delhi proved peaceful, the news from the Punjab grew worse daily. In East Punjab (the Indian portion of the partitioned province) attacks on the Moslem minority had been carefully planned. It was evident that the RSS (a militant Hindu semi-Fascist organization) and the Sikhs had organized a deliberate campaign to exterminate the Muslims – a reprisal, so they maintained, for Muslim attacks on Sikhs and Hindus earlier in the year round Rawalpindi. There was some truth in this con-tention; in March I had been in Rawalpindi to take the Staff College entrance examination, and seen for myself flames coming from Sikh and Hindu properties. But the retaliation in the East Punjab was on a far larger scale and ruthlessly executed. On the Pakistan side Muslim reprisals against Hindus and Sikhs naturally followed. Soon the trouble spread to Delhi, where appalling massacres took place in which the police, and regrettably some of the Indian Army, joined. Dehra Dun followed the general rule and, a week after independence, anti-Muslim riots broke out in the city and spread to the surrounding countryside.

For the IMA the 'tactical' situation was complex. Those most likely to cause trouble were some 10,000 Hindu and Sikh refugees from the West Punjab, housed in a former prisoner of war camp 800 yards down the road from the Academy. The local Congress politicians regarded the inhabitants of the camp as victims of Pakistani persecution, but this view was an over-simplification. The camp contained military deserters, bandits, criminals and thugs of all kinds, inextricably mingled with genuine refugees. Arms varied from LMGs brought in by deserters to Sikh swords and homemade bombs. All political groups from RSS to Communists were represented, but combined in a single object, the desire to liquidate as many Muslims as possible. Tactical direction came from a so-called Refugee Welfare Committee; this group was helped in creating disorder by having access on 'refugee' matters to the local officials and politicians, besides policy direction from an underground RSS HQ in the hill station of Mussoorie, ten miles from Dehra Dun. It was a well conceived, evil plan, which took time to unravel; as usual, in such circumstances, there was at first little or no information, so the security forces, merely reacting to situations, were at first ineffective.

Why were operations against the enemy 'concentration' in the refugee camp not immediately initiated? If the camp had been raided, its occupants screened and their illegal weapons removed, there might have been no trouble in the Doon valley. Unfortunately, however, the Provincial Government felt unable to take action against the 'refugees' for fear of political repercussions; repeated requests by the Army to raid the camp were either shelved or disallowed. The local officials were either indifferent or secretly sympathized with the RSS and encouraged attacks on Muslims. Only when continued lawlessness threatened the stability of their whole country did attitudes change. At first, however, a mixture of inexperience, incompetence, disinterest and intentional sabotage prevented effective measures against disorder.

The first active trouble near the IMA occurred in Premnagar village outside the main gates. A 'commando' of 'refugees', armed with swords, clubs and the odd homemade bomb, attacked the shops of Muslims in the village, looting and setting fire to houses. Panic followed and the victims of the attack, surprised and unprepared to fight back, fled into the jungle. The Commandant immediately ordered a mixed platoon of cadets from the mobile column into the village. Order was restored by a bayonet charge and the arrest of several members of the 'commando', one of them a particularly voluble member of the Welfare Committee. Our action was, of course, in complete contravention of all pre-15 August training on internal security, but undoubtedly had an impact on the opposition.

People may wonder why we did not employ the police and forgot the doctrine of minimum force. We did in fact call upon the police to function. However, the IMA officer sent to liaise with the police found that the entire staff, led by the sub-inspector, had locked themselves into a cell of their own station. When invited to emerge, they replied that it was much safer in there and that nothing would induce them to move until law and order had been restored. In such circumstances, a correct operation, Staff College style, in aid of the civil power was impossible and more direct methods inevitable. After the conclusion of the 'police action', we sent out several fighting patrols and carrier sweeps to restore order in the neighbourhood. The patrols put out some fires and forcibly repatriated the odd member of the opposition to their base in the refugee camp, but were otherwise uneventful.

It was now obvious that hopes of avoiding communal violence in the Doon valley would be disappointed. On 9 September the Commandant decided to suspend training and to reorganise the Academy on an active service basis for impending operations. We informed Supreme HQ in Delhi; telephone conversation with them was uncertain, due to sabotage, while signals took seven to eight days. They accepted our decision and wished us luck. We had a previously arranged plan for this contingency and five companies of infantry (cadets) plus a composite company of permanent staff were quickly organized. In addition to enough motor transport to make two companies fully mobile, we had two sections of carriers as a reconnaissance outfit. This reorganization was all we could do for the moment, since the civil authorities obstinately declined to demand military assistance. The police, their morale sapped by threats from the RSS and previous maladministration, had collapsed completely, but still there was no co-ordinated emergency HQ; for the next few days troops were committed in 'penny packets' as requested by the local magistrate. His requests bore no relation to any military plan and were mainly designed to protect the property of prominent locals.

Our clearing of the village outside the Academy gates had, however, affected the 'enemy's' plans. The Welfare Committee organized a deputation to wait on the local magistrates to protest against our action in attacking a legal procession! This diplomatic offensive, supported by some leading local lawyers, managed to obtain the release of the arrested members of the Welfare Committee. It also established an undesirable precedent for the future release of those captured by the Army whenever they reached the hands of the civil authorities. Nevertheless our action forced new tactics on the RSS command. Appreciating that pogroms under the eye of the Army were dangerous, they turned their attention to the countryside, hoping to do as much damage as possible before military assistance arrived. For about four days, therefore, a series of well planned attacks took place against scattered Muslim villages. The form was identical. The attacking gang would surround the village selected for attack, fire in the air to create panic among the inhabitants, and, when the latter ran out of their houses, either mow them down with LMG or rifle fire or cut them down with their swords. After disposing of the more able bodied of the population, the attackers then closed in on the village and killed the surviving old people and children. The operation would be completed by removing available stocks of grain and setting fire to the village.

There was little we could do at first to interfere with such operations except prepare for future action and urge the civil authorities to allow us the opportunity to restore the situation. Fortunately the Provincial Government were at last becoming alarmed at the deteriorating position and found themselves under pressure from the Centre, where the Prime Minister, Nehru, was appalled by the violence and the unfavourable impression created by the carnage. At last, on 18 September, over a month after independence, the Army finally received instructions to intervene in the Doon valley.

An experienced commander, Brigadier D.A.L. Mackenzie, assumed command of the whole Dehra Dun area. He divided his zone into three sectors, maintaining a strong reserve under his own hand. The Indian Military Academy constituted Sector 'B', with our own resources augmented by two companies of 1st/5th Gurkha Rifles still under their British officers. We reorganized the Academy as a Brigade HQ with me as its Brigade Major; an efficient signals organization and intelligence section were immediately established.

Our sector was large. It comprised the Doon valley from Dehra Dun itself eastward to the River Jumna (about thirty miles). The valley is 20 miles broad, bounded on the north by the foothills of the Himalayas and on the south by the Siwaliks, a long range of comparatively low hills, rising to 3,500 feet. Apart from a metalled main road from Dehra Dun to Chakrata, communications in the valley were poor at the best of times. In September, with the monsoon at its height, tracks to the villages were only occasionally jeepable; even the metalled road would be out of action for two or three days at a time. It was hard to cope with an elusive enemy, who, at first, held the initiative.

We suffered, too, from a lack of adequate intelligence. Plenty of information was available, but was seldom accurate or up to date. There were constant rumours, and panicky stories poured in without ceasing from the police and elsewhere. Above all we required a flow of reliable information. We therefore established a network of standing patrols, each with a radio, stationing them with reliable owners and managers of tea estates. It entailed dispersion to make the system work; nevertheless we soon had a regular flow of sound information. Progressively, as enough intelligence was obtained to enable us to strike accurately, the standing patrols were withdrawn and just small wireless detachments left behind. We supplemented this information network with energetic patrolling, on foot, but also in carriers and other motor transport.

At first our operations had a 'bull in a china shop' character. We kept a reserve of one company and a section of carriers in hand to deal with un-expected situations, while the remaining forces patrolled as energetically and widely as possible. Though this involved hard and often fruitless work on the part of the troops, we convinced our opponents that lethargy had been replaced by determination and activity. We also set ambushes every day on tracks likely to be used by our opponents. Many of these, like traps laid by the police for speeding motorists, were unproductive; some were given away by the locals. We achieved one spectacular success. A Gurkha ambush captured two complete lorry loads of armed Sikhs, including an LMG, a mile from their base in the refugee camp. It was a great coup and we were delighted two days later to get a letter from the Refugee Welfare Committee, complaining of the high-handed action taken by the military against refugees going out to help their Muslim brethren till their crops!

Ten days of intensive operations confirmed what we had known all along – that the refugee camp was the main enemy base in the area. Finally there was permission to clear it. We produced such clear evidence that it would have been hard for the local politicians to refuse; moreover, by now they were starting to realize that genocide was no solution to their economic problems. The virtual disappearance of the Muslim community had seri-ously affected many undertakings. There were, for example, no butchers; the gangs, who worked on maintaining the railway, the tailors and boot-makers no longer functioned. The Provincial Premier, Pandit Pant, a high Congress figure, came to Dehra Dun and put the skids under the local political leaders. Official policy changed dramatically; from now on everyone became anxious to restore order and persuade the key Muslim minority to remain in the Doon valley. Finally we mounted our long-awaited operation (Exercise Groppi) against the refugee camp.

We employed a complete Gurkha infantry battalion, supported by a troop of tanks and numerous carriers used to block the escape routes from the camp. We planned it carefully, concealing our assembly within the IMA grounds and arriving suddenly at first light. The operation went off without a hitch and retrieved a satisfactory haul of illegal weapons and ammunition. We would certainly have got even more but for the delay in launching our assault; the delay had allowed many weapons, and their users, to go under-ground. However, the use of tanks convinced the territorial leaders that even their own politicians meant business. In fact, Operation Groppi marked the end of organized disorder in the Doon valley.

I have been critical of the equivocal attitude of the police and civilian officials towards the attempt of the RSS and the Sikh extremists to exter-minate the Muslims in the Doon valley. One should record that the attitude of the Indian officers of the Army was different. The British officers, very much in a minority by now, received complete loyalty, support and co-operation from their Indian brother officers during this difficult period.

From General Cariappa downward (he was then DCGS India and later C in C) who paid us a visit during our operations, all evinced loathing for the measures employed by the terrorists and acted resolutely to restore law and order. These officers were acting against their co-religionists and, in some cases, perhaps even their relatives; at least two IMA cadets had relations in the refugee camp. Their impartiality and lack of communal feeling deserves high praise; the cadets, too, displayed great restraint, even though some of them received news during the operations that their families had been attacked and killed by mobs of the opposite community in the holocaust raging further north in the Punjab. One day the discipline and sense of duty shown by the Armies of India and Pakistan may show the way to enduring peace between the two countries. In 1947 their attitude was about the only encouraging feature in a grim picture.

The communal trouble I have described in the Doon valley was on a small scale compared to the massacres in the Punjab. Even so, from the Doon valley alone, we found ourselves faced with the movement and protection of 100,000 refugees who now wished to move to Pakistan. It was a difficult job, since flooding in the Punjab interrupted road and rail communications for three weeks, causing great suffering and many deaths. Our job in the Doon valley was relatively simple; we had merely to organize protected convoys of refugees and deliver them safely to the troops in the Punjab responsible for their onward movement. Though much hard work and planning was involved, we had no special difficulties and only isolated incidents with which to deal. By early October, in fact, the IMA was virtually back to normal and we were starting again to think of our December passing out parade and the final partition of the Academy.

By now Groppi and the senior British officers had decided to leave India when they could obtain a passage. One could not help sympathizing with them; many had been away from home since before 1939, were exhausted and deeply distressed by what was happening in India. It was different for me, who had no emotional attachment to the country and regarded my service there as just another job. I did everything I could to get the British officers and their families away; about this time, too, I learnt that Joe McGarrity was a candidate for the job of Academy RSM at RMA Sandhurst and it was vital he should not miss the chance. Had I known then, as I discovered later, that the other front runner was Jacky Lord, I might have given different advice. Fine man though McGarrity was, he lacked Jacky Lord's special range of attainments, and clearly Sandhurst made the right decision.

On 12 October I had an early call from Supreme HQ in Delhi. I was to come at once to Delhi by car, telling no one except the Commandant that I had been sent for. They could not tell me on the telephone what it was about for reasons of security. I was to report to the Director of Military

Training, Brigadier Guy Burton, who would brief me fully. I told Groppi, packed a suitcase and Hazara Singh got the Humber ready. I needed an escort and decided to take with me two of the IMA cricketers, Azhar Sadik and Kemal Rabanni; at least we would have something to talk about on the drive. Wisely, we took some rations, and Attar Singh provided thermoses of tea and Bovril. Soon we were off, Hazara Singh driving like Jehu through Dehra Dun, over the Mohan Pass and on route to Delhi through Meerut. The first 120 miles to Meerut were uneventful; we dozed, talked about cricket, our recent tour, and the latest IMA gossip. We stopped at Meerut to get petrol and discovered that the Jumna had come down in flood and that the Meerut-Delhi road was impassable. There was no option but to drive south through Aligarh to Muttra and hope to cross the river there – a detour of 250 miles. My meeting with Guy Burton looked decidedly uncertain; I left a message with the local HQ to be telephoned to him and we drove off on our detour. It was a ghastly drive on crowded roads, and, often, a hopeless feeling that one would never get through. I tried to conceal my worry from my companions and hope I succeeded, or perhaps, by the time we reached Aligarh, we were all too tired to notice. We stopped there to give Hazara Singh a break and gulped down some tea and sandwiches. By now it was dark, the road was unknown and we had no idea if the bridge at Muttra was still intact. I felt impotent, irresponsible for not having made a better plan, and frightened.

It was daybreak as we reached Muttra; the bridge was still just intact, though there was water on the approach road and Hazara Singh had to go carefully and in low gear so as not to get water in the distributor. Once across the Jumna, I knew we were safe; it was just a steady flog north on the main road to Delhi. I went straight to the Secretariat and reported to Guy Burton, wonderfully calm as a good staff officer should be; if he had been anxious about my non-arrival, he was too nice to show it, and the news he had to give me was too important for recriminations.

Guy told me that the Pakistan Government had made representations to the Auk about the safety of their cadets at Dehra Dun. Relations between India and Pakistan were now so bad that hostilities between the two countries were quite possible; in such circumstances, Pakistan felt they could no longer leave some ten key officers and 120 cadets in Dehra Dun at the mercy of the Indian Government. They demanded their immediate return and the Auk did not feel able to deny their request. The matter was urgent and must be kept secret lest Indian extremists got to hear of the planned move and tried to interfere. Here was the plan; I was to return at once to Dehra Dun and arrange for the Pakistan element of the Academy to be at Saharanpur airstrip by 1000 hours on 17 October. At that time ten Dakotas of 31 Squadron RAF would arrive to fly the party to Lahore. I could brief Groppi when I got back and he, in turn, could inform Brigadier

Mackenzie. Otherwise no one else was to know till twelve hours before the time of the move from the Academy, by which time it would be too late for the RSS or anyone else to intervene. We could ask Brigadier Mackenzie for protection on the route to Saharanpur, using Gurkha troops only. Baggage was to be limited; everything not within the permitted allowance would follow by sea. Were there any questions? The situation was so shattering that I could not think of any, and I doubt if even Guy Burton would have known the answers. We fixed a code name between us – Operation Exodus; we were luckier than Moses in having 31 Squadron RAF in support, Guy Burton remarked, as he wished me luck. I raced back to the car park and onto the road to Dehra Dun.

This time we drove north along the Grand Trunk Road towards Panipat, turning right past Saharanpur airfield towards the Mohan Pass about 120 miles or so north of Delhi. It was longer than our normal route through Meerut, and slower too, since the flow of bullock carts on the Trunk Road was similar to that in Kim's day, with the drivers hugging the centre strip as jealously as ever. I searched for a convincing excuse for our rapid return from Delhi, knowing that Azhar Sadik and Rabbani would be quizzed remorselessly about their trip when we got back to the IMA. A half-truth helped me; the Commandant's passage home had been advanced, I said. The Auk wanted to see him before he left, and he had some evidence to give to a Reconstruction Committee. It was unconvincing, but the cadets knew me well enough to realize that I was not being devious just for the sake of it. We circled Saharanpur airfield, while I calculated how many troops we needed to cordon it off. No problem here with the cadets – I told them there would be a parachute demonstration next month and we needed to think about the arrangements. Over the Mohan Pass at last, back to the Academy, and I thought hard about what needed doing.

I first briefed Groppi about Operation Exodus and the background to it I had gleaned from Guy Burton in Delhi. It was a bombshell for him and could hardly have come at a worse time, as he and Marjorie were struggling to pack up their house. Their plan had been for Marjorie to go home at the end of October and for him to follow in December after the official division of the IMA. There was no point now, he felt, in his remaining; he considered that his duty to the Academy would be discharged with the departure of the Pakistan cadets. We drafted a signal to ensure a place for him with Marjorie on the troopship from Bombay at the end of the month, before deciding how we should handle Operation Exodus itself.

The tactical and administrative plan was simple. The IMA had more than enough transport to move the Pakistan party the 60 miles over the Mohan Pass to Saharanput. I rang John Elliott, our competent MT officer, and told him that the Commandant planned to have an MT inspection on 17 October. All available transport must be present for his inspection, which meant no outside details should be accepted. The route to Saharanpur would require to be protected; Groppi drove round to Brigadier Mackenzie and fixed a battalion of Gurkhas to picket the Mohan Pass. The usual arrangements for protecting a refugee column on its passage through Dehra Dun were easily organized; our own IMA carrier force could do the close protection of the column as far as the Mohan Pass. Once over the top the country was open and I had no worries. We would need a force to protect Saharanpur airfield and this was a good job for our own mobile column.

No problems, tactically, therefore. How, though, to break the news to the Academy, given that Operation Exodus could not be divulged further till 5 p.m. on 16 October? We planned two conferences for that evening and decided to break the news to officers and cadets simultaneously. The Commandant would hold a Commissioning/Order of Merit meeting in his office that evening at 5 p.m.; at the same time I would talk to the Under Officers and cadets in their ante-room. It was vital that no hint of Operation Exodus should leak before the deadline; we ensured that the normal Academy routine remained unaltered and that planning for future events and exercises continued. I sent a signal to Guy Burton in Supreme HQ; "Operation Exodus no problems". I hoped my optimism would not turn out to be misplaced.

Meanwhile, it was vital that life within the IMA appeared unaltered, so that no hint was given of our plan. Luckily, the competition for the Governor General's Banner (the sporting championship of the Academy, involving all the major sports) was reaching its climax. There was only the football event to complete, with the Academy Cup Final due to take place on 16 October, the afternoon before Operation Exodus. I fixed the kick off for 2.30 p.m. with Taskin-ud-Din, the cheerful Pakistani instructor in charge of football, and accepted his invitation to referee the match. Though football was not then a major Indian sport, it was making steady headway at the IMA, being a game you could play throughout the monsoon. I had been coaching the IMA side and we had become the best team in Dehra Dun; the Academy Cup Final was therefore attracting keen interest. Attar Singh kept me posted about bazaar opinion on the various teams and players. It was a splendid contest, so much so that, ten minutes from time, the scores were level at 1–1. I glanced at my watch and realized that we might be faced with the agonizing prospect of extra time. The extra thirty-five minutes which this would involve risked putting the whole timetable for Exodus in jeopardy. I have never longed so urgently for a goal; any goal, for either side, at either end. Two minutes from time, Chiman Singh, a defender, and a star of the Academy side, got the ball half-cleared from a corner on the edge of the penalty area. He steadied himself and hit a marvellous shot into the top corner of the goal. His C Company erupted, and Zorawar Singh, the company commander, was ecstatic. Somehow we got through the next two minutes; never has a referee blown a whistle with greater relief. Chiman Singh, the scorer, who preserved the Exodus timetable, later became a three star general in the Indian Army; some thirty years after his winning goal, I wrote to congratulate him on his promotion and hoped he had retained his sense of timing. I raced back home to change and was in position, on schedule, to break the news to the cadets.

Groppi described afterwards the stunned silence which greeted his announcement of Exodus to the officers. I got the same reaction from the cadets; they were shocked, uncomprehending and desperately sad. Until that moment, they had not understood the implications of partition; at the back of their minds they must have hoped that things would settle down and that relations between the Indian and Pakistan armies would be no different than those between friendly, if competitive, regiments. Such, of course, was the way it should have been, and as the Auk must have hoped it would be. For all of us, in fact, Exodus, and its implications, marked the end of something of real value and potential. Perhaps, from the Auk downwards, we had been unrealistic in thinking in terms of a unified defence of the sub-continent after independence. All the same, it was a worthwhile objective and I do not regret having nurtured and encouraged it in others. Happily, I have been able to remain neutral as between India and Pakistan all my subsequent life, and managed, too, to retain friendships in both countries. But, for the cadets, and for their Indian and Pakistani officers, the ability to dissociate themselves from events was impossible; for them the break was irreparable and their whole future uncertain.

The blow surprisingly seemed worse to the Indians, though they were remaining behind in their own country and would retain possession of the Academy. The Pakistanis were going, if not to a promised land, at least to a new country, for which their co-religionists had fought, and whose establishment represented some sort of triumph. I doubt if sophisticated Muslim officers like Attiqur Rahman thought that way; they were too intelligent, too Western-minded, not to see the politico-military dangers of a divided sub-continent. But others, like Tikka Khan, must have experienced a sense of relief; no longer would they have to compete with cleverer Hindu counterparts and could devote themselves to their profession more easily. The Hindus, by contrast, gave the impression of losing a member of their close family; perhaps rather a tiresome member, but one they recognized as such, and by whom it was something of a humiliation to be repudiated. Both parties, though, felt emotional about the sudden break up; all have told me since, at different times, about their reactions to the shock of the announcement and about the discussion which took place that night during the rush and haste of packing.

Next morning John Elliott had got the convoy well organized. The IMA system worked perfectly and soon staff cars, filled with Pakistani officers and their wives, arrived to join the cadets, emerging from their company blocks, their effects carried for them by Hindu and Sikh friends. It was a dramatic scene and I felt it too, though I am not normally emotional; "Your head rules your heart, Jim," Farhat Rahman, Attiqur Rahman's perceptive and often critical wife, had remarked to me over the dinner table not so long before. Attiqur Rahman, as the senior Pakistan officer, acted as commander of the vehicle column; with him in charge, the train or its equivalent would run to time. I told Groppi I would go ahead to Saharanpur airfield, checking the security arrangements as I went. It was a sad moment for him and he looked, suddenly, an old man. I was glad his sea passage had come through early and happy for him that he would be leaving Dehra Dun himself within a day or two.

It was a silent drive over the Mohan Pass that morning. Except for Hazara Singh, I was on my own, alone with my thoughts, save when I stopped to check timings with the Gurkha battalion protecting the Pass and to confirm the convoy would be along shortly. One's reflections do not always produce a positive response. Often they merely generate nostalgia, but this time they led me to a definite conclusion – I had done what I could at Dehra Dun and it was time to move on before inertia set in. I had arranged to go on to Delhi to report the completion of Exodus to Guy Burton in Supreme HQ. There would be a chance there to find out if anything else challenging was on the horizon. Otherwise? It would be back briefly to the regiment, and then possibly the bar, law examinations, and ordinary life.

At Saharanpur airfield, apart from the cordon of Gurkhas protecting it, I found an efficient RAF party from 31 Squadron manning the broken-down control tower and ready to organize the embarkation. I handed over the nominal rolls, typed overnight by Mr Sood, and relaxed till the convoy arrived. The aircraft were already airborne from Palam, their base outside Delhi; it was a toss up whether they would arrive before the IMA convoy. Exodus could hardly be going more smoothly and I breathed a sigh of relief – a long wait at Saharanpur, shifting from foot to foot in anxiety, had been something I feared.

In the event it was almost a dead heat, the last Dakota touching down as the first vehicle of the convoy escort arrived. John Elliott marshalled the vehicles; the cadets dismounted and fell in, with their hand baggage. The RAF coped perfectly with the officers and their wives; we detailed a baggage party from the cadets to help load the Dakota 31 Squadron had allotted us for luggage. It was all smoothly professional. I could not help feeling proud of the British side of the operation; if we were leaving India, 31 Squadron were doing so in style and I knew their performance would not be forgotten by the cadets or their officers.

It took about 20 minutes to get the aircraft loaded. I shook hands with Attiqur Rahman, Tikka Khan, Bilgrami and the others; a de Gaulle like

153

wave to the cadets as they emplaned and soon the first Dakota was airborne. Within 10 minutes Saharanpur airfield was deserted as if Exodus had never happened. John Elliott organized his vehicles to return to Dehra Dun; I congratulated him and the drivers on their move, thanked the RAF ground party and left with Hazara Singh for Delhi. I felt drained and aware of anti-climax, as Hazara Singh, dodging the bullock carts like a wing three-quarter, made his way down the Grand Trunk Road towards Delhi and Supreme HQ.

It was mid-afternoon when we fetched up in a parking space outside the Secretariat. Soon afterwards, I had reported the successful completion of Exodus to Guy Burton and listened as he rang the various top people in Supreme HQ to tell them how well our plan had worked.

While I was with Guy Burton his telephone rang. I was to see the Auk at 5 p.m., and before that, briefly, his Chief of Staff, Arthur Smith, at 4.45. "The Supreme Commander wants you to stay the night," warned Guy. "You will not want anything special. It is always just supper these days." This was typical of the Auk and the way he encouraged the young. I had stayed with him before, of course, initially thanks to Robin Ridgway, but later because Shahid Hamid, his next private secretary, had also become a friend and ally. By now Shahid, a Muslim, had left for Pakistan, where our paths were to cross frequently in the next two years. Guy Burton, sadly, left the Army when his service in India finished that December; he would have proved a marvellous commander in Malaya, had the British Army system been flexible enough to have absorbed him. His son, Michael, became a rifleman, and did national service in Malaya with The Rifle Brigade ten years later, he later became an Ambassador and a reminder of how talent often runs in a family.

The Auk was still in the house he had occupied with such distinction as C in C. But, despite his high-sounding title of Supreme Commander, his power and glory had largely evaporated. Mountbatten had given him an impossible task. I have already mentioned the disastrous expedient of the Boundary Force, given responsibility without power to maintain order in the Punjab. The task of achieving a fair division of military assets was proving equally impossible. The Indians never intended to provide Pakistan with their fair share of the military equity; their political masters had conceded the principle of Pakistan only reluctantly. Now that India was independent, they did just the minimum to implement the agreement. Supreme HQ quickly became unpopular in Delhi, with the *Hindustan Times* carrying hostile articles and sarcastic cartoons about its role and necessity. On 13 October, two months after independence, the Supreme Commander wrote officially to Mountbatten, as Chairman of the Joint Defence Council, informing him that the task of Supreme HQ was becoming impossible and proposing the liquidation of his HQ before the end of the year. It was no coincidence that the plan for Operation Exodus had originated on this same day; the Auk considered that, in the circumstances, he could no longer be responsible for the safety of the Pakistan cadets at the IMA. Previously he had opposed requests from the Pakistan Government for their earlier movement, arguing that it would be a pity unnecessarily to interfere with a key stage of their military education. Hence the Auk's personal interest in Operation Exodus, over and above the support for the IMA he had always evinced.

I told him our story and thanked him for the support we had received from his staff and 31 Squadron RAF. The Auk was relieved; so much had gone wrong with his plans for dividing the Army since 15 August, practically none of it his fault, that a success was overdue. I was glad the IMA had not let him down. "Thank you, Jim," said the Auk as I finished my tale. "And now what do you plan to do next?" Though this was typical of his interest in individuals, I had not expected the question. After all, I was in the British Army; presumably my regiment would look after me, while there was an admirable Major General, 'Bolo' Whistler, specially attached to Supreme HQ, who had the task of watching the interests of British service officers. I hesitated, before giving an incoherent answer. I would go back to my regiment, see my friends again, and afterwards consider how and whether I could get back to being a barrister. I explained that while I had been at home briefly in 1946 I had been over to Rhine Army on a flying visit; I had not liked what I saw and doubted if soldiering in Germany would suit me after the scope the IMA had provided. "I think we can do better than that," remarked the Supreme Commander. "Stay in for dinner tonight. I want you to meet Douglas Gracey. He is off to Pakistan as Chief of Staff, his MA (Military Assistant) is leaving soon. There could be a chance for you."

I was excited and any feelings of anti-climax disappeared. I had met Douglas Gracey, who had visited the IMA briefly to see what we were doing, and to judge what sort of young officers might emerge from the newly reformed Academy. I had liked him then, been impressed by the questions he asked and by his approach to military life. I knew, too, that his 20th Indian Division had been an outstanding formation in the Burma War and that he had a great professional reputation. I looked forward to meeting him again and hoped I might suit his requirements.

That evening, fortunately, went well. I had been warned the Chief might be depressed and that he was no longer easy to talk to. I did not find him so; perhaps the fact that it was a small group relaxed him. We did not discuss partition, but the older people looked back at what life in India had been like when they were young. I listened quietly, but turned the talk when I could either to the 1914–18 War, the campaign in Mesopotamia or the North-West Frontier, all subjects which interested me as a military historian. Over a glass of beer before we went to bed – early because the big men had to work next day – Douglas Gracey remarked, "I hear you are in no hurry to go home. Come up to Pindi next week to see if we can fit you in." It was a splendid offer and I accepted at once, grateful for the chance to see Pakistan Army Headquarters and examine its possibilities. I drove back to Dehra Dun more cheerful about my immediate future. For me, Operation Exodus had turned out a bonus in disguise.

Others have written at length about Auchinleck. Some knew him better than I did, or served under him in the desert in 1941–42. In India he was an inspiring Commander in Chief, whom I admired greatly and who went out of his way to help and encourage the young. I owe him much, as I hope I have explained. He was a fine man of integrity and with a great presence. People did not always find him easy; he had little small talk and could be shy and reserved. Perhaps he was not a good chooser of subordinates, and his staff often included too many owing their positions to his loyalty rather than their own ability. He was handicapped by not knowing enough talent outside the Indian Army; the British Army did not always send him its best material either to the Middle East or later to India. As a field commander, I doubt if his service in India had prepared him technically for command in the desert. He had never, for example, commanded a modern division and acquired the basic techniques which such an experience would have given. But he was a man of great courage, twice intervening in the desert at critical moments to save the situation. His decisions to remove Cunningham in November 1941 during the Crusader offensive and Ritchie in June 1942 after the fall of Tobruk were those of a brave commander, and won him the respect of his opponent Rommel. I doubt, however, if he could have fought a set piece battle at El Alamein with Montgomery's professionalism, and even the Auk's admirers must concede that Montgomery was his technical superior as an Army Commander. Equally, however, Monty could not have developed the Indian Army into the superb machine which reconquered Burma. If Monty was the better battlefield commander, Auchinleck was the greater human being; I am proud to have served under him, and grateful for his many kindnesses.

Back in Dehra Dun, it was time to say farewell to Groppi and discuss with Mahadeo Singh, his successor as Commandant, the adjustments needed to cope with the departure of the Pakistani officers and cadets. Groppi insisted on his departure being low key; the partition of the IMA had saddened him and he was in no mood for a formal ceremony. Mahadeo did not press the issue, but quietly made plain his gratitude for what Groppi had achieved. We discussed my own position; happily, there were natural successors available. We decided that the Adjutant part of my job should go to 'Smoky' Malhotra who had shown himself an outstanding company instructor. With high personal standards, he was a fine role model and I had no fears about his success in the appointment. We have remained friends since, and it was a delight to me when he was appointed Adjutant General of India in 1975, before finally retiring as a three star general in 1980. Mohan Thapan, a brilliant staff officer, inherited my mantle as personal staff officer to the Commandant; we created a new appointment for him, and as a grade one staff officer he became the IMA's official Chief of Staff. Mohan, too, had remained a friend; trenchant in his views, a perfect user of the English language, he now farms with typical efficiency in Gurgaon District about 30 miles north of Delhi. He too reached three star rank, commanding a Corps before retiring as Vice Chief of the General Staff.

My visit to Pakistan the following week proved fruitful. Douglas Gracey confirmed that my face would fit with the Pakistan authorities; I suspect that a word from the Auk and the success of Operation Exodus had helped. Rawalpindi was chaotic, with the situation in Kashmir already starting to overshadow everything else. I shall discuss this issue later, but Terence Glancy, from whom I was to take over as Douglas Gracey's personal staff officer, left me in no doubt about its implications. Terence could not have been kinder or more helpful; his father had been a distinguished Governor of the Punjab and had retired only the year before. Thus Terence had exceptional knowledge of Pakistan and I picked his brains for all I was worth before he left in mid-December to start a new career as a farmer in Kenya. Sadly, his move to Africa merely led to his exchanging one emergency for another; all too soon Terence was snatched from his farm to run the War Emergency Committee in the Rift Valley during the Mau Mau troubles. Typically, he worked himself to the bone in this capacity, and his sudden death early in the sixties was due to this. Between us, we agreed a timetable for my move to Pindi before 31 Squadron flew me back to Delhi for a final three weeks' tidying up at the IMA.

The Academy settled down quickly after Operation Exodus. With people like Thapan, Iyappa, Zorawar Singh and Malhotra at the helm, there was plenty of talent around. The difficulty was to provide junior officers to fill the gaps as platoon instructors left by the departure of the British and Pakistanis. Mohan Thapan and I put our heads together, before discussing our solution with Mahadeo. We both agreed that it was vital for the IMA to maintain the special atmosphere which had developed over the last two years. We doubted if young Indian emergency commissioned officers would grasp this necessity, or have the necessary background to do so. It followed that we needed to import a quota of outstanding cadets from the first course, who were dedicated IMA graduates, to fill the gap. No matter, in our view, that they would have only a year's commissioned service. After all, I had myself been an instructor in the Oxford University OTC six months after being commissioned from Sandhurst. It had not damaged my professional career and I hoped it had not been too bad for the OTC either. Mahadeo needed little convincing; we contacted Army HQ and in mid-November our selected group began to arrive.

Krishen Kaul, the previous year's Senior Under Officer, was an obvious choice; Ramesh Chandra came, and would help John Dalvi with the cricket. Pathania, a hockey player, and two others made up the quota. All subsequently reached at least the rank of Brigadier, and none were failures as instructors, a result which speaks well for the quality of those we selected, as well as for the IMA system which had produced them.

By the end of November, however, it was time for me to leave. Mohan Thapan pulled my leg mercilessly about my 'conversion to Islam'; as a good professional, he opposed the creation of Pakistan on the grounds of its strategic folly as much as anything else. An educated soldier, he saw the defence of the sub-continent needed to be regarded as a whole and that the two new Dominions would not enjoy a sufficiently friendly relationship to permit effective co-operation. So far events have proved him right, but, as I argued at the time, there was no real alternative. Pakistan was the child of Jinnah's determination and Nehru was right to accept the inevitable.

I had a tearful parting with Attar Singh – one could not take a Hindu servant to Pakistan – and Hazara Singh drove me for the last time over the Mohan Pass to Palam airfield. My heart was full as we drove; the IMA had been an experience I shall never forget. It was a privilege to serve alongside so many, both Indian and Pakistani, who have since made impacts on their country's history; happily, too, they have remained my friends, and our exchange of news each Christmas and New Year, reinforced by my visits to the sub-continent since 1974, have given me great pleasure. I have been back to the Academy three times; on the occasion of the fiftieth anniversary, in 1982, the Commandant asked me if I would present my portrait to the Academy. I was deeply flattered; Coralie Kinahan, briefly breaking the sequence of Northern Ireland Ministers she has so skilfully portrayed, produced a likeness of me as I may have looked at the age of 26. The IMA, happily, liked the result, and it now hangs in the library near Smoky Malhotra, my successor. To be honoured in India in this way means much to me, and I am properly grateful.

In 1947, naturally, all this would have seemed impossible. Nevertheless, I had a lump in my throat as I said goodbye to Hazara Singh, and it stayed with me till I reached Rawalpindi, where Terence Glancy and a different challenge was waiting.

Chapter Nine

PAKISTAN

It was a different world to which Terence Glancy introduced me next day after a cheerful dinner with the Graceys on the evening of my arrival. The Graceys accommodated Terence and myself in their large house; we paid a nominal sum for the 'run of our teeth', and signed a book for drinks we consumed. It was a good arrangement for a bachelor, and greatly preferable to a room at Flashman's Hotel, which was the alternative. From Douglas' point of view, he had someone close to hand, when the pressure was on, as was often the case.

I settled quickly into the routine of Army HQ. As MA (Military Assistant) to the Chief of Staff, I was at the hub of events, and Douglas Gracey was a boss who liked things done without delay. Terence Glancy explained his own routine, which so obviously worked well that I slipped into the groove he was vacating. The day began at 8 a.m. with the Chief of Staff's morning meeting, attended by the Principal Staff Officers and the Joint Financial Adviser. In November, when I arrived, these were all British, professional staff officers from the Indian Army, with the exception of the Financial Adviser, Mumtaz Mirza, whose job was difficult and unenviable. Pakistan's administrative capital was in Karachi, the commercial centre of the new country, and capital of Sind, a difficult province and with different interests to the rest of Pakistan. Poor Mirza had limited authority, since Pakistan had few funds. India was supposed to make over an agreed percentage of the old Government of India funds, which, thanks to the sterling balances accrued from the British Government during the war, were considerable. Delhi, however, dragged its feet over the financial transfer, partly because of inertia, but also as a method of putting pressure on the Pakistan Government. Mirza had an impossible task. On the one hand he was assailed daily with requests for financial approval of projects all essential to the Army's well being; on the other, his superiors Ghulam Mohamed, the

Finance Minister, and Mohamed Ali, the Secretary General, in Karachi instructed him to avoid all expenditure till they could arrange a basis for funding Pakistan. I felt for Mirza and we quickly became friends; sometimes I could ease his problems by putting requests into a better order of priority; Douglas Gracey, as Chief of Staff, was too busy and indeed dynamic to bother with such detail. He was happy for Mirza and I between us to negotiate compromises between Karachi and the hungry Principal Staff Officers at Army HQ.

It did not help that Naval and Air HQ were sited away from the Army with the embryo Ministry of Defence in Karachi. Joint planning hardly existed and there was a tendency for the Army to feel that the Pakistan Navy and Air Force got preferential treatment in financial matters because they were near the source of supply. The Defence Secretary, Iskander Mirza, did his best to referee these disputes; I soon learnt to respect his ability to get things done, even if his methods were unorthodox. Iskander was a master at playing both ends against the middle, a technique he had acquired in his career as a Political Agent in the North-West Frontier Province. Stories of his achievements there were legion, many apocryphal. A favourite tale centred round his dealing with a procession organized at Mardan in support of Khan Abdul Ghaffar Khan, the Red Shirt leader, known to the press as the 'Frontier Ghandhi'. The Red Shirts supported the Congress; the procession had great potential for trouble, since it was opposed to Jinnah's supporters in the Muslim League. The school solution would have been to ban the procession, call out the Army in aid of the civil power and suffer a week of disorder until the participants were exhausted or developed a new ploy for embarrassing the Government. Iskander Mirza played it differently; to the Red Shirts' surprise, he told them he welcomed 'such expressions of democracy'. The administration would therefore supply drinks and refreshments at an appropriate stage on the procession's route; the Red Shirt leaders gratefully accepted Iskander's offer in the spirit in which they thought it was intended. They should have known better; Iskander's refreshments were subtly laced with castor oil. Thus, when the procession reformed after their break, its progress came to a halt half a mile further on, as urgent calls of nature overcame political thinking. There was nothing the Red Shirts could do; their fellow Pathans, to whom Iskander arranged for the story to be leaked, considered the affair so funny that any Red Shirt protest would merely have made them appear ridiculous. Seven years later Iskander Mirza had retained both his resourcefulness and sense of humour; these qualities were much in demand in those chaotic early days.

At first, I needed to learn how an army was run with my mentors the British PSOs I met daily at the Chief of Staff's meeting. My job was to record their deliberations and produce minutes by 10.30 each morning, so their characteristics are relevant. Taffy Davies, Chief of the General Staff, was the most important. He had been a star of the Burma campaign, first as a Staff Officer and later as a Divisional Commander. He had a quick brain and was highly persuasive, especially on paper. His lucidity was alarming, his tolerance of fools non-existent and his capacity formidable. Sadly, service in Burma had left him a sick man; he only remained a short three months in Pakistan before being replaced by a cosier successor in Reggie Hutton. The Quartermaster General, Sam Greeves, had served in Douglas Gracey's 20th Indian Division in Burma; he had been a respected Brigade Commander, rough in manner, sometimes uncouth, but with a heart of gold beneath his brusqueness. Luckily, cricket was his second love after soldiering; he knew about the IMA tour, was a regular spectator at the Rawalpindi Club matches each Sunday and liked to talk about county cricket whenever he found a chance. As QMG he sometimes lacked polish, but never common sense; he was seldom at a loss in those early days when all materials were in short supply or non-existent. The Adjutant General, John Dalison, soon left to go back to England on retirement; he was an expert on personal services, especially pay and allowances, which led to much friction with Mirza, whose blocking technique in this field was considerable. Alan Whiteside, the Master General of the Ordnance (MGO), was more reserved; he was, however, persistent and competent, especially in developing vital ordnance factories for Pakistan.

Douglas Gracey's superior was Frank Messervy, whom Pakistan had inherited as C in C, since before partition he was GOC in C Northern Command with his HQ in Pindi. He had a reputation for gallantry as a fighting commander and first came to notice as a dashing commander of a mobile column, Gazelle Force, in the 1941 campaign to liberate Abyssinia. Subsequently he commanded 4th Indian Division and 7th Armoured Division in the Western Desert; while holding the latter command, his Headquarters was overrun by the Afrika Corps and Messervy himself captured during Rommel's May 1942 offensive. Messervy removed his badges of rank and masquerading as an elderly private soldier, escaped to rejoin Eighth Army. With the arrival of Montgomery in the desert, command opportunities for Indian Army officers disappeared; Messervy returned to India, commanded 7th Indian Division in the Arakan, and subsequently a Corps in XIVth Army's drive to Rangoon. Messervy was an Etonian, an Indian Cavalry soldier, a polo player and a traditionalist. He found it hard to accept that if one served an independent Pakistan, this entailed carrying out the policy of that country's Government, whatever one's views on its wisdom. His personality was impressive and he possessed undeniable presence; Douglas Gracey and he, however, were poles apart temperamentally, and it was no surprise when, early in January 1948, Messervy announced that he would be leaving Pakistan on retirement in a month's time. Some

Pakistanis were sad to see him go, especially the cavalry whom he knew well and who liked his approach to soldiering. But I doubt if Messervy was flexible enough to have coped with the politico-military situation resulting from the Kashmir problem, and Pakistan's military involvement in it. Before he left Frank Messervy kindly asked me to his house for a drink; by now the Pakistan Government had decided to appoint Douglas Gracey to succeed him as C in C. Messervy asked me if I intended to stay on with Douglas Gracey as his Private Secretary. Doing so would involve my being promoted, temporarily of course, to the rank of Lieutenant Colonel at the age of 26, but he (Frank) advised me not to do so. I would get involved in the complexities of the Kashmir problem and he doubted if to stay in Pakistan would further my career. I listened politely and thanked him for taking an interest in my affairs. I did not, however, take his advice and never regretted my decision; the next fifteen months were an education in politico-military life and the experience I gained was invaluable.

Independence on 15 August 1947 had allowed the States to opt for either India or Pakistan, and, after great persuasiveness by Mountbatten in the Chamber of Princes, almost all did so on realistic grounds, regardless of whether the Ruler was Hindu, Sikh or Moslem. Significant exceptions were Kashmir and Hyderabad, both of which felt themselves large and powerful enough to sign standstill agreements with India and Pakistan, hoping to retain a measure of their former status. A third, Junagadh, a small Kathiawar state of 700,000 Hindu inhabitants, but with a Moslem ruler, perversely opted for Pakistan, thus challenging the whole accession concept. The details of the Junagadh issue are unimportant; everyone recognized its absurdity and the Pakistanis did not object seriously when the Indians incorporated Junagadh into India by force. Kashmir, however, was a different matter. The Ruler's refusal to accede to either India or Pakistan before the transfer of power caused a major crisis and the affair still bedevils relations between India and Pakistan over fifty years later.

After 15 August the Muslim majority in Kashmir began rising against the Hindu ruler; by early September the position in the State was dangerously unstable. Throughout September uncertainty continued, the Kashmir government complaining that Pakistan was failing to provide supplies of essential commodities and sponsoring border raids into Kashmir in support of local risings against the Ruler. The reason for the crisis was, of course, the indecision of the Ruler, whose procrastination proved disastrous to himself and the people of his State. Finally, using the example of Junagadh as justification for their actions, the Pakistanis took the law into their own hands and connived in a large-scale invasion of Kashmir by tribesmen from the North-West Frontier Province.

I was still in India at the time of this invasion, but, in any event, I would not have known how the operation was organized, or who decided to launch it. Certainly no one at Army HQ was consulted; Terence Glancy told me that neither Frank Messervy nor Douglas Gracey had any inkling of what was intended, nor can I believe that the Governor of the North-West Frontier Province, Sir George Cunningham, was given previous warning. Rumour maintained that the operation developed politically through the Muslim League and that military planning was the responsibility of former Muslim officers in the INA (Indian National Army) who had settled in Pakistan. The INA had been formed under Japanese auspices from Indian Army Officers and soldiers captured in Malaya who surrendered at Singapore. The Japs never trusted the INA and allotted them a minor role when they launched their invasion of India in 1944; the INA performed ingloriously, most of them surrendering to the British/Indian forces at the earliest opportunity. Later in 1945 the Congress and Muslim League, for political reasons, attempted to build the INA up as heroes; their efforts never achieved great success with the Indian public, and once the political leaders, Nehru and Liaquat, became Prime Ministers of independent countries, were discontinued. Regular officers, whether Indian or Pakistani, had no time for those who had joined the INA; they held them in contempt as traitors and strongly opposed any idea that former INA officers should be allowed to rejoin the Army.

Whoever organized the invasion of the tribesmen, it proved a disaster for Pakistan. The tribesmen were undisciplined and interested only in looting. The proper military objective for anyone attempting to invade Kashmir from Pakistan was the airfield at the capital, Srinagar. With the airfield in the hands of the invaders, no outside help could have arrived in time to save the Vale of Kashmir from being occupied and its Moslem community left free to opt for Pakistan. Instead the raiders delayed on the route, pausing at Baramula to sack a nunnery, while their numbers diminished as pillaging individuals went home to the tribal areas with their booty.

The invasion of the tribesmen finally forced the dithering Maharaja off his fence of indecision and on 24 October he signed a letter of accession to India. The Government of India accepted Kashmir's accession and the Ruler left Srinagar, accompanied by his family. Next day an Indian infantry battalion was flown to Srinagar and, advancing to Uri, managed to hold the tribesmen there, though they suffered considerable casualties, including the loss of their Commanding Officer. Secure in the possession of Srinagar airfield, the Indians built up their forces in Kashmir, while the tribesmen, incapable of matching the regular troops of the Indian Army in positional warfare, began to disintegrate and return home.

Jinnah, whose involvement in launching the tribal invasion remains unknown, now faced a dilemma. As Governor General of Pakistan, he could not afford to see Kashmir, even if it had legally acceded to India, simply occupied by the Indian Army. Opinion inside Pakistan would never accept the subjugation of their fellow Muslims without an attempt to help them. Such an outcome would create a resurgence of communal violence within Pakistan, quickly spreading across the border to affect the vulnerable Muslim community in India. Furthermore the Muslim area of Kashmir, with Poonch as its centre, contained the headwaters of the rivers running into the West Punjab, Pakistan's main agricultural province, dependent on irrigation for its prosperity. Jinnah therefore gave orders to his Defence Ministry for regular Pakistan troops to move into Kashmir. The order reached Douglas Gracey on 26 October in Rawalpindi, where he was acting Commander in Chief in the temporary absence of Frank Messervy in the UK. Gracey, aware of the implications of Jinnah's order, replied that he could not issue any such instructions without the approval of Auchinleck, the Supreme Commander. He then contacted the Auk in Delhi, persuading him to fly to Lahore, where Jinnah was staying with Mudie, the Punjab Governor. Auchinleck arrived in Lahore on the morning of 27 October; he told Jinnah that to send Pakistan troops into Kashmir, now that the state had acceded to India, would constitute an act of aggression. In such circumstances, he, the Supreme Commander, would order the immediate withdrawal of the British officers serving with the Pakistan Army. Since such action would have made it impossible to re-form and reorganize the Pakistan Army, which depended to a far greater extent than the Indian Army on retaining the services of British officers, Jinnah reluctantly accepted the Supreme Commander's decision and cancelled his order.

Nevertheless Pakistan still needed to defend the Muslim areas of Kashmir. A fiction arose by which this territory became the responsibility of a local militia, known as the Azad (Free) Kashmir Forces, commanded by a regular Pakistani officer, who used the 'nom de guerre' of General Tariq. Elements of the Pakistan Army found a clandestine way into the Azad Kashmir Forces in sufficient numbers to stabilize the military situation. British officers were strictly prohibited from taking part and were not permitted to enter Kashmir. Messervy and Gracey were both aware of the reinforcement of the Azad Kashmir Forces by the regular Pakistan Army; neither, however, gave instructions or advice to General Tariq, who dealt directly with Iskander Mirza, the Defence Secretary, and through him with Liaquat Ali Khan, the Prime Minister and Minister of Defence.

Though this clandestine involvement of the Pakistan Army in Kashmir was unsatisfactory, in practice it worked quite well. Much credit for avoiding a major conflagration over Kashmir must go to the two Prime Ministers, Nehru and Liaquat, who remained determined to avoid full-scale war between Indian and Pakistan. It helped too that on 22 December, the Indian Government, accepting a suggestion made by Mountbatten, decided to appeal to the United Nations Organization. The Indian complaint, accusing Pakistan of having organized the original aggression by the raiders, and of continuing to support them, induced restraint on both sides within Kashmir itself. Furthermore the Indian commander in Kashmir, Kalwant Singh, finding his superiority in man and weapon power offset by the weather and the terrain, wisely pursued a policy of limited further involvement. From our point of view in Pindi, India's referral of the problem to the UN meant that there was now less danger of full-scale war between India and Pakistan. Army HQ involvement in the defence of the key areas of Kashmir thus became more overt, with Sher Khan, the able Director of Military Operations, giving clearer direction to the Azad Kashmir Forces.

Messervy was not prepared to soldier on in this equivocal situation. Douglas Gracey, more pragmatic, if sometimes politically naïve, had fewer reservations; he developed a compromise by which resources were given to General Tariq to maintain a defensive role in Kasahmir. Gracey retained overall control of the Army, and, importantly, the task of defending Pakistan should India attack West Punjab. Though there was still a British Commander in Chief in Delhi until the end of 1948, Roy Bucher's operational responsibility was less than Gracey's in Pakistan. In India, unlike Pakistan, there were enough senior officers able to function without British support. Pakistan therefore had to reckon with the possibility of a surprise attack by India, though this was unlikely while Mountbatten remained as Governor General.

Douglas Gracey was fortunate to have as Deputy Chief of Staff Bill Cawthorn, formerly Director of Military Intelligence in undivided India. Cawthorn was an Australian, a brilliant staff officer with a flexible mind. He worked in Karachi, where he provided professional advice to Iskander Mirza and Liaquat, obtained their instructions and passed these to us in Rawalpindi. As I have indicated, my boss, Douglas Gracey, disliked politics and wanted to get on with his main interest, training the Pakistan Army for war. Thus, the job of dealing with Bill Cawthorn devolved considerably on me, inexperienced as I was. Ross McCay, Gracey's successor as Chief of Staff, another Australian officer from the Indian Army, kept himself remote from politics. He had a full-time task wrestling with the administrative complexities facing Pakistan Army and had no time for politico-military complications. Bill Cawthorn was a fine teacher, assuming always that one was more intelligent than I often appeared. I am grateful for what he taught me and also for the way he relied on me to keep Douglas Gracey briefed about Karachi affairs. This was not always easy, though I found my boss a good listener on our car journeys; he was a quick reader, too, and not too fussy about letters drafted for his signature, provided these were explicit and unambiguous.

The assassination of Gandhi on 30 January gave us a period of acute anxiety. I remember hearing the radio news and recall our intense relief when we heard that the assassin was a Hindu, not a Muslim. Gracey was at his best in such situations and seldom over-reacted. "Never take counsel of your fears," he used to say, an expression he had acquired from Bill Slim, and his calmness then, and in other crises, was exemplary.

Nevertheless Douglas Gracey found the last few days before Messervy's departure a strain. Their temperaments were alien, Messervy's phlegm contrasting sharply with Gracey's dynamism. Messervy liked to delay decisions and present procrastination as wisdom. Gracey's philosophy, by contrast, was one of instant, almost instinctive, decision. He maintained that a brilliant operator would do well to get 50% of decisions correct; in the case of 30% the decision probably mattered little. The 20% of wrong judgements would, with luck, fall into the correct category next time; meanwhile the worst one had done was to create a new situation!

Messervy's establishment and style were more British than Gracey wished his to be. The Private Secretary, PS(C), had been John Wainwright, like Terence Glancy a 19th Lancer. Wainwright had a quick mind and much charm; unlike Terence, however, he lacked 'gravitas', and the Pakistanis found him hard to pin down. The senior ADC, Hew Hamilton Dalrymple, a Grenadier, made up for John Wainwright's levity by combining regimental 'gravitas' with his excellent manners. Together they formed a strong team and would be hard to follow.

We combined the Chief of Staff's Secretariat with that of the Commander in Chief into a single unit, headed by me as PS(C). Below me, Major Inayat Khan, a sound staff officer, worked directly to Ross McCay, the Chief of Staff. As the second staff officer in our Secretariat, we acquired Dick Learmonth, who had worked in Delhi under Robin Ridgway for the Auk. Dick had been a tower of strength there and proved as good in Pakistan. He specialized in tour programmes and relations with the Air Force about our Dakota; there was then only one VIP aircraft available in Pakistan, and much forethought was needed over itineraries. Douglas Gracey at once accepted my idea that we should have two Pakistani ADCs; I had known them at the IMA, where they had been Under Officers on the first course. They were both cavalry officers, but different in character and outlook, Wajahat Husain, delightful, courteous and well educated, came from Aligarh in the United Provinces. His parents were well known to Liaquat, the Prime Minister, whose provincial origins were similar. In the circumstances of the new Pakistan, this link proved helpful, and Wajahat often, always tactfully, provided useful input to our deliberations. Wajahat was a fine horseman; he had won the equitation prize at the IMA and became a good polo player. Wajahat had a distinguished subsequent career, leading to command of his regiment, an armoured brigade and a division; he was Commandant of the Staff College in Quetta at the time of General

Zia ul Haq's coup against President Bhutto in 1974. Wajahat's background made him, in Zia's opinion, unsuited for high military command in his dictatorship. Instead, because of Wajahat's own qualities, and also – a nice touch – because they had been brother officers in the Guides Cavalry, Zia transferred him to the Foreign Service. Wajahat became Ambassador in Athens, where my wife, Jean, and I gave him lunch on one of our business tours, and subsequently in Australia, where he achieved great success and was a fine representative of his country. Happily Wajahat has kept in touch, and Jean and I always enjoy entertaining him and his wife whenever they come to England.

Bashir Babar, the other ADC, from Probyn's Horse, was a Pathan from a 'country gentleman' style family near Nowshera in the North-West Frontier Province. Like Wajahat, he was beautifully turned out and with impeccable manners. Though also intelligent, he was more extrovert than Wajahat, and Douglas Gracey found him admirable company; Bashir had a great sense of the ridiculous and regaled us with the latest gossip from within the HQ, and our various tours. Bashir was also a fine games player, with tennis his speciality. Most evenings, after work, he and I engaged in closely matched contests, usually over three sets, though sometimes darkness intervened to prevent a decision. Bashir, too, had an excellent later career; tragically, it was cut short by his death in a helicopter accident, while he was acting as Chief of Staff of a division at an unusually early age. Otherwise he would surely have risen higher and been a challenger for posts at the very top of the Pakistan Army. Like Wajahat, Bashir Babar was someone of high quality. I was lucky in serving with them both.

Douglas Gracey liked to start work early, but refused to sit in the office waiting for paper to arrive. He disliked drafting and reading files. He liked simple papers, on not more than a page and a half of foolscap, with a conclusion which he could either accept or reject. We developed a technique which suited him and allowed him to get the maximum done in the office in the shortest possible time. He was not a great man for seeing his staff, preferring to get the bad news (in my experience staff officers seldom come to you with good) processed through Ross McCay, the Chief of Staff. We always had some paper available for Douglas to work on as soon as he reached the office. While he devoured this first instalment, I would tackle the overnight quota of paper with Miss Hassan, our rapid steno-typist, reducing files and papers to the form which Douglas Gracey liked. By 9 o'clock there was a quota of new documents for Gracey to master, and a brief breathing space while he did so. By then, too, Dick Learmonth would have worked out the interviews for the day, fixed to start at 9.30, while Miss Hassan and I were at work turning the earlier notes into letters or official memoranda for Gracey to sign before he left the office. By 10.30 there was often a second lull and, leaving an indication of my whereabouts with the

ADC on duty, I would walk round the HQ, discover what was cooking, have a word with my friends, and aim to warn the boss or Ross McCay about any special difficulty. I varied the circuit, but Sher Khan, Director of Military Operations, was always a port of call; so, too, was Sam Greeves who had a nose for trouble and much ability in heading it off. Raza, the Adjutant General, who had relieved John Dalison, had a specially difficult job. Unlike other Pakistani senior officers, he was short of operational experience and, for this reason, Douglas Gracey often underrated him. But Raza had high principles, was determined to get the discipline of the new Army correct and took special interest in the selection and training of the next generation of officers. My IMA experience was a help here and I sometimes found myself involved in liaison between Raza and the largely British military training staff. A new Academy with a British Commandant was starting at Kakul, and, with its nucleus of former IMA instructors like Attiqur Rahman, Tikka Khan and Bilgrami, was soon on the right lines. Raza was not always popular with other Pakistanis, who considered him pedantic; I respected him, however, and was not surprised when, as Ambassador of Pakistan in China for over ten years, he later played a major role in developing a special relationship between Peking and Islamabad; the Karakoram Highway linking Pakistan directly with China owes much to Raza's patient diplomacy.

Douglas Gracey was, by temperament, an outside General and liked to be away from Rawalpindi on tour as much as possible. These tours were fascinating and I needed no encouragement to set them up. It was stimulating to see a new Army taking shape and, the defensive battle in Kashmir apart, there was an operational plan to make for the defence of the West Punjab. Douglas Gracey quickly managed to get it appreciated that Pakistan had no hope of emerging victorious from a war with India. The latter's resources were much greater; the only hope of success would be if India attacked first, became unbalanced trying to capture the huge city of Lahore, and so vulnerable to a well timed counter-attack. All here depended on correct positioning of Pakistan's only armoured brigade and the timing of its move by rail over the Jhelum Bridge before deploying into the Punjab plain. In 1948 Pakistan had no Corps HQ; Gracey planned to direct operations himself, much as Auchinleck had done with Eighth Army in the desert in 1942 after the departure of Ritchie. It might just have worked, but only if the Indians had made major mistakes, and I am glad our plan remained a concept and was never implemented.

Our military tours therefore fell into two different categories, those to the field force involved in the Punjab battle plan, the remainder to units and establishments training for the future. The key operational formation, 7th Division, to which the main counter-attack role would fall, was stationed round Rawalpindi. It was commanded until 1949 by a British general,

Loftus-Tottenham, a 2nd Gurkha; solid and sensible, Loftus reminded me of Evelegh, my previous commander in Italy. His common sense gave everyone confidence, while his deliberate tactical approach well complemented Gracey's fiery temperament.

The defence of Lahore fell to 10th Division, commanded by the outstanding Pakistani general of his generation, Iftikhar Khan. 'Ifty' was an excellent commander, with a personality matching his military attainments. Tough, sensible and versed in regimental soldiering, he quickly built up morale in his formation; he also understood the need for the Army to keep out of politics. It was a disaster for Pakistan when 'Ifty', shortly after he had been selected in 1950 as the first Pakistani C in C, was killed in an air crash together with Sher Khan, by then promoted Major General. The loss of these two brilliant officers affected the whole course of Pakistan's history. I doubt if Iftikhar would ever have entertained the possibility of a military takeover. He was a big enough man to have imposed such a philosophy on the Army and it is Pakistan's misfortune that he was denied the opportunity.

Iftikhar retained a British GSO 1 (Chief Staff Officer) to help his division train on sound lines. He was lucky to have Derek Milman, formerly in charge of tactical training at the IMA. Derek, later to transfer to the British Army and command, successfully, the Bedfordshire and Hertfordshire Regiment, was a high grade staff officer with solid wartime experience in both the Middle East and Burma. He formed a great partnership with his Divisional Commander and 10th Division was the formation to which we most enjoyed a visit. Ifty also had good Brigade Commanders; Musa, the commander in Sialkot, admirably practical, later became C in C Pakistan, while Sher Ali, brother of the Nawab of Pataudi, who commanded 14th Parachute Brigade located on an airstrip 30 miles north of Lahore, was a character with views of his own, which he was never backward in expressing. As a soldier, Sher Ali reached the position of Chief of the General Staff before falling out with Ayub Khan, at that time C in C. Subsequently Sher served with distinction as a diplomat, representing his country in Malaysia and Jugoslavia. Afterwards he was a Minister in the Central Government of Pakistan, has written several books and even spent a period in detention at the hands of one of the Pakistan regimes because of his hostility to its policies. Sher had known my wife, Jean, well when he was a junior officer in the early years of the war; we have remained friends and Sher's conversation and views on life are still stimulating.

Quetta was an important military centre, housing the Staff College and a number of other training establishments. Here the general was Akbar Khan, a sound, steady, person, whose lack of operational experience – he had been in the Royal Indian Army Service Corps (RIASC) – made him suspect in the eyes of more thrusting Pakistanis like Sher Ali. But Akbar was a good administrator, with much common sense; he did an excellent job in Quetta and watched carefully over the interests of many British officers attending the Staff College, both as instructors and later as students. Ian Lauder, an admirable professional, quickly got the Staff College well organized and it still prospers. Visits to Quetta were always relaxing; Douglas Gracey had served at the Staff College as an instructor and enjoyed returning, whether to lecture or discuss the instruction. Since I hoped soon to go to the Staff College myself, having managed to pass the Entrance Examination while I was still at Dehra Dun, I studied the Quetta form carefully and found the knowledge useful at Camberley later.

Our most regular destination was, however, Karachi. We went there for meetings of the Defence Council, the Commander in Chiefs' Committee, and also routine visits to Liaquat, the Defence Minister, and Iskander Mirza, his Permanent Secretary. I liked the bluff Admiral, Jefford, who was determined to keep the small Pakistan Navy efficient and was against over-hasty expansion which might prejudice its standards. He wasted little energy in watching what the Indians were doing; he stressed the need for Pakistan to turn its face westward and aim to be a significant force in the Gulf area. Thirty-five years later President Zia enunciated a similar philosophy to me, so doubtless Jefford's vision was right. In 1948, however, the Pakistan Navy had a difficult task in trying to maintain sea communication between East and West Pakistan. It was an aim hard to achieve in the face of a hostile India. Thus Jefford's influence on relations between Pakistan and India was for the good; he inclined to moderation and often proved a restraining influence on more hotheaded advocates of an anti-Indian policy.

If the Pakistan Navy had a difficult task, that facing its Air Force was even more daunting. The first Air Commander, Perry-Keene, was an admirable administrator, and as a former AOA (Air Officer in charge of administration) India had been selected to oversee the question of getting Pakistan's share of air equipment fairly transferred. It soon became obvious that, in the climate of the Kashmir dispute, a fair division of stores would not happen. Perry-Keene therefore left after nine months and was replaced by the very different Atcherley. The latter was one of a pair of twin brothers, both famous in the RAF for their skill as pilots, for their operational record and for the various escapades into which their adventurous natures had led them. The fledgling Pakistan Air Force could not have had a better leader at this stage of its development; morale soared, new types of aircraft came into service, while problems, previously thought insuperable, now became merely obstacles to be overcome. Like attracts like; Atcherley's presence meant that a number of other high-grade airmen came to Pakistan; the most distinguished was Sam Elworthy, then a Group Captain, later to become a Marshal of the Royal Air Force and Chief of the Defence Staff.

Since Douglas Gracey was a four star general and the Pakistan Army the largest of the three services, he was the natural choice to be Chairman of the Commander in Chiefs' Committee. This was fortunate for me as I became its Secretary, a sphere where one had to learn quickly. I remain grateful for the tolerance given me by the other two services and for the generous way in which they brought me into their affairs. Sometimes, too, when Iskander Mirza found himself short of a civil servant to act as Secretary of the Defence Committee of the Cabinet, which Douglas Gracey regularly attended, I was pressed into service in this capacity also. This might have been alarming, but Liaquat, as Chairman, was invariably kind and courteous and I did not find it so.

Our visits to Karachi, where accommodation was limited, presented problems which Wajahat and Bashir invariably managed to solve, often, however, at the last moment. Douglas Gracey was good humoured about the various expedients to which we found ourselves forced; nevertheless he was frequently less comfortable than he deserved to be and understandably disliked trips to the capital, especially since they often came at short notice. It was different for me; I found the atmosphere of Karachi exciting, was flattered at being entertained by members of the diplomatic community and stimulated by the wider horizons of the work itself.

Perhaps our most significant tour was to East Pakistan, which now forms the separate state of Bangladesh. In 1948, however, inspired by Jinnah's achievement in realizing Pakistan, the East Bengalis visualized their future as equal partners with West Pakistan in a federal structure. One can see now that this concept was unrealistic. The population of East Pakistan was already in 1948 equal to that of the West, and the Bengali birth rate much higher. Thus any form of democracy would have given East Pakistan increasing dominance – a situation the West Pakistanis could not accept.

At this time Punjabis, especially, held Bengalis, if not in contempt, at least in some disrespect. After all, they, the Punjabis, were a 'martial race', the Punjabi Mussulmans traditionally forming the hard core of the Indian Army. Their main city, Lahore was a great social and cultural centre, with a University and a magnificent Mosque, a wonder of the Moslem world. By contrast, the capital of East Pakistan, Dacca, seemed to them provincial, and its inhabitants unruly, argumentative and undisciplined. There was, in fact, too little in common between the two wings of Pakistan for Jinnah's concept of a united state to develop harmoniously, and the flimsy structure was bound to collapse.

In 1948, however, such thoughts lay in the future. The British Governor of East Pakistan, Sir Frederick Bourne, was an example of the old ICS at its best; he kept a close eye on the administration and maintained good relations with the locals, while the leading politician, Kwaja Nazimuddin, subsequently Governor General of Pakistan, advocated union with the

West. Nazimuddin was a delightful man; a Cambridge graduate, his rotund appearance concealed many other skills. He was one of the best shots in the country, especially where duck were concerned; in earlier life, Bashir Babar told us, he had been a tennis player of distinction.

Iskander Mirza and Douglas Gracey thought hard about the Pakistani general to command in East Pakistan. They chose Ayub Khan, despite his modest operational record comparing unfavourably with his contemporaries and even some of his juniors. Ayub, however, was a good administrator; he had also shown signs of political ability, first as the senior Muslim officer involved in personnel selection before partition, and afterwards as the Pakistani Military Adviser with Peter Rees' ill-fated Boundary Force. Ayub had a good appearance and presence; I had first met him when he visited the IMA before partition to satisfy Moslem politicians that a Sikh Defence Minister, Baldev Singh, did not discriminate at Dehra Dun against Muslim cadets. I remembered Ayub's courtesy and embarrassment at being given such a ridiculous task, and he was easily reassured. He proved outstanding in East Pakistan; in his time there were few operational problems since Bourne, the Governor, ensured good relations were maintained with the Indians in West Bengal. Ayub concentrated on creating an East Pakistan element of the Pakistan Army. He won the goodwill of the Bengalis, so that, when Iftikhar' sudden death in 1950 removed the chosen successor to Gracey as C in C, Ayub was the only real alternative. As a soldier, Ayub had high standards and demanded them from others. I never saw him in action as a politician and cannot therefore judge his ability in that field or comment on his decision in 1956 to replace the political leadership of Pakistan by military rule.

The Joint Defence Council meetings in Delhi also took up much of our time, even if the encounters were unproductive. The Joint Defence Council stemmed from the original partition agreement; its principal task was to supervise the division of the armed forces between India and Pakistan, including the sharing of military assets. In this capacity, the Joint Defence Council, under the chairmanship of Mountbatten, was responsible to both Governments. When Mountbatten originally established the Joint Defence Council he hoped it might evolve into an Indo-Pakistan Defence Community, providing for the joint defence of the sub-continent. The Kashmir dispute, however, put paid to this concept, and the role of the Joint Defence Council soon degenerated into machinery for the distribution of military assets. Here, from Pakistan's standpoint, the influence of Kashmir proved malign; understandably, the Indians were reluctant to release assets which might be used against their own soldiers in Kashmir. The more overt Pakistan's involvement in Kashmir the greater became Indian determination not to transfer anything significant. By April 1948 Liaquat had resigned himself to the fact that Pakistan would get nothing more from India. He and Iskander Mirza found other more reliable means of re-equipping the Pakistan armed forces; the financial situation, acute in Pakistan's early days, was starting to ease slightly, as West Pakistan's agricultural strength boosted the economy. The April 1948 meeting of the Joint Defence Council was, therefore, the last formal encounter under the Council's original terms of reference; wisely, however, the two Defence Ministers responded to Mountbatten's suggestion that they should continue to meet periodically to discuss matters of joint concern. The continued existence of such joint understanding was important; it allowed informal links between the Indian and Pakistan armed forces to continue, and these arrangements proved ultimately vital in achieving a ceasefire in Kashmir.

Liaquat, Douglas Gracey, and I stayed with the Mountbattens on our April visit to Delhi for the Joint Defence Council meeting. I had never previously advanced beyond the ADC's room in the Viceroy's house; in the Wavell days there were kindred spirits around and it was a good port of call for tea and gossip. But the idea of staying there would have been well above my station. I had therefore been looking forward to our visit to Delhi and enjoyed our night in the Governor General's House. The Mountbatten organization was formidable; before every dinner party, the ADC's Room provided a card for the Governor General on each of the guests, giving his background and interests. Mountbatten could absorb this information while changing for dinner, and bring it out during the course of the evening. On this occasion, I helped the ADCs write the cards for our Pakistan party; it was fascinating later to see this input professionally employed.

The Secretary of the Joint Defence Council was Vernon Erskine-Crum, a Lieutenant Colonel in the Scots Guards, whose job on Mountbatten's staff was Conference Secretary. I had not met Vernon before; like me, he had been at Oxford, where he had rowed in the University boat race, he was four years my military senior and our paths had not crossed. Vernon was impressive; I envied the speed and accuracy with which he produced reports of meetings and discussions. I decided to copy his technique and profited considerably from his example. Vernon himself had a distinguished career and was a young Lieutenant General when selected in 1971 to succeed Ian Freeland as GOC Northern Ireland. Tragically Vernon suffered a fatal heart attack soon after his arrival; his death was a sad loss to the Army. He would have been good in Northern Ireland, and subsequently even higher posts would surely have come his way.

Despite Mountbatten's undoubted charm, neither Liaquat nor Douglas Gracey liked the Governor General. Liaquat had warned us beforehand that, in his opinion, Mountbatten had been 'brainwashed' by Nehru and the Congress, and that the Kashmir issue had finally turned him against Pakistan. Though Mountbatten might profess to be impartial, Liaquat had no confidence in his good offices and considered he should not have remained on, after independence, as Governor General of India. His role, even as a constitutional Governor General, made impartiality impossible, while Mountbatten's continued presence and influence with HMG operated to Pakistan's disadvantage. Liaquat conceded that Mountbatten had originally offered to act after independence as a constitutional Governor General for both the new states; in his view, however, this offer had been unrealistic, since Pakistan required its top honour and appointment for Jinnah, whose health prevented him becoming Prime Minister. Liaquat also blamed Mountbatten for his failure to force the Ruler of Kashmir to decide about accession before 15 August 1947; at that time Kashmir would doubtless have acceded quietly to Pakistan, a decision which Patel, the most communally minded of the Congress leaders, would then have accepted. Liaquat also criticized Mountbatten for accepting Kashmir's accession to India in October 1947. Here Liaquat was on less good ground; Pakistan's folly in permitting the tribal invasion had provoked a situation in which only Indian troops could have prevented the sack of Srinagar, and accession by Kashmir to India was the only way they could be deployed.

Gracey, too, had little time for Mountbatten. Their relationship had soured in September 1945, when Gracey's 20th Indian Division, in the wake of the Japanese surrender, had been given the task of sorting out the tangled situation in Indo-China. Since I have heard only Gracey's side of the story, later confirmed by French sources, it would be wrong of me to offer judgement. Gracey, however, felt that, faced with chaos in Saigon, he had acted quickly and pragmatically, and made it possible for the French, under General Leclerc, to return and attempt to re-establish their position. Gracey and Leclerc had remained friends; both felt that Mountbatten's attitude had been equivocal, and that they had not been given the moral support they deserved by their Supremo. Where Kashmir was concerned, Gracey considered that Mountbatten used his influence unfairly with HMG to put pressure on British officers serving with Pakistan. Here Douglas was on good ground; nevertheless, the influence of the High Commissioner in Karachi, Laurence Grafftey-Smith, coupled with the visits to Pindi of Defence Adviser, Johnnie Walker, a shrewd product of the King's Own Yorkshire Light Infantry, considerably mitigated this factor.

I thus enjoyed our stay with the Mountbattens more than either Douglas or Liaquat, though at dinner I recall the latter delicately pulling our host's leg. "I have a problem, Your Excellency, where I believe your special talents can really help Pakistan," began Liaquat disingenuously. At once Mountbatten was all attention. "We simply cannot come up with a proper national anthem," continued Liaquat. "Perhaps Your Excellency's experience of ceremonial could solve our dilemma." Mountbatten was full of expedients; he would involve the whole machinery of British military music in the act, musical directors of the Royal Marines and the Brigade of Guards would give the matter their immediate attention, no ceremonial stone would remain unturned. Liaquat thanked him kindly without batting an eyelid; I hope no one outside the Pakistan party noticed his quiet wink across the table at Douglas Gracey, who was still enjoying the incident in the aircraft on our way back to Pindi next morning.

It was the first time I had met Mountbatten and I was impressed. I could understand how his technique and powers of persuasion had swept the Congress politicians off their feet in the run up to independence. Clearly he achieved less impact on Jinnah, though it was a great feat to have persuaded the Qaid-e-Azam to settle for the truncated, 'moth-eaten' as he described it, Pakistan which came into being on 15 August 1947. I doubt in fact if anyone except Mountbatten could have brought the operation off; those who criticize him for the speed with which the transfer of power was executed fail to take account of the danger of anyone of several groups 'ratting' on the fragile agreements so hardly won. Nevertheless I have never regretted not working for Mountbatten, then or later.

I was lucky, though, to see something of Lady Mountbatten, whose work on behalf of refugees had won everyone's admiration in the dark days of the previous year. About an hour before we were due to leave, I got a message to call on her in her writing room. Could I somehow get her a Jinnah hat? Clearly I should have to make my purchase with discretion and return the product to Delhi by diplomatic bag. Wajahat Husain bought me the best version he could in Lady Mountbatten's head size in the local Pindi bazaar. We sent it by bag to Delhi and Lady Mountbatten got it just before she left for England. I hope she wore it, as she told me she intended, walking down Sloane Street between Harrods and Peter Jones. Liaquat would certainly have seen the joke, though it might have been beyond the Qaid-e-Azam.

I got away on leave to the UK that summer, flying from Karachi by KLM Dutch Air Lines; it was good to be away briefly from the atmosphere of the sub-continent, and I relaxed happily in London, absorbed in the build up for my sister Priscilla's wedding at St Paul's Church Knightsbridge in July. She was to marry another rifleman, Julian Wathen, though, by then, he had abandoned the black buttons of the 60th Rifles for a career in the overseas part of Barclays Bank – Dominion, Colonial, and Overseas. It was a lovely wedding on a glorious London summer's day and proved the gateway to a very happy marriage. I am lucky to have a kindred spirit as a brother-in-law; we share many interests, enjoy each other's company and often work together to further our joint concerns.

There was little change in the Kashmir situation on my return to Pakistan. Instead, the position in Hyderabad now held centre stage. The Hyderabad situation was a mirror image of that obtaining in Kashmir, but with the communal angles almost exactly reversed. Hyderabad, the largest, richest, and most powerful of the Indian states, had a Muslim ruler, the Nizam, said then to be the richest man in the world. He was certainly one of the meanest; Lord Wavell recounts the agonies it cost the Nizam to provide champagne for dinner on the night of the Viceroy's first dinner, and his subsequent distress when all three bottles produced from the cellar were flat. Nevertheless before independence the Nizam's state was well ruled and administered; there was normally a good Prime Minister, and relations with HMG, through the Resident and the Viceroy, presented few problems. Below the Nizam there existed a Muslim upper class, prosperous, rich and sophisticated. Some followed a career in the Indian Army, and, by 1947, were starting to do well in their profession. Abid Bilgrami, an instructor at the IMA, one of those evacuated to Pakistan in Operation Exodus, was one of them; the Baig family, army officers, polo players, and in one case, Abbas Ali Baig, an international cricketer, provided further instances of the influence wielded by Muslims from Hyderabad in top Pakistani circles.

But the ruling Muslim element in Hyderabad represented just 10% of the States' population. The remainder, predominantly Hindu, had accepted their inferior position during the British 'raj'; settled conditions in Hyderabad permitted Hindu traders and businessmen to become prosperous, and the opulent middle class, despite their lack of political power, had little reason for complaint. Congress had, however, infiltrated the non-Muslim working class, and would have won an easy victory in any democratic process. Significantly, too,there was a strong left-wing element in Hyderabad; some were adherents of the Congress left-wing leader, Jai Prakash Narain, while there also existed a growing Communist party.

Altogether, therefore, Hyderabad offered great potential for agitation. Had the Nizam been decisive enough to have acceded to India before 15 August, as Mountbatten advised him to do, much trouble might have been avoided. But decision was not in the Nizam's nature; instead, like the Ruler of Kashmir, he procrastinated, using negotiators like Sir Walter Monckton to seek special terms for Hyderabad. His advisers also recommended early accession to India, but the Nizam clutched at any excuse for delay. It was political Micawberism at its worst and inevitably events developed their own momentum.

While Mountbatten remained in Delhi, the Nizam could be sure that the Governor General's influence would prevent the use of force by India to compel Hyderabad's accession. Sardar Patel, the Home Minister, was happy to bide his time. Throughout 1948 he and V.P. Menon, Permanent Secretary in the States Ministry, occupied themselves in tidying up the affairs of those States who had acceded to India before 15 August. Operating like master draughts players on a board set for their advantage, they brilliantly incorporated the various states into the Indian Union.

Every political expedient in the book was used; federations, larger group-ings, association with neighbouring provinces – all were cleverly deployed. By mid-June, when Mountbatten left, and was replaced by C.R. Rajagopalachari, Patel and Menon were ready to deal with Hyderabad.

Inside his state the Nizam had combined indecision with unwisdom amounting to folly. The normal Defence Force, about a division in size, was supplemented by gangs of Muslim auxiliaries known as Razakars. The Razakars' leader, Razvi, was the type of thug who flourishes in conditions of uncertainty; his followers were undisciplined, communal and out to oppress and threaten the majority Hindu population. The Indian press produced a series of atrocity stories, all of which increased the pressure on the Delhi Government to end Hyderabad's pretensions. The attitude of the Pakistan Government made matters worse. Understandably, they sympa-thized with the ruling Muslim party in Hyderabad; moreover, as I have indicated, there were refugees from Hyderabad inside Pakistan, who brought the situation there to public notice whenever possible. Such propa-ganda tended to misrepresent the prevailing political position and dangerously to exaggerate the chances of Hyderabad being able to offer effective resistance to an Indian invasion. Articles in *Dawn*, the leading Karachi daily, reflected the value to Pakistan's cause of having a 'Trojan horse' inside Indian territory. Such sentiments were, of course, absurd, besides offering Patel and Menon opportunity to turn the argument on its head and advocate an early invasion of Hyderabad in the overall interests of Indian security. Towards the end of the summer, Pakistan suggested a loan to Hyderabad, even offered the use of Pakistan territory as a base from which arms could be flown to the beleaguered state, blockaded by India and without communications to its landlocked territory.

In fairness, Liaquat and Iskander Mirza themselves, despite the pressures on them from press and public, remained cool and balanced. The Commander in Chiefs' Committee had early advised that there was nothing Pakistan could do to help Hyderabad militarily. Neither the Navy nor the Air Force had the resources to influence events; the Army, already stretched by Kashmir, would just about be able to defend West Punjab against an Indian attack if the Indian Command were to launch one. To invade India would be military folly and would also, as Gracey reminded his political masters, result in the immediate withdrawal of all British officers. Pakistan could only sit tight and await developments. The only crumb of comfort one could offer was to point out that, technically, an Indian invasion of Hyderabad would amount to formal aggression. If India were to be guilty of such action, their behaviour would take some heat out of accusations being brought against Pakistan for its earlier 'aggression' in Kashmir.

Nevertheless, Liaquat's ministerial colleagues continued to invite him to save Hyderabad and he was forced to refer the question once more to the

Defence Committee of the Cabinet. The Prime Minister took the chair himself, with Iskander Mirza in support; unusually, Zafrulla Khan, the Foreign Minister, who had so eloquently advocated Pakistan's cause over Kashmir in the United Nations, was also present. I felt more than usual diffidence acting as Secretary with so much talent around. As usual, the agenda and supporting papers had been prepared by Iskander's staff in Karachi. Douglas Gracey and I had just thirty minutes to read them before the meeting assembled. The Army paper was splendid, bearing the hand of Bill Cawthorn in its preparation; Douglas would have no problems in speaking to it. The Naval paper was also straightforward. Item 3, however, appeared different. "Possibility of independent air action in support of Hyderabad," it read; "Bomb Delhi?" had been added in pencil on our copies of the agenda. Plainly we were in for an unusual session.

Liaquat opened the meeting in quiet fashion. The Government, he explained were under pressure to do something to help the Muslim regime in Hyderabad; *Dawn* had an article almost daily complaining at our in-activity. Even Jinnah, the Qaid-e-Azam, was starting to express his anxiety. Though he, Liaquat, had complete confidence in the advice given him as Defence Minister by his Commanders in Chief, he felt bound to satisfy himself once more that no possibility of aid to Hyderabad had been over-looked.

Joe Jefford, supported by his Pakistani Chief of Staff, Commodore Chaudhuri, had no problem with the naval angle. East Pakistan stretched his resources to the limit; there was nothing the Navy could do to assist a landlocked state. Douglas Gracey had slightly more difficulty with the Army issue, but Liaquat and Iskander both understood the position well and realized that any land threat to India would be folly. Would it be possible to mount a limited offensive in Kashmir, perhaps in an area where the activity could be ascribed to action by the Azad forces? This was a dangerous concept, but, fortunately, Gracey got support from Zafrulla, the Foreign Minister. Any further aggression in Kashmir, or indeed any activity capable of being construed as such, would pull the rug from under his feet at the United Nations; he felt he could vindicate Pakistan's position, but the matter was delicate and we could afford no conduct which was not completely above board.

There remained Item 3. Liaquat turned to Sam Elworthy, a Group Captain, but one of clear distinction, Commander of Mauripur Station, the principal base of the Pakistan Air Force. He was attending the meeting in place of Atcherley, who was temporarily out of the country. Elworthy already possessed the dignity and 'gravitas' which were later to take him to the summit of the Royal Air Force, to the rank of Marshal of the Royal Air Force, to the post of Chief of the Defence Staff, and finally to the House of Lords. "There are others in this room better qualified to pronounce on the moral and legal aspects of this item," he began. "I propose therefore to confine myself to the purely air implications," he continued. "Forces potentially available for the operation – three Halifaxes. Aircraft currently serviceable – one Halifax. Estimated chance of reaching target – 50%. Estimated chance of hitting any significant target – 25%. Likely chance of returning safely – 20%. In the circumstances, the Committee will recognize this is not an operation I can commend to them from a professional standpoint." There was silence for about thirty seconds after Sam Elworthy had finished speaking. His moderate manner and perfect logic left even Iskander Mirza speechless. There was no more to be said. It was an easy minute to write. "The Committee considered this item, and decided it was not an option to be pursued," I recorded. I have often admired the way senior RAF officers put their points in public. Sam Elworthy's example was an object lesson in the value of understatement; it marked a stage in my politico-military education which I still remember.

Soon after this meeting the Indian Government put us all out of our misery by launching their invasion of Hyderabad. Roy Bucher gave us preliminary warning; the Indian General Chaudhuri's armoured division made no mistakes, while the Nizam's armed forces, spaced widely round the frontiers of the state, offered little resistance. The Razakhars, true to type, disintegrated, and Chaudhuri, as Military Governor, quickly restored law and order. It was a triumph for Sardar Patel and marked the completion, inside fifteen months, of his successful policy towards the States. The invasion of Hyderabad was a relief, too, to the Pakistan Government, who could now concentrate on their own affairs, of which the death of the Qaid-e-Azam was the next dramatic event.

No one, except perhaps Liaquat, fully recognized that Jinnah, even before independence, was mortally ill. He had periods of sickness, but these were ascribed to exhaustion; Miss Jinnah, his sister, looked after the Qaid-e-Azam carefully, conserving his energies so that he gave a false impression of vitality and vigour on public appearances. Though Liaquat was too loyal to the Qaid-e-Azam to admit it, Jinnah had, in fact, shot his bolt when Pakistan obtained its independence. He was a lawyer without experience of administration; I doubt if he had expected to obtain even the truncated Pakistan which came into being in August 1947. Certainly he never expected his new country to be granted its freedom so early, nor had he anticipated the administrative difficulties which so nearly overwhelmed Pakistan in those chaotic first days. After his fateful sortie to Lahore in late October 1947, Qaid-e-Azam seldom ventured away from Karachi, except for visits to Quetta, where his health seemed better, and the political pressures less demanding. He took no part in the Kashmir negotiations after the early stages, and, apart from expressing his anxiety over the fate of Hyderabad, remained in Baluchistan throughout that particular crisis.

179

Significantly, he only once, in March 1948, visited East Pakistan, nor do I recall him coming to Pindi to visit his Army Headquarters.

Nevertheless, the news of Jinnah's death in September 1948 came as a shock to his whole country. Everyone plunged into mourning; newspapers appeared ringed in black and full of foreboding about the future. It seemed that Pakistan, bereft of the Qaid-e-Azam, might simply fall apart through lack of leadership. Such fears were groundless; Liaquat formally assumed the political leadership he had in practice been exercising for the past twelve months, and, so far as the administration of the country was concerned, no one felt more than a tremor. Qaid-e-Azam's successor as Governor General, the delightful Nazimuddin, came from East Pakistan. Relations between him and Liaquat had always been good and for the next three years there seemed a genuine prospect of unity between the two wings of the country. The assassination of Liaquat in 1951 sadly interrupted the development of this fruitful partnership and, with the West Pakistanis increasingly inclined to adopt a patronizing pseudo-colonial approach towards their Bengali partners, it was not long before the seeds of the future dissolution started to be sown.

In September 1948, however, everyone's thoughts were on Jinnah's funeral, with Liaquat determined on a ceremony to honour Qaid-e-Azam as he deserved. Earlier that year, in Delhi, Gandhi's funeral had attracted huge crowds; though these were orderly and respectful, the sheer weight of numbers had produced situations of real danger to the participants. In Pakistan we had read accounts of the dangerous surges towards Gandhi's funeral pyre which had threatened the Mountbattens, Pandit Nehru and other principal mourners. Liaquat made up his mind that Qaid-e-Azam's funeral would be military in style and that the Karachi crowds would be kept at a safe distance from the procession and the funeral service itself. Bill Cawthorn came on the telephone from Karachi with Liaquat's wishes so far as the Commanders in Chief were concerned. He would like them to walk in the second rank of the procession, immediately behind Qaid-e-Azam's personal staff; the Head of Protocol would give detailed instructions on arrival at Government House. Iskander Mirza's common sense, and security considerations, dictated that Liaquat, a vulnerable target, would go independently to the burial place by car. There appeared less threat to the three British Commanders in Chief, who would therefore represent the Defence Ministry and services in the procession itself. It would be a three-mile walk, Bill Cawthorn warned us; not exactly a marathon, but taxing in full uniform and the heat of a Karachi September. There were no problems about Douglas Gracey or the Air Marshal; both were incredibly fit, but the Admiral's form on the flat was uncertain. Having warned me to walk in the procession with him, Douglas told me to make a contingency plan in case the Admiral had problems over going the distance.

Joe Jefford was a square, rotund, character, his figure suited to the quarterdeck, but less so to the line of march. Bashir Babar and I made a plan; we decided that he, with the C in C's Cadillac, would follow Liaquat's car to the site of the funeral itself, moving parallel to the cortege, and, in military terms, a tactical bound behind the Prime Minister. Thus Bashir provided a fall back position in case of difficulties en route, and was well placed to secure our ultimate withdrawal when that stage in the funeral service was reached at which the presence of non-Muslims was no longer appropriate. It would be difficult for us as laymen to determine the right moment; Bashir, therefore, undertook to appear at this time and lead our party to the Cadillac and his selected withdrawal route.

I had full confidence in Bashir's ability to execute his part in the enterprise and, equally, knew his sense of propriety would ensure our withdrawal at the correct time. It was a privilege to be involved in such an occasion and I felt proud that Liaquat should have selected British officers to be so prominent. Forming up at Government House was admirably organized; the Head of Protocol was on top of his job and no time was wasted in getting people into their proper positions in the procession. Punctually at ten o'clock Qaid-e-Azam's coffin was carried out of Government House and placed on the naval gun carriage. The Guard of Honour's Royal Salute and Present Arms were magnificent; the mounted escort of the Governor General's Body Guard took post in front of the gun carriage and we were in motion. For the first mile, in the more open part of Karachi round Government House, walking in the procession was like appearing as an actor in a film spectacular; the bands, Chopin's funeral march, the troops, perfectly turned out, lining the route, the magnificence of the Body Guard – it was wonderfully impressive, and, as Liaquat intended, a total contrast to the confusion in Delhi nine months earlier.

After about a mile, however, the route led us through a narrower sector of Karachi; the crowds were huge and pressed closely on the procession in an effort to get a last view of Qaid-e-Azam. There were some halts; sensibly the Body Guard was withdrawn and their place taken temporarily by an infantry guard of honour. Despite the press of people, the halts were not alarming; even so for about three-quarters of a mile our progress was as slow, and the crush as great, as finding one's way to the Underground down Wembley Way after a Cup Final. The discipline of the troops was marvellous and their patience and bearing superb. Gradually the way was cleared, and finally we came to an open stretch of country, not too far from the sea where the final interment was to take place. The site is now marked by an imposing monument to Qaid-e-Azam, with a memorial next door to his chief assistant in founding Pakistan, Liaquat; I was privileged to lay a wreath there in 1983 when I revisited Pakistan. In 1948, however, there was just a low hill, not more than 100 metres high, but sufficiently above the surrounding countryside for all involved in the ceremony to be able to see and hear properly. Sadly, I could hardly follow the speeches in Urdu, and even less of the prayers in Arabic. I remember thinking this situation anomalous, for Jinnah, founder of Pakistan, invariably thought and spoke entirely in English. He never made a speech in Urdu, a language he hardly knew, but on this occasion it was right for the national language to be used. Suddenly, after we had been sitting for about forty minutes, I saw Bashir threading his way through the other mourners. "Time to go, Colonel Jim," he remarked, as he saluted the Commanders in Chief. They, in turn, gave a final salute to Qaid-e-Azam, and, following Bashir, we found our way back to the car. We were a silent group driving back to Karachi; it had been a moving morning, marking a changed era for Pakistan.

There was a lull that autumn after Jinnah's death. In GHQ we welcomed the stalemate in Kashmir, and worked steadily on the military presentation to the United National Commission for India and Pakistan (UNCIP), whose arrival to establish the facts of the Kashmir situation was expected shortly. It may have been this factor which, early in December, precipitated a final flurry of fighting. The Indians, for several months content to sit quietly in Jammu, began to move forward towards Poonch, a key Azad Kashmir centre, and home to many of the best known Muslim bearers in pre-independent India. The Indian advance, parallel to the frontier with Pakistan, was threatening on two counts; not only did it jeopardize a vital Muslim area, but it renewed the danger of the headwaters of the Punjab rivers falling into Indian hands. Since Pakistan's future prosperity depended so greatly on West Punjab, where irrigation was the key to further development, Pakistan could not allow India to control the water supply. Something had to be done, and quickly.

Fortunately the Indian advance towards Poonch provided the military circumstances for Pakistan to make their point. Kalwant Singh, the Indian commander in Kashmir, was well known in Rawalpindi; before partition he had been Frank Messervy's Brigadier General Staff in Northern Army. Everyone liked Kalwant, but he was not renowned for military ability and, on this occasion, his advance was untidy and unbalanced. We learnt afterwards that Kalwant had been pushed into the operation against his will; the Indians were alarmed at a successful operation in the far north, led by a young Pakistani Lieutenant Colonel, Aslam Khan, later to succeed me as PS(C). Aslam had moved across the mountains from Gilgit to capture Skardu, surprising its garrison and threatening further problems in an area where, because of its proximity to China, the Indians felt vulnerable. Kalwant's move on Poonch was intended by Delhi to warn Pakistan off further adventures in the northern sector. Jhangar was the key. It was an important road centre but not much else. The Indian advance had made it a traffic shambles with too many lorries and establishments crammed into a confined space. It was an obvious artillery target and, just inside the Kashmir border, could be engaged from gun positions on Pakistan territory.

Quickly, a plan to exploit the situation was evolved. The whole of 7 Division Artillery, Pakistan's one Army Group Artillery, and three other field regiments were quickly assembled. Soon Pakistan had some 200 guns, including three regiments of medium artillery, able to engage Jhangar. Quietly the target was registered, and the necessary ammunition placed in position. Pakistan air OP's, keeping within Pakistan's airspace, were there to control the fire. One morning, with the confusion in Jhangar at its height, the Pakistan artillery opened up. The result was devastating and the consequences immediate. That afternoon Roy Bucher, the British Commander in Chief in Delhi, telephoned. He had the Indian Government's approval to suggest an immediate truce in Kashmir on the existing positions; he proposed a meeting in Delhi on 1 January 1949 between the two C in Cs and their staffs to record these arrangements and to convert the truce into a formal ceasefire pending the outcome of the negotiations for the future of Kashmir through the United Nations Commission. We got in touch with Liaquat through Bill Cawthorn and Iskander Mirza; soon Douglas Gracey was instructing me to ring Delhi with Pakistan Army's agreement to the Indian Army's proposal.

Douglas Gracey, Sher Khan and I, representing Pakistan Army, flew down to Delhi on New Year's Eve for the ceasefire meeting next day. We were excited and relieved; the Kashmir operations had been a running sore for the last fifteen months and it was good to have the threat of a disastrous war with India finally lifted. The atmosphere in Delhi was friendly and we were beautifully looked after in the Governor General's House. It was the first time we had met the new incumbent, Rajagopalachari, Mountbatten's successor, and he charmed us all by his warmth and the affection he evidently bore for Liaquat, the former ministerial colleague in the pre-partition Interim Government. Though it seemed unusual to visit the former Viceroy's house and not find a British occupant, we realized at once that "Rajaji", as everyone called him, was an ideal Governor General. He had breadth of view and a sense of historical perspective, while his simplicity and lack of pomposity were also attractive.

That evening the Indian Army gave a reception for the Pakistan party in the Gymkhana Club. The atmosphere was agreeable and one met a whole host of old friends. To my delight, all former IMA cadets from the Delhi area had been invited to the reception, and I enjoyed seeing them again and hearing their news. Mahadeo Singh was proving an ideal Commandant, while 'Smoky' Malhotra was equally well suited as his Adjutant. In general, morale in the Indian Army seemed excellent; the problems which fifteen years later culminated in the disastrous confrontation with China on the north-east frontier of India were still in the future.

Next morning, New Year's Day, we arrived punctually to start our meeting with our Indian opposite numbers. By coincidence, the day was Cariappa's first in office as Commander in Chief; Roy Bucher, who was staying on for three months as special advisor to the Defence Minister, gracefully abdicated his chairmanship of our meeting in favour of his successor and, after much press photography of our small conference, we began to work on the details of the ceasefire. Cariappa proved an admirable Chairman, Douglas Gracey was his practical self, while Chaudhuri for India and Sher Khan for Pakistan were sensibly professional. Everyone knew each other well, and their Staff College training, Quetta or Camberley, provided a common language. It became obvious that, despite a formidable agenda, we would not run into any snags, and by the time we adjourned for lunch, with Roy Bucher as host in his New Delhi house, the back of the task was broken. After lunch Roy Bucher took me aside and we walked up and down his lawn for five minutes. He kindly asked me about my future plans, letting slip that I would almost certainly be selected for the 1950 Camberley Staff College course. This was news to me; though I knew, of course, that Douglas Gracey had recommended me, I had not expected to get such an early vacancy. Roy Bucher remarked that, in his view, I would be wise to get back to the British Army, however briefly, before I went to Camberley. I was grateful for his advice and promised I would consider its implications carefully. It was nice of Roy Bucher to have taken so much trouble; though he and Gracey never hit it off, because of their very different personalities, Bucher had played an important role in keeping the Kashmir War within bounds, and much of the credit for the ceasefire must go to him for recognizing that the political conditions were right for a truce. Roy Bucher was an underrated soldier; an Indian cavalryman, he had little opportunity during World War II to show his ability. Afterwards, however, he did brilliantly as acting Commander of Eastern Command in dealing with the Calcutta riots of 1946, and, after independence, his influence on the Indian Army favoured moderation and common sense. Bucher was not charismatic, but he served India well and Pakistan was fortunate that such a politically astute soldier was in New Delhi to keep the military situation from boiling over, as, at times, it had threatened to do.

We quickly finished off the rest of our conference agenda after lunch and I was left with my Indian opposite number to commit the proceedings to writing. I remembered what Vernon Erskine-Crum had taught me the previous year about the duties of a Conference Secretary; we soon agreed a draft, and, with the help of an excellent trace of the respective dispositions provided by Sher Khan, had no difficulty in drawing an agreed ceasefire line. I remain proud of this achievement; the ceasefire line we drew that

New Year's Day in 1949 has stood the test of time. Over fifty years later our line is still an official demarcation in Kashmir, having survived several vicissitudes during the two major Indo-Pakistan conflicts in 1965 and 1971.

Next day Douglas Gracey and Sher Khan left early by air for Rawalpindi to transmit ceasefire instructions to the Pakistan Army troops in Kashmir. I was left behind in Delhi to check the production of the conference records; after lunch, the C in C's Dakota was to return to Delhi to collect me and the conference papers, which I was to deliver to Bill Cawthorn and Iskander Mirza in Karachi that evening. I would fly back to Pindi the following morning on a scheduled civilian flight. My work on the conference records did not take long. I relaxed in my room in the Governor General's House, enjoying a rare morning of idleness and the chance to read a book. My telephone rang; it was the ADC's Room. The Governor General, Rajaji, would like to see me at midday; he had a message he wanted me to take to Liaquat in Karachi. When I met the Governor General, he asked me to sit down and began to talk. Our discussion covered a wide field and revealed Rajaji's wise views about the sub-continent as a whole. He realized the folly of bad relations between Pakistan and India. His own relations with Liaquat had always been good, he told me. The letter I was to take would tell Liaquat that he (Rajaji) would do everything he could in Delhi to improve the situation; Liaquat could also write to him whenever problems arose. He asked me what I saw as the main problem. It was easy to answer; Kashmir was, of course, the stumbling block, and I did my best to explain Pakistan's feelings on the subject, and how they felt they had been cheated out of a territory they considered part of their birthright. The Governor General nodded his head, indicating understanding, if not necessarily agreement. "The trouble is," he remarked. "Panditji (Nehru) has a block about Kashmir. His family come from there and it is hard for him to see the issue without emotion." He turned to the role of the British in India, remarking that we had much to be proud of, not least the way we had managed to unify the country. Our literature, too, had enriched and educated several generations of Indians; he, personally, owed much to Shakespeare, Milton, and our poets. I remarked, impertinently I now think, how beautifully he used our language, and how much I envied him his ability to choose exactly the right words for particular concepts. "But," I remarked, "this is rather silly of me. I expect like your opposite number in Karachi you have a first class degree at Oxford or Cambridge." Rajaji sighed a little sadly. "No," he said. "I have never been to England. I am like a lover who has never seen his lass." It was a delightful note on which to end our conversation, and I said goodbye, realizing how lucky I had been to talk to such a great man for so long. If Rajagopalachari had been at the head of the Congress Party in 1947 partition might not have been needed. But he had no political base outside his state of Madras and, by the time he became Governor General,

Nehru was too firmly established to tolerate such a moderate. Thus Rajaji, admired and respected though he was, never developed the political clout his intellect and ideas deserved.

I discussed Roy Bucher's advice to me with Douglas Gracey. He was sympathetic, but not so categoric as Roy Bucher. He suggested that I should stay until the end of April, when I was due to go home for two months' leave. We could review the matter in the light of how I found matters back in the UK, and how urgently The Rifle Brigade wanted me back. This proved an excellent compromise, and the Military Secretary, Bob Mansergh, confirmed it in March when he paid a flying visit to Pakistan to check the way British officers were being treated in the newly independent country. Douglas Gracey's compromise allowed me to play a part in briefing and handling the United National Commission during their first visit to Pakistan.

Dealing with UNCIP was fascinating, and the experience helped me later in my career when I found myself on the other side of the fence in Cyprus as a UN Force Chief of Staff. The UN member given the task of establishing the facts on the Pakistan side was a Belgian, Harry Graeffe. He spoke good English, but found my knowledge of French a help; he was youngish, thirty-five or so, and we got on well. The job of taking Harry Graeffe around gave me a chance of getting into Kashmir to see something of the military situation there for myself. Normally British officers were strictly forbidden to go into Kashmir, we got special permission in this case from the UK High Commission in Karachi and I found my visit to the Kashmir front very interesting.

The military position was like a quiet sector of the front in the mountains of Italy, except that the features were higher and the communication problems consequently greater. Some of the jeep tracks made by the Pakistani engineers were hair-raising; incredibly narrow, they perched on ledges with a sheer drop of a thousand feet or more. It was fatal to look down and I admired Harry Graeffe for the stoical fashion in which he submitted himself to the vagaries of a driver with whom, knowing no Urdu, he was unable to communicate. We explained to UNCIP the importance to Pakistan of the sector of Kashmir which our forces held; Graeffe, too, was able to understand that to expect the scratch Azad Kashmir irregulars to defend such territory was unrealistic. Whatever the theoretical position in International Law, in practice Pakistan had no option but to intervene as we had done.

Explaining the facts and giving the background to UNCIP was straightforward. It was different, however, when it came to persuading the Commission to set up a plebiscite in Kashmir, which was the Pakistani objective. Though the Indians also paid lip service to the concept of a plebiscite, one could understand their objections to implementing it. They were aware that an impartial vote would then have favoured Pakistan;

Indian public opinion, however, would never have accepted the territory's transfer to Pakistan after the effort and casualties sustained by the Indian Army in securing their hold on the area. Moreover, as Rajagopalachari explained in Delhi, Nehru had an emotional block on the subject which made him unable to think in terms of any concession. It became obvious, therefore, that the best the UN Commission could hope to achieve was a perpetuation of the 'status quo', and, in effect, Pakistan had to settle for such a limited solution. Only rarely is it possible for the United Nations to achieve solutions to problems; very often, therefore, the result of UN intervention is to 'freeze' a situation in the state in which their intervention found it. Sometimes, as in Kashmir, such a result is of value because it avoids more serious consequences. But, as I was to find myself in Cyprus later, to expect practical solutions from UN intervention, however good their motives, is normally too much to hope for.

When I was not dealing with UNCIP, cricket occupied much of my remaining time in Pakistan. The game had given me great pleasure all my time in Rawalpindi. I usually had a net in midweek and there was invariably a match on the Saturday and Sunday. There were some good local players. Mohamed Nissar, former fast bowler for the All India team in England of 1932 and 1936, was a pillar of our side. A delightful man, his figure, embellished by many a good pilaff, was no longer as lissom as when he was a Test player; nevertheless, his pace was still sharp enough to make our opponents hurry their strokes. Jehangir Khan, another former Test player, a Cambridge blue, more famous now perhaps as uncle of Imran Khan, also played regularly. His bowling was as accurate as ever, while his attitude to the game and his sportsmanship made him much admired. We had a brilliant future Test player in Maqsood, a fluent stroke player, who would have done even better but for his enjoyment of life and the good things which go with it. But Pindi's secret weapon and local hero was Miran Bux, the groundsman, who doubled his job with bowling off spinners at almost medium pace. He bowled off the wrong foot, but his delivery was suspect. He certainly threw his faster deliveries, which were hard to detect. He was also shameless in preparing wickets which took spin; with Miran Bux on our side, Pindi were hard to beat and there were few drawn games.

The West Indies, who toured Pakistan and India that winter of 1948–49, presented us with a dilemma. Douglas Gracey, a keen cricketer himself, was raising a C in C's XI to play the West Indies over two days in Pindi. Should Miran Bux, suspect delivery and all, be allowed to play against the tourists? We took careful soundings and consulted Jehangir Khan, who was to lead the C in C's side. We concluded that to omit Miran Bux on his home ground would be impossible, but Jehangir and I decided to have a word before the match with John Goddard, the charming West Indian captain, who we hoped would appreciate the delicacy of the situation we faced. The

West Indies behaved impeccably and played beautiful cricket to win the match handsomely by seven wickets. Miran Bux chucked cheerfully away for nearly 30 overs in their first innings and took five wickets; it was made clear, however, that this appearance must be his swansong in representative cricket unless he could completely redesign his technique. To his credit, Miran Bux accepted the position; he had indeed no option, for press photographs left no doubt about the impropriety of his action. He continued to play for Pindi at the weekends, since no local umpire would have dared to question such a well known local figure; the pitches also continued to favour spin bowling and when I went back to Pakistan in 1983, though Miran Bux himself was dead, I was told his successor had maintained the bias.

I found myself involved in Pakistan's approaches to the then Imperial Cricket Conference to establish Test Match status. Apart from Jehangir Khan and Justice Cornelius, a judge of the Lahore High Court, I was the only member of MCC in Pakistan at that time. We duly approached Lords for guidance and received prompt help and encouragement. There was no lack of talent in Pakistan at that time. The star performer, Fazal Mahmood, was a fast medium bowler, who became later a world-class performer. He often came to Pindi and we played frequently against him in Lahore; I saw him again in 1983. He was then a Deputy Inspector General of Police, responsible for the traffic in Lahore; driving in that city has always been chaotic and I doubt if Fazal can be blamed for his failure to effect any great improvement. Back in 1949, however, the existence of players like Fazal was a great help in getting Pakistan into the Test Match fold; their first tour of England took place in 1954, and, incredibly, Pakistan, after being outclassed in the earlier matches, won the final Test Match at the Oval by a margin of 30 runs. It was a great start for the new country's cricket, and I felt pride in their success, besides delight that the bowling of my friend Fazal Mahmood had played a vital part in their first victory.

By April 1949, however, I began to feel it was time for me to leave the sub-continent where I had served for nearly four years. It was important to restore my regimental roots; moreover, my own team of Douglas Gracey's personal staff was breaking up and it was right that a new PS(C), a Pakistani, should have the task of training their successors. First Wajahat Husain and, the following month, Bashir Babar returned to their regiments. Though Douglas Gracey kindly pressed me to stay till the end of the year, I was anxious not to outstay my welcome and spent my last weeks going round as many places as possible to say farewell to my friends. The Pakistan Air Force gave me a memorable Dakota flight down the gorge of the Indus to Gilgit with unforgettable views of the Himalayas and Nanga Parbat, and there were other nostalgic occasions before I left for home early in May.

I found it hard to organize my thoughts as I flew back home. I was more optimistic then about Pakistan than subsequent events have proved. It seemed at the time that the new state, having survived its chaotic early weeks, and overcome the loss of its founder, Qaid-e-Azam, might settle to a period of steady development under a balanced and liberal successor in Liaquat Ali Khan. The economy, after its initial uncertainty, looked to be developing well; there was already an agricultural surplus in West Pakistan, and the prospects, involving increased use of irrigation, were good. Politically the ceasefire in Kashmir, the hope that UNCIP might be able to promote the conditions for a plebiscite, and the removal of Hyderabad as a source of misunderstanding, promised better relations with India. Though it was obvious that it would not be easy, for reasons of geography alone, to achieve an integrated relationship between West and East Pakistan, the appointment of a Bengali, Kwaja Nazimuddin, as Governor General, and his successful start in the job, gave good hope for the future. Tragically, Liaquat's assassination by a fanatic in 1951, coupled with the earlier deaths in an air accident of Iftikhar Khan and Sher Khan, removed too much talent too suddenly for Pakistan's promising start to be maintained. These losses were disastrous in themselves and produced gaps at the top of the country's affairs which meant people being employed in spheres for which they were unsuited. Mahomed Ali, for example, brilliant civil servant and masterly Secretary General, was never meant to be a political leader and found the task too much for him. If Iftikhar had become Commander in Chief, I doubt if he would have permitted the Army to get involved in politics; Sher Khan, too, would have proved an important force working for sanity and moderation.

Nevertheless the contribution of the British officers to Pakisan's early development was a worthwhile achievement. Perhaps we made mistakes, but it would have been surprising if we had not. Douglas Gracey and his fellow Commanders in Chief laid sound foundations. I am glad I was there and grateful to have had the scope and opportunity serving Pakistan presented.

Chapter 10

RETURN TO ORTHODOXY AND

COLONIAL INTERLUDE

I never felt a sense of anti-climax on my return from India and Pakistan. I needed to restore my regimental roots, and did so as a Company Commander in 1 RB in 1949 and 1951, with a year's intermission at the Staff College in 1950. My two years at regimental duty in BAOR and the tour which followed as Brigade Major 91 Lorried Infantry Division (part of 11 Armoured Division) were a delightful period. I learned a lot, made some splendid friends and hugely enjoyed it all.

Fifty years later, however, I doubt if these experiences, essentially part of the Cold War, are of great interest or relevance to the present generation. By 1954, indeed, I felt it was high time The Rifle Brigade was removed from the specialist motor role which had served us so well during World War II and the first years of the Cold War. I saw that operations like those in Malaya and Kenya were more significant than the next Rhine Army exercise or horse show. Together with other similar thinkers, I resolved to do what I could to change the situation.

Luckily The Rifle Brigade's Colonel Commandant was then Monty Stopford. His war had been in Burma and I decided to approach him to get The Rifle Brigade removed from our specialist motor role as soon as possible. I received a sympathetic hearing and guessed that Monty Stopford would raise the matter with Bill Slim, then CIGS, under whom he had served in Burma. Bill Slim visited 91 Brigade on an exercise in the summer and dropped a hint that he had appreciated Monty Stopford's point. Soon afterwards I heard from Dick Fyffe, about to take over command of 1 RB, that the battalion would be leaving Rhine Army. We were to go to Bulford in Salisbury Plain, re-train as ordinary infantry, and our likely role would be Korea. Since by then the Korean fighting had come to an end with the signing of an armistice, there was, however, every chance that our destination would be altered. Meanwhile I was to brush up on the infantry techniques we had learnt so laboriously ten years before in Italy. The future looked different, and more challenging.

When I rejoined 1 RB in February 1954, we were an ordinary infantry battalion at Bulford re-learning our trade. Our accommodation was cold, draughty and uncomfortable; the spring of 1954 was one of the coldest on record and the summer seemed just continuous rain. We grumbled about the conditions, but were usually too busy to bother about them.

There were frequent distractions. We played a part in a spectacular demonstration of Combined Operations near Portsmouth. There was a royal visit by our Colonel in Chief, the Duke of Gloucester. There were exercises on Salisbury Plain in which we acted as enemy to Territorial Army formations. In July we spent three weeks running the Bisley rifle meeting. Many of these activities were frustrating and all of them interfered with our training, but it was silly to complain.

We were lucky in the quality of the riflemen sent us that summer, while the national service officers, always good, were even better than usual. My own team included two stars in Charles Baker-Cresswell and Ned Ram, while the fact that we were going abroad meant that no one was due for release in the next twelve months. Thus we had some stability and a chance to develop the corporate morale to which one was used in wartime.

Dick Fyffe had been a good battalion commander in war; in peace he was even better. He had organizing ability, patience, and took great trouble with individuals. He was a good delegator, allowing his company commanders to get on with their jobs. In David Alexander-Sinclair he had an able Adjutant who ran the day to day activities of the battalion with precision, and could do *The Times* crossword over breakfast fast enough to compel everyone's admiration. Without this sensible direction, Bulford would have been worse; as it was, we survived, and by the time John Hoskyns left for the Far East on the advance party, we were ready to face a winter in Korea, however dreary this might be.

No sooner did John Hoskyns and his group reach Singapore than they were recalled. Our destination had been changed to Kenya, where the CIGS, John Harding, was determined to bring the emergency to an end. It was a change much for the better and we started to re-train for our new task. We needed to discover as much as we could about the country, its history and the background to the emergency. The situation was more complicated than we imagined.

Kenya had a reputation for beauty; we knew it was situated on the Equator. We had heard about the settlers, and some of us were aware of the Happy Valley in the White Highlands, the venue during the war of a spectacular murder trial. About the African inhabitants of the country we knew little, since press coverage of the emergency had hitherto seemed irrelevant.

In 1954 the African population of Kenya was eight million. There were 40,000 European settlers and some 150,000 Asians. European settlement dated from the turn of the century, at which time the British Government took over the territory as a Protectorate, converting it later into a Colony. The Government encouraged settlement, hoping to bring stability and wealth to the country. The settlement process mainly occurred on land grazed by pastoral tribes, but sometimes settlers took territory previously occupied by agricultural tribes, like the Kikuyu. The Kikuyu, with their close relations the Meru and Embu, made up the largest tribal group in Kenya; at the start of the emergency they numbered about a million and a half. Their tribal area ran down the east side of the Aberdare Mountains and round the southern and eastern side of Mount Kenya. The Mau Mau revolt centred round this region and the next door settled areas; it was a small area, 100 miles from north to south, and rather less from east to west. Mau Mau affected only the Kikuyu, Meru and Embu tribes; the remainder of the African population were not involved, disliked the Kikuyu and co-operated with the Government to end the rebellion.

The emergency area covered three different sectors, the Kikuyu reserve, the settled areas next to the reserve, and those Kikuyu who lived in or near Nairobi. Not all Kikuyu joined Mau Mau, or were even sympathetic to its aims. Many remained loyal to the administration, and to the Chiefs and Headmen appointed by the colonial Government. Some changed sides, often more than once, during the course of the fighting – usually because they were uncertain who would win, but often because they suffered from a clash of loyalties. It was often hard to know who was supporting whom at any particular moment.

The origins of the Mau Mau rebellion lay in dissatisfaction over the way in which some original Kikuyu tribal territory had been occupied by the settlers, but Mau Mau had no definite policy. I doubt if Kenyatta and the more intelligent members of his party, the Kenya Africa Union, thought in terms of forcing Europeans to leave the country. More likely, Kenyatta was merely using the land question to increase his political dominance of the Kikuyu people. Those who joined the fighting organizations, based in the forests of the Aberdares and Mount Kenya, were younger and less sophisticated. Many became terrorists out of a spirit of adventure; few of the gang leaders were educated, though some, Dedan Kumathi for example, displayed great powers of leadership. Control and recruitment of the gangs was exercised by oathing, a feature of Kikuyu tribal life. The oaths binding terrorists to their gang involved loathsome rituals and the terrorists believed that disaster would follow anyone breaking his oath. There was no real control of the rebellion and gangs, usually some two hundred in number, normally had no contact with each other. They were based on a particular locality, with an 'active' wing living in the forest which only emerged for activities like thieving cattle, burning farms, or murdering opponents. The 'active' gangs drew supplies and support from 'passive' wings in their area of origin. Nairobi, the capital, was a centre of this 'passive' support, supplying ammunition or medical supplies in addition to food.

Mau Mau had taken the administration by surprise. In 1952 Kenya had been looking forward to a visit to the colony, early in the year, by Princess Elizabeth and the Duke of Edinburgh. The visit was to have been the swan-song of a distinguished Governor, Sir Philip Mitchell. Though the colony's intelligence services, and some perceptive District Officers, recognized there might be trouble ahead, the Governor deliberately disregarded such portents. Kenya, he considered, had earned its royal visit, and he was deter-mined that it should go off peacefully,. In the event, sadly, the visit was overshadowed by the death of King George VI; Princess Elizabeth received the news while at a game reserve, Treetops, near Nyeri, and returned to London at once to assume her duties as the new Sovereign.

The political situation in Kenya soon deteriorated. There were Mau Mau-inspired atrocities, as gangs began to assemble in the forests of the Aberdares and on the slopes of Mount Kenya. The most spectacular was the murder of Chief Warahiu, a senior Kikuyu loyalist; it indicated the way in which the leadership of the tribe was being undermined by the growing strength of the terrorists. In October 1952 the Government arrested Kenyatta and leading members of the Central Committee of the Kenya African Union; Kenyatta was placed on a 'show trial' for conspiracy at Kapenguria in the far north of the colony. The arrests hardly affected the developing unrest. Members of the Central Committee were replaced; the new Committee continued the existing methods of its predecessor and considered itself responsible for the direction of the Mau Mau movement. The Government were finally forced to declare a state of emergency at the end of the year.

The declaration of the emergency found the British Army ill-equipped to deal with the situation. Its limited resources were already stretched to the limit and a new colonial crisis, coming on top of existing commitments in Korea and Malaya, was unwelcome. Nor was the command set up in Kenya geared to an emergency. The GOC, Cameron, was a sapper, appointed to supervise the establishment of a strategic base, McKinnon Road, near the port of Mombasa. He was unsuited to running an anti-terrorist campaign, but six months elapsed before he was replaced by an experienced commander. Nor were the Lancashire Fusiliers, or other British battalions arriving during 1953, trained for their new role. The campaign was regarded as a sideshow, largely irrelevant to the Army's main task of defending Western Europe. It took time for Bobby Erskine, the new C in C, to get Kenya organized and develop a plan for ending the emergency.

In 1954 the tide began to turn as Erskine's plan, supported by a steady flow of information, started to work. In principle, Erskine developed operations along the lines which had proved successful in Malaya. Proper links were established at every level between the administration, police and the military – the doctrine of the 'three-legged stool'. The administration undertook the task of winning the hearts and minds of the Kikuyu themselves, with the aim of denying the gangs in the forests the supplies and reinforcements they needed. This process was hard and unspectacular, and entailed grouping the Kikuyu in villages, where they could defend themselves through their own Kikuyu Guard, and be protected from the threats of the terrorists. This policy of 'villageisation' proved the key factor in reversing the trend against the gangs. The Kikuyu themselves played a main role in defeating Mau Mau; in doing so, they displayed courage and determination, surprising the other tribes of Kenya, who had not hitherto had much regard for Kikuyu martial prowess.

It was also essential to use the regular forces available properly and Erskine correctly established his priorities. Top of the list came a massive screening operation in Nairobi, and the shanty towns in the suburbs from which the forest gangs drew supplies and food. This needed good planning and continued for six weeks after its launch in April 1954. Meanwhile, Erskine accepted that the situation in the Reserve and in the settled area round Nyeri and Nanyuki would not improve; the best he could hope for was to contain the position. It required moral courage on Erskine's part to maintain his strategy; throughout the year he was criticized by settlers and others who did not understand the basis of the plan, but who were anxious to see progress in their own area. It is obvious now that Erskine's priorities were right; then, however, it was not so clear, as the results of the Nairobi operation took time to become apparent.

Erskine also organized the training of the Army for its role in the attack on the forest gangs he intended to launch early in 1955. A battle school was established at Nanyuki and attention paid to a wider understanding of the emergency's background. To combat Mau Mau one needed to understand the Kikuyu mentality and to appreciate how their minds worked. Troops arriving from the UK required also to realize they were not fighting to safeguard the interests of the settlers; like other colonial territories, Kenya was being prepared for ultimate independence with restoration of law and order an essential preliminary.

1 RB's Operational Training Party left Blackbushe Airport in Hampshire on 9 October 1954 bound for Kenya. Our party, led by Paddy Boden, consisted of eight officers and five NCOs; our task was to gather knowledge

of local conditions and pass it on to the main body of the battalion, who, following by sea, were arriving six weeks later. I was the only Company Commander in the party, so my job would be to concentrate on the tactical and operational aspect, while others, largely specialists, mastered their own techniques.

The air journey to Kenya, by chartered Hermes, was comfortable and uneventful; we landed in Nairobi just over twenty-four hours after leaving England. We got a great welcome, especially from the Kenya Regiment, a territorial unit composed of Europeans living in Kenya. The regiment was dispersed so that the experience of its members, who knew the country and its language, could be available to the Army, the Police and the Kikuyu Guard. 1 RB had a Kenya Regiment Sergeant attached to each rifle company; we relied greatly on them for advice and they proved admirable teachers and guides. The Rifle Brigade were fortunate since the Kenya Regiment was affiliated to our sister regiment, the 60th Rifles, so giving us a special foothold in the colony.

After a night in Nairobi, we set off northwards towards the emergency area; our destination was the Buffs, at that time operating in the Embu Reserve, on the southeast edge of the Mount Kenya Forest. On arrival our party split up and I worked with my opposite number, a Company Commander in the Buffs. The Buffs were kindness itself and we learnt much from them, and from their neighbours, the Devonshire Regiment. The Buffs, who had been in Kenya since the early days of the emergency, had been given no chance of studying conditions beforehand. They were catapulted straight into operations and learnt by experience as they went along. They had done splendidly, but admitted they would have liked to make more impact on the terrorists. Their tactical disappointment was due, in our view, to reluctance to adapt their organization to tribal warfare in Africa. They remained a normal infantry battalion, working in conventional companies and platoons, and taking little account of the methods of Mau Mau. Though this seemed obvious, the remedy was less so – otherwise it would have been adopted long before. The Buffs' frustration was shared by others and the subject clearly required careful study.

Two days after our arrival with the battalion we took part in a 'sweep' in the Kikuyu Reserve. The operation involved the whole of the Buffs, plus over 500 Africans, either police or members of the Kikuyu Guard. The principle of the operation was simple; one third of those involved acted as beaters, the remainder, surrounding the area, carried out the role of 'stops'. The concept was not a success; the thick country made it impossible to control the beaters and the terrorists either lay low or slipped through the encircling cordon. It was easy to decide that 'sweeps' were to be avoided, but we continued to search for better alternatives.

I next took part in a forest patrol. We carried too much equipment and, though we covered a great deal of ground, going right up to the moorland at a height of about 12,000 feet, the operation was abortive. I admired the physical strength of the patrol commander and the determination he displayed. I was less impressed, however, by his navigation in the jungle, or by his tactical approach to our task. It seemed we should have been looking, slowly and methodically, for signs of Mau Mau activity, following the tracks which they might have been using and pausing frequently to listen and watch for anything which might have given a clue to an enemy presence. Instead we pressed on regardless; if we had encountered any opposition, we would all have been too exhausted by our heavy packs to have shot accurately at a fleeting target. Furthermore, our patrol seemed to be a one off affair; it was not based on proper information, nor was a follow up planned had we run into a Mau Mau gang. I thought we were just gong through the motions, and when we returned to base, apart from the physical satisfaction obtained from climbing and descending some 6,000 feet, I felt our efforts had achieved nothing. There must surely be a better way.

My next forest patrol, this time into the Aberdares, with a King's African Rifles battalion, proved more instructive. We moved more methodically, halting regularly to listen, and there was something, too, to learn from the elegance with which the African soldiers negotiated the forest and followed the tracks through the bamboo up towards the moorland. Again, however, I felt that our patrol took place in a vacuum; so far as I could see, it was unrelated to any intelligence, nor was it part of an operational pattern. On our return I heard someone describe our activity as a 'routine patrol'; this description seemed to me a contradiction in terms and I determined to avoid patrolling for its own sake. If pursuing forest gangs was like looking for a needle in a haystack, at least we could concentrate our activities on haystacks where there might be needles and avoid those where no needles existed.

The Buffs arranged for us to fly over the operational area we had been allotted in the Aberdares in a Pacer aircraft of the Kenya Police Air Wing. These light aircraft played an important part in the emergency; they were extensively used for controlling operations, for reconniassance and often for the dropping of supplies. This last technique was informal; the pilot first identified his target and then dived steeply towards it. At the right moment the passenger opened the cabin door and hurled the load out. It was so simple that the forest patrols had come to rely too much on it. The gangs had learnt to watch the activities of the Pacers carefully; a supply drop indicated the presence of a security force patrol and it was simple for the gang, once aware of a patrol's location, to avoid contact. My B Company never used this system; I decided to invent a more imaginative method and began to consider using our own 'passive wing' following the example of our opponents.

The Aberdares were to feature largely in B Company's existence for the next year and merit a short description. The forest itself began at 8,000 feet; the land below that level had mostly been cleared for agricultural purposes. In the settled area, north of Nyeri, ranching was the main activity, varied with mixed farming, pyrethrum often the main crop. In the Kikuyu Reserve the red earth, reminiscent of Devonshire, and abundant rainfall provided ideal conditions for smallholdings of all sorts. The Kikuyu were natural cultivators and used the land intelligently; their use of terracing to avoid erosion was a model for others.

The lower level of the forest up to 9,000 feet was beautiful, with the trees a feature. There were masses of game; it was impossible to walk anywhere without seeing every sort of buck, while there were colobus monkeys in the trees and on the game tracks. There were herds of buffalo, too, which were best avoided, and occasionally elephant and rhino, though these usually stuck to the bamboo and avoided the lower forest, except at night when, especially if there was a salt lick, they would come down to one of the pools or rivers to drink. Even on the hottest day the lower forest was cool; it was an idyllic area and to traverse it on patrol a delightful experience.

The bamboo above, which extended for the next 2,000 feet, until petering out at 11,000 feet, was different. It was thick, dark and invariably damp as one climbed through it along a game track, crouched down to make one's way through. Movement was tiring, unpleasant and sometimes hazardous, especially if a rhino also wished to use the track and was going the opposite way. One did not invariably meet a rhino; there were, however, enough about for nearly everyone who operated in the forest to be charged by one at some time. The technique for avoiding rhinos was simple; a body swerve borrowed from Rugby football would normally do the trick, and, since rhinos are half blind, avoiding the initial charge was all one needed to do. One would often find elephants on the track; these, however, are intelligent animals, no more anxious to make contact with human beings than we with them. The drill here was to halt when you saw them and allow them to get your wind; when they did, they would move away politely off the track, crashing into the bamboo on one side or the other, allowing you free passage.

The Kikuyu regard Mount Kenya as a god, something easy to understand as one looked across at its snow-capped summit in the early mornings when the weather seemed always to be clear. Cloud started to build up during the later morning and by the afternoon the peak was usually shrouded in mist. Operationally, the Aberdares provided more scope, since the gangs there were nearer to their sources of supply in the Reserve, and so larger and better organized.

By the time the main body of the battalion arrived, our Operational Training Party had obtained a good knowledge of the emergency area and our task. I was still unclear how our forest patrols should operate and accepted having to learn by trial and error. We had, however, made progress in our attitude to intelligence, and for this Frank Kitson, also of The Rifle Brigade, who had developed an understanding of counter-revolutionary war well beyond his contemporaries, must take the credit. Frank had been in Kenya for some twelve months before we arrived. He had been sent out from Germany the previous year to serve as a DMIO (District Military Intelligence Officer) and soon won a deserved reputation. He put his specialized knowledge at our disposal and we were ready learners. Frank's own speciality – the development of pseudo-gangs formed from surrendered ex-terrorists – had given him special insight into the Kikuyu mentality. There was no way we could rival Frank's expertise, but we learnt from him how to acquire information and, importantly, not to waste it by inefficiency after we had obtained it. One required the confidence of the young Kenyans who were the key intelligence operators, not always easy in view of their low opinion of the security forces. I went over several times to talk to Frank at his camp, where he lived with one other European, Eric Holyoak, surrounded by ex-terrorists, who slept in an adjoining room next door to Frank himself. Twice Frank kindly asked me to dinner; it was odd to have one's meal served by former Mau Mau, all of whom had taken binding oaths to kill people like myself but had since changed allegiance. I admired Frank's cold courage and the leadership he displayed in persuading terrorists to change sides and maintain their new allegiance.

Frank Kitson taught us how to obtain information and make good use of it, but not even he could advise us on patrol techniques to contact gangs in the absence of definite intelligence. At first, therefore, we employed traditional patrolling methods, using common sense to adjust these to local conditions. I decided, however, to increase our mobility in the forest by making new motorable tracks wherever possible. These need not be elaborate; if they could be negotiated by a landrover, this would be enough for us to get patrols into the bamboo quickly and unobserved.

By mid-November, when the main body of 1 RB arrived, we also knew about our first operation. Bobby Erskine reckoned that by the end of 1954 he would have broken the back of the Mau Mau rebellion in Nairobi, the settled area and the Kikuyu Reserve. 1955, therefore, would see the security forces concentrating on the forests, the only refuge left to the terrorists. The Director of Operations, 'Loony' Hinde, a veteran of 7 Armoured Division in the desert, decided to tackle the Aberdares first. It was to be a major operation, code name, HAMMER, involving most of the infantry, British and King's African Rifles, available. The principle was simple; the troops involved would establish bases on the moorland and patrol slowly down through the bamboo until they reached a stop line on the border of the lower forest. Hinde hoped this intensive patrolling would put the terrorists under such pressure that they would be forced out of the forest altogether, and that, by saturating the forests with troops, the gangs' food supplies would be severed. On paper the plan looked sound; in practice, however, I doubted if it would work. The gangs, I felt, would simply split up, lie low until the patrolling had passed them by and then reassemble elsewhere. Nevertheless the operation would prove a good exercise for a new battalion like 1 RB; whatever its tactical deficiencies, Hammer would certainly familiarize us all with the forest. Later, no doubt, we should develop a better tactical plan; for the moment, though I doubted the Hammer concept, I could not conceive a better alternative.

1 RB were allotted the Aberdare Forest north of Nyeri as an operational area. We were given a 28-day period of acclimatization to get used to operating at over 8,000 feet, and also to learn about our territory. B Company were fortunate in drawing Squair's Farm as our base. The farmer, Harry Squair, a Scotsman, with a Glasgow accent so pronounced it would have made Harry Lauder sound like a Cockney, allowed us to use his guest house as our Headquarters. We had a view across the floor of the valley to Mount Kenya thirty miles away, and, importantly, good initial access to the forest through a track from Squair's Farm itself which petered out after a mile where it was no longer useful for logging purposes. I decided to use our acclimatization period to develop this track so we could reach the moorland by landrover. Dick Fyffe arranged a labour force of sixty Kikuyu each day, armed with pangas. We set them to work to clear a path through the bamboo, having first decided on the route our track should follow. It was no motorway and the drainage arrangements were primitive by sapper standards. Nevertheless our efforts worked; by the end of the month we had a motorable route up to the moorland, from where we had a memorable view of Tortoise, the highest point in the Aberdares. Our track ended on a ridge, some thirty yards or so wide; it was a good place for our Company HQ and also for radio. We were proud of our track and numerous visitors came to see it and use our viewpoint, known as Tortoise View.

Tortoise View provided a good moment. Patrolling the sector of bamboo below Tortoise View was preceded by pattern bombing of the area by the RAF. Since the forces available amounted to six obsolete Lincoln bombers, supported by a few Harvard trainers, this display of air power was not particularly formidable. We felt cynically that the RAF's real aim was to use up their stocks of World War II bombs, which would otherwise have had to be destroyed in situ as they became unserviceable. The chances of doing harm to the Mau Mau seemed small and we reckoned that the main result would be to make the buffalo and rhino in the target area angrier than usual and the patrolling risks correspondingly greater. Nevertheless, the bombing promised to be a spectacle, and an impressive array of top brass, led by the

Air Commander, Air Commodore Beiseigel (B Company nickname Bomber Bike), assembled at Tortoise View to watch the bombing. Dick Fyffe, who was proud of his earlier service in the RAF, and still maintained his flying logbook, encouraged us to think in joint service terms; moreover the Air Commander was a nice man, who had once played cricket for Leicestershire, and who owned, in RAF Station Eastleigh, 1 RB's favourite football opponents. Spot on time over came the Lincolns, flying in formation, to drop their bombs on the bamboo; the Harvards, following up, dropped a 250 lb bomb each and then energetically machine gunned the area. It was magnificent, but useless counter-revolutionary warfare. As the Air Commodore turned to leave, I thanked him, politely I hope, for the RAF support. I remembered, too, an important Camberley lesson about air power. "It must have been quite a job, Air Commodore, to win the air battle against the Mau Mau," I remarked, my face as straight as I could keep it. Mike Carver, then a full Colonel and Deputy Chief of Staff at GHQ in Nairobi, overheard my remark and gave it higher marks for humour than for producing inter-service spirit. Dick Fyffe, however, was not amused and I remained in the jungle for a day or two until my frivolity had been forgiven.

Despite the effort involved, Operation Hammer was a failure. Few terrorists were killed or captured, and once the operation had been launched, the gangs found little difficulty in either lying low or moving to areas outside the net of the security forces. It was, in fact, a wasted three weeks and demonstrated the futility of large-scale anti-terrorist operations. From B Company's point of view, however, it had an admirable consequence. Bobby Erskine, visiting Operation Hammer, realized that the pattern of forest operations was wrong and that more could be achieved by fewer, better trained, patrols operating in the forest, while the remainder of the troops practised an organized food denial policy in the Reserve and settled area. One company from each battalion therefore was to be withdrawn from the operation on Mount Kenya to train as a specialized Tracker Company. B Company were chosen for the task and we began to think how to operate.

Since the task of the tracker companies was to engage the Mau Mau on their own ground in the Aberdares and on Mount Kenya, it seemed to me that to overcome the terrorists' guerrilla tactics, we needed ourselves to become counter-guerrillas. It would be necessary for us to keep our own operations as secret as those of the terrorists; like the Mau Mau, our bases in the forest should be concealed. There could, for example, be no smoking in the forest, since we knew that the Mau Mau had developed an acute sense of smell. Equally the smallest bit of litter, even a discarded sweet paper, would tell the terrorists that our patrols were around. Supply dropping was out, since the Pacers would give away our positions. There were in fact two main requirements for a forest company – to track and patrol well enough to obtain contacts, and to be certain of killing once contact had been obtained. We set to work with these two aims in view.

Earlier, Charles Baker-Cresswell, Ned Ram, Sergeant Arnold, and I spent three weeks with Venn Fey, a farmer on the Kinangop, the Rift Valley side of the Aberdares, learning his patrol technique. Venn Fey was a third generation Kenyan, whose family had come to the colony at the start of the century. During Operation Hammer, while the main body of the Army were toiling away on the other side of the Aberdares, Venn had taken heavy toll of gangs who had crossed to his side of the mountains and, thinking themselves secure, given their positions away. Venn taught us to work across the grain of the country, allowing our trackers and tracker dogs full scope to search for tracks. These, once discovered, were followed up energetically or ambushed. It all made sense and at last we now had a simple technique to follow which would provide us with the contacts we required. It was good of Venn to accept B Company at face value; he had been arguing hotly for some time with the authorities and, like most Kenyans, thought little of British regular soldiers. Perhaps B Company's disillusion with what we had been asked to do on Operation Hammer helped to make us credible; certainly Charles Baker-Cresswell, Ned Ram and Sergeant Arnold, in their different ways, all possessed star quality and obvious enthusiasm. Our later success owed everything to Venn's tracking technique.

Thanks to Venn, B Company now possessed a tracking technique. The other requirement, that of shooting straight, was simpler. We were lucky in being chosen to carry out troop trials on the new automatic FN rifle. Though slightly heavier, the FN had a higher muzzle velocity than the old .303; it was powerful enough to knock over any terrorist with one hit, and greatly added to our confidence. We wasted no time on Bisley style marksmanship; instead our jungle range, based on moving targets and the principles of 'Annie Get Your Gun', was pragmatic. The tracker teams shot on the jungle range every day; no one went into the forest unless they were in form, and anyone, of whatever rank, who was unfit or out of touch was ruthlessly dropped.

B Company abandoned the traditional platoon and section structure which did not fit our new pattern of working. Instead each platoon was divided into two tracker combat teams, each of eight men, commanded either by an officer or a sergeant. One of the two teams in each platoon possessed a tracker dog and handler. B Company thus fielded six tracker combat teams, three of them including a tracker dog. The balance of soldiers not selected for tracker teams were used to protect forest bases or as porters, the latter organized in a 'passive wing' under CSM Fosker. It was the job of the 'passive wing' to deliver rations to the tracker teams anywhere in the forest. It was not a simple task, since tracker teams had to be able to exist in the forest for long periods without the Mau Mau gangs being aware of their presence. Fosker used great ingenuity in making his deliveries; if using a cache by the side of the track, for example, the supplies would be carefully camouflaged to avoid drawing attention to them. The 'passive wing' group would then carry on up the track for a further half hour or so to make a dummy delivery to deceive the opposition about where our patrols were operating. We worked on the assumption that all our moves inside or outside the forest were watched and reported; a deception element was required in every plan. Inside the forest rigorous routines and strict patrol disciplines were essential. Rouse was at first light – 0600 hours – and the tracker teams got on the move by 0630 in order to take advantage of the early morning moisture which reflected tracks more clearly. Our patrols were lightly equipped, with just a camouflage smock over a shirt and jungle green trousers. We wore rubber jungle boots which gave some hope in a contact of being able to move fast enough to get in a shot at what was invariably a fleeting target. Patrols moved slowly while looking for tracks; we found the African trackers worked best if allowed to do so at their own speed. There was a half-hour halt about midday for lunch – biscuits and chocolate only, with just water to drink. No hot drink till dinner in the evening, when it was dark enough to make a fire in the bamboo whose smoke would not be visible to the terrorists. The evening meal was a good one, prepared during the day by the group responsible for protecting the bivouac area. Afterwards the patrol and trackers together would sit round the fire, discussing the day's events. The African trackers were superb mimics; my own idiosyncrasies, and nickname of Bwana Football, frequently figured in their imitations. Then sleep, protected by a sentry whose other job it was to keep the fire going all night; not only did this deter animals from coming near the base, but the fire would be needed for breakfast next morning. Such a routine at heights of between 8,000 to 10,000 feet needed the riflemen to be really fit, and capable of a high standard of marksmanship at fleeting targets, the range usually between 50 and 200 yards.

While we were training at Squair's Farm we also had an operational task. With the help of the tracker platoon from the Royal Northumberland Fusiliers, our task was to keep the Aberdares north of Nyeri free of large gangs while the rest of the security forces were involved in Operation FIRST FLUTE on Mount Kenya across the plain. Our first success came on 9 March, the result of accurate shooting by Sergeant Arnold's team while following up a well sustained bit of tracking by Charles Baker-Cresswell the previous day. Significantly it took 14 rounds at a range of 200 yards to dispose of this particular terrorist. Mau Mau often seemed immune to rifle bullets, the scientific explanation being that they were less affected by shock than Europeans.

By the end of the month we had developed confidence in our methods and it was time to leave Squair's Farm and find an area with more terrorists. Throughout April, therefore, we operated on Mount Kenya, while the rest of the battalion concentrated on the unspectacular tasks involved in Operation HUNGER STRIKE, a food denial plan intended to cut off supplies of food to the terrorists in the forest. Hunger Strike played a vital role in increasing pressure on the forest gangs. Shortage of food caused them to take risks to obtain supplies; it was not long before B Company, this time Ned Ram and his tracker team, were able to profit from such a situation.

Ned and his team were on patrol in the lower forest of Mount Kenya, searching for tracks in the way Venn Fey had taught us. They heard the sound of cattle and of terrorists chattering about 400 yards away on the other side of a steep valley. Ned determined on a careful stalk; so good was his fieldcraft and so quietly did his team move that they managed to get within 20 yards of a gang of twenty. The terrorists were killing and cutting up some cattle and, for once, had no sentries posted. Ned opened fire and two of the gang were killed immediately; a third, who ran straight into the patrol in trying to escape, met his death shortly afterwards. It vindicated B Company's tactics and Ned's team had made the most of their opportunity.

On 16 May we were told to stop operations on Mount Kenya and to prepare for a new assignment in the Aberdares. Since the end of March the Aberdares, south of Nyeri and opposite the Kikuyu Reserve, had been a closed area. No patrols had been allowed into the forest, nor had the RAF been permitted to fly over the area. Serious surrender talks between Special Branch and the Mau Mau leaders were in progress; so well did the discussion go at first that a deputation of terrorist leaders actually visited Nairobi in order to achieve a permanent ceasefire. By mid-May, however, the talks seemed certain to end in failure; the leaders either had too little control over their rank and file to persuade them to surrender or were using the talks as a chance to gain face and relief from the pressure of food denial. Chief Muhoya, a prominent loyalist, told me later that Mau Mau propaganda in the Reserve maintained that the surrender talks had been instigated by the Government; it was the security forces, so the terrorists claimed, who wished to come to terms with Mau Mau. To continue the talks would serve no purpose.

An operation south of Nyeri was therefore planned to follow the ending of the talks. Its aim was to engage the terrorists in the previously closed area before they dispersed or severed their contacts with the passive wing in the Reserve. GIMLET involved a night move into the forest by four battalions of KAR with a British tracker group, under my command, operating on their northern flank. My tracker group consisted of B Company, the forest company of the King's Own Yorkshire Light Infantry (KOYLI), two

Kikuyu tribal police units and a police General Service Unit (GSU). Mike Tippett, who had earlier shown great flair in forest operations during Hammer, came to run B Company for this operation, leaving me free to direct the remainder of my mixed force.

B Company's initial plan for Gimlet sounded simple. We would drive, in the dark, 50 miles south from our camp on Mount Kenya near Nanyuki, and establish four tracker teams deep in the forest before dawn. No previous reconnaissance was allowed, but the existence of the National Park track made deployment easier. Provided the weather was friendly, trucks could drive up to the moorland, which gave us a chance of getting our tracker teams into the forest unknown to the terrorists.

The final order 'Gimlet on' came through for the night 20/21 May. We left our Mount Kenya camp on a night as dark as any I can remember, but completed our move with very little hassle. By first light our HQ had occupied its new site on top of Nyeri Hill and we settled down to await news from the tracker teams. Nyeri Hill was a splendid place for the HQ; it stood straight up from the surrounding Reserve and provided excellent communications by short range VHF set to the patrols in the forest. These could talk clearly to Company HQ from their secret forest bases, and during Gimlet we never needed air contacts for control purposes. This was a great advantage, both for convenience and in keeping our forest bases secret. We received an unintentional cover plan; the KAR battalion on our left relied on air supply, which encouraged the Mau Mau to make for our area, where they could see there was no air activity. We kept our set on Nyeri Hill open throughout the 24 hours, but the patrols in the forest opened up only to pass their 'sitreps' – normally between 1600 and 1900 hours each day, and to receive their instructions for the next day, normally at 2000 hours, after all the 'sitreps' and information available from the area had been carefully considered. It says much for the reliability of the sets, and the competence of the operators, that this system worked so well.

The first day's returns were exciting. Charles Baker-Cresswell's team had contacted a small food-carrying party at the top edge of the lower forest. Two terrorists had been killed, though we did not find the body of the second until a week later. Again, the value of pausing to listen while following tracks stood out. In this case Charles stopped to do so and heard voices at the bottom of the hill; he split his patrol, leaving the trackers and the dog on the higher ground and embarking on a stalk himself with a corporal and two riflemen. So silently did they move that they got within 30 yards of the gang before opening fire. Equally satisfying was the contact of a single terrorist by Sergeant Burrell up on the moorland; here the range was 200 yards and reflected cool accurate shooting at a height of over 10,000 feet. These two contacts were the first terrorists killed on Gimlet and made a good start for us with the KAR Brigade, who, though polite and friendly, had been sceptical of our tactics and the reasoning behind them.

The Mau Mau, surprised by the scale of Gimlet and unaware of its boundaries, remained at first in the areas where they had been living comfortably during the ceasefire talks. The two tribal police units under our command took advantage of the terrorists' indecision and secured seven kills between them before the gangs changed their tactics. They now moved up onto the moorland, where they lay low for a while, relying on existing stocks of food and hoping that the security forces would be deceived by the absence of tracks in the bamboo and lower forest and would call the operation off. Our tracker teams experienced a short lull, with few fresh tracks for the next few days. During this period, however, Charles Baker-Cresswell's team found Dedan Kimathi's Government House, and a church nearby with seating for eighty to 100 terrorists. This was a coup for B Company. Dedan Kimathi was the most daring of the gang leaders still in the field and the leader of the Aberdare elements of the rebellion. He and his followers had evidently been living comfortably in recent weeks; Dedan Kimathi himself had a desk and primitive office furniture. On his desk there was an ivory paperweight, which Charles and his team kindly gave me; it sits on my writing table to this day. Charles also captured minutes of the Mount Kenya Parliament; though of no great immediate operational significance, these aroused great interest in GHQ. Charles' discovery attracted the attention of the BBC, whose Middle East correspondent, carrying a TV camera, made his way to Government House and delighted the riflemen at the prospect of appearing on TV.

B Company was in the thick of things and on 30 May 6 Platoon tracker team, commanded by a young Kenya Regiment sergeant, D'Adhemar, took part in a rare pitched battle with an aggressive and well armed gang. A patient piece of tracking led the patrol to a hollow tree about 3,000 yards from the forest fringe; a search revealed seven notebooks, including a diary of the emergency kept by Dedan Kimathi himself, and further minutes of the Mount Kenya Parliament. This capture was another valuable intelligence coup and we delivered the documents to Special Branch in Nyeri that night. After getting rid of the papers, Sergeant D'Adhemar settled his patrol for the night, using a log cabin conveniently close to hand.

At about 2000 hours, about an hour after dark, one of the African trackers went outside to answer a call of nature. He had hardly begun when a bullet flashed past him; he returned to the hut and warned the patrol, who stood to and awaited developments. Soon a full-scale attack developed, about forty Mau Mau being involved. About sixty rounds were fired by each side, but the shooting in the dark was poor and there were no confirmed casualties, though Corporal Smithers, manning the Bren, shot a terrorist in the stomach at a range of 15 yards, but saw him pulled to safety before the patrol could get out of the hut to capture him. The Mau Mau used a variety of weapons from a .303 to a .22. Many of the weapons were homemade, and, fortunately, had too little kick to penetrate the timber walls of the hut. Two more attacks took place during the night, but without visible result, despite the expenditure of much ammunition. Next day B Company was too slow; it was partly my fault, for it took too long to establish what had happened. The likelihood of a patrol being attacked at night had seemed so remote that they did not usually come on the air on the morning before moving off. On this occasion Sergeant D'Adhemar and his patrol were slow in reporting what had occurred; by the time I reached the scene it was too late to organize a proper follow up. Nevertheless, we learnt some valuable lessons, not least the danger of over-confidence; we arranged, in future, for patrols to open up briefly on the air at 0630 each morning before they moved off, and added an extra Bren to the base element of each patrol. A high-level terrorist, probably Kimathi himself, had been in the area; no one else would have ordered such an attack, or pressed it home with such determination.

These adventures, however, kept B Company in the news, and on 1 June Gerald Lathbury, the new C in C who had taken the place of Bobby Erskine, visited us on Nyeri Hill. Gerald Lathbury brought with him *The Times'* military correspondent and his GSO1, Hugh Hope, of the 60th Rifles. We gave him a description of our methods; he was interested in our briefing and made an appointment to see a tracker team in the forest. A week later he visited the joint base of 5 Platoon's two tracker teams below Rohoruini Hill. It was a fortunate visit since Sergeant Arnold had killed a terrorist the previous day after a skilful 48-hour ambush on a game snare about 200 yards from the platoon base. The rest area had been well sited; the terrorists went within 20 yards of those of the patrol off duty before running into the ambush, so indicating the value of good battle discipline and suggesting that Mau Mau had little idea of how we were now operating.

Gerald Lathbury was altogether B Company's kind of general; I hoped he enjoyed his visit to us as much as we did. He was a good listener, not only to the simple theory on which we operated, but, more importantly, to Charles Baker-Cresswell, Sergeant Arnold and their riflemen. Gerald had made his name as a Parachute Brigade Commander; he had been at Arnhem, besides having previously learnt his trade as an infantryman in The Rifle Brigade's sister regiment, the Oxfordshire and Buckinghamshire Light Infantry, soon to be joined with us in the Royal Green Jackets. Thus he was at home in the forest with the riflemen and, by his informality, able to get the best from them. When Gerald left us, I guessed he had drawn the right conclusions from his visit. It was not long before the B Company organization became the universal pattern; we had stressed particularly that there was nothing special about B Company. We were lucky that Venn Fey had shown us how to track methodically; the rest was applied common sense and good leadership by the patrol commanders. We followed again Sir John Moore's formula of the 'thinking fighting man'; as usual, the riflemen had responded to the challenge when it was presented to them and, by being encouraged to think, surprised everyone by their ingenuity.

As Gimlet increased the pressures on the terrorists' food supplies, the gangs started to split up into small groups of five or six. They became hungry and disorganized, and further successes came our way. On 13 June Corporal Taylor, leading a patrol in the Treetops Salient, captured and wounded a terrorist in another well sited ambush. I was proud of this success, since the Treetops area was full of game, and for a young Londoner, only 19 years of age, to lead a patrol in such circumstances, with buffalo and rhino all round, was a fine achievement. Next day Sergeant Burrell, following up tracks from this incident, killed a terrorist sitting in a tree. For the next week there were daily contacts. We were not always successful; sometimes bad luck or bad control of our trackers prevented us getting value from an operation, but we were learning all the time. On 19 June Charles Baker-Cresswell's team brought off our best coup so far, killing four terrorists out of a gang of six; following up the next day, Ned Ram shot another terrorist and recovered a quantity of .22 ammunition. On 27 June, after I had allowed the KOYLI to operate round Treetops, Ned Ram went into their territory further north and scored yet another success. When Operation Gimlet came to an end on 4 July, we had proved to our own satisfaction that our tactics were sound, and that our officers, sergeants and junior NCOs could all get results. We returned to 1 RB at Maro Moru for a month's rest and re-training, proud of our efforts, but also anxious to help others to do as well.

During our break from operations, I tried hard to get people away from the forest. By now The Rifle Brigade had made friends among the settlers and we received many invitations, often from places far afield and not affected by the emergency, like Kitale, Sotik and Mau Narok. In B Company we had a rule that the officers never accepted an invitation unless two corporals or riflemen were invited too. At first our hosts were surprised at our attitude, and perhaps fearful that the riflemen might not feel at home. They need not have worried; the riflemen were admirable guests and the conversation, if sometimes following unusual channels, never flagged. Lord Portsmouth kindly asked a B Company party to stay on his farm at Kitale. When they returned, I asked Corporal Baker, my sophisticated signal NCO, how his safari had gone. "Smashing," was the reply. "But Lord Portsmouth's champagne was a little too dry for my taste," he added in an enquiring but not critical tone. There were many similar conversations, and it was good to see how people enjoyed each other's company in these situations. Each group learnt from the other, and the exchanges were as valuable for those from the Old Kent Road as for the members of Kenya's exclusive Muthaiga Club, often our generous hosts. The riflemen were struck by how hard the farmers worked and how difficult their job was; equally our hosts learned to respect the British soldier, and the intelligence of the riflemen.

We returned to operations on 6 August, this time on Mount Kenya. Our camp was near what was then the Mawingo Hotel, nowadays the exclusive and expensive Mount Kenya Safari Club. We made an airfield with Kikuyu labour, a football ground, and pioneered new tracks up Mount Kenya. We had a huge operational area, stretching right round the northern edge of Mount Kenya as far as the border of the Meru Reserve. There was a forest frontage of 40 miles, and, with such a large area to cover, our task was different to the role we had undertaken during Operation Gimlet. Now our role was to keep our stretch of forest clear of gangs, so that the farmers in the settled area outside could get on with ranching without the distraction of stock thefts. It was a wise change of policy, reflecting the success the security forces had achieved in breaking the back of Mau Mau.

B Company had a quieter time in Nanyuki than had been the case on Nyeri Hill. There was more time for leisure and a chance to consider what we had learnt during the past year. David Alexander-Sinclair came to us as second-in-command, and I aimed to hand B Company over to him when I had to leave at the end of October to go as a member of the Directing Staff to the Staff College. I developed an agreeable routine those last three months. It was not difficult to get the day's work done by 1030 in the morning; we usually had only two patrols in the forest, which meant we had plenty in reserve to follow up unexpected situations arising anywhere. From 1030 to 1200, therefore, I donned my tracksuit and coached our very good battalion and company football teams. The weather was splendid; the rains were behind us and the winter rains not expected till November. A light lunch, and into the landrover to call on the police, a local settler, or check on some piece of intelligence. Back by four, at which time the Pacer, with Derek Helens usually its pilot, had arrived and we would overfly our area to check that all was well. During our flight we would contact our forest patrols, hear about any tracks they had found and plan their activity for the following day. Back to Nanyuki for tea, after which we encouraged local farmers to drop in for a drink and a gossip. It was a relaxed life and there was for once time to get to know the riflemen really well and listen to their reactions. I learnt more from the riflemen than they can have gleaned from me; perhaps the main lesson was the judgement and common sense which the ordinary soldier brings to any problem, provided he is briefed properly and kept informed. In B Company I adopted a system copied from the Indian Army, where a weekly 'durbar' is the normal practice. I talked for ten minutes on what we were trying to do operationally and opened the meeting to the customers. No topic was barred, provided the suggestion was constructive; 'whinges' were not encouraged, and, in any event, were ill received by the audience. It resembled a civilised version of Prime Minister's Question Time and I think we all enjoyed it. Since people understood the reasoning behind the rules there was virtually no crime, yet another argument in favour of the philosophy of the 'thinking fighting man'.

Despite our more relaxed approach, we continued to have our share of success. Charles Baker-Cresswell still excelled, and celebrated his impending departure for home with two brilliant patrols resulting in the deaths of another four terrorists. Our African trackers were outstanding, and we had learnt by now to make effective use of the tracker dogs. We treated our African trackers just like riflemen; though they had their own separate area in camp, they had similar rights of access to the management as British soldiers. Many good ideas emerged from this joint consultation; at first all communication was through our Kenya Regiment sergeant, but soon we learnt enough Swahili to be able to make points for ourselves. The Africans, though initially not very skilful, quickly became fanatical footballers; by combining with the dhobis, who did our washing, they formed their own platoon football team, Trackers and Dhobis Athletic. The riflemen supported them loyally when they took the field, at first against the reserve sides of other platoons, but later, more ambitiously, against local African teams from outside. Though our trackers came from several tribes, Nandi, Kipsigis and Samburu for example, we had no tribal problems; it was good that they identified so strongly with B Company and The Rifle Brigade.

Early in B Company's life as a tracker company, I decided a special tactical sign would provide a focus for the high morale, which was a main element in achieving success. Inside the hollow square which represented B Company's normal tactical sign we therefore painted a large footprint; it was meant to represent the track left by Man Friday for Robinson Crusoe. We became proud of Man Friday's Foot, and our drivers enjoyed explaining its origins when they visited Nairobi. On my own landrover, Joe Lewis, my driver and the battalion's brilliant goalkeeper, attached a small football to the large foot to indicate B Company's prowess at football.

I was sad to leave B Company, since I knew that this would, sadly but inevitably, be my last command at this level, and felt nostalgic at the thought. A company is essentially a personal command; it is the last level at which one knows all about everyone for whom one is responsible. A company, directly, reflects one's own personality; looking back at my career, I realize how lucky I was to have spent so much of my life at this level of command. I have the happiest memories of B Company, Man Friday's Foot and those who supported me so loyally. But I recognized it was time to move; if I had stayed much longer, there was danger that

B Company would degenerate, as Green Jacket outfits sometimes do, into a mutual admiration society. It is easier to think one is good than to remain so, and B Company probably needed the stimulus of a new leader. Under David Alexander-Sinclair Man Friday's Foot continued to be successful operationally, and B Company maintained its high morale and sense of humour.

Chapter Eleven

THE STAFF COLLEGE, THE ROUND BALL
AND A HAPPY MARRIAGE

I stayed in Cyprus with my sister Priscilla and her husband, Julian Wathen, on my way back from Kenya. The EOKA emergency was in its early stages; the administration seemed to have been taken by surprise. There was no effective intelligence organization, the police were overwhelmed, and the military headquarters was out of touch. While I was in Limassol, the Governor, Sir Robert Armitage, was replaced by Field Marshal Sir John Harding, who had just retired as Chief of the Imperial General Staff, and, at once, a different approach obtained. Tom Acton, a fellow rifleman, came out with John Harding as his Military Assistant and told the Field Marshal that I was in Limassol. I was flattered at being asked to lunch at Government House in Nicosia to discuss my time in Kenya, but my contribution only confirmed what the Field Marshal already knew.

I worried about my brother-in-law, Julian Wathen. A fluent Greek speaker, and Manager of Barclays Bank in Limassol, he was busy helping the embryo intelligence organization and it was likely that before long he would become a target for EOKA. His job as a bank manager made him follow a fixed routine, making an assassination attempt easier. There was little I could do to help; it would have been wrong to alarm my sister unnecessarily and Julian was well aware of the risks he was running. I did, however, have a word with Tom Acton about my anxieties. A murder attempt on Julian occurred the following February, but fortunately merely wounded him in the shoulder. Tom Acton intervened at once to ensure Julian was properly protected in hospital after the shooting; I rang Barclays Bank in London from the Staff College and, quoting John Harding, persuaded Julian's employers to bring him home immediately before EOKA could organize another murder attempt.

I soon settled into the agreeable routine of the Directing Staff at Camberley. My first Commandant was 'Splosh' Jones, under whom I had served in 7 Armoured Division. The Staff College itself, however, was not in such good shape as I remembered it as a student five years before. In 1955 the curriculum had altered little since 1950; the course still taught, admirably, the lessons of the Second World War, but did not reflect the new challenges facing the Army, of which Kenya and Cyprus were examples. The Commandant had already recognized this weakness and I found myself a member of a 'cold war' team, charged with introducing new subjects and exercises to reflect these different priorities.

There were outstanding colleagues in developing these new themes. Richard Clutterbuck, later to build a second career as a professor at Exeter University in the special subject of counter-revolutionary war, was well ahead of his time in understanding intelligence. David Willison, a critical sapper, was another stimulating influence. Later he was to become Deputy Chief of Staff (Intelligence) and a leading expert on all aspects of intelligence work.

The cold war team acquired a further reinforcement in Jacques Brulé, the liaison officer from the French Army. Jacques was an officer in the Foreign Legion; he had served recently in Indo-China and came to the Staff College from his regiment in Algeria, where the rebellion, starting in 1954, had by 1956 gathered momentum. It was obvious that the Algerian emergency was on a much bigger scale than those in Malaya and Kenya with which the British Army had dealt successfully. The French Army's failure in Indo-China and the disastrous episode of Dien Bien Phu had left them humiliated. Jacques explained that they were determined to make full use of the lessons learnt in Indo-China; they could not afford another military failure in Algeria and were confident of their ability to suppress the rebellion.

My friendship with Jacques Brulé, his membership of the cold war team and the support of the Commandant brought me an invitation to lecture at the Ecole de Guerre, the French equivalent of the Staff College, on the Kenya emergency. I was offered an interpreter, but decided that my French could be made good enough to deliver my talk in French. My fluency in French dated from my time in Algeria and Tunisia between 1942 and 1944. Thus my accent was nasal like that of the 'colons'; though my French friends politely described it as 'Belgian', they knew and so did I that my tone was that of a 'pied noir'. Socially my French accent had disadvantages; professionally, however, I gained from its idiosyncrasies since it was so unusual for a British officer to talk French with a pronounced colonial accent that my audience listened attentively. It was as if a French officer had come to Camberley, speaking colloquial English with a pronounced Liverpool accent. Though my lecture at the Ecole de Guerre was programmed for the afternoon, and followed an excellent lunch, my audience remained flatteringly awake. I guessed that the main attraction had been my Algerian accent, and possible affronts to the French language and the Académie française, the institution responsible for its continued purity.

Professionally, the French were interested in the tactics of colonial emergencies; the younger officers, and especially those who had served in Indo-China or Algeria, enjoyed my strictures against large-scale operations and realized the value of continuity in command structures. The Commandant of the Ecole de Guerre, General Lecomte, had already identified the views of these younger middle-piece officers. He asked 'Splosh' Jones if I could be spared for a period of study in Paris itself and for a full-scale visit to Algeria later. 'Splosh' accepted enthusiastically; not only was it good for Camberley's image that the French admitted they had something to learn from us, but our own studies would gain from a look at French methods in Algeria.

The Suez operation caused my Algerian trip to be postponed till January 1957 and, so scathing were French criticisms of the British performance at Suez, nearly led to its cancellation. Fortunately, however, Lecomte kept his sense of proportion, realizing that the French Army had little to lose from my voyage of exploration. I flew to Paris, stayed a night with Diana and John Beith in their Gate House at the Embassy and left next evening with my '*compagnon de voyage*', Colonel Jean Craplet, for Algiers. From my point of view Craplet was a superb choice as bear leader; he spoke some English, but not much, but this was not important. What mattered was Craplet's approach to soldiering, sense of humour and fundamental friendship for the British. In the early days of Monty's time as C in C Western Union – about 1948 – Craplet had served the Field Marshal for a year as one of his ADCs; he had enjoyed the experience, learnt much and emerged with a fund of good stories. Craplet had earlier learnt his trade in the Chasseurs Alpins, a regiment whose approach to life, including a quick step, a liking for bugles and informality, had much in common with The Rifle Brigade. We became friends, and I was not surprised by Craplet's subsequent career. In Algeria he commanded first a Brigade, then a Division; next he served as Commandant of St Cyr before retiring as C in C of the French Army in Germany. Sadly, he was to die soon after his retirement, falling asleep at the wheel of his car after a visit to a battalion of his regiment, of which he was Colonel.

The Algerian rising had taken the French by surprise when it began in November 1954 with scattered incidents of arson, bomb throwing and ambushes. The bulk of rebel activities occurred in Eastern Algeria, particularly in the Aures Mountains. The French were dumbfounded; Algeria had been quiet since a brief abortive rising in 1945, ruthlessly suppressed with some 1,500 Muslims killed in the process. Though there had been active nationalist agitation in neighbouring Morocco and Tunisia, the Muslim population in Algeria seemed unaffected. Algeria was prosperous and the idea of disloyalty had not occurred to the French authorities. Indeed, at first, the French considered that the first outbreaks of trouble in Eastern Algeria were the work of Tunisian nationalists, anxious to stir up trouble elsewhere to divert attention from the insurgency in Tunisia itself. Thus, the French military command treated the situation as a small local tribal revolt and were slow to recognize its scale.

Only in March 1955 was a State of Emergency declared, and it was August before the emergency regulations applied universally. The French were heavily committed elsewhere and, like the British, victims of military overstretch; in May 1955 there were barely 100,000 soldiers in Algeria. It was not until the autumn of 1956 that a total of 400,000 soldiers, the number then estimated as necessary to crush the rising, was even contemplated. The Suez crisis meant that this figure was not reached till early 1957. The French command found they could only contain the rebellion during 1956; my first visit to Algeria coincided with the French being able at last to plan their campaign.

By the end of 1956 the French had evolved a military strategy. It was based on 'quadrillage' or grid system of deployment. Quadrillage involved the garrisoning of major towns and cities in strength, while other smaller towns, villages and even individual farms were similarly protected, though, of course, in lesser strength. Quadrillage absorbed large numbers of troops, leaving relatively few for mobile operations; nevertheless, it ensured the security of the main centres of population and communications. Quadrillage also involved full co-operation between police, military and the civil administration; in this way it followed the British doctrine of the 'three-legged stool' which had proved effective in Malaya. As the quadrillage became effective, operations were linked to a civil development programme, based on building roads, clinics and schools, projects undertaken as soon as the Army smothered guerrilla activity.

It was the right recipe for military success, once the necessary troops were available, while the Government in Paris provided the massive sums the programme would cost. Jean Craplet and I set out on our voyage of discovery, optimistic that the French would be successful militarily, even though we both had our doubts about the political environment within which any purely military achievement would have to take place. In other words, as I had been warned beforehand in a perceptive briefing by Michael Palliser, then Second Secretary at the Embassy in Paris, there was danger of an arid military achievement, which would leave matters no better than before and the French embittered by their failure.

Our first visit outside Algiers was to Constantine, an area I knew well from having lived near Philippeville for nine months in 1943 and 1944, while 6 Armoured Division re-trained after the Tunisian campaign. In January 1957 the French military situation in Eastern Algeria was unhealthy. The French held the main towns, Constantine, Bône, Setif, Philippeville, and the main roads between them securely, but large areas of the 'bled', or open countryside, were dominated by the rebels. The main roads in the area were open, at least by day, but one needed an escort, in our case of two armoured cars from the Gendarmerie, and often a section of infantry as well, to travel safely. Usually Jean Craplet and I, therefore, as privileged visitors, travelled by light aircraft or helicopter, which, though convenient for us, reflected the difficult security situation. Moreover, the boundary with newly independent Tunisia presented special problems. Just across the border, centred on Sakiet Sidi Youssef, the ALN maintained bases for training and recruitment for their forces in the field in Algeria. The French were forbidden to attack these ALN bases and diplomatic pressure on Tunis was unproductive. The future therefore appeared bleak, though the military commanders we met remained positive in their intentions.

We had a memorable flight to Bir el Ater, about 40 miles beyond the important centre of Tebessa, and not far from the Tunisian frontier. Here we saw the work of the 'Services Arabes Speciales', a new group formed mostly of young officers, nearly all under 30, whose task was to administer large sectors of the country which had previously existed without formal control. The setting of Bir el Ater was pure Beau Geste; an oasis with palm trees, a neat white fort with a small military garrison, the outpost presided over by a captain aged 28, accompanied by his pretty wife, who helped him in many of his activities. We were given a marvellous lunch, washed down by excellent Algerian wine, followed by delicious dates. Over the meal our host explained his responsibilities – security, education, development of agriculture, communications, water supply and administration of justice. It was a superb job for an intelligent young officer and the 'SAS' officers were well chosen. After lunch we met the local Arab leaders, who were an impressive bunch, though understandably anxious to end up on the winning side in the emergency. I had to say a few words, and, mindful of my earlier briefing from Michael Palliser, managed to do so without, I hope, being too equivocal. I could certainly sincerely wish them and my host good fortune; sadly, many of those who co-operated with the French must have been killed later as collaborators after the establishment of an independent Algeria.

My programme took me all over Algeria, with visits to Tlemcen and Colomb Béchar perhaps the highlights. In Algiers I met the famous General Massu, just embarking on a large-scale operation to clean up the Kasbah; this area, right in the middle of Algiers, had become a 'no go' area and was the centre for much terrorist activity, besides being a base for logistic support. Massu's plans for the Kasbah reflected the same stage in the

Algerian emergency as Operation ANVIL against Mau Mau elements in Nairobi during our Kenya campaign. It took Massu longer than he had anticipated to sort out the Kasbah and it was nine months before he reported success.

I was due to meet General Salan, the C in C in Algiers, but just as Craplet and I were about to leave the Aletti the telephone rang. It was a harassed junior staff officer from General Salan's Headquarters. Our appointment was off; ten minutes earlier a bazooka fired from a building across the road had smashed in Salan's offices, killing his Chef de Cabinet and wrecking much of the building. Though Salan himself was uninjured, he was clearly in no mood for interviews with visiting British officers, and, in the circumstances, I was relieved to be spared the ordeal.

Before we left Algiers, Craplet established that the attempt on General Salan's life had been carried out by right-wing Europeans, probably from the group who subsequently developed into the OAS (*Organisation Armée Secrete*). It was ironical that the attempted assassination should have come from this quarter in view of Salan's later leadership of the OAS; at that time, however, Salan's views on Algeria had not fully developed and the extremists regarded him merely as yet another French general with 'soft' views about the emergency.

I continued to keep touch with the French Army and gave a presentation on Algeria to Camberley, which I hope encouraged the study of counter-revolutionary war. To some students, like Frank Kitson, I was preaching to the converted, but it was not easy to obtain a balance with the requirements of BAOR, which remained the British Army's principal contribution to European security.

I managed to pay a return visit to Algeria in July 1958, soon after General de Gaulle had assumed power following the virtual collapse of the Third Republic. General de Gaulle's presence as Head of State gave France a stability and confidence which had previously been lacking. My own second visit to Algeria took place a month after de Gaulle's visit to Algeria; there can seldom have been a more Delphic utterance than his famous "*Je vous ai compris*" statement in Algiers. De Gaulle, who knew Algeria well from his time in Algiers in 1943 and 1944, understood the settlers and their state of mind exactly; the converse, however, was not true and his audience, including many leading soldiers, totally failed to grasp its implications.

All this was unknown to me as I flew to Algiers on 10 July 1958. This time my companion was Lieutenant Colonel de Boisheraud, like his predecessor Jean Craplet an instructor at the Ecole de Guerre. We got on well and I enjoyed his company and support. Like me, de Boisheraud enjoyed the good things of life; we dined agreeably and well together, with plenty of the local Algerian wine to wash down our repast.

The tension in Algiers had totally disappeared. Traffic flowed normally, the drivers hooted their horns as in any other French city, and the streets were crowded and animated. The new features were posters everywhere of General de Gaulle and the Cross of Lorraine; often these were accompanied by either "Vive Salan" or "Vive Massu". A striking poster, reflecting the thinking at the time of both 'colons' and the Army, was a map of France stretching from the northern frontier with Belgium right down to the Sahara. There was an effective caption: *"De Dunkerque à Tamanrasset – Tous Français"*. Cinemas, public transport and restaurants, all crowded, worked smoothly. There was no evidence of hostility towards the French or other Europeans like myself, and the young Arabs in the city wore the jeans and sported the Tony Curtis haircuts which then were the uniform of Western youth. On 14 July (Bastille Day) I went to bathe at Alger Plage (20 miles from Algiers itself) and found the beaches as crowded as they would have been at any seaside place in Metropolitan France.

It was no surprise, therefore, to find General Marguet, Chief of Staff to Salan at HQ 10 Region, in an optimistic frame of mind. Marguet stressed the significance of General de Gaulle's accession in improving the overall position. The events of 13 May had helped the Army in many ways. In particular, now that the Army controlled the civil administration, the power of the *'gros colons'*, the large settlers lobby, was much less. There was more confidence among the civil Arab population, so much so that the ALN were finding recruitment difficult and the desertion rate from the terrorist bands had risen significantly. The French Army's propaganda was clearly proving effective; the ALN had recently introduced an automatic death penalty for anyone in their ranks found guilty of listening to the French radio or even reading a French leaflet.

My first two visits – to the Corps area responsible for the Algiers sector, and to the Ninth Infantry Division at Orleansville, the formation responsible for the Ouarsenis Mountain Massif – confirmed what we had been told at HQ 10 Region. But the real transformation was along the frontier with Tunisia. Eighteen months before, it was impossible to move outside the towns without an escort; I recalled that even to go to the airfield five miles away we had been given a jeep escort of armed gendarmerie. Now it was normal to travel on the main Route 16 from Bône 400 miles south to Negrine in the desert without any escort, even at night; since, throughout its length Route 16 parallels the Tunisian frontier, it was obvious that the danger from gangs crossing from Tunisia had been eliminated. Traffic moved perfectly normally and at typical French high speed just as it would have done in Metropolitan France. In Bône itself, there were no incidents of any kind during my time there, and I was told there had not been one for the past three months. Relations between Moslems and French appeared good and there was a noticeable atmosphere of calm without the slightest evidence of tension.

I studied the barrier along the Tunisian frontier which had so completely changed the situation. Known as the Morice Line, it consisted of a five-hundred-volt electric fence, 12 feet high, protected on either side by a normal double apron wire obstacle. The Morice Line ran from the Mediterranean all the way to Negrine 400 miles south in the Sahara. In places the fence was doubled, and for much of the way even trebled. Thus a terrorist gang wishing to pass through the barrier needed to cross three separate electric obstacles during the course of a single night. The fence was patrolled by French mobile forces mounted in armoured cars or half tracks. These mobile elements were equipped with searchlights and operated even more intensively by night than by day. There was a simple system which established at once when and where the barrier had been cut. Sensibly, the French did not regard the Morice Line as providing an absolute obstacle to the passage of the gangs. The aim was rather to provide a steady stream of accurate and up-to-date information about frontier crossers.

The frontier barrage in fact provided the accurate intelligence needed for the intervention of mobile reserves. The latter, pre-allotted to various sectors of the barrage, intervened almost automatically; there seemed little need for difficult command decisions. No less than 50,000 troops were employed at that time in maintaining the barrage; a feature of the French tactics was that only 10,000 of these troops were tied down on static duties, the remaining 80% being available for mobile operations. The barrage was covered by artillery, with great use being made of radar both to provide information and to direct the fire of the guns. By today's standards the radar sets were fairly primitive – normal anti-aircraft equipment for the period. Nevertheless, even those sets were able to pick up a man or a patrol at a range of 12 kilometres. Having identified the target, they were able to follow it up to a distance of 30 kilometres.

The barrier altered the whole state of the Algerian emergency. By making life difficult for line-crossers, the rebels in Algeria became increasingly isolated from their supplies and reinforcements in Tunisia. The Morice Line was the chief single factor in producing the military conditions which finally ended the emergency. I have often wondered what would have happened in Northern Ireland if we had been able to contemplate a similar frontier barrier along the frontier with the Irish Republic.

I also owe to the Staff College my involvement with what proved an enduring and enjoyable extra-mural activity. I have always been fond of football, whether as player, spectator or, later, coach. While at Camberley, I became a committee member of the Army Football Association. Soon I was on the Executive Committee, and almost at once, as a member of the Selection Committee, associated with the Secretary, Gerry Mitchell, in the management of the Army's representative teams. Those were the days of national service and the Army side contained the cream of the country's young footballers, Scots, Welsh and Irish, as well as merely English. It was a privilege to be involved in the management of so much talent. During my time in management the Army team included Bobby Charlton, Manchester United and England, Alex Parker, our captain, Everton and Scotland, Cliff Jones, Tottenham and Wales, Gerry Hitchens, Aston Villa and England, and John White, Tottenham and Scotland – to name but a few of the outstanding players at our disposal. So good was our side that even the combative Dave Mackay, later to win great fame, sometimes found himself reduced to the substitute's bench. It was a memorable experience for a football fanatic like myself, and the journeys north by sleeper to Scotland, Merseyside and elsewhere are firmly fixed in my memory. So, too, are the informal drink parties on the return journey, with Gerry Mitchell's ability to absorb Scotch whisky a feature, especially when, as often happened, the Army had won a famous victory.

My role with the Army representative football team led to my becoming for a period Football Correspondent of the *Sunday Times* and to remaining a correspondent with that newspaper until 1990. In 1957, under the Kemsley regime, the *Sunday Times* was essentially a rugby football paper. That code was well covered by several excellent writers; football, in contrast, hardly got a mention. I suspect that Denis Hamilton, an outstanding Editor but then still Personal Assistant to Lord Kemsley, spotted the gap in the paper's sports coverage and resolved to rectify matters. At all events I found myself approached at a cocktail party given at Minley Manor by Douglas Darling; the suggestion came from Roger Mortimer, then the Racing Correspondent, who had been a prisoner of war in Germany and knew The Rifle Brigade well. I was delighted when Ken Compston, the Sports Editor, rang the Staff College while I was chairing a syndicate discussion the following week. Would I cover Arsenal v. Manchester City next Saturday? He feared he could only afford a fee of ten guineas on top of my expenses, but hoped that I could understand that, as yet, I was an untried journalist. Hardly able to believe my luck, I gasped my acceptance of the terms and returned in a state of euphoria to my syndicate. It was October 1957 and I continued to write on Saturdays for over thirty years.

But the most important, and by far the happiest, event to occur during my time at Camberley was my marriage to Jean, who was brave enough to take me on at the advanced age of 37 and has given me a married life of wonderful happiness. Our meeting owed much to chance. Diana Beith's mother, Victoria Gilmour, Tor-Tor as she was known, had been incredibly kind to me over the years. While I was at Camberley I used to go over to her lovely Mulberry House at Bentworth near Alton for lunch, dinner and frequent weekends. Tor-Tor's hospitality was magnificent and the company frequently well above my level. On this occasion, for once, my enthusiasm for a visit to Mulberry was less than total. Tor-Tor had asked me to make up a party for a charity ball in Winchester, not really my scene at all; I was busy with my Algerian plans, the demands of football management and my burgeoning career as a football correspondent. Nevertheless, I gathered from Tor-Tor on the telephone that this was a three-line whip and accepted with a good grace. There was to be a dinner party beforehand at Mulberry and this I would undoubtedly enjoy.

When the dinner party assembled, I could hardly believe my luck. Among our party of six to go on afterwards to the dance at Winchester was the most lovely girl; she was apparently the first cousin of Diana Beith, and, by extension Tor-Tor's niece. There was a snag; Jean had a partner, a nice enough gunner major, fortunately not known to me. During dinner, I debated with myself the extent to which, in however ungentlemanly a fashion, I could cut him out. "All is fair in love and war," I reflected, while W.S. Gilbert's advice about faint hearts and fair ladies came to mind. In any event, it would be up to Jean herself; at worst, I would be risking a brush off, and the stakes made this a risk worth taking.

Happily my luck was in. During dinner Jean and I got on well. We had much in common; Jean knew India – her father had been Governor of Madras – and conversation flowed on this and other topics. Jean even knew about football; her father had once been Member of Parliament for the Aston division of Birmingham and attendance by his daughters at Villa Park had been part of their electioneering duty. Greatly daring, I broached the subject of her escorting gunner. Great was my relief when I found that he was not, in any sense, a 'steady', just an acquaintance brought along as a companion for the evening.

Jean and I drove to Winchester together, danced or sat out continuously at the Guildhall, and spent an evening so happy that I am reminded of it whenever I go near Bentworth or to Winchester. Our paths, however, had to divide on the return journey, for I had to return to Mulberry for the night, which meant Jean's original partner taking her home to her house at Tunworth near Basingstoke. During the evening I had given Jean my address, and thought I could discover hers by looking up her father in *Who's Who* and writing to her there. This I did the next morning, posted my letter and hoped for the best in terms of a favourable reply to my suggestions and plans for future meetings.

Sadly, there was no reply. Perhaps I had been overeager or brash in my suggestions. Perhaps, though I thought this unlikely, the gunner major had launched a successful counter-attack. I did not like to ring up Tor-Tor to get Jean's Hampshire address, lest either of these fears might turn out true. I fell back on Micawberism, the last refuge of the timid and incompetent.

Luckily Jean was more resourceful than me. After an interminable ten days or so I found a letter from her waiting in my pigeonhole at the Staff

College. It contained an invitation to supper at her house at Tunworth, which I accepted at once.

Our supper together was a delight. Jean proved a marvellous cook and chose a lovely white wine to wash the meal down, a delightful Montrachet, which must have cost the earth at the time, and is well above our level today. After dinner we listened to music; Brahms Violin Concerto, the Brahms Haydn variations and some Beethoven. It turned out that Jean's father was desperately ill with cancer, and likely to die at any moment. The address in *Who's Who* to which I had sent the letter was therefore no longer operative; sure enough, I got it back a day or two later endorsed "Not known at this address". But for Jean's initiative, our first meeting might have been still-born. I shudder when I think of what I might have missed. My friends have always envied my luck, and this was undoubtedly its prime example. We were married on 3 October 1958 and have lived happily together ever since.

Chapter Twelve

RMA SANDHURST AND A CHANGE
OF REGIMENTAL ALLEGIANCE

After the Staff College I was lucky to get a final spell of regimental soldiering as a Greenjacket – as second in command of what was still The Rifle Brigade in Wuppertal. It was a good time; we worked hard to build a battalion of regular soldiers and set the tone for the future.

I do not, however, intend to write much about this period here. Forty years later, what then seemed important now appears either irrelevant or so obvious as not to require re-stating. Nevertheless we did our best to lay sensible foundations for the future and the continued success of the RGJ suggests we did not do too badly.

Professionally, however, I was marking time until my next job. In April 1960 I heard I had been selected to be GSO 1 (Chief of Staff) to the Royal Military Academy, Sandhurst, considered a plum appointment. Somehow, though, I had doubts about how much I would enjoy myself and how well suited I would be to Sandhurst. When I had been at Camberley at the Staff College I had been unimpressed by the RMA and doubted if I could adjust easily to being part of that establishment.

The difficulty was that Sandhurst fell between two stools, military and academic. However one attempted to rearrange the furniture, the problem remained. I found the problem insoluble then, and equally intractable twelve years later when as a Major General I served as a member of a committee reviewing officer training; doubtless some of the same dichotomy exists today. The problem was bedevilled by nostalgia and tradition. Sandhurst is seen by some as a sacred cow; thus attempts to reform it ran into trouble then, and perhaps still do.

It seemed to me that we were attempting to square a circle. It would have been better, and much less expensive, for the Army to have recognized the dilemma, made Sandhurst into a purely military training establishment, with the flourishing military history department its one surviving academic activity, allowing the Universities, including the Army's own University at Shrivenham, to take on the academic training of those cadets with the potential to become graduates. To an extent, this has now been done; had we progressed along this path earlier, much controversy and expenditure would have been avoided.

There also seemed something wrong with the Sandhurst ethos. Sadly, cadets did not seem to enjoy being at the RMA. Most regarded it as a tedious ordeal, and viewed the two-year course as the price for becoming an officer. A few were actively unhappy, but perhaps they were unsuited to the Army anyway. But, by comparison with my own happy time at the age of 18–19 at Oxford and while being trained for three months at Sandhurst, modern young seemed to enjoy life less than I had done. I also compared them with the cadets I had known fifteen years previously at the Indian Military Academy. The contrast did not favour Sandhurst. Most IMA cadets enjoyed their time there and regarded it as a high point of their early lives. It seemed to me sad that Sandhurst had become an ordeal to be survived rather than an experience to be savoured. One is nineteen only once; something was wrong with a place which was either boring or counterproductive, or both.

In principle, therefore, I found myself out of tune with the Sandhurst atmosphere and frustrated at being unable to change it. Reluctantly I decided that it was wasting energy to kick against the pricks; instead I would try to improve those areas where progress was possible and one could move forward without squabbling with the traditionalists.

It was not easy to work with a Commandant quite different to me in outlook and personality. Geordie Gordon-Lennox was a Grenadier, who did not share my iconoclastic approach to military life. During the Second World War Gordon-Lennox had won a reputation as an outstanding Commanding Officer; brave, determined and a master of detail, he had won his reputation in fierce infantry fighting in Tunisia and later in the Anzio beachhead. He had been sent to Sandhurst by Frankie Festing, then the CIGS, 'to make the trains run to time' and restore standards which Frankie felt had been allowed to drop. Gordon-Lennox was well suited to this side of the job; by the time I arrived any inefficiency no longer existed. The place ran well, though the atmosphere seemed humourless and unspontaneous, reflecting the personality of its Commandant; I realized it would be difficult to serve someone inherently conservative and whose affection for Sandhurst prevented him implementing the change of atmosphere the place needed.

Luckily the Deputy Commandant, Monkey Blacker, was imaginative, and, for me, easier to work with. Blacker had been a DS at Camberley; he was an international show jumper, had taken part in the Olympic Games, ridden in the Grand National (and once during a journalists' strike written about the race too), and loved games and sport. He was also an excellent artist and good at encouraging similar interests in the young. I liked him at once and we got on well, deciding early to do as much as we could between us to improve the Academy by stealth, avoiding confrontation with the establishment. An immediate area for improvement was the tactical training, which needed a lighter touch, and exercises either abroad or in remoter parts of the United Kingdom. Monkey understood the importance and value of team games; between us we did what we could to improve the standard of the Academy's representative sides and make more time available for cadets to pursue sporting interests in depth.

Neither Monkey nor I, however, were able to do much at first about the dead hand of the foot drill, for which Sandhurst was famous, but which, in our opinion, took too much time and consumed too high a percentage of the military timetable. Fortunately the Adjutant, Philip Ward, from the Welsh Guards, and fifteen years later a successful Commandant of Sandhurst, was liberal, broad-minded and helpful. Moreover, the Academy Sergeant Major, Jacky Lord, who had been a Company Sergeant Major at Sandhurst when I had been a wartime cadet, was a wise and balanced man. With understanding from both these quarters, we adjusted the timetable to permit time for other more challenging military training.

Halfway through my time at Sandhurst I heard from Frankie Festing, Colonel Commandant of The Rifle Brigade, that I was not to command The Rifle Brigade when I left the RMA but was to go instead to the XX Lancashire Fusiliers. I was at first disappointed since every regimental soldier's ambition must be to command his own regiment; it did not take me long, though, to realize that the decision was wise and would widen my horizons by providing different opportunities.

I was fortunate that the Lancashire Fusiliers agreed to accept me. The Regiment had a great reputation; its most famous achievement was winning six VCs before breakfast at Lancashire Landing on Gallipoli. I had seen much of the regiment's 2nd Battalion, a distinguished part of 78 Division, in both Tunisia and Italy. I also knew that Wolfe, the victor of Quebec in 1759, had commanded the XX for some seven years, and that many of the regiment's traditions were based on his example. My own family had links with Lancashire and Manchester, while the XX shared my passion for football, and I soon heard that this factor had played a part in my selection. If I had to leave the Green Jackets, I could not have hoped for anything better. I soon got to know my new regiment, and their recruiting area in Lancashire – Bury, Salford and Rochdale.

By the time I left Sandhurst for 1 LF I felt myself accepted as part of the XX. Nevertheless it is never easy to take over command, and that of a battalion, with its family atmosphere and special loyalties, presents special problems. Even if I had not been a newcomer, the task would not have been easy; coming from outside, and especially from the Green Jackets, there were obvious pitfalls. Though my Divisional Commander, Tubby Butler, an old friend from my time at the Staff College, had warned me that changes were needed, I resolved to make no alterations for a month. "Time spent on reconnaissance is seldom wasted" runs the military adage, and, though the saying may be a cliché, it retains its truth.

Tubby Butler told me I had inherited a battalion with great potential, but which was frustrated because the Rhine Army system did not seem to provide an outlet for its talent. The problems stemmed from incorrect priorities; there was too much emphasis on drill and ceremonial and not enough on allowing scope to the excellent young officers to train their platoons in their own way. A tradition for Trooping the Colour on Minden Day had been allowed to interfere unduly with other activities. Practicing for the event consumed much time, while the entertainment following the parade was expensive and a burden on the limited funds of both Officers' and Sergeants' Messes. The emphasis on ceremonial had its effect on other military activity besides developing NCOs who excelled at drill but little else. I was asked early on for my views on Trooping the Colour; coming from a regiment like The Rifle Brigade, which had never possessed any colours and, if it had, would certainly not have trooped them, I had no problem about my conclusion. We would not undertake this activity while I was around; I arranged with Tubby Butler that while we were in his division an exercise would be arranged annually to prevent Trooping the Colour, and this expedient worked admirably.

Militarily, the XX were professional. I thought, however, their approach to military life was too serious and quickly made it clear that a lighter touch would be actively encouraged. I wanted the Fusiliers to enjoy their soldiering and to discover that there were other spare time activities besides drinking, of which there was too much. I decided to get the military work done before lunch, leaving the afternoon free for games or other activities. We also found time for the young officers to lead and train their platoons. We arranged for platoon commanders to take their platoons right away from Osnabruck for a week; they could use their platoon transport, but I left it to individuals to do what they wished with the time given them. The young officers, and their Fusiliers, blossomed when given their heads, and I have been delighted to see how well they have done since. I was lucky to inherit my second in command, Kevin Hill, born and brought up in Bury, and, like me, a veteran of the Italian campaign. Kevin's common sense complemented my approach to life; later, after a period on the staff, he succeeded me in command and the battalion flourished, as I knew it would. My first Adjutant, Ian Cartwright, was a great support; a determined prop forward, Ian was a pillar of the XX's excellent Rugby team and a great spirit in the Rugby Club, run, without reference to rank, on the same basis as a similar club in ordinary life. He clearly possessed much military talent and I was surprised to find that arrangements had not been made for him to go to the Staff College, though he had passed the entrance examination. Tubby Butler helped me to get this rectified; a vacancy emerged for Ian at the Indian Staff College at Wellington, from which he graduated the following year. Subsequently Ian proved an admirable Commanding Officer and followed me as Deputy Colonel for Lancashire of the Royal Regiment of Fusiliers. It was good to further Ian's military career and also that of his successor as Adjutant, Jeff Straw, who also became an excellent Commanding Officer. There was no lack of talent in the battalion, with other future Commanding Officers in Michael Hayley and Chris Berry among the subalterns; nor, once we had explained the new priorities in the Sergeants' Mess, was this ability confined to the officers. I decided I needed a new RSM and in Frank Burrows found the intelligent flexibility we needed to make our approach to soldiering work smoothly. The Bandmaster, Tony Richards, was another great individual with a flair for military music; it was good to see him, a year later, selected for a commission as a Director of Music, and later go even higher as Director of the Household Cavalry Mounted Band.

Our next posting was to Worcester, Norton Barracks, formerly Depot of the Worcestershire Regiment. By now 1 LF was extremely fit and proud of its ability to march long distances and, on occasions like the Nijmegen Marches, a great Dutch tradition, even for enjoyment. We decided to make use of this skill as part of our return from Osnabruck to Worcester. Two platoons of volunteers were selected to march across Germany, Holland and England to our new station. Marching 18 miles a day, with a rest day every three days, the journey would take them three weeks. Bill Litstiz and George Carter, the officers commanding the platoons, reconnoitred their routes from Osnabruck to the Hook of Holland, arranging where to stay each night and for hospitality and publicity on the journey. We decided that the platoons should march on slightly different routes to provide variety, coming together every three days for a rest period and administration. The project caught people's imagination and we received support from many quarters, not least the German and Dutch areas through which we marched.

The marchers experienced numerous highlights en route, the first being at the Dutch-German frontier some 80 miles west of Osnabruck. TV cameras from both Holland and West Germany were present; the XX Band played three national anthems, the Minden March and the British Grenadiers as the two platoons, their drill sharpened beforehand by a short session under Frank Burrows just down the road, swung smoothly into

Holland. We received a great welcome from the Dutch; at the frontier it took the shape of an enormous currant loaf about six feet long, which proved not only an attraction to the photographers, but also extremely good to eat. The Fusiliers had a royal progress through Holland; in Gouda, famous for its cheese, Fusilier Joe Mahon, a star of the battalion's concert party, was thought by the locals to be one of the Beatles in disguise. Bill Litstiz found himself next morning marching the first two miles surrounded by a fan club, who only dispersed when the Dutch police persuaded everyone that the Fusiliers were just allied soldiers and no more.

This good publicity got 1 LF off to a flying start in Worcester and we decided to exploit our success by a tour of Lancashire to coincide with the Annual Gallipoli Service in Bury Parish Church. We combined some ceremonial aspects, like laying up the battalion's Old Colours in Bury Parish Church, with football matches against Bury and Bolton Wanderers and a series of visits and demonstrations in our recruiting area. Our approach to soldiering, novel in those days, though it has since become more accepted, seemed to catch the imagination. The *Daily Mirror*, not always a help to the Army, ran a positive article about our informality and the high morale and cheerfulness of the Fusiliers. The result was a remarkable flood of recruits; the graph in Terry Shaw's office at Regimental HQ in Bury showed a peak of forty-three recruits in a single week. Our manpower problems were now behind us and the quality of those we attracted was high.

We had a busy summer at Worcester training for many possible destinations, especially the Radfan. Matters were made easier in some ways because there then was no effective command set up in the United Kingdom. The local Territorial Brigade were detailed to keep an eye on our activities, but were unequipped to do so. They were occupied with their own problems, and the Brigadier left us alone. We came under West Midland District in Shrewsbury for purposes of administration, but they, busy with running the Territorial Army, had little time for our affairs. It was no use complaining about the lack of support; the situation was symptomatic of the way in which the overseas deployment of the Army was neglected in favour of the Rhine Army, still very much the top priority.

By autumn my own future was starting again to look uncertain; I had been two years in command and would be likely to move on soon after August 1964. I heard from the Military Secretary that I would be promoted Brigadier to command an Infantry Brigade in the late summer of 1965. It was the plan before then that I should go to the Naval War College at Greenwich on what would be a disguised sabbatical. Meanwhile I arranged with the Ministry of Defence for my battalion to go to British Guiana for nine months, their emergency tour to start in January. Since the Governor and Commander in Chief of the colony, Dick Luyt, was an old friend and had been my cricket captain at Oxford in 1940, I hoped it might be possible for me to take the battalion out to Guiana, settle them in and then hand over to my successor, Kevin Hill. The future in fact looked as secure as it ever does in the Army; it was not surprising, therefore, to find this pattern abruptly changed.

The news reached me in an unusual way. I had arranged, as part of our recruiting offensive in Lancashire, for the band to play at a floodlight evening game at Old Trafford on 17 September. It was a fine match, our band excelled themselves and were warmly applauded; afterwards I was enjoying a glass of champagne with Matt Busby in the Directors' Room when someone came in with a message; Colonel Wilson was to ring the Military Secretary immediately. My immediate reaction was that the telephone call stemmed from an ingenious effort at a leg pull; I gave whoever it was full marks and sent Jeff Straw, who was with me, off to tell the originator to jump in the Irwell, or whatever the nearest river happened to be. Three minutes later a shaken Jeff returned. "It really is the Military Secretary," he gasped. "You had better take the call at once." I accepted the proffered telephone. It was Drew Bethell, an old friend and contemporary at the Staff College; he had a key job on the Military Secretary's staff and the call was plainly for real. I was to hand over the battalion as soon as Kevin Hill could be extracted from his job in Cyprus and go as a Brigadier and Chief of Staff to the United Nations Force in Cyprus. How long this assignment would last Drew had no idea; the mandate for the Force was due for review on 20 December, after which its future was uncertain. I would be unaccompanied and should be ready to move in three weeks' time.

The next three weeks proved a nightmare of conflicting interests. I went to London for a first briefing, but returned little the wiser except that the UN Force Commander would be the Indian general, Thimayya, whom I had met briefly at the IMA Dehra Dun. I asked my XX driver, the admirable Corporal Macdonald, to come with me to Cyprus and was delighted when he accepted. There would be a friendly Fusilier face around in the United National HQ when I arrived.

I reflected on my period of command. I had made some sweeping changes and the atmosphere which Kevin Hill inherited was different to two years ago. I hoped it was better, but wished I had been given longer to lay firmer foundations. The most rewarding aspect undoubtedly lay in the friendships Jean and I had developed, especially among the younger officers and the Fusiliers. A great battalion character was Corporal Johnny Blaney, the trainer of our football team, and in that capacity my right-hand man. Known universally, even by generals like Tubby Butler, as Spartacus, he was a great man; a fanatical supporter of Everton, he had the warmth and sense of humour of the best Liverpudlians. He liked to win, of course, but, far more important in his view, was whether or not we had played our best. He is joining the Royal Hospital as I write, and will surely prove a great Pensioner.

It would be wrong to give the impression that the talent amongst the Fusiliers existed only amongst games players. The Band was a storehouse of ability, developed brilliantly by Tony Richards, who was an exceptional leader as well as an excellent musician. Tony appreciated that musical skills were improved by good personalities; he spent much time, therefore, in looking after the interests of his bandsmen and one saw them blossom under his influence.

The Corporals' and Sergeants' Messes were also full of talent. Frank Burrows, the RSM, was later commissioned and reached the rank of Major. His wife, June, taught herself to become an artist and for several years sustained a profitable small business in this field, catering for tourists in Cyprus. John O'Grady, a fine boxer and tough but fair front row forward, also later reached commissioned rank after a distinguished tenure as RSM. Jack Nash was yet another later to be commissioned; the standard of intelligence was high and we made good use of it.

It was altogether a wonderful two years which I shall never forget.

Chapter Thirteen

THE BLUE BERETS

I said goodbye to the XX on 16 October, confident it would be in good hands. There is often a difficult period after giving up command and the resulting depression is known as 'post command blues'. No such symptoms occurred to me; there was no time for them to develop.

I was comprehensively briefed about UNFICYP and my role there before leaving London. The time given me by Mike Carver, Director of Staff Duties, and Victor Balfour, Director of Military Operations, was invaluable. Mike Carver had until July been Deputy Commander and Chief of Staff to the UN Force; he was not only completely up to date, but also, knowing me well, warned me of pitfalls into which my extrovert character might lead. He reminded me, too, how stretched the Army's resources were; there would be no question of UNFICYP getting any more, while anything I could surrender would be welcome. Victor Balfour reinforced this aspect, explaining how our contribution to UNFICYP fitted into our role in the Near East. He did not expect the UN Force to solve a problem which had baffled everyone for the past fifteen years. He would be content if we merely managed to maintain the "status quo"; like Alice in *Through The Looking Glass*, we would need to run hard to stay in the same place.

I also had a Foreign Office briefing, pleasantly opaque after the brisk realities expounded to me earlier. Clearly, in diplomatic terms, one would be walking on eggs; I resolved to make friends at once with the UK High Commission in Nicosia and to learn about their activities. No one could tell me much about the UN, and how it operated. Though this surprised me at the time, I now understand why. The UN has no 'persona' of its own; it resembles a mirror reflecting the international situation. If one does not like the projected image, the remedy is to change the picture by diplomatic action; one achieves nothing by attacking the mirror.

Nevertheless I was still puzzled as I said goodbye to Jean in the Cromwell

Road air terminal before going out to Heathrow to catch the flight to Cyprus. Following Mike Carver was a daunting prospect; it would be no use trying to emulate him and I would need to develop my own technique.

It felt strange at first. Corporal Macdonald was already there, a corrective against any tendency to pomposity. He, though too polite to say so, clearly thought my new red tabs as funny as I found them unfamiliar. Hitherto I had always been a regimental soldier; now I found myself on the other side of the fence and needed to readjust. Colin Yeo, a courteous gunner, did his best to explain things to me. He hinted tactfully that my tendency to oversimplify might end in tears; it was not, he briefed me, a normal assignment and nothing in Cyprus was ever remotely as it first appeared. Admirable advice, which I remembered whenever I felt tempted to lay down the law. Nothing in Cyprus was ever simple, and Colin was right to emphasize that fact.

I spent the days, while Colin Yeo was still around, clambering in and out of a helicopter flying round the island familiarizing myself with the trouble spots. Though the principles of the communal problem in Nicosia, Famagusta, Larnaca, Limassol and Paphos were much the same, there were differences, historical or dependent on personalities. In Cyprus personal animosities and friendships are vital; Frank Kitson, with whom I had spent an entertaining and helpful hour in London, had emphasized this aspect. Earlier in the year he had been Mike Carver's intelligence officer in Nicosia; he provided some unusual and valuable personal contacts and I quickly followed up his leads. Frank had warned me of the danger of seeing situations through the pro-Turkish eyes of many British involved in the issue; their passion for fairness led them to sympathize with the community they saw as underdogs. For the moment the Turkish Cypriots were underdogs in the island itself; in the area as a whole, however, the mainland Turkish military bases of Mersin and Iskanderun meant that the Greek armed forces in Cyprus were in the weaker position. Their weakness was pronounced where air power was concerned; the Turks possessed overwhelming air superiority, which was a key element in the military situation. The Turkish command of the air was not continuously evident; it was often necessary to remind the main Greek Cypriot actors, Makarios, Grivas and Georghadjis, of this vital military factor.

The Zurich agreement of 1960 had made Cyprus an independent sovereign Republic. Two areas on the south coast of the island, round Akrotiri and Episcopi and further east round Dhekelia, remained under British sovereignty and were known as the Sovereign Base Areas. Akrotiri was an important RAF establishment, while Episcopi contained the Joint Service Headquarters covering all British activity in the Near East. Dhekelia was an Army base, with large-scale administrative facilities, whence the UN Force was admirably supplied. The Treaty of Guarantee, signed by the

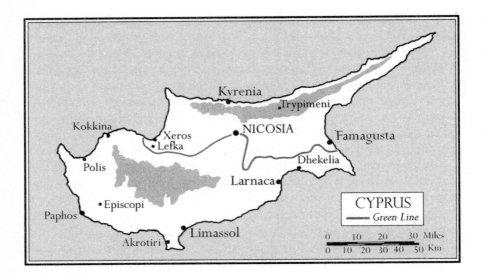

three guarantee powers, Britain, Greece, Turkey, and also by the Republic of Cyprus, required Cyprus to remain independent and to respect her constitution. The treaty expressly forbade any activity directed either towards Enosis (Union with Greece) or partition of the island. The guarantor powers guaranteed the independence of Cyprus within the latter's constitution. The Treaty of Alliance, of which Britain was not a signatory, allowed Greece and Turkey each to maintain token military forces on Cyprus, the strengths being limited to 950 and 650 respectively. Ostensibly these two national contingents were meant to train the fledgling armed forces of the Cyprus Republic. They also represented an additional guarantee of the island's status and a hope for good relations between the Greek and Turkish communities.

The Constitution laid down an independent Republic with a presidential system of Government. There was to be a Greek Cypriot President, and a Turkish Cypriot Vice-President, each elected by their own communities. The Council of Ministers would have ten members, seven Greek Cypriot and three Turkish. One key Ministry, Defence, was to be held by a Turkish Cypriot. Though decisions within the Council of Ministers were to be taken on a majority basis, a power of veto was vested in both the President and Vice-President. A similar proportional basis (70% Greek Cypriot, 30% Turkish Cypriot) was to operate both in the House of Representatives and in the civil service.

It proved impossible to operate this carefully designed system of checks and balances without genuine will to co-operate between the two communities. By the end of 1963 a state of deadlock had developed. The Greek Cypriot leadership decided the Constitution must be amended in order to limit the power of the Turkish Cypriot minority to obstruct the processes of orderly government. Amid rising communal tension, the Turkish Cypriots reacted strongly against President Makarios' Thirteen Point proposals, which they saw as a deliberate attempt to destroy the safeguards for their community. They objected especially to the proposal to end the power of veto vested in the President and the Vice President, regarding this concept as vital to maintain their position. By now relations between President Makarios and Vice-President Kutchuk had broken down and the lack of mutual respect prevented rational discussion of the President's proposals. Any hopes of compromise disappeared on 7 December 1963 when the Turkish Government announced in Ankara that the Makarios Thirteen Points were quite unacceptable to Turkey and must, therefore, be rejected.

Violence was now inevitable. Severe fighting broke out on 21 December and continued for several days, defying all appeals for a ceasefire. The Greek Cypriots probably began the violence; they were certainly the more prepared and got the better of exchanges. On 26 December the guarantor powers intervened with a proposal that the British, Greek and Turkish forces on the island, operating under British command, should be given the responsibility for keeping the peace. It proved impossible to use either the national Greek or Turkish contingents in a peacekeeping role; the task thus devolved on the British who welcomed at first, soon became unpopular, especially with the Greek Cypriots. No one wished the British, so recently the colonial power, to undertake the sole burden of peacekeeping indefinitely. Nevertheless it was not till February 1964 that the parties agreed to take the issues to the Security Council. Once this action was taken the Security Council acted quickly. A resolution on 4 March 1964 established a UN Peacekeeping Force to take over from the British. Soon the first contingents were on their way to the island, and by the end of June, four months before my own arrival in Cyprus, the UN Force (UNFICYP) was in business.

British participation in the Force diminished as other national contingents arrived to take their place. When I arrived in Nicosia the military strength of UNFICYP was just over 6,000; the British contingent provided 1,200, its main components an infantry battalion, an armoured car squadron and the Force's vital helicopter support. The Sovereign Bases were responsible for the UNFICYP's logistic supplies, catering brilliantly for national idiosyncrasies within the international force. Other military contributions to UNFICYP came from Canada, Denmark, Sweden, Ireland and Finland. Each of these produced an infantry battalion or its equivalent; the Irish also provided a further infantry group for the first nine months or so of my time as Chief of Staff. Canada furnished a Brigade Headquarters, which was valuable at this stage of the Force's development, before Force HQ achieved its later standard of professional cohesion.

The island was divided into military zones and districts, with a national contingent responsible for each. The Canadian Brigade HQ was responsible for the key area, Nicosia Zone. Under the Canadian Brigade were the Canadian battalion, and the Danish and Finnish contingents. Nicosia Zone included the two most tricky military problems. In Nicosia the Greek and Turkish Cypriot fighters faced each other along the so-called Green Line dividing the two communities. The Green Line owed its name to the first British Peace Force Commander, Peter Young, who had drawn an arbitrary, but happily sensible, line across his map of Nicosia. Because he used a green chinagraph, the line was known as the Green Line and the title stuck. The other area of confrontation lay astride the main road from Kyrenia to Nicosia, where the Turkish Cypriot fighters, controlled by the Turkish national contingent, opposed the Greek Cypriot National Guard. This area of the Kyrenia Hills was important because the direct route for an invader from Turkey followed the main road; earlier in the Emergency, 16 British Parachute Brigade, part of Mike Carver's Peace Force, had established good boundaries between the contestants. The Parachute Brigade Commander, Roley Gibbs, a fellow Green Jacket, fortunately possessed excellent tactical sense. Though there was constant sniping between the two sides, the boundaries he determined stood the test of time and were unaltered until the Turkish invasion in 1974 altered the whole situation on the island.

Nicosia Zone's Canadian Commander, Norman Wilson-Smith, an experienced infantryman, used his Canadian infantry battalion to control the Kyrenia Road confrontation, appreciating that the opponents in this area, directed by Turkish and Greek professionals, would prefer being 'umpired' by fellow NATO allies. The Danes were deployed along the Green Line in Nicosia; their patience and sense of humour suited the conditions exactly. The Danes never made an issue where no problem existed and smoothed ruffled feelings tactfully. In Brigade reserve, and responsible for the rural part of Nicosia Zone, were the Finns, excellent soldiers; their Commander, Ensio Siilasvuo, was one of UNFICYP's best officers.

If Nicosia was the chief trouble spot, Famagusta ran it close in causing problems. At first it was an Irish responsibility, and I saw at once that the situation was being well handled. The Irish understood the Cypriot mentality well; they were masters at turning an appropriate blind eye to situations which they judged less than vital. Sometimes their tendency to 'play both ends against the middle' could land them in trouble; generally, however, they handled affairs calmly and well.

The Swedes, by contrast, found it harder to come to terms with Cypriot life. Their officers had more experience than others in peacekeeping operations, but this was of limited help. The Cypriots of both communities liked to be a law unto themselves; they reacted against concepts successful elsewhere, and especially to any solution drawn from an African precedent. They regarded themselves, whether Greeks or Turks, as Europeans, and, in argument, were often too much for the deliberate Swedes. In October 1964 the Swedish contingent, under the excellent Carl Gustav Stahl, were responsible for the western end of the island. Their sector included the trouble spot of Kokkina, a small Turkish bridgehead on the north coast opposite Turkey. Militarily, the Kokkina bridgehead was indefensible; it was totally overlooked, while the tiny harbour, suited only to fishing boats, was vulnerable to observed artillery fire. Kokkina's importance was psychological. The garrison, mainly composed of students from the Turkish mainland, was under the command of a regular Turkish officer. He maintained iron discipline, and, despite its military weakness, the Kokkina garrison possessed high morale. In September some members of the Swedish contingent had been caught by the Cyprus police running arms and ammunition into Kokkina. Though the quantities were small, the Cyprus Government reacted strongly, abandoning a demand for the withdrawal of the Swedish contingent only when they realized that such a request could cause the removal of the whole UN Force. Thimayya worked hard to take the steam out of the issue, but friction persisted locally between the Swedes and the Greek Cypriot National Guard. It was my first major problem; Thimayya and I decided to exchange the Irish and Swedish contingents. To maintain their prestige, the Swedes had to be given another sector of equal importance. The British, at that period still unpopular because of the legacy of the original Peace Force, could not be moved from Limassol, so the Irish were the only candidates. To Thimayya's and my relief, they agreed to give up the comforts of Famagusta for the wilder area round Polis and Kokkina; though the move itself proved a complex logistic operation, the Irish achieved wonders in their new area and the Kokkina problem became less acute. The change helped the Swedes also; the intricate responsibilities round Famagusta and Larnaca were better suited to the Swedish approach. Soon the Swedes were handling Famagusta with great competence and Thimayya and I were delighted with the re-deployment.

Apart from being Force Chief of Staff, I was also Commander of the British contingent and responsible to Thimayya in both capacities. My first British battalion, the Cheshires, were commanded by an old friend, Mike Dauncey; ten years before, he had been my GSO3, when I was Brigade Major in 91 Brigade. We resumed our friendship and my visits to his admirable battalion were always a delight. At first the Life Guards, under Ronnie Ferguson, provided the armoured car squadron, before being relieved by another squadron, Ajax, from 2nd Royal Tanks. Geoffrey Duckworth, the Squadron Commander, was an excellent regimental soldier and proved himself a diplomat too. Since Ajax squadron were the main element of UNFICYP's reserve, it was vital for them to establish close links with the remainder of the Force. We held a series of simple exercises to practice such co-operation, with many new friendships resulting.

I had been warned about the need for the British to maintain a low profile. Fortunately, the British Limassol sector was ideal for avoiding the limelight. A better atmosphere existed in Limassol than elsewhere, largely thanks to the excellent District Officer, Mr Benjamin. His Turkish Cypriot opposite number, Ranadhan Jemil, was also a relaxed character. He had been a friend of my brother-in-law Julian Wathen, when, ten years before, the latter had been Manager of Barclays Bank in Limassol. Such contacts helped to establish the right atmosphere in Limassol district; so, too, did the good relationships and friendships which existed between the Sovereign Base Areas in Episcopi and both communities in Limassol. By the time Mike Dauncey's battalion were due to depart, I no longer had any reservations about deploying the British contingent anywhere on the island where its services were needed. This extra freedom of action was later to prove invaluable; it only developed, however, through the tact, common sense and judgement exhibited by the British during that first winter.

At UN Force HQ, Thimayya, the Force Commander, was a splendid boss. He had reached the top of the Indian Army before resigning his position as Chief of Staff in protest against unsound positions and policies forced on the Army by their political masters. After Thimayya's resignation, the wisdom of his representations became clear when fighting broke out on India's North-East frontier, and the Chinese exploited the weaknesses in devastating fashion. 'Timmy' was a man of principle, who quickly won respect as a UN Commander. Sensibly, he did not bother much about detail, though he knew enough about particular issues to see him through. Because he kept out of day-to-day matters, he had time to see critical areas for himself. Bluff, disarming and a fund of common sense, he was an admirable Force Commander.

His health, however, was a worry. He suffered from a heart condition, contracted earlier in his career through operating at great heights in Kashmir; he needed to take care of himself, but, since he loved a party and liked to stay up at nights, he seldom followed his doctors' advice. There was, fortunately, an excellent specialist in the British Military Hospital in Dhekelia, while successive British Chief Medical Officers in UNFICYP kept Timmy's condition under review, but plainly he was living on borrowed time. His wife had decided not to come to Cyprus. Mireille, his daughter, kept house for him in Nicosia, and, with the help of his ADC, Fateh Singh, did her best to persuade him to look after himself. Thimayya was under no illusions. "I like the job," he told me, "and feel I may be making a contribution. I would be bored stiff back in India." Sometimes when Tom D'Arcy, our understanding Chief Medical Officer, showed me photographs of Timmy's heart condition, I debated whether he should continue. But I decided it was none of my business, and, from the UN point of view, Thimayya's contribution was unique. When Jean came out to join me, she became as devoted to Timmy as I was; between us, we had many a talk about India, and Madras Province in particular, which Jean knew well from having lived there for six years while her father was its Governor. I am sure it was right to allow Thimayya to die in harness, as I know he wished.

The Secretary General's Representative, and head of the political side of UNFICYP, Carlos Bernardes, was also a good appointment. Carlos was Brazilian, a professional diplomat, who had reached the top of his country's foreign service. He had served at the United Nations in New York, and on occasion taken the chair in the Security Council. He had charm and ability, though sometimes he became frustrated by the negative attitudes of the two communities. He recognized, however, that a settlement to the Cyprus problem was probably out of the question. Too many interests were content with the situation as it was; immobilism was, therefore, probably the only practical policy.

I got on well with Bernardes; like most Brazilians, he loved football, and this was something we had in common. He was perfectly turned out, usually wearing a well-tailored grey flannel suit and presenting a pleasantly English front. He would arrive at the office about ten thirty each morning and settle down to read *The Times*. He liked to talk about world affairs; I often dropped in at about twelve to brief him on the military situation and found myself sidetracked into talking about British politics. Early in his career Carlos had been his country's consul in Glasgow; he enjoyed the experience and acquired an affection for the British. Bernardes' relaxed approach was invaluable to UNFICYP. Though, when the situation required it, he could be quick and incisive, he did not believe in creating work, nor did he seek to make mountains out of the many Cypriot molehills.

George Sherry, UNFICYP's Political Secretary, was a different type. An American and a professional UN Civil Servant, he saw himself as Ralph Bunche's personal representative in Cyprus, with great admiration and affection for his patron. George's UN service had been largely spent in the UN building in New York; his experience there, and especially his knowledge of the personalities on the 38th floor of the UN building, was invaluable to UNFICYP. George was a workaholic, who revelled in telegrams, and was miserable if there was nothing to report. Since my main aim was a quiet life, Sherry's search for crisis could be tiresome, but he had a good intellect and was at his best in troubled situations. Later, in 1965, when UN Headquarters considered Cyprus to be less critical, Sherry returned to New York. His successor, Remy Gorgé, a calm Swiss lawyer, proved a congenial associate and a great source of strength to UNFICYP.

The outstanding character on the island was the President of the Cyprus Republic, Archbishop Makarios. At first I saw little of His Beatitude, Thimayya wisely considering that the less his British Chief of Staff was exposed to Makarios the better. Later, and especially after Thimayya's death in December 1965, I came to know the Archbishop well and found him fascinating to deal with. He constituted a mass of different personalities rolled into one; one never knew which of his characteristics would be dominant on any particular day. As a politician, he liked to resemble a freedom fighter who had won independence from the British and was resolved to maintain his country's hard won status. In this mood, Makarios behaved much as Pandit Nehru had done when I had seen him in India not quite twenty years earlier, there were the same attacks on imperialism, a similar emphasis on non-alignment. Makarios was not above using his position as Head of the Church to support his role; his sermons were masterpieces of applied theology and worth careful study in their translated form. David Hunt, who became the UK High Commissioner early in 1965, quickly established a special relationship with the Archbishop. He was clever enough, and his knowledge of modern Greek sufficiently fluent, to challenge Makarios' theology, and the Archbishop relished these encounters.

During my time as Acting Force Commander the Archbishop could easily have embarrassed me had he wished to do so, but he never took advantage of my position. He had a splendid sense of humour. At an official lunch, given in honour of Jose Rolz Bennet from Guatemala, a UN Deputy Secretary General, he used it to entertain his guests and perhaps also to tease George Grivas, with whom his relations were never easy. Grivas, seated on my right, had been holding forth to me in French – he declined to speak in English though he understood the language well – about the importance of good formal manners in military affairs. I agreed, for once, with Grivas, and the Archbishop, surprised to see me nodding agreement, asked across the table what we military men had been discussing. I told the Archbishop, remarking that British soldiers nowadays were sometimes lacking in basic military courtesies. "Not at all, Brigadier," countered his Beatitude. "The British have perfect military manners. What other nation arranges for its officers to salute you when they come to put you in gaol?" He then described how the officer from the South Staffordshire Regiment had behaved when given the task of arresting him and the Bishop of Kyrenia; the two clerics were being deported to the Seychelles because of their refusal to condemn the use of terrorism by EOKA. Rising from the lunch table, the Archbishop, using his Episcopal staff as a regimental cane, gave an exact imitation of the young officer's behaviour, salute and Sandhurst style halt included. It brought the house down, except for Grivas, who was not amused.

The key to Makarios was to recognize him as a mediaeval style churchman and not to expect him to behave like a modern Anglican bishop. Lanfranc or Thomas à Becket was nearer the mark; the likeness may even have occurred to Makarios himself. One day in 1966, as Acting Force Commander, I had to call on the President to ask him if he would instruct his Government to make some concessions to the Turkish Cypriot community. The request was, I recall, a familiar ploy from the minority community; I knew that Makarios could not possibly concede it, and that, if he did, he would find himself quickly disavowed by Grivas and his supporters. Nevertheless I had to go through the motions; I arranged an interview with the President and went along to do my best.

It was obvious at once that the Archbishop understood my dilemma. He had even anticipated it. I made my pitch in moderate terms, indicating that I realized what the reply must be. I hinted, however, that the Turkish Cypriots would watch carefully to see how long I stayed with the President. Too short an interview would mean their proposal had not been advocated positively, or fully considered by the Government. An interview of thirty minutes would be needed to deny both these propositions fully. His Beatitude smiled as I explained the problem. "Well, Brigadier, what would you like to talk about?" I doubted if the Archbishop would enjoy discussing Cyprus' football prospects in the forthcoming World Cup; equally, unlike David Hunt, my theology and knowledge of church history was inadequate to support a discussion on the ecumenical movement. I then noticed that on the President's desk there lay a copy of T.S. Eliot's *Murder in the Cathedral*. I grasped at the straw; fortunately I know the play almost by heart, having acted in it as a boy at Winchester. It proved a subject dear to Makarios' heart. Did I, he asked, consider there was anything in common between his personality and Becket's as Eliot portrayed him? I gave the President the answer he clearly hoped for, and our conversation sprouted wings. Which of the tempters who call on Becket in the first part of the play did I think he might find it hardest to resist? There were four I recalled; the pursuit of love, a desire for riches, an obsession with temporal power, and, subtlest of the four, a wish to become a martyr for the wrong reason. Makarios had, of course, as he knew well, the capacity to fall a victim to any of these four temptations. As a young man, he had, by all accounts, been a great one with the girls; he was known to be a brilliant operator of the Cyprus Church finances, allegedly taking the accounts to bed with him as a preferred form of light reading.

Where temporal power was concerned, his position as President of the Cyprus Republic was at that time unchallenged. I considered carefully, therefore, before giving my reply. "Though your Beatitude could, I am sure, be tempted by all four tempters, perhaps a desire for martyrdom for the wrong reason would be hardest to avoid."

My answer struck the desired note. Makarios' face lit up and he embarked on a number of disclosures, some, but not all, vaguely connected with T.S. Eliot. He was revealing about Enosis; he had no intention of embracing any sort of formal union with Greece. He might contemplate a vague association, provided this relationship did not compromise the independence of Cyprus. But any idea of being run as a province from Athens would be anathema. We all suspected this to be the President's stance; one could read between the lines of his speeches to reach this conclusion. Nevertheless, it was unusual for him to be so explicit on any topic while his statement helped me since it confirmed a fundamental divergence between the Archbishop and Grivas, his Commander in Chief, a simple and uncomplicated Enosist.

I looked at my watch. We had been talking for 45 minutes, far longer than was necessary for me to carry conviction with the Turkish Cypriots. Makarios smiled as he accompanied me to my car outside. TV cameras, and a Cypriot version of Robin Day, awaited us. "Well, your Beatitude," he began. "You must have had a very testing interview with the UN Force Commander." "Yes," replied Makarios, bat politically straight. "We had a very illuminating exchange of views."

Usually, however, UNFICYP's negotiations with the Cyprus Government took place with Georghadjis, the Minister of Home Affairs, and his Permanent Secretary, Mr Anastasiou, a former colonial civil servant. Georghadjis was a hero of EOKA; he had won fame, during the earlier emergency, by a spectacular escape from Kyrenia Castle, then the place of detention for key EOKA prisoners. Despite his EOKA background, Georghadjis' relationship with Grivas had become equivocal, as his attitude towards Enosis became closer to that of Makarios. Like others who have been involved in a resistance movement, Georghadjis had a suspicious nature. It took time to get to know him, and I owe Anastasiou much for the loyal way in which he interpreted UNFICYP's activities. Finally an admirable relationship developed; in return, I never mentioned to Grivas the difficulties I knew existed between him and his official political masters.

Grivas was unattractive. One could not forget that seven years previously EOKA had murdered, not only British servicemen, but also their wives and families. Nevertheless, to maintain peace in Cyprus, UNFICYP needed to maintain relations with him. Grivas remained suspicious of the British and it took me time to get to know him. He would not speak English, or accept social invitations from UNFICYP. He did, however, accept a Liaison Officer from us, and this link revealed he would be prepared to meet me regularly provided our conversations were in French and remained informal. I accepted this formula; we met thereafter weekly to resolve military problems. The meetings proved useful and helped to solve misunderstandings between UNFICYP and the National Guard.

Early in his career Grivas was a student at the French Ecole Superieure de Guerre. The French Army then possessed a Maginot mentality, and, though Grivas had served against the Italians in Albania in 1941, his knowledge of conventional war was dated. He had no idea how to defend Cyprus against the superior forces of the Turkish Government. In particular, he did not understand air power, and it was hard to teach him the scale of air attack which the island's defenders would face. It was vital to avoid provoking the Turks; if they intervened, they would certainly win and Grivas could not influence this.

Most of UNFICYP's problems with Grivas concerned the construction of fixed defences round Cyprus. In purely Greek Cypriot areas such defences presented no problems. Elsewhere, at Larnaca and Famagusta for example, Grivas' fixed defences could be interpreted either as against invasion (and so permissible) or as a threat to the Turkish Cypriots, and so outlawed by UNFICYP's mandate. The patient Swedes, especially, adjudicated many such claims; often I would have to see Grivas and get him to accept our ruling. I invariably cleared such decisions first with Anastasiou and Goerghadjis. Grivas refused to accept their authority; they were mere civilians with no understanding of military affairs, but he was prepared to accept my professional competence, even if he did not always agree with my conclusions. Grivas liked to discuss the methods used by the British against him during the EOKA emergency. Field Marshal John Harding he considered too big a soldier for the minor tactics required against EOKA. For Ken Darling, however, he had great respect. Grivas admitted that militarily EOKA had been defeated, as it was bound to be once the right tactics were employed. Finally, after my own departure from Cyprus, Grivas was forced out of the island, the victim of a double cross by the Greek Colonels, who had overthrown the monarchy in Athens and were running their own authoritarian regime. By then Enosis was a dead duck; it was Grivas' misfortune that he could never face this reality. Ironically, Georghadjis also met his end at the hand of the Colonels; he knew too much about their plotting against Makarios and paid the penalty, either for his suspicions, or for his complicity.

The Turkish Cypriot leaders were less colourful. Denktash, their ablest political mind, was then away from Cyprus advising the Turkish Government on how to handle Cyprus. Kutchuk, the Vice President, and titular head of the community, was a nice man, but without push or charisma. Osman Orek, formerly the Defence Minister, was forceful, but touchy in his dealings with UNFICYP. The Turkish Cypriots had no latitude to make their own decisions. They were dominated by Ankara and had always to clear matters with the Turkish ambassador, Osdemir Benler. Luckily the latter was an able operator, with whom I had excellent relations. A key man, too, was Umit Suleiman, a lawyer, who represented the Turkish Cypriots in their dealings with UNFICYP. Umit was intelligent, and straight. He was frustrated by the control exercised by the authorities in Ankara, even if he was too loyal to say so. Umit was always courteous and meetings with him were agreeable, even when unproductive.

I needed to keep in touch with the diplomatic community. Most countries accredited to Cyprus were involved in financing UNFICYP in some degree and their representatives were expected to report on our activities. The UK High Commission helped greatly in this diplomatic activity. I was fortunate in both the UK High Commissioners with whom I had to deal. The first, Alec Bishop, was a former general. A delightful man, he did not enjoy good health and found Levantine life distasteful. "I wish, Jim," he confided to me, "we could sometimes do on this island what we consider to be right rather than having to base all our actions on political expediency." We respected his integrity, but Cyprus was not his scene, and he was pleased to leave in March 1965.

David Hunt, Bishop's replacement, was very different. A don at Magdalen College, Oxford, in 1939 he joined the Army in the Welsh Regiment and made a reputation as an intelligence officer in the Middle East. During the Italian campaign he was Alexander's Chief of Intelligence in Italy; he enjoyed the Army, and, at the end of the war, considered accepting the regular commission which was offered him. Wisely, he decided against, but his understanding of military affairs made him a perfect choice for Cyprus.

David realized that Greek Cypriots, rather like the Indians, have a love-hate relationship with the British. In normal circumstances they enjoy our company and feel at home in our society. In a crisis, however, they often expect us to do more for them than is possible. When we fail to deliver, the ensuing bitterness is the greater because of their high expectations. David understood this factor perfectly, and how to avoid the condition. I relished his acute political ability; his loyal support for UNFICYP was invaluable.

Others on the High commission staff supported David's tactics admirably. Robin Adair, the Deputy, Bill Peters, First Secretary, and Denis Speares, were easy to work with and well versed in UNFICYP affairs. John Drinkall, who took Denis Speares' place, also became a friend; it was a privilege to work alongside so effective a British team.

The strength of the High Commission helped my contacts with other diplomatic missions. Toby Belcher, the United States Ambassador, another fluent Greek speaker, was also a firm supporter; he could appear brash, though UNFICYP did not need to complain on that score. The French Ambassador, a courteous diplomat of the old school, also became a friend; he possessed the best cook in Nicosia and lunch or dinner at his Embassy was a gastronomic pleasure. I needed to maintain close relations with the Greek diplomatic mission, and here again I was fortunate. The Ambassador, Alexandrakis, was a Cretan with a distinguished bearing, much common sense and a great charm. He later became his country's Ambassador in Washington. Most of my dealings, however, were with Alexis Stephanou, the Head of Chancery, Anglophile in the extreme and with a knowledge of Shakespeare which put one to shame. Even Grivas respected Alexis, who often managed to persuade him to exercise restraint.

This diplomatic activity meant that Jean and I, necessarily, became members of the Nicosia evening circuit. We seldom had less than two engagements in an evening and drove hectically from one to another to fulfil our schedule.

Corporal Macdonald, my driver, was adept at ferrying us from one engagement to the next. He also became one of the most popular members of the Nicosia teenage set in the process. Jean and I were delighted to see him one day, while we were being entertained by the Israeli Ambassador, Tuvia Araze, holding court by our car, surrounded by some pretty diplomatic daughters chatting him up. It was a sad day for us all when Corporal Macdonald went back to England to get married. We missed him greatly, but I was lucky in his replacement, a Geordie, Corporal Gibson, still a firm friend.

Contacts with the British bases were also important. The C in C, Tom Prickett, was a downright airman, whose approach to life presented few problems. He loved polo, and, provided the 14th/20th Hussar young officers, in intervals from UNFICYP, behaved properly on the polo field, did not bother too much about the UN. Makarios respected the Air Marshal. When, once I could not convince the President that the Turkish Government were concerned by some Greek Cypriot activity, I asked Tom Prickett to explain to the Archbishop what the term 'runway readiness' signified. His Beatitude got the point and later used the expression himself in our conversations; I wondered, flippantly, how he applied its principles to the Orthodox Church.

Relations with the Army District Commander, Peter Young, were difficult at first. I needed to be tactful with Peter, who had been disappointed to be relegated to the bases when Mike Carver arrived. His successor, Rodney Burges, was a different character. His mind moved quickly and he understood how to be flexible. He took the trouble to study both sides of the communal situation; sometimes people in the bases automatically identified with the Turkish Cypriots, not understanding the other side to the argument. Rodney's understanding proved a great help throughout my time in Cyprus; we became friends and UNFICYP's relations with Episcopi and Dhekelia were always excellent.

The bases provided superb support for UNFICYP in many ways. Their hospitality at Episcopi and Dhekelia was warm, and provided escape and relaxation from the stress of the Cyprus problem. Individuals from UNFICYP's national contingents were generously entertained, and the reputation of the British Army gained greatly. Thimayya, Anglophile anyway, particularly enjoyed an invitation to the bases and felt specially at home there.

For the first six months my living conditions were not ideal. Jean had not accompanied me to Cyprus, since when I left England it was still possible that the UN Force Mandate might not be extended beyond 20 December when it was due for renewal. Thirty-eight years later UNFICYP is still in existence, so this was unrealistic. Nevertheless, since the Force was on a temporary basis, its infrastructure remained on an emergency footing. There was no justification for spending money on accommodation and temporary huts were regarded as adequate. Force HQ occupied a wartime extension of RAF Station Nicosia. It was handy for Nicosia Airport and provided good landing facilities for helicopters, but the site provided few other advantages. It was noisy, uncomfortable, cold in winter and very hot in summer. The logistic staff, housed in a large aircraft hangar, had particularly bad conditions, but never allowed this to interfere with their staff work, excellent by any standards, and much better than in previous UN operations.

As Chief of Staff, I had a small room to myself with a writing table, an armchair and a washbasin. The fifty yards I had to go for a shower was the same as when I was an undergraduate at New College; it was no more uncomfortable than my small caravan had been on exercises in BAOR. Corporal Macdonald looked after me admirably, and, apart from missing Jean and the family, I had little to complain about and was too busy to do so anyway.

My job as Chief of Staff, and especially the diplomatic demands, meant that Jean's presence was important on the social side. The RAF managed to get her out twice in the first six months for a fortnight at a time. I concentrated as many lunch and dinner parties as possible in the two periods, but when Jean was back in England, I missed her increasingly when I learnt UNFICYP was in for a long haul and that I would stay as Chief of Staff for a two-year stint. I owed Thimayya no less, and, by the spring of 1965, it had become evident that his state of health precluded any change of Chief of Staff. Happily, Charles Richardson, the Quartermaster General, came out to Cyprus at the end of March. His Miliary Assistant was Peter Hudson in The Rifle Brigade; arrangements were made for Jean and the family to come out as soon as I could find a house in Nicosia. By now I had many Cypriot friends and we found a small bungalow-type villa near the golf course, on the Green Line between the Government forces and the Turkish Cypriot fighters. We hoisted a UN flag in the garden and painted a UN sign on the roof. Corporal Macdonald and I moved in to get things going before Jean, the family, Corporal Britch, my orderly, married to our Nanny, Pauline, arrived the following week.

The house was hopelessly cramped, and when my stepchildren, Susie and Hugh, came out for their holidays, someone had to sleep on a camp bed in the passage, but we were happy there. We fed brilliantly as usual, while William and Rupert soon settled into the admirable English school in Nicosia. Most afternoons we managed to get away to the beach near Kyrenia; William and Rupert learned to swim that summer, and the sun and fresh air did wonders for us all. I needed to keep in touch with the Operations Room at Force HQ while we were on the beach. Luckily Robert Wythe, Force Signal Officer, produced a landrover crew under the admirable Corporal Tuson, who not only maintained continuous radio contact but also enjoyed cricket on the beach with William, Rupert, Jean and myself. I had a superb personal assistant, Staff Sergeant Graves, who came round to the house each evening at ten o'clock; over a glass of Keo beer, I then dictated signals to New York and the sovereign bases giving details of the day's UN activities, military, diplomatic and social. Staff Sergeant Graves well deserved his award of the British Empire Medal for his reliability, tact, and discretion in handling this important traffic.

My official day began with UNFICYP's Morning Prayers which I never missed if I could help it. The meeting normally lasted fifteen minutes only, but it provided a chance for everyone to be up to date about what was going on, and how UNFICYP and other agencies were influencing events. Each branch of staff would give their plans, probable location, and details of visits for the day. Finally I summed up, giving the policy about the issues which had emerged from the conference as well as my own reaction. The latter was important in view of the international character of the Force; like myself other international staff members had a loyalty to their own national contingents as well as to UNFICYP. Leaks were inevitable; Morning Prayers ensured that at least these were accurate.

After Morning Prayers, and before returning to my office, I slipped briefly into the small British contingent office just inside the hangar. Here Jerome de Salis, my Welsh Guards link with the British, gave me the British papers, instructions from the Ministry of Defence, queries from the bases and relevant diplomatic telegrams sent up from the High Commission. These last provided HMG's slant on our affairs, which were seldom at variance with instructions coming from the UN Headquarters in New York. The absence of dichotomy between my two masters owed much to Brian Urquhart, the British official who brilliantly directed UN peacekeeping operations in New York. Brian had served in airborne forces during World War Two and was a master of clear direction. His telegrams, and the guidance he gave UNFICYP, reflected his comprehension of how the nature of our original mandate limited the options. Sometimes, as Brian Urquhart explained in some of the early cables, our comparative absence of power to use force could prove a positive advantage. UNFICYP was allowed to use force only in self defence, or when one of its posts was directly attacked. Had we possessed stronger powers, there would have been pressure to use them; it would have been impossible to do so without damaging the good relations with both sides we needed to carry out our task.

I kept half an hour from nine o'clock free each morning for meetings with my UN colleagues. It was a chance for national contingent commanders, after attending Morning Prayers, to drop in and talk informally about their local problems. Often I could sort out a difficulty with a telephone call to Anastasiou at the Home Ministry or Umit Suleiman at the Turkish Cypriot leadership. I tried to make such telephone calls in the presence of the national contingent commander concerned so that he would know what I had said and be confident that I had presented the problem accurately. Normally Anastasiou and Suleiman were accommodating and helpful; sometimes, if for example there was disagreement between Grivas and the Government of Cyprus, it would be beyond them to help. It was important for UNFICYP to recognize such situations early so that higher authority (the President, the Greek or Turkish Government) could be invoked before prestige complicated the matter.

The Force Commander arrived in his office at half past nine. He liked a quick briefing about any new significant topic, and especially to be warned where intervention on his level seemed likely to be needed. Our meetings were agreeable; Thimayya had a good military mind and grasped the essentials of a situation quickly. I rarely, therefore, accompanied him if he needed to make a point to either the President or the Turkish Cypriot leadership; it was better for him, and reflected the international character of UNFICYP, for his supporting staff officer to be Canadian, Scandinavian or Irish, rather than his British Chief of Staff.

By ten o'clock or so, therefore, I was normally free to get out on a planned visit of my own. Usually this would be by helicopter; I aimed to visit each of the sector Headquarters on the island once every ten days or so. My visits were informal and I liked to keep them brief. "We are pleased to see you come, and pleased to see you go," I remember being briefed by the RSM on my young officers' course at Tidworth when I joined The Rifle Brigade some twenty-five years earlier. Sometimes, on a national day for example, it was good manners to make an exception, but I tried to avoid staying for lunch if possible, so overwhelming was the hospitality to which one found oneself subjected. Ideally, therefore, I aimed to be back in my office shortly before lunch, when I caught up on the events of the morning and issued instructions as a result of my morning's travels through the Ops Room.

I tried always to lunch at home, where Jean cleverly provided just the sort of family meal we all enjoyed. She somehow fitted in the shopping while I was out visiting each morning. Corporal Macdonald was clever at slipping this engagement into his daily schedule; we had no private car of our own in Nicosia, since our stay on the island, like that of UNFICYP itself, was of uncertain length and one could not afford to become entrenched. Often there was an official lunch for Jean and me to attend. Frequently these were diplomatic occasions, and there were also military commitments, often connected with the arrival or departure of members of the UNFICYP staff. Sometimes, Jean and I were the hosts; on such occasions we took a table at the Jardin des Gourmets, a French-style restaurant in Nicosia which provided excellent food, washed down by the powerful local wines. I hope our lunch parties were as much fun for our guests as they were for us; not only were they enjoyable in themselves, but they provided valuable opportunities for people to meet and exchange ideas. Jean took pains over the seating plans; it required tact to get the diplomatic protocol correctly balanced against the demands of military rank and governmental positions in the Cyprus Administration.

After lunch, during the summer and autumn, we used to go to Kyrenia with the family to bathe. We had a favourite rock just short of Five Mile Beach to the east of Kyrenia, and this was often our destination. You could sit on it with a friend, put the world to rights, and dive in whenever the conversation became too serious. The children soon learnt to swim and by the time we left Cyprus were effective divers too. The sea those days was warm, clean and unpolluted. My radio crew, led by Corporal Tuson, bathed nearby; there was a bare patch just behind the beach where we all played cricket. On Sundays, after church, we often took a picnic lunch to Larnaca, where the beach was sandy and provided even better cricket.

For my first six months with UNFICYP we had a Mediator, Galo Plaza, former President of Ecuador, who aimed to submit his report early in April. Galo Plaza was an attractive man, extrovert and confident. He visited Cyprus in November and December to establish the facts of the communal situation. Bernardes told us the Mediator had done well on an international level in Athens, Ankara, and London especially. Mike Carver, who lunched with Galo Plaza during the latter's visit to London, took the trouble to confirm this impression in a personal letter to me. The prospects for a settlement seemed bright for these few months, during which the general optimism helped UNFICYP considerably to keep the peace.

The honeymoon period induced by Galo Plaza helped me greatly. I was given a proper chance to establish myself as an international Chief of Staff and also to develop a network of friendships all round the island, which were later invaluable. Cypriots are sociable and generous; they like to offer people hospitality and enjoy being entertained.

I worked hard, too, to improve the working of UNFICYP's HQ. We ran the odd exercise, achieved a better level of communication within the force and tidied up the logistic arrangements. By the end of March I was genuinely proud of the way the international force worked. There were few disagreements, while Force sporting events and rifle meetings led to new friendships. Thimayya's character made him particularly good at fostering international unity within the Force; by the end of March UNFICYP was a better organization and more respected than six months before.

Nevertheless, UNFICYP's relations with the National Guard remained difficult. Grivas was at the root of many problems; his policy of improving coastal defences of the island, usually by constructing new pillboxes, caused much trouble. There was a serious incident, however, near Lefka in mid-March. It arose because Grivas wished to improve the National Guard's position against Turkish attack from the sea. Peristonari Hill lay five miles inland; its importance lay in the fact that the feature dominated the approaches to Lefka, a Turkish enclave in an otherwise Greek-dominated area. UNFICYP had appreciated its significance and the Swedes had installed an OP there the previous summer; when the Irish assumed responsibility for the sector, they continued to occupy the position. Early in March, Grivas, reconnoitring his defences, had realized the threat of the Turkish Cypriots in Lefka to the rear of the National Guard positions on the coast. Even Grivas did not contemplate an attack on Lefka itself; any such action would have brought instant retaliation by the Turkish Air Force. He reckoned, however, he might just get away with occupying Peristonari Hill, since this was only the site of a UN OP. Accordingly, choosing a weekend, Grivas gave orders to the local National Guard to seize Peristonari Hill in a night attack; since, apart from the UN section post forming the OP, the feature was undefended, the operation presented no real military problem.

A political storm erupted as soon as the occupation of the hill became known. The Turkish reaction was predictable, but, in view of the need to exercise restraint pending the publication of the Mediator's Report, more moderate than it might have been. Two jet fighters from the Turkish mainland buzzed the area as a reminder that the hill could be made untenable whenever Ankara decided to take action. The Irish sector commander drew the obvious conclusions from the Turkish aircraft; wrongly, however, he withdrew the Irish OP from the feature, not appreciating that the Turks' hands were tied by their undertaking to exercise restraint. Though the Irish decision to withdraw was unilateral and unwise, Thimayya decided there was no point in crying over spilt milk. To have insisted on the Irish reinstalling their OP would have meant humiliation for their sector commander, even if Grivas had been prepared to accept it, which was doubtful. Instead we allowed the Turkish Cypriot fighters to occupy another position, Ghaziveran Hill between Lefka and Peristonari Hill, which we had previously denied them. Grivas' occupation of Peristonari Hill had thus gained him little; his coastal defences may have appeared stronger, but a National Guard infantry company was thenceforth tied up in maintaining the new position.

The Turkish Cypriot defences of Lefka were, however, greatly strengthened by their new positions at Ghaziveran, while the Turkish Air Force had reminded the National Guard that their role would be the decisive factor at Lefka.

Thimayya and I were relieved that the Peristonari Hill affair had ended without more serious consequences. We told the Greek Embassy how dangerous a situation had been provoked by Grivas. We had avoided a major crisis narrowly, and we would not have been so lucky had not the Mediator's Report been imposing a moderating effect on Turkish reactions.

Meanwhile, UNFICYP awaited the publication of the Mediator's Report. Galo Plaza had served us well thus far; we wondered, however, not only what his conclusions would be, but how they would be received internationally and on the Cyprus stage.

Chapter Fourteen

UN FORCE COMMANDER

We expected too much from the Mediator's Report. Our optimism had a fundamental flaw. Regrettably, Plaza, representing the United Nations, possessed no real power. He could hope to persuade, but could not direct the Government of Cyprus. His report would also need the unanimous support of the guarantor powers, Greece, Turkey and Britain. Furthermore, the two superpower members of the Security Council, the United States and the Soviet Union, would have to support his proposals. The odds against overcoming these obstacles were enormous, while there were vested interests happy to see the existing tension continue. Galo Plaza's efforts were therefore destined for failure and we should not have been surprised, a month after the promulgation of the Mediator's Report, to find ourselves in the same position as before.

It is unnecessary to discuss the details of Plaza's recommendations. At first glance, they seemed to favour the Government of Cyprus in indicating the failings of the Zurich agreement, but Plaza's view that the Government should forswear Enosis meant his report would be unacceptable. Makarios himself by now privately endorsed the Mediator's opinion, but he could not admit it; Greek Cypriot EOKA elements, and Grivas himself, would never have tolerated such frankness. Equally the Turkish Cypriots, once they had overcome Plaza's attitude to the Zurich agreement, realized that by welcoming his comments on Enosis they were able to embarrass the majority community. A week after the Report's publication, Suleiman, the most politically aware member of the Turkish Cypriot leadership, told me that he thought Ankara had been unduly hasty in turning down the Mediator's Report; he realized that Makarios would have to undertake a peace offensive and that there might be useful crumbs for his community to glean.

The failure of the Plaza Report allowed UNFICYP to plan properly for the future. Without UNFICYP hostilities would break out again, and, without machinery to restore control, Turkey would launch an invasion to protect the minority community. While Thimayya and Bernardes concentrated on reactions, military and political, to the Plaza Report, I settled UNFICYP's future in detail. There were pressing problems, of which the most important was the future of Irish representation in UNFICYP.

When UNFICYP was formed, the Irish Republic had responded generously to the Secretary General's invitation to contribute a contingent to the Force. During 1964 and early 1965 there were two Irish Lieutenant Colonels' commands, with a total strength of the Irish contingent over 1,000. There was also an Irish Deputy Chief of Staff in May 1965, Carl O'Sullivan, an outstanding officer, later Chief of Staff of the Irish Army. Ireland had, however, assumed that UNFICYP's existence would be relatively short. Thus the Irish, who had proved excellent UN soldiers in the Congo, were happy to contribute strongly to UNFICYP; since opportunities for overseas service in the Irish Army were limited, they welcomed the chance to provide this in Cyprus. A long haul for UNFICYP was different. The Irish contemplated withdrawing from the Force altogether. Thimayya and I were reluctant to see this occur. The Irish contribution to UNFICYP had been high class; the contingent were popular inside the Force and their officers and soldiers had demonstrated great understanding for peacekeeping in the special atmosphere of Cyprus. Though the Secretary General might find another contingent to replace them, the Irish possessed their own style, without which UNFICYP would have been the poorer. I discussed these factors with Carl O'Sullivan, who wished to maintain Irish representation, but understood that it must be at a level which Ireland could sustain. We had, therefore, to reduce the Irish commitment with the minimum disturbance to the remaining contingents, all now settled in their sectors.

There was, however, slack in UNFICYP's Limassol Zone, where the Cheshires and their successors, the Grenadier Guards, had greatly reduced incidents. The tact and good manners of the British, and our policy of keeping a low profile, had ended the hostility inherited from the British Peacekeeping Force. I recommended therefore the next British battalion, who were to be the Royal Highland Fusiliers, should spread westwards and take over the Paphos sector as far as Polis from the Irish. This would leave the latter with a smaller area of responsibility on the key north coast of the island, facing the mainland of Turkey. The Irish would continue to be responsible for the trouble spots of Kokkina, Lefka and Limnitis, where their capacity to avert problems was invaluable.

I now had to sell this concept to the British, who were reluctant to take on extra responsibilities. There was no problem with the soldiers themselves, who would welcome a change of scene. Wisely, Rodney Burges endorsed the proposal, while David Hunt, the High Commissioner, possessed the military background to overcome political objections. It proved a good decision, and, though Paphos still provided its share of problems, the British zone remained an oasis of comparative calm.

We had been lucky to get the Grenadier Guards to replace the Cheshires. They were an outstanding battalion and their arrival put UNFICYP on the right side of the military tracks. The Brigade of Guards are careful about where their battalions go and under whom they serve. The Major General himself, John Nelson, and David Toler, the Grenadiers' Brigade Commander in Germany, both visited Cyprus beforehand to see that Michael Bayley's fine battalion would be in appropriate hands. Luckily John Nelson had served in 6 Armoured Division during World War Two; we had many friends in common and UNFICYP passed its test satisfactorily.

The Grenadiers' successors that autumn were the Royal Highland Fusiliers, the product of a controversial amalgamation between the Royal Scots Fusiliers and the Highland Light Infantry. Various pundits had argued that this was an impossible marriage. How could you combine a Lowland Regiment (the Royal Scots Fusiliers) who wore trews with a Highland one who wore the kilt? How would the gentle Ayrshire soldiers mix with the tough Glaswegians in the HLI? Many similar objections appeared, but the Army Board were obdurate and the amalgamation went ahead. It proved an outstanding success, thanks to the determined leadership of Charles Dunbar, first Commanding Officer of the amalgamated regiment. I was delighted to have the RHF in UNFICYP. The regiment had an outstanding football team and I was anxious for the British contingent to match the Danes, who had monopolized the UN Force Championship for the past year. Moreover, Thimayya had begun his military service by an attachment to the Highland Light Infantry. He knew all about the Jocks and had actually shot the very tiger whose skin was worn by the big drummer in the regimental band. He was thrilled to see his old regiment again and his visits to the battalion were keenly anticipated and much enjoyed. There had been doubts about how the Jocks would view exchanging their bonnets in favour of the UN blue beret, and speculation about how the blue beret would go with a kilt. Gordon Pender, their sensible Commanding Officer, had no time for any such rubbish. His battalion settled down at once and the western end of the island, under the direction of the 'Laird of Paphos', behaved itself even better than before.

I had never served before at close quarters with a Scottish battalion, but soon realized my good fortune. The sense of humour of Gordon Pender's Jocks proved a delight, while the regiment's professionalism gave them a splendid understanding of the Cypriots. I learnt this myself soon after their arrival on my first visit to the battalion. I came upon a section post in Paphos; it was under the command of a twenty-year-old full corporal, a Glaswegian, streetwise, and with a Bill Shankly style accent which sounded like tropical rain landing on a tin roof. I was still a new Brigadier and aware I knew less about my job than the section commander did about his. No matter; senior officers are supposed to cope in such situations, so I pressed on. "I expect you have been briefed about the communal situation and so know why you are engaged in maintaining this boundary between the Greek and Turkish Cypriot sectors?" I was leading with my chin, of course, and realized the fact from the courteous but pitying way in which the young section commander regarded me as he answered. The Scots are adept at bringing Sassenach generals down to size nicely but this was my first experience of the process. "Sir," was the answer. "You don't stay alive in Glasgow for twenty years without knowing the difference between Rangers and Celtic." Game, set and match to the Royal Highland Fusiliers; we were lucky to have such a splendid battalion in UNFICYP.

Much of Thimayya's and my time was spent on adapting the organization of the Force to the long haul which lay ahead. The Finns and the Danes, though extremely loyal, were finding Canadian command irksome. Bruce Macdonald, Wilson-Smith's successor, had become a friend. His staff, however, were less imaginative; understandably, the Danes and the Finns became restive and wanted to have a sector of their own directly responsible to UNFICYP HQ. Thimayya sympathized with their aspirations and we arranged to phase out the Canadian Brigade HQ when Macdonald's tour came to an end in October. We also persuaded the Irish to maintain a reduced commitment and it was good to see these delicate negotiations concluded satisfactorily.

It was satisfactory to find the British contingent now so popular. During the summer a crisis occurred over the relief of the Irish contingent; we asked Makarios if he would mind having the British at Lefka or Kokkina, he expressed his delight. "I would rather have the British there than anyone," he told Thimayya. It was an admirable reflection of the work of the British battalions and armoured car squadrons who had served in the island since UNFICYP's establishment. Even Grivas admitted that his National Guard commanders preferred to deal with the professional British, and our new found popularity certainly eased my own job. I found myself less involved in day-to-day crises and with more opportunity to consider the wider aspects of the Cyprus problem.

The problem still appeared insoluble. Makarios remarked to me that he always worried if he saw two Cypriots in conversation at a party or social occasion. "The outcome," he remarked, "will almost certainly be another three political parties." The intense individualism of the Greek Cypriots certainly made them difficult to lead. Though the Greek Cypriots were reluctant to admit it, only a few extremists still wanted Enosis. They felt that the Athens Greeks looked down on them as country cousins and in the National Guard the Greek Cypriots disliked the control imposed by regular Greek officers with a NATO background and training. Cypriots were not unhappy at the notoriety the Cyprus problem brought the island. Georghadjis once remarked to me, "Of course we all realize Cyprus can never become a world power. All the same we will certainly do our best to go on being a world problem."

UNFICYP began gradually to concentrate on improving the day-to-day security of people in Cyprus. We never openly admitted that we had abandoned attempts to solve the problem. Nevertheless we accepted that we no longer needed to take the initiative and that attempts to do so would probably prove counter-productive and reactivate communal trouble. The Greek Cypriot community, whose position was stronger than ever before, approved UNFICYP's new policy. They could now forget the recent troubles, rely on UNFICYP to keep the peace and concentrate on the Cyprus economy. The Turkish Cypriots also welcomed the improved security climate; they were content to be left alone in their various quarters and sectors of influence round the island. They only reacted when attempts by the Government to restore normal conditions appeared to threaten their military security.

By the middle of August, indeed, UNFICYP's policy of 'live and let live' had reduced incidents so greatly that we came under pressure from New York to reduce the size of the Force. Thimayya, like most military commanders, resisted such proposals on principle. I had more sympathy for such thinking, since each of the national contingents were finding it hard to maintain their strengths. Unless we reduced our demands, we should be faced by the threat of wholesale withdrawals and damage to the balance of the Force. By quiet modifications, we dispensed with the Canadian Brigade Headquarters, accepted battalions with three instead of four companies and removed UN posts in areas where their presence was now irrelevant.

Bruce Macdonald left in mid-September to command a new UN operation set up in India and Pakistan to supervise the establishment of a ceasefire following the 1965 war between those two countries. His departure made it important to have a Canadian in a key role in UNFICYP's HQ, and Drewry, an admirable gunner, was selected to replace O'Brien, the Irish Contingent Commander, as Deputy Chief of Staff early in October. Drewry and I got on well. When Thimayya went on leave at the end of September I acted as Force Commander with Drewry taking on as Chief of Staff. The Force seemed to work well under the two of us and there were no objections from either Greeks or Turks about a British officer acting as Force Commander.

The calm continued in the autumn after Thimayya's return. October was a remarkably quiet month and early in November I was able to get away to the United Kingdom for a fortnight. I needed the break, but the aim of my visit was to plan the next stage of my military career, which had became untidy as a result of my enforced stay in Cyprus. Somehow, so the Military Secretary told me, I had to fit in a period of command at Brigade level in order to qualify me, in due course, for promotion to Major General. I had missed out on my regular command, so would have to do a stint in the Territorial Army. I asked to be given a formation covering a big city, and preferably one in the Midlands and North, where I felt there might be more scope. It was arranged, therefore, for me to relieve Dick Vernon, an old friend and Green Jacket, in command of 147 Infantry Brigade with its Headquarters in Birmingham when I could be spared from UNFICYP.

I had hardly settled down again before, on 11 December, it was Jean's turn to fly to England for her daughter Sarah's wedding. We had to stage our visits so that one or other of us could be in Cyprus to look after William and Rupert. These two, fortunately, were very happy at their Nicosia school and beautifully looked after by our Nanny, Pauline Britch, so my responsibilities were not too onerous.

A happy and relaxed Christmas was in prospect on Saturday, 18 December, Sarah's wedding day back in England, when my telephone rang early. It was Fateh Singh, the Force Commander's ADC, fighting to hold back his tears as he told me he had found Thimayya dead in the bathroom when he called round to his flat to deliver the overnight clutch of signals and cables from New York. Though, of course, I knew of Thimayya's heart condition and realized that death was his constant companion, the news was a shock. His contribution to keeping the peace had been immense; his passing would leave a gap hard to fill. I wondered how I would cope as his stand in, and how long it would be before New York found a replacement.

Fortunately there was little time to take counsel of my fears. I rang President Makarios to tell him the news and arranged to see him at eleven o'clock that morning. I summoned a Contingent Commanders' meeting for two o'clock that afternoon; Thimayya's distinction meant that we should need to organize a lying in state before an aircraft could come from India to carry his body home to Bangalore where Fateh Singh told us he wished to be buried. I remembered, too, the importance of treating the Turkish Cypriots 'pari passu' with the majority community, and set up a meeting with Vice President Kutchuk for the afternoon.

Meanwhile, we needed to devise a way for the diplomatic community to pay their respects. I rang David Hunt at the High Commission in search of inspiration and, naturally, he had the answer. "Get them to sign a book," he said. It was a brilliant solution and filled the gap until we were able later that morning to announce the arrangements for Thimayya's lying in state at Wolseley Barracks the next day. It was fortunate also that the Royal Highland Fusiliers were the British battalion in UNFICYP. Timmy had begun his career in the Highland Light Infantry; there could be no regiment better to guard his body and Gordon Pender made arrangements for this to be done with that special dignity at which the Scots excel. I asked the Canadian Guards, specialists in Ottawa ceremonial, to make the arrangements at Nicosia Airport and to provide the Guard of Honour as Thimayya's body was finally carried to the aircraft. By the evening our plan was firm, the necessary information had been given to the press and television, and there was nothing more to do except mourn our Force Commander.

For forty-eight hours until, escorted by a sad Fateh Singh, Thimayya's coffin left Nicosia on board an aircraft of the Indian Air Force I had no time to think about the future. Then I returned to reality as I wondered how the two communities would react to dealing again with a British Force Commander and especially one much less experienced than Thimayya. Makarios could hardly have been more helpful. He said at once he was prepared to deal with me as he had done with my predecessor; he was courtesy itself, and so were his ministers and officials. David Hunt later explained the background; UNFICYP provided a valuable support to the Cyprus Government's position. By effectively putting the problem 'in the fridge', we consolidated the dominant Greek Cypriot position. So long as nothing was done to provoke an actual Turkish invasion Makarios was secure; he could play the situation long or short as he felt inclined. His error lay in not making concessions to the minority community while he was in this dominant position; had he been able to nerve himself to do so, there would have been no Turkish invasion in 1974 and the overall position would be very different today.

My tenure as Acting Force Commander was of uncertain duration and I did not need to propose a new initiative. Nevertheless it would be unwise to let matters drift; too inert a stance would lead people who wanted to resume the trouble feeling able to do so. It was sensible therefore to pursue Thimayya's defortification policy as energetically as possible. I agreed this with Bernardes and New York; we then let this policy be known, not by a formal press announcement, but by well informed 'leaks', through national contingent commanders, to the diplomatic community. I sought early meetings myself with Makarios and the Turkish Cypriot leadership and sensed their relief at the prospect of the 'mixture as before'. Fortunately Thimayya had always taken the line that defortification achieved at Famagusta must be the prelude to other similar moves elsewhere. At our first interview Makarios confirmed this was his intention also; it looked as if we could make further progress if we could maintain the momentum.

The British Government were understandably nervous of my possible exposure in the tricky role of Acting Force Commander. Nevertheless Rodney Burges gave me strong support; he realized it would take longer than expected to find a suitable replacement for Thimayya. He resisted the temptation to undertake 'back seat driving' from the Sovereign Bases; any such tendency would become known to the Cypriots and destroy my credibility. I always stressed the 'Acting' element in my command of the Force and did not move into the Force Commander's office or use his car. I continued to work closely with John Drewry, my excellent Canadian Deputy Chief of Staff, who enjoyed the extra responsibility and grew in stature as time went on.

I did what I could through UN channels to try and obtain a relief for Thimayya. There were few candidates and most of them possessed snags which made them unsuitable. Macdonald, who had previous experience with UNFICYP, was a possibility. However, the Canadian Government only volunteered his services for three months, since he was needed for a domestic appointment in his new rank of Major General. Bunche felt that such a lack of continuity was unacceptable and floated the names of Gyani, Thimayya's immediate predecessor, and Rikhye, another Indian who specialized in UN appointments. Gyani was, however, unacceptable to the Turks because of his previous performance in Cyprus; there were doubts, too, about Rikhye's lack of military experience outside the UN, and a feeling that he would find it hard to follow a soldier as distinguished as Thimayya. Ankara also indicated, after the Indo-Pakistan fighting the previous autumn, that they would prefer not to have another Indian. It soon became obvious that there was no very obvious alternative, and, after about three weeks, I became reconciled to the prospect of a protracted period of Acting Command.

In mid-January UNFICYP had an opportunity to negotiate an important step forward. It concerned the Kokkina 'bridgehead', long a problem, and which had seen significant fighting in 1964. For the past eighteen months the Turks had maintained their positions at Kokkina for prestige reasons. The place was indefensible; the National Guard refrained from attacking it because doing so would bring down swift retaliation by the Turkish Air Force. The position of the Kokkina garrison had become unenviable, and we knew, from our regular visits by helicopter, that their morale was low. Largely composed of students from mainland Turkey, they had come to Cyprus in the summer of 1964, sustained by a wave of patriotism and a feeling that a full-scale Turkish invasion would soon follow. By now, however, they were frustrated by the siege conditions, there were indications of possible epidemics and action was clearly required.

It was not a surprise when Vice President Kutchuk, having been granted a special interview with Bernardes, asked if UNFICYP could negotiate the withdrawal of the Kokkina garrison. Such a task was just the challenge UNFICYP was established to answer; we replied that we would do our best and had every hope of being successful. Bernardes and I decided to approach Georghadjis; we thought he would be sympathetic, but it left us the later option of involving Makarios should our first proposal not meet with approval. In fact, as we had guessed, Georghadjis, who liked to make quick decisions, accepted the idea at once. There was only one difficulty which he could see. "How am I going to tell Grivas?" he asked with a rueful smile. Given such a start, the detailed negotiations were less difficult than we expected. Once Grivas understood that the Turkish proposal could be presented as a victory for the National Guard, he proved accommodating. The Turks jibbed at first over having to accept the Kokkina garrison completing embarkation cards before their departure, but their condition and morale meant this protest was no more than formal. The actual port of departure would be Xeros, further along the coast, where larger lighters could be used for embarkation. The 500 rifles of the garrison were left in situ in Kokkina with the local Turkish Cypriot muktar responsible for their safe custody and with regular inspections by UNFICYP. In theory there was to be freedom of movement through Kokkina after the garrison's departure; in practice, since we allowed the local Turkish Cypriots to maintain their roadblocks, the Greek Cypriots would have to continue using a diversion. Face was saved by a theoretical need to rebuild the road and Grivas had reluctantly to accept this compromise.

The actual embarkation, handled on the ground by John Drewry, went smoothly. We moved the Kokkina garrison to Xeros after dark in UN transport, efficiently marshalled by the Royal Corps of Transport. The press and television presented a problem; fortunately both the Government side and the Turkish Cypriot radio were equally at fault in breaching security and in their anxiety to claim the evacuation as a victory. The embarkation at Xeros took place under the arc lights needed for television pictures. The press had a good story and made the most of it. With both sides anxious to claim a victory, UNFICYP got its share of credit and increased prestige. The operation formed just the prelude we required for Jose Rolz Bennet's visit the following week.

Rolz Bennet, a Guatemalan, was one of U Thant's two Deputies and was visiting Cyprus to examine the role of UNFICYP. Both Bernardes and I looked forward to his visit, which the completion of the Kokkina evacuation made timely. UN Headquarters in New York needed convincing about the working of their peacekeeping operation, which they recognized was becoming more set in its ways. The funding of the Cyprus operation was a problem for the Secretariat; at that time the Soviet Union, following the United Nations' operation in Korea, declined either to support or finance peacekeeping operations, with the result that the burden fell mainly on the Western powers, the USA in particular. Though it was easy to see that the gradual approach we had developed was the right answer, one could understand the impatience of those who had to foot the bill. Thus it was no longer enough for UN officials to point to UNFICYP's success in stopping the inter-communal violence in Cyprus; they needed also to suggest either a possibility of a political solution, or to demonstrate the dangerous consequences of terminating the UN Force's mandate. The successes of Famagusta and Kokkina were more significant than we realized.

Bernardes and I found Rolz Bennet good company, and his visit was successful and stimulating. Rolz Bennet was quick on the uptake and quite unpompous. His relations with the Cypriots were excellent and gave us the chance we needed to advance some of our ideas and hope that Rolz Bennet might give them extra credence. Our advice was simple. The Government of Cyprus were in the strongest position they could ever hope to achieve. The Turkish Cypriot community were tired of the emergency and the Kokkina evacuation was a reminder of their low morale. Now, while the Government were on top, was the time to make concessions; it was a matter, not merely of generosity, but of common sense. There would, we argued, never be a better opportunity to win friends in the minority community. There was also a note of warning in our counsel. The Ankara Government were in a touchy state of mind. They could not afford more setbacks like Kokkina, and, if pressed, were likely to respond in the only way open to them by the use of force against Cyprus. It was important, therefore, not to try their patience too highly. Rolz Bennet advanced these ideas eloquently, but Makarios, always a gambler, unwisely thought he could do better. Doubtless, too, neither he nor Georghadjis, relished the task of explaining such a policy to Grivas. The latter was more relaxed during the Rolz Bennet visit than at any other time I can recall. He was in especially good form at the official luncheon given by the President for Rolz Bennet, remarking on the President's obvious good health, which Makarios attributed to his profession as a churchman. "The Army is not so bad either," retorted Grivas, "but perhaps I would be even fitter if my parents had made me a monk."

Before he left Cyprus, Rolz Bennet was complimentary about my achievements as Acting Force Commander. He was aware of HMG's reluctance to have a British officer in the role for longer than was necessary. Nevertheless, Makarios, the Turkish Cypriots and Bernardes all seemed to have confidence in my ability, and he did not therefore propose to advocate undue haste in seeking a successor. Bunche and he both considered that UNFICYP was working well; in such circumstances they were in no hurry to tinker with the machinery. Though this opinion was flattering, I continued to advocate the need for a new Force Commander whenever the opportunity arose. It would be fatal if the impression got around that HMG were content for the situation to continue indefinitely.

The island continued quiet militarily, but there was an outbreak of strenuous political activity in the wake of Rolz Bennet's visit. Galo Plaza's earlier job as Mediator had been allowed to lapse at the end of 1965. Bernardes, without adopting the formal title, now assumed the functions of the post and soon achieved considerable momentum. He argued that the continued cost of the UN Force would prove increasingly hard to justify without political progress. All parties therefore must work towards restoration of normal conditions and not be content with the present position. Bernardes' arguments went down well in Athens and Ankara, since the Greek and Turkish Governments were both fed up with the Cyprus problem and their adherents on the island. In Nicosia, however, Makarios only gave lip service to the search for a solution. He was gambling, correctly in the short run, less wisely in the longer term, that the UN Force would continue to be financed and that he would be allowed to continue the gradual erosion of the minority community. Bernardes saw this clearly and found the attitude of the Cyprus Government infuriating. For the moment, however, there was no alternative, Makarios had the Security Council over a barrel, and though, eight years later, his policy was to explode in his face, in that spring of 1966 he looked unassailable.

It may seem that UNFICYP were wrong to acquiesce in such an immobile situation. I doubt, however, if we had much alternative. The risks of a breakdown, and of precipitating a full scale conflict between Greece and Turkey, both fellow members of NATO, were far too great. I do not regret the caution with which UNFICYP proceeded and still consider that we were right to work through and with the Government of Cyprus, despite the limitations so imposed on us. It is a measure of Makarios' failure as a statesman that he failed to take advantage of a situation so heavily loaded in his favour. When he died in 1977 he must have been a disappointed man.

At the time, however, these ideas hardly crossed my mind. From the British viewpoint, Denis Speares, just before he left, attempted, from his position in the UK High Commission, to evaluate the best policy for the future. He concluded there was no alternative but to soldier on with UNFICYP; safer to live with the problems one knew rather than to jump into the unknown. I remember discussing Denis' analysis with him and accepting his views with relief. As Acting Force Commander, I also preferred to avoid too fundamental a reappraisal.

The issues, which exercised us daily, now seem trivial. The more significant stemmed either from the Government's wish to restore their authority over areas in de facto Turkish Cypriot control or their desire to improve freedom of movement. Invariably the Turkish Cypriots interpreted such initiatives as threats to their security, sometimes reasonably, but often on principle. Trypimeni, Knodhara, Temblos, Stavrokono were all issues which caused us great trouble at the time, and where UN patience was sorely tried. I worked hard to get consideration of these disputes carried out at the local level, more often than not successfully. It was important for me not to get involved too early and I preferred to be asked to intervene by Anastasiou on behalf of the Government or the Turkish Ambassador on the other side. A saving grace in these petty negotiations was the essential courtesy of the participants. However tiresome the controversies, it was a satisfaction to avoid people killing each other, and there were few days without this limited feeling of achievement.

Bernardes and I also had to reckon with the possibility of an attempt to overthrow the Makarios regime by force. Our fears were genuine as the coup by Nicos Sampson, which overthrew the Archbishop in 1974, was to prove. Even in 1966, however, UNFICYP needed to have a contingency plan prepared for such an eventuality. Bernardes always felt that Makarios might be complacent about his own position; it was always possible, too, that Ankara and Athens, equally fed up with the President's unreliability, might combine to secure his downfall. Clearly UNFICYP would have to stand completely aside from any such development. We determined, however, that we would continue our task of preventing inter-communal fighting and that Bernardes, as soon as the dust of any coup had settled, would approach the de facto authority for an assurance that no attack was intended on the Turkish Cypriot community. Bernardes cabled in this sense to New York, who supported our view.

At the end of April I heard from New York that they had been able to secure a relief for me as Acting Force Commander. The choice was a Finnish Lieutenant General Martola; aged 69, he might appear old for the job, but his political and fighting credentials, with a distinguished record against the Soviets during World War II, were clearly impeccable. I also heard a day or two later that my own relief as Chief of Staff was to be Michael Harbottle. Martola was to arrive on the island in the middle of May; I would stay for a month as his Chief of Staff before leaving for England to resume my normal military career.

Martola duly arrived as planned on 16 May. I liked him at once; he was easy to get on with and, fortunately, immediately struck up a good relationship with Bernardes. Georghadjis amused me when we met at the airport to receive Martola by remarking in a stage whisper as we walked across the tarmac back to the VIP room in the airport, "Well, he seems a little old to me, but we will do our best not to cause him too much trouble." Next morning it was obvious that Martola had been well briefed in New York; he was open-minded and understood the fundamental obstacle to progress in solving the dispute – the President's disinclination to talk seriously to anyone.

I went with Bernardes on 18 May to introduce Martola to Makarios and we found the President in one of his most relaxed and disarming moods. He promised Martola that he would do everything possible to co-operate with UNFICYP but otherwise kept the conversation on general lines, being clearly anxious to stop Bernardes getting round to more relevant topics. Bernardes succeeded in getting across the important messages which he had brought back with him from New York. The Secretary General wished Makarios to appreciate that, though UNFICYP's mandate was due to be extended for six months from mid-June, this did not mean that its future would be indefinitely assured. Though the President acknowledged Bernardes' message, I guessed he had little intention of heeding the warning it contained. Brinkmanship was his nature and he clearly intended to continue as before, convinced that time would remain on his side.

Kutchuk's table talk when we visited the Turkish Cypriot leadership was below the standard of Makarios. But he and Martola got on well, talking in French, to the frustration of a serious minded Turkish Cypriot delegation, clearly longing to get down to their usual string of complaints. Finally Orek, who had been Minister of Defence in the original Government of Cyprus cabinet, could stand it no longer. "Could we talk English for a change," he blurted out. It was obvious here too that Martola was a good choice. He reminded me more of an old fashioned University don than of a soldier; my only reservation was that he might not be tough enough to resist the pressures, but events were to prove me wrong and Martola soon developed into an admirable UN Commander.

Once Martola had settled down, my main interest was to try and ensure a calm period to give Harbottle, my successor as Chief of Staff, a reasonable introduction. Towards the end of May a top-level delegation from Ankara came over to assess the Cyprus position. I went with Martola to dine in the Turkish quarter to brief them and to explain how UNFICYP viewed the situation. At dinner I found myself next to Ambassador Vergin, the leader of the delegation and a shrewd personality. He confirmed to me that Turkey was now militarily in a position to launch a full-scale invasion of Cyprus whenever it was necessary; this was a situation which had not obtained in 1964 when they would certainly have landed if they had possessed the military means to do so. Vergin admitted that part of the Cyprus problem stemmed from the favourable terms Turkey had obtained at the time of the Zurich Settlement. "Our diplomacy was too successful for our own good," he remarked. Makarios, in his view, had been justified in attempting to modify the Zurich Constitution; his error had been to do so by force. Vergin recognized the present strength of Makarios' position on the island; Turkey would now accept a solution to the Cyprus problem which "if anything favoured the Greeks", provided that there were proper safeguards for the security of the Turkish Cypriot community. In his view some form of 'cantonal' system like that of Switzerland might be appropriate. This seemed positive to me and I passed on his concept to David Hunt, who also liked the idea, but wisely observed that he doubted if Makarios would be strong enough to implement it even if convinced of its wisdom.

Martola and I passed on Vergin's assessment to the President a couple of days later. Makarios took the point at once, assuring us that the Government would go out of their way for the moment not to cause trouble. He knew that talks between Athens and Ankara about Cyprus were imminent and had no intention of being accused of sabotaging them. Certainly the Government exercised unusual restraint for the remainder of my time on the island, even in areas like Trypimeni and Larnaca where they had a better than usual case.

About this time, too, there was a visit by Arthur Bottomley, Secretary of State for Commonwealth Relations, which also helped to keep the Government of Cyprus on its best behaviour. For a number of reasons, and thanks to David Hunt's diplomacy, the British were then remarkably popular. When I took Harbottle to see Georghadjis for the first time, the latter was complimentary about the British contingent, remarking that "only the British got any results". Though Georghadjis was, of course, flattering me as a departing British contingent commander, his attitude, and that of Anastasiou, represented a marked change since 1964. Nevertheless that splendid regiment, the Royal Welch Fusiliers, under an excellent Commanding Officer in John Swift, had certainly made an outstanding start in Limassol and Paphos; the armoured car squadron of the Inniskilling Dragoon Guards, under Mike Swindells, were equally skilful, and helped me to ensure that my departure took place on a happy note.

Despite the admirable atmosphere which surrounded my departure from Cyprus on 22 June, I was not sorry to be on my way. I felt there was little more I could offer UNFICYP and was beginning to find the sterile attitude of all the parties towards a settlement frustrating. UNFICYP had clearly done a good job in preventing a recurrence of fighting, but its role here was negative. Certainly my two years as a UN soldier had an impact on my subsequent military career. For better or worse, I now had a reputation for political dexterity and this factor may have kept me away from purely military assignments. I have no regrets on this score; I doubt how good a formation commander I would have proved in BAOR and, though I should have enjoyed the challenge of Northern Ireland, my UN involvement, and close friendship with the Republic of Ireland officers, might have made for misunderstanding. Though I and my family loved Cyprus, I have not been tempted to return since, apart from a brief stopover in the Sovereign Bases when a great friend in Hew Butler was the General there. I remain sad at the failure of the Cypriots themselves to resolve their problems on the island. The best chances fell to Makarios as I have indicated; the Turkish invasion of 1974, and present state of de facto partition, has made a solution even more difficult.

Appendix to Chapter 14

LETTER FROM U THANT, SECRETARY GENERAL, UNITED NATIONS

15 May, 1966

Dear Brigadier Wilson,

You have served with distinction as Acting Force Commander in Cyprus for nearly five months. Now that your acting command has come to an end with the appointment of General Martola as Force Commander, I wish you to know how very greatly your service to the United Nations is appreciated by all of us here at Headquarters. The task of Force Commander in Cyprus is a delicate and difficult one, requiring a combination of firm leadership and great diplomatic skill and understanding. In filling the gap caused by the sudden death of General Thimayya, you have demonstrated both of these qualities in full measure and have led the United Nations peacekeeping force in an exemplary manner, which has commanded the respect and co-operation of all parties concerned.

Your success in forestalling disturbances by timely negotiations and firm action has been notable in a number of critical situations in the past few months. Your keen understanding of the nature, possibilities and limitations of the United Nations role in Cyprus has made you a most effective commander of the peacekeeping force and has also made it possible for you to maintain excellent relations with all parties.

I send this letter to you by the hand of General Martola.

Please accept my warm congratulations and my heartfelt good wishes for the future.

Yours sincerely,

U THANT
Brigadier A.J. Wilson,

UNFICYP
Nicosia, Cyprus

Chapter Fifteen

EPILOGUE

When I returned to England, and the main stream of the British Army, from Cyprus in 1966, I still had eleven more years to serve, seven of them as a general officer. My life was full, agreeable and constructive; the jobs I was given were well suited to my capacity and I enjoyed them all. In the context of the Cold War, they were significant in helping the British Army to play it part in the ultimate triumph of the West over the Soviet Union.

Thirty-five years later, however, I doubt if reading about the details of this period in my life would prove of great interest to the casual reader. My tasks – as Director of Army Recruiting to fill the Army with officers and soldiers, as Commander of North West District to sell the concept of an Army whose main role would be in Europe, as Vice Adjutant General to oversee the main workings of the Army's personnel policy, and finally as GOC South East District responsible for the largest UK troop command – were absorbing. But they were not dramatic, and if they had become so, it would only have been because I had missed a trick and allowed a situation to develop out of control.

Fortunately for me – since I doubt if I would have found preparing for a battle which, in my judgement, would never happen very rewarding -- my period as a UN Force Commander had disqualified me from further military command in BAOR. There would have been too much technically for me to catch up on and there was no shortage of qualified and talented contemporaries. When briefly it seemed I might go in 1967 to Germany as Commander of BRIXMIS (the British Mission to the Soviet C in C), the door might have re-opened. But Denis Healey, the Secretary of State, and the Adjutant General, Reggie Hewitson, decided between them that for me to do a further job of 'cops and robbers' would not be in my interests or that of the Army. In their view, I would be better employed in a Pied Piper role – to recruit an Army – and I am grateful to them for the opportunity, independence, (and financial responsibility) I was given to do so. When in 1969 I was offered the chance to go to the Royal College of Defence Studies I was deeply involved in reorganizing the Army's marketing system and politely turned down the opportunity. I had been on the panel of lecturers at Seaford House since 1965 – on UN Force Command – and preferred to complete my recruiting task. My decision did not affect my promotion to Major General in 1970; though the RCDS would no doubt have been a great experience, I doubt if a 'sabbatical year' at that stage would have suited me, while I might have found reversion to 'statu pupillari' frustrating.

Our two years in the North West from 1970–72 were a delight. Lancashire, in particular, felt it had been neglected militarily. It was my job to rectify this impression, and I greatly appreciated the chance I was given to do so. It was sad to leave Lancashire, but I was lucky in my next job as Vice Adjutant General.

By great fortune, John Mogg, an old friend and fellow Green Jacket, had become Adjutant General, a job for which he was perfectly suited and where his leadership was outstanding. John liked touring and was at his best on such journeys. He became known as the 'Marco Polo' of the Seventh Floor and required a kindred spirit to 'mind the ship' in his absence. Doing so, and being so completely in John Mogg's mind, was a great experience, especially as there were important personnel decisions to be made at the time.

My UN experience had also, of course, though no one said so explicitly, made it impossible for me to serve in Northern Ireland in an executive role. Though, in theory, it might have seemed an advantage that so much of the Irish Army, and in particular all the key senior officers, had served under me in Cyprus, the media could have drawn the conclusion that Britain was minded to hand over the direction of operations in Ulster to the UN. Nothing, of course, was further from HMG's intentions, but to encourage any such speculation would clearly have been unwise. I was able, however, to visit Northern Ireland regularly as VAG to do what we could to improve conditions for those serving in the province and to develop a great admiration for the manner in which military affairs there were handled.

John Mogg's liking for foreign travel did not prevent my getting away frequently on visits of my own. I went to the Sudan (where the British had recently assumed responsibility for running that country's Staff College), India (to lecture at their request at the IMA), and Oman (to make certain the quality of those we were sending to commands in the Dhofar was as good as we could provide). This last proved a fascinating trip; it was a privilege to appreciate Tim Creasey's touch in handling the war, and later, with the help of another old friend in John Akehurst, to see their bold tactics and fine leadership crowned with success.

John Mogg's successor as AG, Monkey Blacker, also knew me well. The fact that we thought so much alike on military matters enabled him, during my last six months as VAG, to travel widely himself. Essentially practical in outlook and realistic in the aims he set in personnel policy, Monkey was another outstanding AG and the Army owes him much for what he achieved in office.

In South East District, based on Aldershot, I was responsible for much of the Army's basic training, as well as for the Parachute Brigade, the backbone of the strategic reserve. So good, however, were those more directly involved, especially Geoffrey Howlett (as talented a commander at one star level as one could imagine), and Bill Withall at the Royal Engineer Training Brigade, that there was little for me to do other than applaud their efforts.

Life, however, was seldom dull and a number of extramural activities, membership of the Sports Council for example, and Chairmanship of major army sports, cricket and Association football, consumed any spare time agreeably. There was also a demanding Committee on the Re-organization of Regular Army Officer Training (CAROT), which never lacked interest. The President, Allan Taylor, and my fellow member, Rollo Pain, were former colleagues on the Directing Staff at the College. I am sure we did not solve the problems facing us completely; indeed, by that stage, it was probably impossible to do so on a single-service basis. Nevertheless, I doubt if we did much, if any, harm, and, perhaps, by increasing confidence in the system, we may even have improved matters.

Nevertheless, by 1977, when the time came to retire, I was still just young enough (at 56) to learn a new trade, and when head hunters approached me saying they needed someone to work in an 'unpopular industry', and who was not afraid to 'argue with civil servants and Ministers', I accepted the offer gratefully.

Once again I fell on my feet and into a change of career which proved difficult and challenging. Looking back, I had never expected to be a soldier in the first instance, let alone to have been given, while remaining I hope an amateur, such exceptional opportunities and varied experiences. I have, in fact, been lucky all my life, though my friends have usually been too kind to tell me so. Perhaps my main good fortune has been working with so many delightful and talented people; as this record shows, I have had few quarrels, perhaps surprising for someone sometimes considered unorthodox and independent, and who regularly expressed his views freely. If this reflects the tolerance of the British Army, it may also explain something of its strength; certainly soldiering provided me with a memorable thirty-seven years for which I am supremely grateful, as this record makes plain. *"Heureux qui comme Ulysse a fait un beau voyage."* I hope he enjoyed it as much as I did.

INDEX